Richard Sibbes

Richard Sibbes

Puritanism and Calvinism in Late Elizabethan and Early Stuart England

By
Mark Dever

Mercer University Press
Macon, Georgia
2000

ISBN 0-86554-657-6
MUP/P201

© 2000 Mercer University Press
6316 Peake Road
Macon, Georgia 31210-3960

First Edition.

∞The paper used in this publication meets the minimum requirements of American National Standard for Information Sciences—Permanence of Paper for Printed Library Materials, ANSI Z39.48-1984.

Library of Congress Cataloging-in-Publication Data

CIP data are available from the Library of Congress

Contents

Foreword

BY EAMON DUFFY

RECALLING HIS CHILDHOOD religious formation in the reign of James I and VI in the remote village of Eaton Constantine near Shrewsbury, Richard Baxter told of the poor pedlar who had come one day to his father's door selling ballads, but also "some good books." Baxter's father bought one of these, a set of sermons under the title *The Bruised Reed*, by Richard Sibbes, sometime Fellow of St. John's College Cambridge and at the time of Baxter's father's purchase, lecturer at Grey's Inn in London, a key post in the legal and civic life of the city. The young Baxter duly read Sibbes's book, "and found it suited to my state and seasonably sent me; which opened more the Love of God to me and gave me a livelier apprehension of the Mystery of Redemption, and how much I was beholden to Jesus Christ."

For Baxter, Sibbes would remain always one of the foremost exponents of what he liked to call "our old English practical divinity," a doctor of souls ministering to the broken hearts of converted sinners. Sibbes's passionate and tender writing ensured that his works continued to be read within the puritan tradition, and he was one of a select band of seventeenth-century puritan writers who rated a major nineteenth century reprint, remarkable among such enterprises for its scholarly fidelity to the original editions. In the twentieth century, he was recognized by Perry Miller as "the quintessential puritan," and his works were extensively drawn on by the subtlest and profoundest of all modern interpreters of the puritan spirit, Geoffrey Nuttall.

Sibbes himself, however, has largely disappeared from view, his life shrouded in obscurity and misinformation. Less than a generation after his death he had come to be seen as a Puritan martyr, suffering ejection from his College Fellowship for his refusal of conformity to the Prayer-Book, the friend and supporter of radical protestants, who took refuge in a London Lectureship when he could no longer accommodate his dissident convictions within the parochial framework of Laud's church. In the process, he became part of the pedigree of separatist Nonconformity, the ancestor of Congregationalists and Presbyterians, quietly edited out the history of Anglicanism.

Mark Dever's scintillating and penetrating study dramatically redraws this whole picture. He demonstrates that far from being a dissident, Sibbes in the 1630s was virtually the last example of an older breed of Elizabethan conformist puritans, part of a network of the great, the Godly and the good which reached from rural Suffolk, through Elizabethan Cambridge, to the mercantile and legal communities of the Metropolis. He must indeed have been increasingly uncomfortable in a Laudian Church engaged in repudiating or reinterpreting the Elizabethan Protestant inheritance of the Church of England, yet he doggedly maintained to the end a moderating position which played down the structures and externals of the National Church and retreated inwards to emphasize instead the conversion of the heart. Sibbes, it emerges, was never ejected from his Fellowship. Despite serious reservations about the ritual aspects of the Prayer-Book, he subscribed to what was required of him, and moved to London not as a refugee from Anglican intolerance, but in the normal course of a preaching career, to the broadening of auditory and influence which a lectureship in one of the Inns of Court offered. Dever's painstaking unraveling of Sibbes's friendships, patronage networks, and theological affinities demonstrates that although his circle included many who later moved into positions of radical dissent, his links with them were formed when they too were still conformists, and he never abandoned his own conformist position.

Dever's sensitive and surefooted exposition of Sibbes's theological position is equally fresh. Some historians of Puritanism have suggested that English "affectionate divinity" in the age of Sibbes abandoned the pure stream of Calvin's thought for the incipient moralism of Beza, and that between Calvin and the English Calvinists there had opened up a disastrous theological rift. Rejecting any such notion as a key to Sibbes's writing, Dever portrays Sibbes as "one of the last great Reformed preachers of England to believe in theory and know in practice an officially undivided covenant community." He brings to his exposition of Sibbes's subtle and highly personal practical divinity a wide and deep acquaintance with sixteenth and seventeenth-century Reformed theology, but also that rarer thing, a sensibility which is warmly sympathetic to the nuances of Sibbes's writing while remaining sharply and critically alert. The result is a marvelously lucid and persuasive account of a key moment in the evolution of early modern protestant thought, in a period which Sibbes himself described as "the best tymes of the gospel." Read it.

Foreword

BY J. I. PACKER

HE WAS CALLED the Sweet Dropper by reason of his encouraging sermons. He drew admiring crowds in both Cambridge and London. He stammered a little in the pulpit, but his messages were clear, vivid, strong, deep, and basic for Christian living. He came across as a holy man, gentle, firm, humble, cautious, and wise, a lover of Christ, of Christians, and of peace. A couplet that went the rounds after his death ran thus:

> Of that good man let this high praise be given:
> Heaven was in him before he was in heaven.

For three centuries those who have known and cared about him have called him a Puritan, and in light of what Puritans finally became that fits, but in his day the word implied provocative nonconformity, and that was not his style. He saw himself as an Anglican centrist, embodying the Cambridge University version of Reformation faith and life and seeking to spread it despite obstruction from the top—that is, from the Stuart autocrats and William Laud, their pet tiger. Ordained at thirty after a late conversion, he identified with the pastoral brotherhood shaped by such as Richard Greenham, Richard Rogers, William Perkins, and Paul Baynes (the human instrument of his coming to faith): men whose central commitment was to the discipling of all England in the God-fearing, Bible-based, Christ-exalting, spirit-empowered devotion that was always part, if not all, of the Puritan stock-in-trade. (This was the religion reanimated in the next century by revivals on both sides of the Atlantic.) A learned man, and a kind of icon within the brotherhood, as appears from the number of recommendatory prefaces that he wrote for their books, he published not more than three small devotionals; but he regularly wrote his sermons, and left at his death over two million words on paper, which kept printers busy for the next twenty years. When he died in 1635, he had been master of Cambridge's Katharine Hall since 1626, vicar of the town's Holy Trinity Church since 1633 (he had begun preaching there as early as 1610), and stated preacher at Gray's Inn, London, since 1618. He had become a highly regarded clergyman in what he called "this Truly Evangelicall Church of England," where he had positioned himself throughout as a man of peace, a reforming conformist, and a pioneer in good causes for furthering the gospel. His name was Richard Sibbes. He deserves a book to himself and, now at last, he has one.

The Puritan movement, churchly and conversionist, seeking simultaneously the reform of Anglican order, the regeneration of unconverted churchgoers, and the sanctifying of all life, was constantly on the move, aiming to use every situation to advance its cause. Sibbes was typical. The first years of his ministry saw Puritan pastorates multiply and Puritan books flood the country, and Sibbes treated the mounting setbacks of his later years as only temporary, so that separation and emigration were needlessly negative responses to them. He was perhaps fortunate to leave the world before the worst Laudian atrocity (the maiming of Prynne, Eastwick, and Burton) and the eruption of the Civil War. As an "affectionate practical divine" of mainstream Puritan type, he taught constantly the realities of communion with the Father and the Son through the Spirit of assured faith through the witness of the Spirit, and of patient endurance and personal advance by the Spirit's power in the face of all kinds of troubles, appearing throughout as a Bible-man who knew himself to be on the victory side in and through Jesus Christ.

Mark Dever surveys all this with welcome precision and sets the record straight on key points. His book is a fine contribution to Puritan studies, and it is with great pleasure that I commend it.

Preface

The writing of this book has encompassed many days and hours in England and America. It was, in essence, a dissertation written in fulfillment of the requirements for the doctoral degree at Cambridge University. Since I finished working on it in 1992, it has been somewhat revised for publication. This revision process has been helped greatly by the keen mind and sharp pen of Michael Lawrence and by the editors at Mercer University Press.

In its original form, the British government (through Overseas Research Scholarships), the J. B. Lightfoot Scholarship Fund in the University of Cambridge, and, of course, my family all contributed financially to allow me to do this research. Paul Parisi, too, generously gave many hours showing a Puritan how to manage with a computer.

Numerous family members and friends have encouraged and challenged me, even listening to large parts of this dissertation or to ideas in it. Among them, particularly helpful conversation partners have been Jon Hinkson and Elizabeth Catherwood. I have incurred a debt to James L. Price, Jr., Roger Nicole, Timothy George, and R. Albert Mohler, Jr., for friendship and for training me to think theologically. Ligon Duncan discussed my work with me, with welcomed knowledge and interest in both the history and the theology of the period. J. I. Packer has been an encouragement to me, as to so many others, in ways both numerous and unknown to him.

Richard Sibbes referred to a book as a "friend," a "second self" from whom we should take benefit. I have profited from many such friends, a portion of which are acknowledged in the bibliography. Filled with such friends, and more animate ones, Cambridge was an excellent place to pursue this study. The staffs of many libraries kindly answered inquiries, fetched books, photocopied material, explained terms, and suggested other avenues of investigation. Particularly helpful were the libraries of the ancient colleges in Cambridge and Oxford, chief among them the libraries of St. John's College and St. Catharine's College, Cambridge; also the University Library at Cambridge, the Bodleian Library, Oxford, the British Library and Dr. Williams's Library, and the Library of Gray's Inn, London, the National Library of Scotland, and New College Library, Edinburgh. Equally patient with my questions were the staffs of the Public Records Office, London, the Suffolk County Records Office, Bury St. Edmunds, and the Cambridgeshire County Records Office. Of special help in my research were Malcolm Underwood, Archivist, St. John's College, Cambridge, and Elizabeth Leedham-Green, Assistant Keeper of the University Archives, Cambridge.

Cambridge seems to be outstanding for the community that exists among its historians; many willingly shared their books and articles, expertise and insights with me. H. C. Porter's encouragement and criticisms, John Craig's paleographical help and cheer, Professor Patrick Collinson's interest and suggestions all made the work of this study more enjoyable, and the final product, for whatever faults it may still bear, is better than it could have been without them.

Three people to whom I owe a special debt are three church historians who have modeled vital faith and searching scholarship for me. William Nigel Kerr introduced me to Richard Sibbes a decade ago, when I was about to pursue work on John Bunyan. Geoffrey F. Nuttall has made himself and his friendship available to me freely and warmly. There have been some hours with him that taught me more than months in formal study could have done. If I had not been given such a Reformed theological training, he might well have made me wonder if omniscience should not be considered one of God's communicable attributes. And finally, my doctoral studies supervisor, Eamon Duffy, has endured countless queries, provided cogent criticisms and given wise insight with almost uncanny regularity on a wide range of issues related to my study (and beyond). My decision to pursue this study at Cambridge was based in no small part on the prospect of working with him; and my experience fully vindicated that choice.

As in too many other things, in acknowledgements family tend to come last. Perhaps that is because they are more the end of than the means to so much of one's earthly life. Though my parents and more extended family all encouraged us in our time of study in England, particular thanks are due to my mother, who twenty years ago in her typically supportive attitude first encouraged her son to consider study at Cambridge. And most importantly my thanks go to Connie, my wife, who shared with me the joy of reading so many of Sibbes' sermons, the toil of writing about them, and the prospect of life together beyond doctoral studies. Over a decade of the trying combination of xiii

marriage and study she has demonstrated that "love is patient. . . . It always protects, always trusts, always hopes, always perseveres."

Though read first, prefaces are written last. So it is that authors are so often valedictory in tone, saying farewell to a study which has been a constant companion for years. All things considered, this book bears little resemblance to Augustine's *De Civitate Dei* (though its length was similar, before university regulations required retrenchment of the original); yet his closing words well expressed my feelings as I came to the end of this study: "And now, as I think, I have discharged my debt, with the completion, by God's help, of this huge work. It may be too much for some, too little for others. Of both these groups I ask forgiveness. But of those for whom it is enough I make this request: that they...join with me in rendering thanks to God. Amen. Amen."

Would that Richard Sibbes had made acknowledgments.

Introduction

SOMEONE DESCRIBED AS "a rather bland, sweet–natured, mild–mannered, charming, learned and highly respected middle–aged gentleman" may not seem to be a promising prospect for study.[1] Though disincentives and even difficulties may discourage an investigation of him, Richard Sibbes proves to be an inviting subject historically and theologically. Summarily stated, his theology epitomizes the Early Stuart period, and his history illustrates conflicts and consensuses within the English church. Even the neglect he has endured encourages investigation.

Sibbes's style of expressing his theology—his preaching and the theology itself—are typical of the period. His sermons are a paradigm of the practical divinity that so distinguished the English church at the time. Even during his life, Sibbes was recognized as an eminent practical preacher. In 1634 Samuel Hartlib referred to Sibbes as "one of the most experimental divines now living."[2] Rarely polemical (with the exception of occasional attacks on Roman Pelagianism), his preaching was distinguished by its pacific tone, more concerned with comfort than controversy. In the epistle "To the Reader" prefacing Sibbes's *The Glorious Feast of the Gospel*, Arthur Jackson, James Nalton and William Taylor wrote:

> Alas! Christians have lost much of their communion with Christ and his saints—the heaven upon earth—whilst they have wofully disputed away and dispirited the life of religion and the power of godliness, into dry and sapless controversies about government of church and state. To recover therefore thy spiritual relish of savoury practical truths, these sermons of that excellent man of God, of precious memory, are published.[3]

---

[1]William Haller, *The Rise of Puritanism*, (New York, 1938) 163.

[2]Samuel Hartlib, Ephemerides, Hartlib Mss., Sheffield University.

[3]Arthur Jackson, James Nalton and William Taylor, "To the Reader," preface to *The Glorious Feast of the Gospel* by Richard Sibbes (London, 1650); reprint Alexander Balloch Grosart ed., *The Works of Richard Sibbes*, 7 vols. (Edinburgh, 1862-1864) 2: 439.

Later historians have realized Sibbes's ability as a preacher. William Haller has described Sibbes's sermons as "among the most brilliant and popular of all the utterances of the Puritan church militant."[4] Norman Pettit suggested that Sibbes had "the richest imagination of all. Indeed, Sibbes was unique among spiritual preachers, perhaps the most original of his time."[5] Yet if his ability and success were singular, his theology and aims were not.

Perhaps even more than his style and expression, the substance and essence of Sibbes's theological thought epitomize his era, particularly in his central use of the idea of covenant. Sibbes called the covenant the ground of the entirety of the Christian life "both in justification and sanctification."[6] It is this covenantal framework, which many, from Perry Miller to R. T. Kendall, have identified as the central difference between Calvin and his later English followers. Since the generally accepted ideals of English Protestant theology were central to Sibbes, he invites study. Because Sibbes's theological style and substance can be said to be both typical of and unique to the period, they epitomize it. It is not surprising that Christopher Hill should describe Sibbes as "the quintessential Puritan."[7]

Sibbes also invites study because his history illustrates agreements and conflicts within the English church at the time generally, and it does so in ways different than earlier presentations of him might suggest. His life was marked not so much by conflict and deprivation, as by prosperity in patronage, preaching, and preferment. From the age of ten when he began to study at the King Edward VI Free School in Bury St. Edmunds until his death at age 58 as Preacher of Gray's Inn, London, Master of Katharine Hall, and Vicar of Holy Trinity Church, Cambridge, Sibbes was associated with well-known institutions. Thus, as later generations would compile lists or write institutional histories, it was almost impossible that a characterization, or at least mention, of

---

[4]Haller, 152.

[5]Norman Pettit, *The Heart Prepared: Grace and Conversion in Puritan Spiritual Life*, (New Haven, Connecticut, 1966) 66.

[6]Sibbes, "The Rich Poverty; or, The Poor Man's Riches," in *Works*, 6:245.

[7]Christopher Hill, "Francis Quarles and Edward Benlowes" in *Collected Essays*, (Amherst, Massachusetts, 1985) 1:190.

him could be omitted. His positions and situations act as a kind of tour through the historical countryside.

Given his association with prominent institutions and his post-humous reputation, the substantial neglect of Sibbes in the secondary literature is all the more striking. Half a century ago R. P. Stearns noted that there were "no good studies" of a number of prominent Puritans of the early seventeenth century, including Sibbes.[8] Except for a few unpublished dissertations, this neglect has continued, with Sibbes being often cited, but not studied.[9] As an example of the religious situation in early Stuart England, Sibbes can be used to explore and investigate models that have been suggested such as "moderate puritan," "noncon-formist," and "Calvinist." Sibbes certainly did not lead the life of silencings and exile that many of his contemporaries, and even some of his friends, did; yet he has been remembered as a striking example of how even moderate Puritans suffered deprivation under James. It is a purpose of this study to unite the images of Sibbes's life and thought, to illuminate both him and his times.

ALTHOUGH A STUDY of Richard Sibbes may prove helpful, it is not easy. Questions repeatedly out-distance evidence. C. S. Lewis aptly ex-pressed this dilemma of historical study when he observed that "the real historian will allow that the actual *detritus* of the past on which he works is very much more like an old drawer than like an intelligent

---

[8] R. P. Stearns, "Assessing the New England Mind," *Church History* (1941) 10:262.

[9] Besides dissertations in which Sibbes is one of several figures treated, those that this author is aware of are: Frank E. Farrell, "Richard Sibbes: A Study in Early Seventeenth Century English Puritanism" (Ph.D. diss., University of Edinburgh, 1955); Bert Affleck, "The Theology of Richard Sibbes, 1577–1635" (Ph.D. diss., Drew University, 1969); Harold Patton Shelly, "Richard Sibbes: Early Stuart Preacher of Piety" (Ph.D. diss., Temple University, 1972); Sylvia Roberts, "'Radical Graces': A Study of Puritan Casuistry in the Writings of William Perkins and Richard Sibbes," (M.A. diss., University of Melbourne, 1972); Jonathan C. Harris, "Richard Sibbes: A Moderate in Early Seventeenth Century Puritanism" (M.A. diss., University of Melbourne, 1978); Cary Nelson Weisiger II, "The Doctrine of the Holy Spirit in the Preaching of Richard Sibbes" (Ph.D. diss., Fuller Theological Seminary, 1984).

epitome of some longer work."[10] Always true in historical research, difficulties, even unusual ones, abound in the study of this public man. First, Sibbes never married; therefore, there was no obvious family member to write a biography or to collect his papers, letters, or manuscripts. Various letters and manuscripts are divided between London, Oxford, and Cambridge, but no cache of papers either by or pertaining to Sibbes exist for the historical student. The second unusual difficulty in the study of so public a person is the lack of evidence of a funeral sermon for him. Such sermons, often with a memoir of the deceased attached, are important sources of information for the historian. It is known that William Gouge preached the sermon, but it was apparently never published. The lack is supplied, poorly, by a brief contemporary memoir of Sibbes by Zachary Catlin, and another, even shorter, published by Samuel Clarke in *A Collection of the Lives of Ten English Divines* (1652). Besides these two, the only extant contemporary sources are in a few remaining letters by Sibbes, chance references to him in the letters or writings of other contemporaries, and the prefaces written by colleagues to his numerous books, most of which were published posthumously. This last source points out yet another difficulty for the researcher – there is no record of when or in what order most of Sibbes's sermons were preached. Therefore, the reconstruction of any historical progression in his thought is problematic at best.

A PROFITABLE STUDY of Sibbes from the primary sources available, however, is still possible. In the first part of this study, the life of Sibbes is examined in the context of the changing church and nation of which he was a part. By the latter years of Elizabeth's reign, the focus of godly divinity shifted from the controversies of the 1570s to more pastoral, less contentious concerns. Claire Cross observed that "the bitter arguments over the precise form of a Christian church laid down in the New Testament, which twenty years previously had absorbed so much of the energy of Cartwright and Whitgift, had given way to a more pacific school of writers who put far more emphasis on practical Puritan

---

[10]C. S. Lewis, "Historicism," in *Fern-seed and Elephants and other Essays on Christianity*, ed. Walter Hooper, (1950; reprint. London, 1975) 58.

piety."[11] Not that controversies ceased, but there was alongside the controversial literature a growing literature of personal devotion and piety, concerned with preparation for salvation and assurance of it. This is the literature that history has, with reason, taken to be typical of the company of which Sibbes was an acknowledged master usually referred to as the English Puritans.

Though Sibbes's formative years were spent in the last decade of Elizabethan Cambridge, most of his life was lived under the early Stuarts, when the Church of England was moving away from identifying itself with the continental Reformed tradition. The demands of conformity to the church that Sibbes must have considered while an undergraduate at St. John's differed increasingly from the demands of conformity after the Hampton Court Conference and the Canons of 1604, not to mention from the even more alien Church of England of the 1630s. Under the reigns of James and Charles, the more advanced reforming party in the English church was repeatedly defeated, and *conformity to* the national church came to be perceived as at odds with *reformation of* the national church. This study will follow Sibbes's career and his writings (when specific dating is possible) from the early years through the reign of James I and into the different church that was being fashioned under Charles I and Laud.

Perhaps the historical difficulties surrounding the reconstruction of Sibbes's life help to explain why most previous studies have been concerned almost exclusively with his theology with little consideration of his historical context. This study attempts to examine the life and career of Sibbes in his historical context and the theology he espoused and expressed in that context. Was it distinctly Reformed? Was it mystical? Was it nonconformist? If so, how? If not, why has it been seen so? This is the purpose of the second part of the book, in which special concern will be given to the areas that deal with the age–old theological problem of the concurrence of the actions of God and humanity. This is the area in which covenant falls and in which both the theological uniqueness of Puritanism and the distinctiveness of Richard Sibbes's writings have usually been seen. His theology will be examined both in its most Calvinistic, objective expressions (i.e., concerns of predestination and election) and in its most typically Puritan, "experimental" expressions

---

[11]Claire Cross, *Church and People, 1450–1660,* (London, 1976) 161.

(i.e., concerns of assurance and conscience). In the end, Sibbes will be seen to have been, not a moderate Puritan forced into non-conformity by the growing extremity of the Laudian church, but a conformist to his dying day, who yet never ceased striving for the gradual reformation of the church. Thus the theological picture of Sibbes, in which his conformity is seen to be both Reformed and conscientious, becomes consonant with his pacific historical image.

Though some substantial work has been done to clarify and recast the understanding of Puritanism along more accurate theological lines, showing it to be neither a re-incarnation of Calvin himself nor an entirely *novum rei*, there is a need for specific studies that will give careful attention to both the historical and theological tensions. While such sensitivities are always needed in ecclesiastical history, they are particularly needed in the study of this period. This is an attempt at such a study, aiming to be historically and theologically sensitive, and at the same time synthetic.

Considering the increasing "specialization" that marks academic study, Hugh Trevor-Roper noted that:

> Today most professional historians 'specialise'. They choose a period, sometimes a very brief period, and within that period they strive, in desperate competition with ever-expanding evidence, to know all the facts. Thus armed, they can comfortably shoot down any amateurs who blunder or rivals who stray into their heavily fortified field; and, of course ... they themselves keep prudently within their own frontiers.[12]

In one sense, this study of Sibbes is prudently specialized in its object; yet in another it is quite imprudently various. Separate faculties, libraries, and journals have long established the divide between the study of history and that of theology. While many theologians are knowledgeable historians, and perhaps fewer historians, knowledgeable theologians, the intellectual intertraffic of the two in any given study tends to be largely one way. This study has attempted to create something of a dialogue, considering Sibbes's ecclesiology and conformity, his soteriology and his preaching, his career and his

---

[12]H. R. Trevor-Roper, *Men and Events*, (New York, 1957) v–vi.

casuistry together. In the course of the study, some criticisms will be made of both theological studies for their lack of historical knowledge and historical studies for their lack of theological knowledge. Such criticisms certainly leave the present study more, not less, open to criticism from both sides. The words "with what judgment ye judge, ye shall be judged; and with what measure ye mete, it shall be measured to you again," (Matt. 7:2) take on new and existential meaning. Yet any such criticism may be another small step in an increasingly fruitful educational interchange.

In the process the traditional interpretation of Sibbes in particular will be affected. Sibbes begins to seem both less of a nonconformist and less unusual, both more Reformed and more privileged than he has before appeared. His life begins to take on a more obvious consistency with his writings than earlier studies have suggested. The anticipations and tensions of Richard Sibbes as a conforming clergyman in the early Stuart church become more evident, and his relation to what he called in an open letter to a separatist friend the "truly Evangelicall Church of England" more understandable.[13]

More generally, this study suggests a model that relates English Puritanism to its Reformed forefathers with less discontinuity than the interpretation that is regnant. It appears that they were not so much theological, but historical shifts that brought about the markedly experimental Reformed divinity of the English Puritans. In conclusion, Sibbes proves to be a useful study in the relation of Reformed divinity to the demands of early Stuart conformity, and thereby in understanding the religious life of that interesting period when hopes for a thorough reformation were waning, but had not yet mingled with the widespread desperation of the people as fully as they were to do in the decade after Sibbes's death.

IN AN ATTEMPT to make this book more helpful, all references to Sibbes's works are given to the collected nineteenth–century volume edited by A. B. Grosart rather than to the original seventeenth–century texts. Although it was originally the intent to do otherwise, in the

---

[13]"Consolatory Letter to an Afflicted Conscience," in *Works*, vol. I, p. cxvi.

course of reading many of the sermons in the seventeenth–century texts, it became apparent that Grosart had been almost entirely accurate in his collected edition. The advantages of reference to a uniform and readily available standard edition will be obvious. A complete list of seventeenth–century editions of Sibbes's works can be found in the bibliography.

PART I:

"AMIABLE LIVING":[1]

THE HISTORICAL IDENTITY OF

RICHARD SIBBES

---

[1]John Sedgwick, in his "Dedication" to *Beames of Divine Light* by Richard Sibbes (London, 1639); reprint A. Grosart, *The Works of Richard Sibbes*, 7 vols. (Edinburgh, 1862–1864), 5:221).

I

Sibbes's Formative Context, the 1590s

IN THE SPRING of 1559, a poor labourer of Pakenham, Suffolk, died, leaving a young wife, Elizabeth, and two sons, Paul and Robert. He left them a house, a little land, and a few pounds. Robert lived perhaps into his nineties, dying in January of 1637, leaving behind Alice, likely his second wife, and no surviving children. The older son, Paul, became a wheelwright, moved to Tostock, a few miles from Bury St. Edmunds, married Joane, and had six children who survived into adulthood.[1] Richard was the first of the children born to Paul and Joane Sibbes. He was born in Tostock in 1577[2] and was baptized in the parish church on 6 January 1580. While Richard was still young, Paul and Joane Sibbes moved their family two miles west, to the town of Thurston. In his memoir of Sibbes, Zachary Catlin (a contemporary of Sibbes at Cambridge and later rector of the church in Sibbes's home parish of Thurston) records that 'they lived in honest repute, brought up, and married divers children, purchased some houses and lands, and there they both deceased. His father was...a skilful and painful workman,

---

[1]Keith Wrightson has observed that the kind of moving seen here in Paul Sibbes's life (born in Pakenham, lived in Tostock with wife and at least first child, soon afterwards moved to Thurston and settled there) was a common, if temporary "phase of the life–cycle" in Tudor and Stuart England. Keith Wrightson, *English Society 1580–1680* (London, 1982) 42ff).

[2]Significant dates in Sibbes's life often have been misreported. Daniel Neal gave Sibbes's birthdate as 1579. (Neal, *The History of the Puritans* [London, 1837] 1:582). Numerous later authors dependent upon Neal reproduced his error. The most recent printed mistakes of this sort have been those in R. T. Kendall, *Calvin and English Calvinism to 1649*, (Oxford, 1979) 102, where Sibbes is reported to have been born in the year 1572 and to have been admitted to St. John's College, Cambridge in 1591.

and a good sound-hearted Christian."[3] In Thurston, young Sibbes grew up and began his education. All of the other Sibbes children remained in the area throughout their lives. His brother John took up his father's trade and house in Thurston. From John and his wife came a son, three grandsons and a great-grandson that followed Richard in studying at Katharine Hall, Cambridge. John died sometime between 1610 and 1635. Richard's brother Thomas moved to the nearby village of Rattlesden, and married Barabara. The union produced no surviving off-spring. The occupations of the husbands of Richard's three sisters (Susann Lopham, Elizabeth King and Margaret Mason) are unknown. Of all his siblings, only Margaret and Thomas survived Richard.

Richard, however, did not remain in Thurston. Nevertheless, even after he was elected to a fellowship in Cambridge, Sibbes did not cease to be a part of his family's life in Thurston. Perhaps the prohibition of marriage, which was a condition of holding a fellowship of a Cambridge college in the seventeenth century, increased his ties to his own not-too-distant family. Catlin recorded with gratitude that Sibbes would either preach in the parish church, or assist him in distributing communion "whensoever he came down into the Country, to visit his Mother and brethren (his Father being deceased)," which apparently was frequently enough that, Catlin recorded, "wee soon grew wel acquainted. "[4] Throughout his life, Sibbes continued to hold land in the village, eventually leaving it to his brother Thomas and his nephew John. Even after moving to London Sibbes did not forget his familial responsibilities. He offered to bring his mother there to live, but she declined, preferring to remain in Thurston.

But before his election to a fellowship at Cambridge, or his appointment to a prominent pulpit in London, Richard's parents had intended that he settle in the Thurston area. He had been meant to become a wheel-wright like his father. At one point, the elder Sibbes even invested in a set of tools for his son. But the younger Sibbes

---

[3]The Cambridge University Archives have three different manuscript copies of Zachary Catlin's "Memoir of Richard Sibbes" (Add. 48; Add. 103; Mm.1.49). It has been printed twice, once by J. E. B. Mayor in *Antiquarian Communications: Being Papers Presented At the Meetings of the Cambridge Antiquarian Society* (1859) 1:255-264, and once by A. Grosart in *The Works of Richard Sibbes*, (Edinburgh, 1862) 1: cxxxiv-cxli.

[4]Zachary Catlin's "Memoir of Richard Sibbes," printed as "Appendix to Memoir," in *Works*, 1:cxxxv.

seemed ill-suited to it. While he later found in the memories of his father's work a rich store of illustrations, his own early inclination was to study and read.[5] And so it was to the labors of the academy, rather than the wheelwright's shop, that Sibbes devoted his energies. Catlin recorded:

> Testimony of Mr. Thomas Clark, High Constable, who was much of the same Age, and went to schole, together with him, at the same Time.... He hath often told me that when the Boies were dismist from Schole, at the usuall Houres of eleuen, and 5, or 6, and the rest would fal to their pastime, and sometimes to plaiing the Waggs with him ... it was this Youth's constant course, as soon as he could rid himself of their unpleasing company, to take out of his Pocket or Sachel, one Book or other, and so to goe reading and meditating, til he came to his Father's house, which was neere a mile of, and so as he went to schole agen.[6]

For several years, Sibbes walked about a mile to and from the school at Pakenham (just north of Thurston) to be taught by Richard Brigs.[7] This was almost certainly a "petty school"; that is, an arrangement whereby a local vicar would instruct the children of his and perhaps nearby parishes in basic literacy.[8]

After attending Brigs' school at Pakenham, from perhaps as early as 1587, Sibbes walked to the well-known Edward VI Free School at Bury

---

[5]E.g., Sibbes's image of conscience as "a wedge to drive out a hard piece of wood to be cut," (Sibbes, "Witness of Salvation," in *Works*, 7:375) or his presenting "a man out of Christ" as "a stone out of the foundation, set lightly by, and scattered up and down here and there," (Sibbes, "Yea and Amen; or, Precious Promises," in *Works*, 4:123).

[6] *Works* 1: cxxxv.

[7]Brigs had attended St. John's, Cambridge, taking his M.A. in 1585. It is likely that Pakenham was Brigs' first position after leaving Cambridge. From there, he went on to become Master of the Norwich Grammar School in 1598, a position which he held until his death in 1636.

[8]Such schools were not institutionalized and, therefore, have left little documentary evidence of their existence, except for references to them in historical accounts, such as Catlin's account of Sibbes. See Wrightson, 185; Barry Coward, *The Stuart Age* (London, 1980) 59.

St. Edmunds, over four miles from his home. It is unclear how Sibbes came to be one of the few score of students there. Statute 45 in their charter stated that "Poor mens children shall be received in the said school before other" and yet, whether this provision would have applied to Sibbes is uncertain.[9] He must have been examined by the schoolmaster and his assistant and have been found able to write and read competently. The educational process in the Free School was made up almost completely of memorization and recitation. The students were to memorize and recite the creed, and the Lord's Prayer, the Ten Commandments in English and Latin regularly. Through recitation they also learned Latin and Greek, reading works by Erasmus, Ovid, Terrance, Horace, Cicero, Sallust, Virgil, Isocrates, and others—works "such as be most chaste and less meddled with wantonness."[10] The regulations even went so far as to require that "the scholers shall at no time depart from or out of the school to do their necessity before they have recited at their egress three several latin words, and three other at their regress."[11] According to the charter, the only recreation allowed the boys was shooting of arrows, for which purpose they were to bring their bows and arrows to school each day. When trying to find an image to contrast with the judgments of God always being exactly directed, it is not surprising that Sibbes hit upon the image of God's judging not being as "children shoot their arrows, at random."[12] They were taught from 6 AM until 5 PM on weekdays, and until 3 PM on Saturdays and holidays. John Wright (M.A. from Clare College, Cambridge in 1578) had become schoolmaster in 1583 after a considerable controversy had resulted in the removal of the previous schoolmaster. (The prior incumbent had been suspected by some of being unsound in religion, probably of being a papist.) It is, therefore, likely that Wright's religion had been carefully scrutinized by local godly gentry, including Sir Robert Jermyn and Sir John Higham, both of whom had been active in looking after the affairs of the school. The significance of this fact should not be lost. Beginning with Sibbes's time at Bury and continuing during his time at Cambridge, religious

---

[9]See Wrightson, 189.

[10]"March 12, 1583[4] Statutes of King Edward VI Free Grammar School at Bury St. Edmunds" (Suffolk County Records Office, E5/9/201.7) 22.

[11]"Statutes" number 66, 16.

[12]Sibbes, "Judgment's Reason," in *Works*, 4:78.

controversy and concern formed an important part of the context of his academic labors.

Throughout these years Richard's family prospered in Thurston, through wheelworking, farming, and even landholding (renting houses and property in Thurston and Pakenham). Yet even though Paul Sibbes was a yeoman of considerable means,[13] it is clear that Richard's education was felt by his father to be financially burdensome. It was required in the 1583 Statutes of the Free School in Bury that parents must pay the usher (who taught the first three forms) four pence "for enrolling your child's name" and must provide their children with "sufficient paper, knife, pennes bookes, candle for wynter and all other thinges at any tyme requisite and necessarie for the maynetence of his childe" including the bows and arrows for recreation.[14] Paul Sibbes's continued reticence to provide for his son's education is evidenced by a remark in his will, in which he mentions that he had been at "great charges" in the education of Richard.[15] That Sibbes was well aware of this attitude on the part of his father is indicated by Zachary Catlin's inclusion of this fact in his memoir of Sibbes, written well over forty

---

[13]Contrary to what has earlier been suggested (e.g. Frank E. Farrell, "Richard Sibbes: A Study in Early Seventeenth Century English Puritanism" (Ph.D. diss., Edinburgh, 1955) 17) Paul Sibbes was a fairly well-to-do yeoman. In his will (dated January 31, 1610[1]) Paul Sibbes bequeathed to various members of his family his own residence, lands and tools in Thurston, another house, land and pasture by Overstrete in Thurston, a house and lands near the commons in Thurston (at the time being leased) a house and lands (around 10 acres) in Pakenham, a four acre field planted with wheat in "Stocho," 55 Pounds, 10 Shillings, and other personal possessions. Though not wealthy, he was clearly a wheelwright of considerable means. P. J. Bowden has estimated the yearly profit of a yeoman farming 30 acres of land for this period (the acres granted in Paul Sibbes's will total 28) might be on average 14-15 Pounds. See P. J. Bowden, "Agricultural Prices, Farm Profits, and Rents," in J. Thrisk, ed., *The Agrarian History of England and Wales, Vol. IV., 1500-1640* (Cambridge, 1967) 657-659. This profit would have been supplemented by Paul Sibbes's income from his craft as a wheelwright, and perhaps from the rentals on other property he held. For more detail on the status of the yeoman in this period, see Wrightson, 19-38; cf. Maurice Ashley, *England in the Seventeenth Century*, 2nd ed. (New York, 1978) 21-22.

[14]"March 12, 1583[4] Statutes of King Edward VI Free Grammar School at Bury St. Edmunds" (Suffolk County Records Office, E5/9/201.7) 25.

[15]Paul Sibbes's Will, W1/67/176, Suffolk County Records Office, Bury St. Edmunds. Appendix II is a transcription of this will.

years after the elder Sibbes's death.[16] Yet Sibbes did not seem to regret the expense he caused his father, as shown by an illustration Sibbes later used: "Doth that child trust his father, that, besides going to school, thinks what he shall put on? how he shall be provided for, and what inheritance he shall have hereafter? Alas: this is the father's care, and belongs not to him."[17] Catlin recorded that Paul Sibbes was only willing to continue Richard's education as long as he did because of "the Importunity of Friends."[18] Catlin continued, "His father at length grew weary of his expense for booke-learning" and made an investment in some tools for him so that he could be set up in his own trade.

Sibbes's education continued at this point because of the patronage of some local men who had taken note of his predilection for study.[19] And again, this development in Sibbes's education is not untouched by the religious ferment of his day. In East Anglia at the time, but in Suffolk in particular, prominence did not exclude a measure of nonconformity.[20] Leading families of the area that held the advowsons of many of the churches regularly gave them to men who were at least partially nonconforming. In 1597, six parishes (perhaps more) in the Thedwestry Deanery had incumbents that were presented for irregular use of the surplice. One of these was Leonard Graves, the vicar in Thurston from 1589 to 1609 (and like Brigs, a Johnian).[21] Graves was

---

[16]Grosart, due to a misreading of Catlin's memoir, has suggested that Paul Sibbes died sometime before 1608. It is clear now from his will (drawn up in January 1610, and proved on February 15, 1610) that Paul Sibbes died in 1610 [1611].

[17]Sibbes, "The Saint's Hiding-Place in the Evil Day," in Works, 1:421.

[18]Catlin's Memoir, in Works, 1:cxxxiv.

[19]Wrightson, 58ff.

[20]Revolt against the use of surplice was "especially notable in the archdeaconry of Suffolk," (J. F. Williams, ed., Diocese of Norwich: Bishop Redman's Visitation, 1597: Presentments in the Archdeaconries of Norwich, Norfolk and Suffolk (Norwich, 1946) 19).

[21]The others in the deanery who were presented for irregular use of the surplice were the incumbents of Bradfield St. Clare (Richard Grandishe) Bradfield St. George (Lawrence Whitakers) Livermere Magna (John Ward) Hesset (Anthony Rowse) and Whelnetham Parva (James Wolfenden) (Williams, 160–161).

cited in Bishop Redman's visitation of 1597 for reading "Comon prayer manie Sondaies and holidaies omyttinge to weare the surplesse."[22]

Without Paul Sibbes's approval, Graves and "Mr. Rushbrooke," an attorney in Thurston, arranged for a meeting for Richard with some fellows of St. John's College, Cambridge. Among these was Graves' friend, the "Puritan Chief" John Knewstub.[23] Sibbes wrote later, "We love examples of great, noted persons."[24] In Knewstub, Sibbes met perhaps his first "great, noted" person. Knewstub, who was vicar of Cockfield ten miles south of Bury St. Edmunds for forty-five years (1579–1624), had taken his B.D. from Cambridge in 1576 and had been an active supporter of Thomas Cartwright in his days in the University. The "doyen of the Suffolk preachers,"[25] Knewstub had more than once been mentioned for Master in elections at St. John's and was a serious candidate in 1595 upon the death of William Whitaker.

In 1593, as the Elizabethan settlement entered its fourth decade, Acts of Parliament had been passed against both the Puritans and the papists. April of 1595 saw one of the relatively few executions for heresy in Elizabeth's reign.[26] On April 7, the Jesuit Henry Walpole was hanged in York as a heretic. The 1590s were clearly a time of continued religious strife in England, and the Cambridge of Sibbes's undergraduate days was not exempt from this strife. The myth of a wholly puritan Cambridge dissolves in the examination of the frequent religious controversies in Cambridge throughout the reign of Elizabeth. From the controversy over vestments throughout the 1560s, culminating in the Cartwright/Whitgift exchanges, to the storm of protests over

---

[22]Williams, 161.

[23]Edmund Carter, *The History of the University of Cambridge*, (London, 1753) 255. Evidence from a controversy in 1613 about a pew in the Thurston church suggests that Knewstub (Rector of Cockfield) along with Lawrence Whitaker (Rector of Bradfield St. George) Richard Grandishe (Rector of Bradfield St. Clare) William Holden (Vicar of Pakenham from March 1591) and Edmund Gallaway (Rector of Stanton, and one of the Botesdale preachers in 1611) were close friends of Graves. Cf. *The Registrum Vagum of Anthony Harison*, transcribed by Thomas F. Barton, (Norwich, 1963–1964) 2:247–249.

[24]Sibbes, "Angels' Acclamations," in *Works*, 6:321.

[25]Patrick Collinson, *The Elizabethan Puritan Movement* (London, 1967) 218.

[26]According to W. K. Jordan, five people during the reign of Elizabeth were executed for heresy. *The Development of Religious Toleration in England From the Beginning of the English Reformation to the Death of Queen Elizabeth* (London, 1932) 181–182, 236

sermons by William Barrett, John Overall, and Peter Baro in the late 1590s, resulting in the Lambeth Articles, Cambridge had never been the pacific preserve of precisians, or of those fully Reformed. For every Kelke, there was a Caius, for every Aldrich, an Ithell, and for every Chaderton, a Legge.

It was not only the heads who were divided in their theological sympathies; those who lectured and taught did not always lecture and teach the same things. When outspoken Calvinist William Whitaker died, leaving vacant the Regius chair of Divinity in the university, he was succeeded by John Overall (a proto–Arminian), a disciple of Peter Baro, the Lady Margaret Professor. Too, the university lecturers were not the only ones lecturing on theology in Elizabethan Cambridge. Paul Seaver has observed that "What was important for many of the future Puritan clergy...seems to have been not so much what they learned from tutorials and university lectures, from the formal content of higher education, as the experience of hearing the great preachers of the university towns."[27] During Sibbes's time as an undergraduate in Cambridge, while Peter Baro was lecturing in the university as the Lady Margaret Professor of Divinity, William Perkins, one of the only English theologians of the period to have a truly European reputation, was lecturing at St. Andrew the Great. Perkins was a popular lecturer among the students and had wide influence among those in the generations immediately following him. Among those who listened to Perkins were Sibbes, William Ames (one of Perkins' students at Christ's who entered college only one year ahead of Sibbes), and Sibbes's life–long friend William Gouge (whose career ran parallel to Sibbes's in so many ways). The university Sibbes entered in the mid–1590s was clearly a place where scholars could hear widely different understandings of the Protestant gospel.

The controversies surrounding grace in the 1590s, during Sibbes's days as an undergraduate at St. John's, show that deep questions could still be raised in the university about some of the most fundamental aspects of Protestant theology; and they were no less than the Lady Margaret and Regius Professors of Divinity themselves who raised

---

[27]Paul Seaver, *The Puritan Lectureships*, (Stanford, 1970) 182.

them.[28] One of the most well-known Cambridge controversies began on 29 April 1595. On that day, William Barrett, chaplain of Gonville and Caius College (and a disciple of Baro's) preached a sermon at Great St. Mary's in which he openly attacked several tenets of the Reformed faith (especially perseverance of the saints) and even attacked the deference with which so many of his colleagues treated John Calvin's writings. Within a week he was brought before the Consistory Court to answer objections that had been raised to the sermon. Five days later he read a recantation in Great St. Mary's, but even this in a way which at least 56 of his fellow dons felt was insufficient. By July Barrett had revoked his recantation, and the two sides seemed to harden in their antagonisms toward each other. On 7 July Barrett's mentor Peter Baro was called before the Consistory Court to face questioning about his theology. In the same month, Robert Some, Master of Peterhouse and the person who had presided over the initial hearing concerning Barrett's sermon, publicly attacked Barrett in a sermon at Great St. Mary's. This, however, was something of a tactical error. In the Elizabethan church, it seemed that the attacked usually got the sympathies and support of those in authority because of their understandable interest in maintaining the status quo.

Whitgift knew the Cambridge controversy could all too easily exceed the bounds of the university and cause increased unrest in the national church. Some was called to Lambeth Palace and reprimanded for his sermon by the Archbishop. Whitgift was not, however, oblivious to who had started the present disturbance. In September he drew up eight examination questions for Barrett. On 12 September Barrett was examined upon these eight points by a committee of five Cambridge heads of houses: Duport (Master of Jesus and the one who might perhaps be sympathetic to Barrett's theology), Whitaker of St. John's, Tyndall of Queens', and Chaderton of Emmanuel (all of whom would be quite antagonistic to Barrett), and Barwell of Christ's. After Whitgift had been informed of the proceedings, he replied by simply forbidding further sermons on the matter and convening a meeting of Whitaker, Tyndall, and Barrett at Lambeth to discuss it further. Notwithstanding the Archbishop's instructions, on 9 October Whitaker preached a

---

[28]See H. C. Porter, *Reformation and Reaction in Tudor Cambridge* (Cambridge, 1958) 281-287, 335-390, for a narrative of the events surrounding the theological controversies of Cambridge in the 1590s.

sermon at Great St. Mary's in which he clearly advocated the Calvinist positions on election, reprobation and perseverance. In the next year, Robert Some published his *Three Questions Godly, Plainly and Briefly Handled* in which he asserted perseverance and definite atonement (both positions which Barrett and Baro had controverted). After his meeting with Barrett at Lambeth Palace, Whitgift himself lost patience with Barrett and, along with Whitaker and Tyndall, drew up and signed the Lambeth Articles on 20 November. On 24 November, he sent them to the Vice-Chancellor of the University "praying you take care, that nothing be publicly taught to the contrary."

It was in 1595, perhaps due to Knewstub's influence, that Richard Sibbes matriculated at St. John's College, Cambridge, under the mastership of Whitaker.[29] Thus Sibbes's education began under the tutelage of the Johnian, Richard Briggs, continued under the supervision of John Wright, and advanced through the advocacy of the nonconforming Johnians, Leonard Graves and John Knewstub, it reached its apex. And all along the way, religious controversy was the ever present context.

In the closing years of Elizabeth's reign, Cambridge, along with the rest of England and Wales, was experiencing something of a building boom. Trinity College, the new foundation of Sidney Sussex College, and Great St. Mary's had major building projects underway during Sibbes's early years as a student in Cambridge. At St. John's, Sibbes's reading was carried on amid the sounds of workmen building a new court for the college. The foundation was begun on 2 October 1598, and the north range was completed in the following year. By 1602 the entire court was finished. But before this new court had been begun, Sibbes

---

[29]"It was mainly on the recommendation of Knewstub that Richard Sibbes . . . entered St. John's in 1595" James B. Mullinger, *St. John's College*, (London, 1901) 84. James and J. A. Venn, *Alumni Cantabrigienses*, part I, vol. IV, (Cambridge, 1927) 73, lists Sibbes as matriculating "c. 1594," but there is no evidence for this earlier date from contemporary records. The "Alumni Sheet" in the library at St. John's, Cambridge, lists Sibbes as having matriculated "c. 1594" but there is no record of this in the college archives. Since the "Alumni Sheet" is of fairly recent date, this author assumes that the date "c. 1594" was simply taken from Venn. Along with Mullinger, Clarke's memoir of Sibbes supports the 1595 admission date. Samuel Clarke, "The life of Doctor Sibs" in *A general martyrologie, containing a collection of all the greatest persecutions which have befallen the church of Christ...Whereunto is added the lives of thirty-two English Divines*, 3rd ed., (London, 1677) 143.

had certainly already seen a college in greater flux politically and religiously than it was in physically.

St. John's was Knewstub's college. It had a tumultuous history of ardent Protestantism, including a surreptitious meeting in the college, which some had deemed a presbytery. Peter Lake has written that "by the early 1590s St John's was divided into mutually exclusive and antagonistic groups" thanks, in no small part to William Whitaker.[30] Soon after Sibbes's arrival there, St. John's College was bereft of its master. On his way back to Cambridge from Lambeth on 4 December, 1595, "illness supervened" and Whitaker died.[31] On 10 December, Whitaker was buried. Within a few days, twelve of the fellows wrote to Sir William Cecil, Lord Burleigh, Elizabeth's trusted and powerful Secretary, and complained of the desperate state of the college, citing Whitaker's lack of attention to college matters. They also complained of the supporters of Cartwright in the college and the disproportionate influence they had.

---

[30]Peter Lake, *Moderate Puritans and the Elizabethan Church*, (Cambridge, 1982) 191. Whitaker, mentioned above, was a renowned theologian of the English church. Mullinger describes him as "the most distinguished leader in England of that growing party which accepted the doctrine of Calvin and Beza, and, while on friendly terms with Cartwright, he spoke disparagingly of his most admired productions," (Mullinger, 73). Notwithstanding Mullinger's testimony, it is interesting that Laurence Chaderton, Master of Emmanuel, and Whitaker's brother-in-law, was uncertain enough of Whitaker's stand on predestination that he personally and specifically questioned him on the topic before Whitaker went to Lambeth in November 1595. "No English divine of the sixteenth century surpassed Whitaker in the estimation of his contemporaries," wrote Mullinger (75). To illustrate this statement, Mullinger records that Whitaker's theological opponent, Bellarmine, "so much admired his [Whitaker's] genius and attainments that he kept his portrait suspended in his study." His expositions of Christianity reached the students of Cambridge through his lectures as Regius Professor of Divinity. (He was appointed to the chair in 1579, when William Chaderton, its previous occupant, left Cambridge in order to be made Bishop of Chester.) Whitaker exerted his influence more widely through his published works and through his co-authorship (with Whitgift and Humphrey Tyndall, President of Queens') of the Lambeth Articles. For more on Whitaker see F. G. M. Broeyer, *William Whitaker (1548-1595) Leven En Werk Van Een Anglocalvinistisch Theoloog*, (Utrecht, 1982); also Lake, 93-115, 169-226.

[31]Mullinger, 74.

The election of successor to Whitaker was a difficult one, involving several candidates, one of whom was John Knewstub. Knewstub's candidacy was vigorously supported by John Overall, Master of Katharine Hall, and Whitaker's successor as Regius Professor of Divinity. Two other fellows of St. John's were candidates—John Bois, well-known for his proficiency in Greek (and the Latin orator at Whitaker's funeral in the college chapel), and Thomas Playfere, the popular college prelector in Hebrew. In the letter of twelve fellows to Burleigh, they wrote that "the colledge is so full of such like men [reformers like Whitaker], as they are the greater nomber of the societie: and so if the newe master be chosen by them, we must needes greetly feare what they will doe."[32] Burleigh's decision was to delay the election.

During the delay, the other Cambridge heads declared for Laurence Stanton or "Dr. Webster" (with most supporting Stanton). Meanwhile, the fellows of the college were not inactive. Within two weeks of Whitaker's death, "two petitions were sent from the college to Burleigh in support of Henry Alvey, signed in all by twenty-nine Fellows, out of a total number of about fifty."[33] Alvey, Whitaker's assistant in college matters, seemed to be the candidate with the most support among the fellows. On 14 December, fearing the prospect of an Alvey mastership, several fellows of the college wrote to Burleigh denouncing Alvey as too ambitious. The next day, twenty-four fellows wrote to Burleigh, asking him not to deprive them of their right of election. They listed the following as candidates acceptable to them: John Reynolds, dean of Lincoln, Webster, Richard Clayton (Master of Magdalene, and former fellow of St. John's), Knewstub, John Ireton (a fellow of Christ's College), Alvey and Roger Morrell. Burleigh nominated Clayton and Stanton as the two from whom the next master should be elected. Elizabeth preferred Stanton (the heads' choice) but would allow the society at St. John's to choose between the two. Clayton was the only candidate who seemed acceptable to both sides. In the end, Whitaker was succeeded by one considerably less sympathetic to the more radical reforming party than Alvey, Knewstub, or Whitaker had been. On Monday, 22 December, within a month of Whitaker's death, Richard Clayton was

---

[32]Lansdowne MSS. vol. LXXIX, no. 69 (cited by Porter, 202). See also Mullinger, 88; and Porter, 202–203.

[33]Porter, 202.

elected as Master of St. John's College.[34] While it is unclear how much of all of this a first year undergraduate would have known about, it is clear that Sibbes had entered a setting in which college sermons, divinity lectures, and conversations in the hallways must have revolved often around issues of religious conformity, with implications that seemed to go far beyond simply the attire of the Vicar of Thurston. The college that Sibbes entered was theologically turbulent and socially unruly.

Within the university, too, controversy continued. Baro, undoubtedly emboldened by the success of his disciples, preached a University Sermon (at which it could reasonably be assumed Sibbes was present) on 12 January 1596, in which he directly contradicted the Lambeth Articles. (On that same Sunday, William Perkins preached a sermon at St. Clement's Church in which he opposed Overall's election as the new Regius Professor of Divinity.) That week Baro was called before some heads of houses, and the next before the Consistory Court for the sermon. Goad, Provost of King's and Vice-Chancellor, debated with Baro, but was unsure of what to do with him. When he wrote Lord Burleigh for advice about Baro, Burleigh wrote back, objecting to the treatment Baro had received and even going so far as to agree with Baro on the disputed points. This startled the heads. After several weeks of deliberation, they (Goad, Some, Legge, Preston, Neville, Tyndall, Montagu, Barwell and Chaderton) replied to Burleigh, objecting more generally to the "popery" in the lectures and teaching of Baro. As the dispute widened throughout the year, Baro became less certain of the security of his position. By the autumn of Sibbes's second year in Cambridge, Baro resigned his chair and fled from Cambridge. Thomas Playfere, fellow of St. John's, was elected to succeed him.

In 1597 William Barrett fled from Cambridge to the continent. There he joined the Roman Catholic Church, fulfilling some of the Reformed fears about the natural consequences of his doctrinal deviations. Peter Baro died in April of 1599. Still, theological controversy over Calvinism was not extinguished during Sibbes's latter student days at St. John's. In June of 1599 objections were again lodged with the university about Overall's preaching and teaching, with Robert Some once again leading the way. In September he preached a sermon in which he clearly

---

[34]For a full account of this election, and its setting in the life of St. John's College, see Porter, 183–206.

attacked Overall, and succeeded once more in getting the university astir. On 20 October Overall was called before the Consistory Council for questioning, but no further action was taken against him.

If this represents the controversial atmosphere and the exceptional context of Sibbes's Cambridge, what was the more regular context? What kind of education would he there have obtained? Certainly Cambridge was recognized by the Elizabethan period as being among the first rank of European universities, thrust from its previous relative obscurity by the convulsions of the reformation. Academically, Sibbes's formal undergraduate education would have consisted largely of the Latin and Greek classics, rhetoric and logic. Reading Aristotle, attending disputations, and giving special attention to moral, natural, and metaphysical philosophy would round out the last two years of his studies before taking his B. A.[35] Studying would have taken place mainly in his own chamber, probably his tutor's room and in shared meetings with other of his tutor's students.[36] There would have been both university and college lectures to attend, and Saturday afternoons would have been spent in the college chapel being catechized.[37]

During his years as an undergraduate at St. John's, Sibbes was financially supported by his father who provided only slightly over eight pounds per year. This was supplemented with additional aid from Knewstub, Graves, and a subsizarship from the college.[38] As a sizar, Sibbes again experienced the benefits of patronage at a young age. Sizars were "men who only indirectly benefited by college endowments to the extent of, perhaps, receiving rooms and tuition free, but were attached to a Fellow or Fellow Commoner of the College who in return for some kind of service provided them with funds for maintenance, the service and help being undefined."[39] As some of these sizarships at St.

---

[35]For more on the typical course of B. A. studies for a Cambridge undergraduate of the period, see John Twigg, *A History of Queens' College, Cambridge 1448–1986* (Cambridge, 1987) 98.

[36]Twigg, 94.

[37]See "An. 1588. Maii 17. A Decree, by Will. Whitaker, Master, and the seniors," printed in *Reports from the Select Committees: Education of the Lower Orders* (London, 1818) 4:405.

[38]Catlin's Memoir, in *Works*, 1:cxxxv.

[39]R. F. Scott, "Some Aspects of College Life in Past Times" in *The Eagle*, 162; rpt. in Scott, *Notes from the Records of St. John's College, Cambridge*, 4th series, (privately printed, 1913–1934) item XI. Cf. Twigg, 89ff. At least at Queens'

John's became endowed, the unendowed sizarships became known as subsizarships, though the difference of names indicated nothing other than the source of the financial allowances. No trace has been left either of the Fellow to whom Sibbes was attached or of the duties he performed for him.[40]

In *Bowels Opened*, Sibbes noted that some words in Romans 11 "should stir us up earnestly to take our part in that Christ hath provided, because we know not how soon the table may be taken away. When men see the dishes in removing, though before they have discoursed away much time of their supper, yet then they will fall fresh to it."[41] This scene of men rushing to finish their supper was one that would have naturally been in Sibbes's mind as one who had eaten in common halls almost all of his adult life. One duty he certainly would have performed as a student in late Elizabethan Cambridge would have been waiting at tables in college. Other duties were probably menial chores for the Fellow to whom he had been assigned, varying simply at the Fellow's discretion. This is not to suggest that sizarships were demeaning positions in the college. Often they were the primary means of financial support for students who could not otherwise have afforded a university education. Scott wrote, "The Subsizer was not a poor student, depressed to the footing of a servant, but generally the son of a clergyman, small yeoman or farmer elevated to the rank of a student by a kindly and richer friend without whose help he could not have come to the University."[42] Whatever the exact nature of Sibbes's financial support, it was sufficient to see him through his first degree.

College in this period, Twigg has written that "Because scholarships were meant only for the truly deserving, their holders were obliged to take the BA degree at the earliest possible opportunity—four years after admission—or else forfeit their scholarships. Payments ceased automatically three years after the BA, or, immediately after taking holy orders, at which stage it was felt that scholars should secure either a fellowship or a parish living." (Twigg, 91).

[40]A decree in the college statutes, enacted 6 November 1605, states that "no fellow shall have above one subsizar, except allowed by the master and seniors," enjoining a fine for any that violated this rule. What if any implications this may have for the number of subsizars per fellow, or their having been in some sense exploited remains unclear.

[41]Sibbes, "Bowels Opened," in *Works*, 2:35.

[42]Scott, 165. The continuing importance of the position well into the Stuart period is shown by a decree of 1625 published by the Vice-Chancellor and heads which forbad the employment of women and illiterate boys and men to

Sibbes commenced B.A. from St. John's College in 1599,[43] thus concluding the four years in which he first entered into the wider world of Elizabethan England. Yet that England was changing. The same year which saw Sibbes commence from St. John's saw Burleigh, a friend of moderate reform in the nation, church, and university, die. With Burleigh's death, and the deaths of Elizabeth and Whitgift in the next few years, the trio of those who had held together the Elizabethan settlement more than any others for the previous four decades passed from the scene. But this was after Sibbes's initial period in Cambridge. During his first years as a student there, the Lambeth Articles, for all the disregard they later suffered, did serve to create the climate of a clear soteriological Calvinism which the Church of England and the universities espoused and taught. No doubt his future conformity was influenced by the patronage he had enjoyed and the controversies he had observed while a student at St. John's.

---

do these tasks which were the only source of livelihood for some (though not all) of the sizars.

[43]Figures compiled by John Twigg for this period suggest that as many as three-fourths of all sizars at Cambridge took a degree, compared to only one-fourth of fellow commoners during the same period. Among other things this might suggest, it certainly suggests the greater necessity of a degree for the livelihood of sizars, than for their social superiors, the fellow commoners. (See Twigg, 104).

II

Sibbes and Conformity, 1601-1617

WITHIN TWO WEEKS of the death of Elizabeth I, James VI of Scotland journeyed south from Edinburgh with great anticipation. On his way south in April 1603, James was made directly aware of one area of discontent in his New Kingdom—its religious life—by the presentation of the Millenary Petition.[1] By the conclusion of the meeting of the Hampton Court Conference several months later, James had been "impressed by the puritans as agitators and conspirators...but not with the gravity of their demands. The more moderate, even trivial, their case, the less excuse for disturbing the peace and unity of the church."[2] Having attended to their complaints, James now expected conformity to the law of the church, as it was soon expressed in the Canons of 1604. That which was particularly the cause of "so much broyle in the Church and hart burninge"[3] were the Three Articles of Canon 36, which affirmed the ecclesiastical supremacy of the king in England, that the

---

[1]Reprinted in J. P. Kenyon, *The Stuart Constitution: Documents and Commentary*, 2nd ed., (Cambridge, 1986), 117–119.

[2]Patrick Collinson, "The Jacobean Religious Settlement: The Hampton Court Conference," in *Before the English Civil War*, Howard Tomlinson ed. (London, 1983) 44. Cf. Kenneth Fincham and Peter Lake, "The Ecclesiastical Policy of King James I," *Journal of British Studies* (April, 1985): 24:171. While Professor Collinson seems to take a more skeptical view of James' deliberate use of moderate Puritans than have Fincham and Lake, there is nothing inherently inconsistent between James' being both irritated by these Puritans, moderate and radical, as trouble makers, and yet having found a politic and quite natural way of dealing with them, as Fincham and Lake have suggested. See also, Frederick Shriver, "Hampton Court Re-visited: James I and the Puritans," *Journal of Ecclesiastical History* (1982): 38:48–71.

[3]Stephen Egerton, "Address to Convocation, urging a revision of the newe booke of common prayer," cited in S. B. Babbage, *Puritanism and Richard Bancroft*, (London, 1962) 79.

Book of Common Prayer and the present structure of the Church of England were in no way contrary to the word of God, and that "he himself will use the form of the said book prescribed in public prayer and administration of the sacraments, and none other," and that the 39 Articles were biblical. The Canon continued:

> To these three articles whosoever will subscribe, he shall for the avoiding of all ambiguities, subscribe in this... form of words, setting down both his Christian and surname, viz. 'I *N.N.* do willingly and *ex animo* subscribe to these three articles above mentioned and to all things that are contained in them.

A lack of conformity, even after subscription, was ground for suspension and, "if obstinate," excommunication.[4] The campaign for conformity, which followed "proved to be the end of the puritan movement in the form of a concerted effort mounted from within the Church to alter the fundamental terms of the Elizabethan settlement by political means."[5]

There were, however, other ways of achieving reforms in the church, one of which was undoubtedly through the training of young ministers in the universities. A former Cambridge fellow, reflecting on the leading role of his *alma mater*, wrote that "Cambridge is or should be, as an eye to all our land: so that the alterations that fall out there cannot but bee felt of all parts."[6] Yet Cambridge was not *semper eadem*; the university and the colleges changed with the changing national church. The Earl of Essex was succeeded as chancellor of the university by Sir Robert Cecil, who, if not less Protestant, was at least more fully the Queen's tool than Essex had been. The deaths of William Perkins

---

[4]Canon 38.

[5]Collinson, "Jacobean," 45. Cf. Patrick Collinson, *The Elizabethan Puritan Movement* (London, 1967), 448-467; Peter Clarke, "Josiah Nichols and religious radicalism 1553-1639," *Journal of Ecclesiastical History* (April, 1977), XXVIII/2:145-150.

[6]William Ames(?), "Preface" to Paul Baynes, *The Diocesans Triall*, (London, 1621), 2. Cf. Rosemary O'Day, *The English Clergy: The Emergence and Consolidation of a Profession 1558-1642*, (Leicester, 1979), 138-142; Charles Carlton, *Archbishop William Laud*, (London, 1987), 138; Victor Morgan, "Cambridge University and 'The Country' 1560-1640", in *The University in Society*, Lawrence Stone ed. (London, 1975), 1:225-243.

(1602) and Thomas Cartwright (1603) seemed further signs of the changing of the church. More alarming to many was the new King's reference to the Church of Rome as a "true, but corrupt church"—an idea that had previously been roundly condemned in both the universities—in the opening speech to his first Parliament on 19 March 1604. Paul Baynes, Perkins's successor as lecturer at St. Andrew the Great, fell victim to the increased drive for conformity in the universities after the King's "Memoriall" of December 1604. In 1607 Baynes was forced to resign his fellowship for refusing to subscribe and conform. In 1610 another fellow of Christ's, William Ames, was silenced for remarks in a sermon critical of the "usual Christmas license" and card playing and eventually went to the Netherlands as a chaplain to English merchants there.

Even as the changing bounds of conformity fell across many godly consciences, they seemed at the same time to be enlarged to embrace many whose opinions previously would have been considered beyond the theological pale in a Reformed church. Notably, in 1604 William Laud took his B. D. at Oxford affirming the necessity of baptism for salvation. In 1605 Lancelot Andrewes was made Bishop of Chichester and was succeeded as the Master of Pembroke College, Cambridge by Samuel Harsnett, a fellow of the college. Although Harsnett was not popular, he was a chaplain of Richard Bancroft's, the successor of Whitgift as Archbishop of Canterbury. The vacancy created by Harsnett's election was filled with a disciple of Andrewes's, Matthew Wren, who was later to be Master of Peterhouse. That same year, Bishop William Chaderton of Lincoln was pressured into silencing Arthur Hildersham for nonconformity. Four years later, in 1609, Lancelot Andrewes was given the long-vacant see of Ely, and Harsnett again followed Andrewes, being made Bishop of Chichester. Also in 1609, after a disputed election for master at Christ's College, the election of the Puritan fellow, Pemberton, was disallowed. In his stead, James ordered Valentine Carey, a fellow of St. John's and former fellow of Christ's to be made master. Finally, on 8 January 1610, Nicholas Rushe, a fellow of Christ's was ordered by the Vice-Chancellor's court to disavow an offensively Puritan sermon he had preached. When he refused, he was expelled from the college and the university. Such was the flavor of the Early Stuart church, and in all of this, the shifts of the national church were clearly being felt in Cambridge.

Sibbes, however, had been in Cambridge for ten years before James had come to the throne, or Bancroft to Canterbury. The Cambridge Sibbes first knew was the late Elizabethan Cambridge, with Burleigh as Chancellor. It had been populated, agitated, and excited by William Whitaker, William Perkins, William Ames, Paul Baynes, and Robert Some. By the time James issued his "Memoriall" to the universities, Sibbes had commenced B. A. and M. A. He had attended Perkins's lectures at St. Andrew the Great before he commenced B. A. in 1599 and continued to attend when they were later given by Paul Baynes. In 1602, after the mandatory three years of further residence in Cambridge, Sibbes was created M. A., along with 105 other students.[7] The year before, on April 3, 1601, Sibbes was one of nine admitted as Foundress Fellows of St. John's. He was admitted as fellow for his native county of Suffolk. Though only twenty-four years old, Sibbes was not the youngest of the fellows.[8] While being made a fellow was the mark of a good college career in early seventeenth-century, it was perhaps also an indication of no other immediate prospects.

What did he do as a fellow of St. John's College? Generally, one may assume that Sibbes kept up the typical fellow's functions, foremost among which would have been tutoring. While no statutory limit was set on the number of students one fellow could tutor, the students outnumbered fellows in St. John's by five or six to one (though not all fellows were resident[9]). Admissions registers did not begin for the college until 1629, but a noted dated 1608 in the college archives in a Prizing Book (a book recording the valuation of rooms in college) states

---

[7]British Library, Harleian Manuscript 7038 f.83.

[8]Edward Miller, *Portrait of a College*, (Cambridge, 1961), 30.

[9]On 24 February 1601, in an effort to either discourage non-residency among fellows, or at least reward residency, "It was decreed, by Rich. Clayton, Master, and the seniors, that from thenceforth the gain of the bakehouse and brewhouse, together with the fellows part of corn-money (detriments being discharged) should be divided weekly, as the scholars corn-money then was, among those fellows only, that do remain at home, & are continuing, when the weekly division is made, or have continu'd the greater part of the week, . . . " from "The Statutes of St. John's College Cambridge," printed in *Reports from the Select Committees: Education of the Lower Orders*, vol. IV, (London, 1818), 405.

that "Mr [Abdias] Ashton" a fellow, "has five pupils."[10] From these books it is also clear that the room Sibbes held in college from 1611 until 1614 had five studies above it for his pupils.[11]

The fellow's responsibility included convincing the master of the college to allot rooms for his students, certainly privately instructing the students, and writing progress reports to their fathers. The tutor, being *in loco parentis*, also had financial duties to their students, which would include keeping their money for them and even lending money (or credit) to them on occasion. Mornings after chapel would usually be spent free from the students, as they attended college and university lectures. Afternoons were for tutorials, and evenings would be concluded by gathering the students into the fellow's rooms for evening prayer.[12] In his later sermons, he would refer to both Titus and Timothy as Paul's "scholar," and more than once to the Holy Spirit (or even the law) as the "tutor" of the Christian "scholar."[13] Other than his teaching in college, Sibbes would have acted in various fiduciary capacities, whether financially for the college (his signature survives on a deed of sale of college land at Radwinter from 1611) or morally for his scholars (he stood surety for one of the undergraduates involved in the riot at Trinity's Great Gate in 1610).

The fellows to whom Sibbes prized his rooms may give some hint of the godly sub-community in St. John's of which he was a part. Most interesting in this regard is Sibbes's final room exchange in 1616.[14] He was succeeded in E South by Abdias Ashton and succeeded John Allenson in Second Court F. Both Ashton and Allenson, had signed the articles against Peter Baro some twenty years earlier. Ashton, Allenson and Reginald Braithwaite (from whom Sibbes took his rooms in 1605)

---

[10]St. John's College Archives, C12.1, 176. I am indebted to Malcolm Underwood, Archivist of St. John's College, Cambridge, for guidance and explanations given to me.

[11]St. John's College Archives, C12.1, 176.

[12]See Miller, 39.

[13]Sibbes, "Bowels Opened," in *Works*, 2:13; "Fountain Opened," in *Works*, 5:459; "The Excellency of the Gospel above the Law," in *Works*, 4:223; "The Pattern of Purity," in *Works*, 7:516; "The Excellency of the Gospel above the Law," in *Works*, 4:299; "Fountain Opened," in *Works*, 5:468; "Divine Meditations and Holy Contemplations," in *Works*, 7:195.

[14]The Prizing Books at St. John's provide a continuous record of which rooms in college fellows occupied from early in the seventeenth century.

all signed the letter sent to Burleigh upon the death of Whitaker asking for St. John's to be allowed a free election for their master and were generally active in the godly party of St. John's during this time of transition.[15] That Sibbes should have been associated with such a group in the college is hardly surprising, considering that it was John Knewstub who had first introduced him into the society of St. John's.

At the same time, it appears from the Rental Books of the college that Sibbes was a very engaged and successful fellow and that he served in a variety of posts in college both before and after his involvement with the Trinity lecture began.[16] Within the first decade or so of his fellowship, the records show that Sibbes was elected by the master and senior fellows Fell Chaplain and Sublector (1603), Examiner (subject unspecified; 1604–1608), Lady Margaret Chaplain (1612–1618), and Dr. Thompson Chaplain (1612–1618). From his chaplaincies (pre–Reformation foundations), Sibbes merely drew extra income and perhaps had specific, regular duties in chapel. That it was something of an honor, because of the limited number of these chaplaincies in the college, and even partial remuneration for Sibbes's other activities in college, might well be suggested, for his responsibilities as sublector and examiner entailed a significant amount of labor. As a sublector in 1603, Sibbes's main duty would have been to assist the principal and (other) college lectors in the morning with practical arrangements, perhaps including substituting for them sometimes. As an examiner for four years, Sibbes would have been engaged in questioning the college's undergraduates for one hour a day on the lectures in the subjects of either rhetoric (classics), dialectics (logic), mathematics, or philosophy. That most of these honors and responsibilities were given to Sibbes by the master and seniors of this period is notable, considering that it was of Richard Clayton (Master of St. John's 1595–1612) that Thomas Baker wrote, it was "owing to his government, that Puritanism, that had taken such deep root, was now in great measure rooted out of the college."[17] St. John's

---

[15]Thomas Baker, *History of the College of St. John the Evangelist, Cambridge,* ed. J. E. B. Mayor, (Cambridge, 1869), 2:607; cf. 606–608.

[16]The record of Sibbes's positions in college are to be found not primarily in the college registers, but in the college rental books for 1600–1618 (SJCArchives SB4.3) and for 1619–1633 (SJCArchives SB4.4). Almost all of these offices were by annual election of the master and seniors.

[17]Baker, 1:196.

for Sibbes must have been not simply a training ground in Reformed divinity, but in Reformed divinity exercised with politic restraint.

By his final years of residency in Cambridge, Sibbes was elected to three of the most important posts in the college. In the year 1615 Sibbes was elected both Senior Dean and Lector Domesticus of the college.[18] As Senior Dean, Sibbes would have been the final authority in the administration (other than the master and seniors) of all aspects of the students' lives, from matriculation to commencement, including their religious, academic, moral, and social lives. From marshalling students to presiding over exercises in the hall and in chapel, Sibbes, in conjunction with the Junior Dean (Daniel Horsemanden), would have been very involved in and absorbed with college life. The position of Lector Domesticus is less well understood, but it is perhaps to be identified with the position of Principal Lector of the college. If that were the case, Sibbes would also have been obliged to deliver lectures throughout the week in the college hall on various subjects (probably including logic, rhetoric, and philosophy). Such positions not only brought Sibbes into more intimate contact with the running of his own college, but also, no doubt, gave him opportunity to interact with prominent visitors. Most prominent of all among these visitors would have been the king himself. As Senior Dean, Sibbes would probably have been minutely concerned with the royal visitation to St. John's in May 1615, though the specifics of his involvement do not survive.

With Sibbes's departure for London in 1617, he no longer filled such important practical roles at St. John's. Nevertheless, the most important role in the college to come to Sibbes was that of senior fellow. In 1619, after Sibbes had gone to London, he was elected to that post. As part of the general reforms of the university in the wake of the Cartwright/ Whitgift controversies of the 1570s, St. John's statutes were rewritten in 1580, and power over college matters was transferred from the master and fellows in general, to the master and senior fellows in particular.[19] The practical importance of the senior fellows was the virtual control of college offices they held in tandem with the master. Their privilege was

---

[18]Baker referred to the offices of lector and dean as usually falling "upon men of learning," as the other offices (e.g. bursar) "fell upon men of business," (Baker, 1: 206).

[19]On the Statutes of 1580, see James B. Mullinger, *St. John's College*, (London, 1901), 67–71. Cf. Miller, 29–34.

to have a share in the dividends of the college, which was about eight times as large as the share enjoyed by the junior fellows. Knowledge of the positions held by Sibbes in St. John's helps to explain his later election as Master of Katharine Hall, Cambridge. No extraordinary patronage is needed to account for the election. Given the other posts he had held, being a senior fellow of St. John's would no doubt have quite naturally suggested Sibbes as a likely master of a college.

In the larger sphere of university life, Sibbes was also active. He served as Taxor for the university in 1608. The Taxor was charged with the responsibility of seeing that just weights and measures were used by the town merchants in their selling of goods to the students. It was usually a position held by someone who was making the university his career. By holding such a position as a Cambridge fellowship and by being ordained, Sibbes had clearly risen in social status; he had become a member of the gentry. In this, Sibbes evidences the rapid social change that was typical of late Elizabethan and early Stuart England.[20] His grandfather had been merely a laborer, and his father a yeoman; Richard Sibbes was a gentleman—or at least an academic.

However, Cambridge was, for Sibbes, not only a place for career, but also for conversion. Elizabethan Cambridge had many things to commend a serious contemplation of religion, from regular sermons to monthly communion, from required prayers to outbreaks of the plague. At some point, probably soon after he became a fellow of St. John's, Sibbes was "changed." Sometime during this period in Cambridge, "It pleased God to convert him by the Ministry of Master Paul Baines, whilest he was Lecturer at Saint Andrews in Cambridge."[21] Baynes was, as Sibbes described him after his death, "of a sharp wit, and clear judgment: though his meditations were of a higher strain than ordinary, yet he had a good dexterity, furthered by his love to do good, in explaining dark points with lightsome similitudes."[22] Sibbes later

---

[20]Keith Wrightson, *English Society 1580-1680*, (London, 1982), 17–38.

[21]Samuel Clarke, "The life of Doctor Sibs" in *A general martyrologie, containing a collection of all the greatest persecutions which have befallen the church of Christ...Whereunto is added the lives of thirty-two English Divines*, 3rd ed., (London, 1677), 143. This is the only contemporary statement about Sibbes's own conversion.

[22]Sibbes, "To the Reader," in Paul Baynes, *A Commentary Upon the First Chapter of the Epistle... to the Ephesians*, rpt. in *Works*, 1:lxxxv. See also Keith

wrote, "As the minister speaks to the ear, Christ speaks, opens, and unlocks the heart at the same time; and gives it power to open, not from itself, but from Christ."[23] There is no reason to think this conversion was dramatic. In fact, Sibbes's lack of allusion to his own conversion and his repeated reference to its gradual nature may reflect the fact that he was one whom he described as "those who have kept themselves from the common pollutions and gross sins of the time. It pleaseth God that faith comes upon them, though they know not how for the time."[24]

On 21 February 1608 Sibbes was ordained deacon and priest in the Church of England at the age of 30 (well above the canonical minimum age of 24). Why he waited for over six years after he had reached the canonical age for ordination is not known. One reason for his delay would undoubtedly be that he did not consider himself converted until sometime after 1602. If he did present papers of testimony from "credible" persons who had known his life and behavior for three years previous (as some who were ordained were asked to do, according to canon 34) then Sibbes might well have wanted to wait for three years beyond his conversion (thus suggesting that his conversion occurred in 1605). The normal rush of college business and academic life could also have prevented him from either deciding to seek ordination or from actually seeking it once he had decided. Though the act of being ordained deacon and priest on the same day was officially prohibited in the church (as were any ordinations outside of the Sundays following an Ember week), it was a common practice. In fact, Sibbes was ordained with eight other young men that day, and he was not the only one to receive both offices in the same day. In the entry in the episcopal ordination register for this service Sibbes is listed first, and is the only one designated as fellow of a college.[25]

The ordination service was performed not by the Bishop of Ely, Martin Heton, but by the bishop of Sibbes's native diocese, Norwich, John Jegon (former Master of Corpus Christi, Cambridge). The service

---

Sprunger, *The Learned Doctor William Ames: Dutch Backgrounds of English and American Puritanism*, (Urbana, Illinois, 1972), 37, 192–193.

[23]Sibbes, "Bowels Opened," in *Works*, 2:63; cf. "Fountain Opened," in *Works*, 5:469.

[24]Sibbes, "Witness of Salvation," in *Works*, 7:375-6.

[25]Norwich and Norfolk Record Office ORR/1/2, ff.80–81. Thanks to John Craig for this reference.

took place in the parish church of Ludham. Ludham was the village in which the Bishop of Norwich had his main residence, excepting Norwich itself, and it was allowed canonically for the bishop to perform ordinations in the parish church of any of his residences. For two days before, on 19–20 February, these nine young men had been examined by two priests—John Curteis, M. A., and a Mr. West, M. A. If this ordination was done according to the Canons of 1604, those who had examined them would also have been the ministers who assisted the bishop in the service of ordination itself. Too, this would have been the time at which Sibbes would first have had to subscribe to the Three Articles. Considering that he was ordained, though no record of any subscription at this point survives, it would seem that Sibbes did subscribe.

Once ordained, and licensed as a preacher[26], Sibbes quickly gained a reputation as a good preacher among the people of Cambridge. Zachary Catlin records that when he became minister of Thurston in June of 1608, Richard Sibbes was already "a Preacher of good note in Cambr.... "[27] How would he have acquired such a reputation? Having been ordained early in 1608, and as a fellow of a Cambridge college, it is not surprising that he would have had some opportunities to preach or lecture in town or nearby country churches. Indeed, one of William Whitaker's complaint twenty years earlier against another fellow of St. John's, Everard Digby, had been that "he never preacheth any sermons more than of necessity he must neither at Cambridge nor else where for anything we know."[28] Grosart suggested that Sibbes began a preaching ministry in London between 1602 and 1607,[29] yet Grosart's only evidence for this was Catlin's mention of his reputation having already been established in 1608 and a mistaken reading of the introductory material to The Bruised Reed. Most probably the source of his reputation was simply the public sermons he would have preached in St. John's College chapel. In the records of St. John's College it is stated that

---

[26]Whether licensed by the university through the Vice-Chancellor's Court, or by the Bishop of Ely, and when, cannot be told because the relevant records either were not kept, or have not survived for either the university or the diocese.

[27]Zachary Catlin's Memoir of Richard Sibbes, printed as "Appendix to Memoir," in Works, 1:cxxxv.

[28]Letter of William Whitaker to Lord Burleigh, dated 26 October 1590, St. John's College Library.

[29]Alexander B. Grosart, "Memoir of Richard Sibbes, D.D.," in Works, 1:xxxv.

Sibbes and Robin Lane were elected as College Preachers (often referred to as St. Mark's Preachers) on 1 March 1609 and that Sibbes continued to serve in this capacity throughout his time as a fellow of the college.[30] According to Fisher's original statutes for the college, the responsibility of these preachers was to preach in English for the good of the townspeople. The original statutes provided for eight such preachers. The later Elizabethan statutes are unclear in the number of College Preachers to be elected, though the office was to continue, and one-quarter of all the fellows of the college were to preach. A decree by Richard Howland (Master of St. John's) and the seniors in 1584 in the college statutes stated that "there shall every first Sunday of every [kalendar] month, be a Communion with a private sermon, by the preachers allow'd by the College, in the morning betwixt the houres of 8 & 9; and the same day, after noone at one, a publick sermon by the sd. preachers.... "[31] The "private sermon" referred to would have been for members of the college only; the "publick sermon" however, at one in the afternoon, would have been in English, and open to townspeople. Presumably, this is the context in which the College Preachers were to function. Since his preaching could not have begun before February 1608, it seems certain that, if Catlin's memory served him correctly, Sibbes quickly became known as a good preacher, primarily through these English sermons delivered in the college chapel.

The year 1610 saw Sibbes being recognized by both the university and the town of Cambridge. The first recognition came from the university. In 1610 Valentine Carey, Joseph Hall, and Samuel Ward were created Doctors of Divinity in Cambridge. In the same exercises, fourteen M. A.'s were created Bachelors of Divinity. Among those was Sibbes, who by that time had been a fellow of St. John's for almost a decade. To be created B. D., the M. A. had to preach one public sermon in English, and one in Latin to the university; he had to answer all questions put to him by members of the university on two points of divinity in the open schools for two hours; and, finally, he had to reply against someone else on two different topics on separate days in the

---

[30]St. John's College Archives SB4.4.
[31]"Statutes of St. John's," *Second Report*, p. 404.

same place, all the above activities taking place within one year.[32] Perhaps because of his reputation as a preacher, Sibbes was chosen out of the fourteen to be the B. D. "responder" at the commencement exercises. He was to respond to the two propositions: (1) *Romana Ecclesia est apostatica.* (2) *Dei Decretum non tollit libertatum volun-tatis.*[33] Sibbes, then, commenced B. D., defending two beliefs common to the moderate Puritans of the day.

The second recognition, and that which has been far more significant in shaping later historians' perceptions of Sibbes, came from the town. In 1610 the minister, churchwardens, and twenty-nine other parishioners of Holy Trinity Church established a lecture by popular subscription to be held in the church at one o'clock on Sunday afternoon. On 22 November they wrote to Richard Sibbes as follows:

> To Mr. Sibs publique pracher of the Towne of Cambridge. We whose names ar heer Underwritten the Churchwardens and parishioners of Trinity parishe in Cambridge, with the ful & fre consent of Mr. John Wildbore our minister, duely considering the extream straytnes & divers other discomodities concerning the accustomed place of your exercises, & desireing as much as in us lyeth the more publique benefit of your ministry, doe earnestly entreat you wold be pleased to accept of our parishe churche, which al of us doe willinglye offer you for & concerning the exercising of your ministery & awditorye at the awntient and usual daye & howre. In witness hereof we have heerunto set to our hands this 22nd of November 1610.
>
> Joh. Wilbore, Minister.
> Edward Almond,
> Thomas Bankes, Churchewardens
> [Signed also by 29 Parishioners.][34]

Sibbes is called "publique p'cher of the Towne of Cambridge" not as a reference to his having held a public lectureship previous to this one

---

[32]William Harrison, *The Description of England,* ed. G. Edelen, (Ithaca, New York, 1968), 73.

[33]British Library, Harleian Manuscript 7038 f.88.

[34]C. H. Cooper, *Annals of Cambridge* (Cambridge, 1845) 3:229.

established at Holy Trinity Church,[35] but simply in that he was a public preacher (ie., a preacher in English) in the town of Cambridge. The mention of "the extream straytnes & div'se other discomodities concerning the accustomed place of your exercises, & desireing as much as in us lyeth the more publique benefit of yor ministry" is intriguing. Where was his "accustomed place of your exercises"? It seems clear from the decree for "publick sermons" mentioned above, that the "accustomed place of your exercise" was the chapel at St. John's. It is not surprising that townsmen such as the petitioners would consider a college chapel discommodious, and the small size and arrangement of seating in a collegiate chapel would be less than ideal for a popular lecture. Wherever it was, it was a place which at least these parishioners considered a less convenient place than Holy Trinity would be. The "awntient and usuall day and hour" were Sundays at one o'clock in the afternoon, the same time as the university lecture at Great St. Mary's and, more significantly, the same time at which these townspeople had almost certainly heard Sibbes preach his "publick sermons" at St. John's chapel. For his troubles, Sibbes's was to be paid 40 pounds per year, raised by public subscription.

Sibbes's lectures at Holy Trinity were evidently crowded with listeners—so crowded, that a new gallery needed to be built to accommodate them. In order to finance this gallery, subscriptions were obtained.[36] That this lecture was for the town of Cambridge, rather than simply the parish of Holy Trinity, is suggested by the fact that these later subscribers came from eight other parishes (including two butchers

---

[35]As J. Barton has suggested in "Notes on the Past History of the Church of Holy Trinity, Cambridge," *Cambridge Antiquarian Society Communications* (Cambridge, 1869–1870), 4:319. He posits that Sibbes had succeeded Chaderton and Bentley as the lecturer at St. Clements, and that it was St. Clements which the townsmen were referring to as being discommodious. There is, however, no evidence for this.

[36]Records survive of a new gallery being built in Holy Trinity, apparently to accommodate the crowds, in March 1616. For the list of subscribers for the erection of the gallery, see the Parish Records of Holy Trinity, P22/6.2, Shire Hall, Cambridge. A few of the names are the same as those which signed the request to Sibbes some five years earlier. Listed amounts of subscription ranged from 3 shillings and 4 pence (an amount given by three different donors) to 2 Pounds (given by Mr. Davers of St. Benet's Parish). Cf. Barton, "Holy Trinity," 313–335.

from St. Edward's Parish and a shoemaker from St. Benet's Parish). Furthermore, by 1630, this same lecture was referred to as "a publick Lecture serving for all the Parishes in that Town (being 14 in number)" and as the "Towne Sermon."[37] This town lecture was evidently popular not only with the town subscribers, but also with the students. Clarke wrote:

> And when Master Sibs had been Master of Arts some while, he entered into the Ministry, and shortly after was chosen Lecturer himself at Trinity Church in Cambridge: To whose Ministry, besides the Townsmen, many Scholars resorted, so that he became a worthy Instrument, of begetting many Sons and Daughters unto God, besides the edifying and building up of others.[38]

Through Sibbes's preaching at Holy Trinity in 1612, John Cotton reported that God had been pleased to convert him. Cotton, though already an ordained clergyman, had long struggled with his being unmoved by the passion of Christ. William Perkins' preaching had been particularly disturbing to him. Yet Sibbes's more hopeful preaching encouraged Cotton. Through attending Sibbes's lectures at Holy Trinity, and through some personal conferences in which they discussed what one could do in order to be saved, Cotton gained an apprehension of his own salvation. Through him, John Preston was won from "witty" preaching over to "true," plain, spiritual preaching. Through Preston's newly reformed preaching, Thomas Goodwin, who had also attended Sibbes's lectures, was converted.[39] To the younger

---

[37]Letter from Dudley Carlton, Viscount Dorchester to Vice-Chancellor Butts, dated 11 May 1630, reprinted in Cooper, 3:229.

[38]Samuel Clarke, 143, cf., 218; also, Larzer Ziff, *The Career of John Cotton: Puritanism and the American Experience* (Princeton, 1962), 30f.

[39]R. Halley, "Memoir of Thomas Goodwin," in *The Works of Thomas Goodwin*, (Edinburgh, 1861), 2:lix–lx. Goodwin himself stated that at one point prior to his conversion, instead of going to "St. Mary's, where the flaunting sermons were . . . for eight weeks together I went with the Puritans of that College to hear Dr Sibbs, whose preaching was plain and wholesome; and to improve my time the better before sermon began, I carried with me Calvin's Institutions to church, and found a great deal of sweetness and savouriness in that divinity," (lx).

members of the university, Sibbes presented a formulation of Calvinist doctrine that had been widely accepted by the time he arrived in the university. Ironically, it was his influential presentation of what he had learned as a conforming theology that may have helped to gain for Sibbes a reputation as a nonconformist. Though Preston preceded Sibbes in death by seven years, Cotton and Goodwin (along with Sibbes's friend John Davenport) all freely admitted their indebtedness to and reverence for Sibbes, yet all separated from the established church within Sibbes's lifetime, preferring instead the congregational way. The nonconforming Goodwin was to be one of the chief editors of Sibbes's works. The nonconforming Cotton, although across an ocean much larger then than now, always kept "the picture of that great man [Sibbes] in that part of his house where he might oftenest look upon it."[40]

Given such disciples, it is not surprising that Sibbes has been presented as an early Stuart preacher who neither approved nor practiced kneeling in communion, wearing the surplice, or signing the cross in baptism, and yet who remained within the established church. He was constantly troubled by Laud. Doubly deprived, censured and silenced, Sibbes became a model for his numerous disciples—such as Goodwin, Davenport, and Cotton—who would later find their way into dissent. It has been supposed that only the power of his lawyer-friends and noble patrons allowed him to retain his later ministry at Gray's Inn for almost two decades. After his death, his writings became almost entirely the possession of nonconformists, and Sibbes came to be read through separatist spectacles. Although remembered as espousing a robustly Reformed theology, it was his moderation that was particularly admired by those who followed him. Sibbes seemed to stand above the tumult of the times, "to preserve the vitals and essentials of religion, that the souls of his heareres, being captivated with the inward beauty and glory of Christ, and being led into an experimental knowledge of heavenly truths, their spirits might not evaporate and discharge themselves in endless, gainless, soul-unedifying, and conscience-

---

[40]Cotton Mather, *The Great Works of Christ in America* (Hartford, 1853), 1:255.

perplexing questions."[41] So the perception of Sibbes has remained—a paradox of tumultuous, conflict-filled career and arrestingly "sweet," gentle writings.

In his introduction to Sibbes's *The Glorious Feast of the Gospel*, Arthur Jackson wrote that "We need say nothing of the author...his memory is highly honoured amongst the godly-learned."[42] The celebrity that had come to Richard Sibbes by 1650 was only heightened by the memory of his conflict and suffering to remain both godly and conforming. With Laud as his antagonist, Sibbes was named by Prynne along with "Doctor Staughton . . . D. Taylor, D. Gouge, M. White of Dorchester, M. Rogers of Dedham, with sundry more of our most eminent preaching orthodox Divines" as having been "brought into the High Commission and troubled or silenced for a time, by his [Laud's] procurement upon frivolous pretences: But in truth, because they were principle Props of our Protestant Religion, against his Popish and Arminian Innovations."[43] Laud did harass Sibbes once in London for his involvement in circulating a letter that was deemed politically inexpedient, and more pointedly, for his involvement as a leader in the Feoffees for Impropriations. But the picture of the harassed Sibbes went beyond even that. It reached back into his days in Cambridge. Thomas Ball, in his "Life of the Renowned Doctor [John] Preston" (used by Samuel Clarke in *A generall martyrologie* [1651]) reported that when Preston feared that Buckingham's support for him was waning, his attention turned to Lincoln's Inn for "a kind of freedome & exemption; for he saw that holy & blessed Dr. Sibbs was outed both of fellowship & Lecture in the university, yet by the goodness and prudence of Sr. Henry Yelverton...he was received & reteyned at Grey's Inn unto his death."[44] Ball does not state that Preston is reported as actually having said this to anyone, rather simply that Preston "saw" the way an Inn of Court was Sibbes's refuge when "outed both of fellowship & Lecture in the university."

---

[41]Simeon Ash, James Nalton and Joseph Church, "To the Reader," in Sibbes, *A Heavenly Conference Between Christ and Mary after His Resurrection* (London, 1654); rpt. in *Works*, 6:415.

[42]Arthur Jackson, James Nalton and William Taylor, "To the Reader" in Sibbes, *The Glorious Feast of the Gospel* (London, 1650); rpt. *Works*, 2:442.

[43]William Prynne, *Canterburies Doome* (London, 1646), 362.

[44]Samuel Clarke, *A general martyrologie* (London, 1651) 108.

Was Sibbes really outed? In neither of Sibbes's memoirs nor in any of the introductions to thirty posthumously published volumes of his works are these two deprivations mentioned. Zachary Catlin's memoir of Sibbes, written at the request of Sir William Spring in 1652 omits any reference at all to Sibbes's lectureship at Holy Trinity church. The other contemporary memoir of Sibbes was that by Samuel Clarke — "The Life of Doctor Sibs" — published in *A martyrologie* (1652). This brief memoir was based upon Clarke's own knowledge, information gleaned from introductions to Sibbes's works, and conversation with William Gouge, a particularly important source. As an old friend of Sibbes in Cambridge and London and the preacher of Sibbes's funeral sermon, he would have known of any deprivations Sibbes suffered, especially if they caused his removal from Cambridge to London.[45] Yet in this memoir, Clarke made no allusion to Sibbes's Cambridge deprivations, even after he had edited Ball's life of Preston the previous year, in which both deprivations were mentioned.

In fact, no seventeenth-century memoir of Sibbes records any such deprivations. Indeed, the only accounts of them are as an aside in a memoir of John Preston, which could have been written as late as 1650. Is it likely that this additional information about Sibbes in Ball's account reflected his more accurate knowledge of Sibbes than Catlin or Clarke had? Or, do the silences of Catlin and Clarke bring into question the accuracy of Ball's mention of Sibbes's loss of his fellowship and lectureship? That Ball's account of Sibbes is more full is certainly not the case. Sibbes actually appears very little in Ball's life of Preston. That Ball's information was more accurate than Catlin's or Clarke's also seems doubtful. Ball was in Cambridge as an undergraduate during the final year and a half of Sibbes's lectureship at Holy Trinity. Whether he attended his lectures, we can only guess. Certainly he would have known of Sibbes's leaving and going to London, and undoubtedly rumors would have circulated as to why the popular preacher had left. Although Catlin was a personal friend of Sibbes, his memoir actually gives little time to recounting Sibbes's life in Cambridge, therefore it would be only slightly surprising that these deprivations should be omitted. Clarke, however, would be likely to have known about such deprivations had they occurred, since his memoir of Sibbes was at least

---

[45]Samuel Clarke, in *A general martyrologie*, 144, mentions having spoken with Gouge about Sibbes.

partially based on conversations with William Gouge. Furthermore, writing in 1651 or 1652 Clarke would have no reason to omit such a reference, especially when he had published it the previous year by his inclusion of Ball's memoir of Preston in his *A generall martyrologie*. So, from these considerations alone, the weight given to the idea by repetition notwithstanding, one might wonder whether Sibbes's deprivations actually occurred.

Sibbes was not deprived of his fellowship at St. John's in 1615. We have already noted Sibbes's election as a Senior Fellow of the College in 1619. The Rental Books of St. John's College mentioned above record quarterly payments to R. Sibbes as a fellow continuously from 1601 through the first quarter of 1626, the year in which Sibbes became Master of Katharine Hall.[46] His quarterly payments from the college as a College Preacher and commons and livery allowances continued into 1626 as well.

The question of his having been "outed" from the lectureship is more ambiguous. It is certain that he was asked to begin the lecture at Holy Trinity in November of 1610 and that he was chosen Preacher of Gray's Inn, London, in February of 1617. But there is no reason for accepting the commonly reported fact that he was deprived of this lecture in the year 1615. That date was first suggested due to a misreading of a statement based on an assumption based on a mistake.

The 1615 date (or early 1616 as Grosart would have it) for the suppression of the Holy Trinity lecture is called into question by an instrument for the construction of a new gallery in the church, which is dated 4 March 4 1615 (Old Style).[47] That the lectureship was suppressed or that Sibbes was simply deprived of it at all in 1616 is made almost impossible by an edict of James that, though undated in its copies in both the Cambridge University Archives and in the Public Records Office, London, nevertheless, almost certainly was issued on 3 December 1616. On that day, James met with the Heads of Cambridge Houses in Newmarket to discuss ecclesiastical matters in the university. The digest of their conversation matches almost exactly with the written

---

[46]St. John's College Archives SB4.4 f. 163.
[47]Cambridge Shire Hall, Parish Records, P22/6.2.

edict, which follows it immediately in the State Papers Domestic.[48] The content of this edict does not seem to include (as has often been suggested) a suppression of the lecture at Holy Trinity. It was only to forbid lectures which conflicted with the catechizing in the colleges, an exercise that was done from 3:00 to 4:00 P.M. on Sunday afternoons. The lecture at Holy Trinity was held at 1:00 P.M. and so was not affected by the edict.[49] In the conversation with the Heads, James had apparently expressed his desire that students should attend the university lecture at Great St. Mary's, rather than other lectures at the same time, but this was only directed to the students, and even so it was not repeated in the written directions given to the Heads.[50]

These directions were quickly followed. There appears in the records of the Vice-Chancellor's Court a memorandum dated 6 December 1616, just three days after the edict was issued by the King. The memorandum reads:

that Mr Sibbs was asked by Mr Vice-Chancellor whether he would subscribe to the 3 articles required to be subscribed unto by the Canons. He refused to subscribe, and diverse questions being asked he made these answers:

[Now in Sibbes's own hand] I said that the signe of the cross [in baptism] was dangerous. My meaning was in regard of those that be not well instructed and not otherwise. I said that there is

---

[48]Public Records Office, State Papers Domestic, James I, SP14/89, f.113–114. Cf. James' "Memoriall" of twelve years earlier, (State Papers Domestic, James I, SP10/68).

[49]See CUA Mm.1.38, 137 for a reference in a letter from Viscount Dorchester to Vice-Chancellor Butts dated 11 May 1630 about the lectureship at Holy Trinity. In the letter Dorchester mentions that the lecture has "for many yeares past... been held at one of the clocke in the afternoon...", the same time as the University Lecture was held in Great St. Mary's. This letter has been reprinted in Cooper, 3:229–230.

[50]Is this also the occasion to which Thomas Ball refers in his memoir of John Preston, where he writes, "About that time the lecture at Trinity-church, and the sermons at St Andrews, were prohibited, and the scholars all confined to St Mary's .... "? Thomas Ball, *The Life of the Renowned Doctor Preston*, E. W. Harcourt,ed. (Oxford, 1885), 42–43).

nihil impie in the booke of ordination. I add it is not contrary to the word of God, but allowable. R. Sibbs.[51]

Either this is the record of Sibbes's subscription to the Three Articles or he met with the Vice-Chancellor again later the same day and subscribed. The next day, John Hills, Master of Katharine Hall and Vice-Chancellor, wrote a letter to James Montagu, Bishop of Winchester (who, as former Master of Sidney Sussex was frequently James's agent in dealings with the university) stating that

> The two Town Lecturers, Mr. Sibbs, and Mr. Bentley, have beine before me, and the Heads of colleges; Mr. Bentley readily without fear or doubt hath subscribed and promised his conformity to all things approved or allowed in our Church; Mr. Sibbs at first made Some Quastion and Seemed lesse Setled in Opinion, but upon a Second conference he also Submitted and Subscribed and the reason of his delay, as we gathered, was rather for ~~feare to displease~~ [inserted instead, "misdoubting the censure of"] his ~~erasie~~ auditors, than out of any resolution or opinion he had against the Articles or anything in them contained, for he hath also promised to administer the sacraments of baptism and the Lord's supper according to the order and words prescribed in the Book of Common Prayer.[52]

Hills's initial reference to Sibbes's "feare to displease his crasie auditors" is probably a reference to Sibbes's concern that some might misunderstand the sign of the cross in baptism, a concern he had voiced the previous day in the Vice-Chancellor's Court and with which Hills evidently had little sympathy. The importance of this letter, however, is that it shows that Sibbes did indeed conform (or at least subscribe). The fact that he was even asked to conform and that he was referred to in Hills letter as a "town preacher" proves that Sibbes was still lecturing at Holy Trinity in December of 1616. It was less than two months later that

---

[51]CUA Vice Chancellor's Court I.42. f. 202. See Victor Morgan's reporting of this incident in his "Country, Court and Cambridge University: 1558–1640: A Study in the Evolution of a Political Culture," (Ph.D. diss., University of East Anglia, 1983), 2:208.

[52]CUA Lett. 11.A.A.8.d.

he was chosen Preacher of Gray's Inn, London. While the possibility exists that Sibbes was deprived at some point later in December or January, this seems unlikely, and there is no evidence for it beyond Ball's mention of it. It begins to appear, therefore, that Sibbes was deprived neither of his fellowship nor of his lectureship.

Why would Ball have reported these deprivations? Why would he have supposed them to have taken place? Because he cited no sources for his assertion, the modern historian can only guess.[53] Perhaps Ball had heard, as a student, that Sibbes was called in to subscribe, that there were some questions about the matter, and that soon afterwards he left for London. That, added to the clear divisions of the 1640s, which could easily have been read back carelessly into the 1610s, could plausibly explain Ball's references to Sibbes being "outed both of fellowship & Lecture in the university" which became the basis for re-making this otherwise moderate puritan into a nonconformist, another example of a Protestant "martyred" by the Laudian church.[54]

Ironically all of this legend has led to a very different impression of Sibbes than one would gather from reading his writings and reading about his character and temperament from his contemporaries. The very fact that Sibbes did subscribe to the Three Articles in December 1616 disproves the idea that he was an open nonconformist. Sibbes was a hesitater, and a questioner, but not a dissenter. Yet with these deprivations removed from the foreground, the conciliating tone of his writings begins to appear more consistent with his own person, and his later preferments become more understandable. The picture of

---

[53]Ball's memoir is not altogether accurate in other respects. For example, Preston is said to have been elected preacher of Lincoln's Inn, London in 1622 when that post fell vacant by John Donne's death. Donne, however, did not die until 1631. Cf. Irvonwy Morgan, *Prince Charles's Puritan Chaplain*, (London, 1957), 117–124.

[54]While there is no certain date for the composition of Ball's life of Preston, it would seem to have been composed sometime well after Preston's death in 1628; perhaps it was specifically written for Clarke's "lives of sundry modern divines," where it first appeared in 1651,(Samuel Clarke, *A general martyrologie...Whereunto are added the lives of sundry modern divines*, [London, 1651]). The mistaking of the date for John Donne's death (as 1622 when it was 1631), the reference to "very many yet alive" which can witness to Preston's manner of life, the reference to Henry Yelverton's and Sibbes's death, and the explanation of what the obligations of Charles' royal chaplains were to him, all show that the composition was well removed from 1628.

Sibbes—as a reformer, but a cautious reformer, as a Puritan, but a moderate Puritan—is consistent with the rest of Sibbes's life and activities in Cambridge and London.[55]

---

[55] For a fuller treatment of Sibbes focusing on the question of his having been deprived of his lectureship at Holy Trinity Church, and his fellowship at St. John's College, see this author's "Moderation and Deprivation: A Re-appraisal of Richard Sibbes," *Journal of Ecclesiastical History* (July, 1992): 43:396–413.

III

Sibbes and the Communion of

Saints, 1617–1635

As we see creatures of the same kind,
they love and company one with another;
doves with doves, and lambs with lambs;
so it must be with the children of God,
or else we do not know what the communion of saints means.[1]

ONE OF THE most striking aspects of Richard Sibbes's sermons is his frequent and powerful reference to friendship. "What makes the life of man comfortable? There is a presence of God in meat, in drink, in friends."[2] In his treatment of Psalm 42:11, he delivered one of the most beautiful and passionate sections of these sermons in what amounts to a verbal rhapsody on friendship.[3] He said:

There is a sweet sight of God in the face of a friend; for though the comfort given by God's messengers be ordinarily most effectual, as the blessing of parents, who are in God's room, is more effectual than the blessing of others upon their children,

---

[1]Sibbes, "The Church's Riches by Christ's Poverty," in *Works*, 4:521.
[2]Sibbes, "A Breathing after God," in *Works*, 2:228–9.
[3]Sibbes, "The Soul's Conflict with Itself," in *Works*, 1:191–193; cf. "Bowels Opened," in *Works*, 2:36–37; "The Excellency of the Gospel above the Law," in *Works*, 4:262.

yet God hath promised a blessing to the offices of communion of saints performed by one private man towards another.[4]

Godly friends were walking sermons.[5] Sibbes described God himself as "the great Friend,"[6] and Christ was characterized by "a winning, gaining disposition," which was to be in his followers.[7] Sibbes proved to have such a nature. By 1624 his ministry in London had been so well-received at Gray's Inn that, just as at Holy Trinity Church, his auditorium had to be enlarged. As one somewhat estranged from his father, removed from his family, and unmarried, Sibbes could well appreciate the value of friendships. Furthermore, the "communion of saints" was readily available to Sibbes throughout his life. He had risen by friends (Knewstub, Yelverton, potentially Ussher, possibly Goodwin), and the places to which he rose required friendships to be important. From the age of seventeen or eighteen Sibbes was not only a bachelor, but lived in communities of bachelors—St. John's, practically Gray's Inn, Katharine Hall.[8] A person in Sibbes's position might well have found himself, after the better part of a lifetime in Cambridge and London, never more than once or twice removed from a great part of the university-educated clergy of the time and from the greater part of the political and financial nation.

As important as friendships may have been, the problem remains of how the historian can reconstruct them accurately. Realizing their potential aid in reconstructing Sibbes's history, Nicholas Tyacke has suggested that prefacing works of Paul Baynes and Ezekiel Culverwell (both suspended for nonconformity), dedicating a work to Sir Horace and Lady Mary Vere, "major patrons of refugee Puritan clergy in the Netherlands," having his own works posthumously edited by "the two

---

[4]"The Soul's Conflict with Itself," in *Works,* I:192; cf. *ibid.,* p. 191.

[5]Sibbes, "The Bride's Longing," in *Works,* VI:560; cf. Sibbes's "Angels' Acclamations," in *Works,* VI:321; "The Pattern of Purity," in *Works,* VII:515; "The Rich Poverty; or, The Poor Man's Riches," in *Works,* VI:237; "The Soul's Conflict with Itself," in *Works,* I:192.

[6]Sibbes, "The Saint's Hiding-Place in the Evil Day," in *Works,* I:411; cf. "Bowels Opened," in *Works,* II:37.

[7]"The Excellency of the Gospel above the Law," in *Works,* IV:262; cf. "The Bruised Reed and Smoking Flax," in *Works,* I:51.

[8]Gray's Inn required its lecturer be unmarried. See Reginald Fletcher, ed., *The Pension Book of Gray's Inn . . .1569–1669* (London, 1901) 139; cf. 224.

radical Puritans," Thomas Goodwin and Philip Nye, and having named Nathaniel Barnardiston (whose chaplain was a nonconformist) an overseer of his will all point to Sibbes's own radical religious proclivities.[9] Is this suggested by Sibbes's friendships? Or do his friendships further corroborate the image of Sibbes drawn in the previous chapter: a cautious, moderate reformer? The difficulties of reaching such conclusions on such evidence, always considerable, are only exacerbated in the case of Sibbes by the lack of historical remains. In Sibbes's case, the extant personal writings that involve him are few, and those have usually survived because of their association with an historically notable figure. Many other relationships have left not a trace. While certain instances and activities, remarks, and attitudes are known, it is necessarily the limits of the historian's knowledge, not of the actual relationships themselves that are being tried in this exercise. Yet, while the extent and nature of any past figures' relationships can never be fully known, it is possible to reconstruct something of Sibbes's friendships. Indeed, it becomes clear that some friendships were particularly close, while others seem to have been simply functional associations. The mere proof of an association yields little of interpretive value, particularly with figures like John Dury and Samuel Hartlib, (both of whom mentioned knowing Sibbes.)[10] Yet with others the result is more rewarding. The task of this chapter is to investigate the remaining evidence, to reconstruct something of the more important associations that marked Sibbes's later life in London and Cambridge and to conclude what may and may not be suggested about Sibbes from them.

---

[9]Nicholas Tyacke, *The Fortunes of English Puritanism, 1603–1640* (London, 1990) 11, 15–16; (cf. Richard Greaves' inclusion of Sibbes in his *Biographical Dictionary of British Radicals in the Seventeenth Century*, [Brighton, 1984], 3:169–171). While Vere did employ radicals such as Ames, Tyacke does not note that Vere was also the means of getting preferment for more decidedly moderate clergy, e.g. James Ussher. See Ussher's letter of 1624 to Lady Vere, (BL Additional Ms. 4274, no. 18).

[10]See John Dury, *The Unchanged, Constant and Single-hearted Peacemaker* (London, 1650) 7; Dury, letter of 24 July 1635 to unnamed custodian of Sibbes's papers (BL Sloane MS 654, fols.351–352); Hartlib, Ephemerides, 1634, 1635.

Circles of Friendship

A good example of the limitation of the remaining evidence is found in what is known of Sibbes's relationship with John Preston. Perhaps no other pair of prominent early Stuart godly preachers had careers that ran so parallel to each other's. Yet little is known of their relationship. Their letters to James Ussher provide some information.[11] In Samuel Clarke's *Martyrologie*, Nicholas Bernard's biography of Ussher reported that Sibbes and Preston were both close friends with Ussher and shared "most entire affections."[12] Clarke's section on Preston (written by Thomas Ball) does not even mention Sibbes (apart from the reporting of Sibbes's having been "outed" from fellowship and lecture in the university). This silence is surprising. Since Sibbes was already dead by the time the memoir was written, there is no obvious reason for Ball's reticence.[13] Inferences of their close association can be drawn from Preston's posthumous consideration of Sibbes. Preston remembered Sibbes in his will, giving him the right to pick a book out of his library[14] and requesting that Sibbes serve as editor and publisher of his sermons after his death.[15] That Sibbes and Preston highly esteemed each other seems certain; beyond that little can be said.

Not only is the extant evidence about Sibbes's friendships obviously partial, but much of it is also ambiguous. For example, the fact that Sibbes can be proved to have cooperated closely on a number of different projects with someone can hardly be taken to be an indication of a close personal friendship. There are probably no two preachers with whom there is more evidence of Sibbes cooperating than there is of

---

[11]Preston to Ussher, 20 July [1621?], in Elrington, ed., *Whole Works of the Most Rev. James Ussher*, (London, 1864) 16:370–372. Preston to Ussher, 16 March 1619; *ibid.*, 373.

[12]Samuel Clarke, *A general martyrologie, containing a collection of all the greatest persecutions which have befallen the church of Christ...Whereunto is added the lives of thirty–two English Divines*, 3rd ed., (London, 1677) 292; cf. Benjamin Brook, *The Lives of the Puritans*, (London, 1813) II:418.

[13]See Clarke, 108.

[14]Irvonwy Morgan, *Prince Charles's Puritan Chaplain* (London, 1957) 43.

[15]Sibbes brought out the following collections of Preston's Sermons: *The New Covenant, or the Saints Portion* (1629); *The Saints Daily Exercise: a Treatise Unfolding the Whole Duty of Prayer* (1629); *The Breastplate of Faith and Love* (1630); *The Saints Qualification* (1633).

his working with William Gouge and John Davenport. Both were
Feoffees with Sibbes, and both signed the circular letter in support of
aid for the refugees from the Palatinate, for which they were together
censured in the Court of High Commission.[16] All three of them were
among the signers of an Instrumentum affirming support for John
Dury's work, and circulated by Dury in May 1631.[17] They are the only
two preachers at whose churches it can be proved that Sibbes
preached.[18] In Hugh Peter's memory, Gouge, Sibbes and Davenport
were the three that remained.[19] If the amount of evidence that survives
were alone the basis for judgment, Sibbes might be taken to have been
equally close to Gouge and Davenport. Yet, after putting this evidence
together with a few other bits of information, reflection suggests a
different conclusion. Davenport was twenty years Sibbes's junior, an
Oxford man, and had only become known during the 1625 plague. He
probably would have seen Sibbes frequently only from 1625-1633.[20]
Gouge, on the other hand, was a contemporary of Sibbes from
Cambridge, whose family was well-known to Sibbes. Together with
Baynes, Gouge is one of only two people Clarke mentions in his short
treatment of Sibbes, styling Gouge a "frequent hearer" of Sibbes.[21]
Furthermore, there is the note in the muniments room at St. Catharine's
College that when William Gouge took his D. D. at Cambridge in 1628,
Gouge, though a king's man, was entertained with a dinner at

---

[16]The letter was dated 2 March 1626[7]. On 30 June 1628, Davenport wrote
to Mary, Lady Vere that their troubles with the High Commission continued. See
Davenport to Vere, *Letters of John Davenport*, I.M. Calder, ed. (New Haven,
Connecticut, 1937) 29-30. Cf. *Calendar of State Papers, Domestic, 1631-1633*. John
Bruce, ed. (London, 1862) 167.

[17]BL Sloane MS 1465, fol. 2. Whether or not the thirty-eight signatories
merely represented individuals supporting Dury, or a more self-conscious
group is unclear. Cf. G. H. Turnbull, *Hartlib, Dury and Comenius*, (Liverpool,
1947) 147. In the Hartlib Manuscripts (MS 5d/10) at Sheffield University, there
is evidence that Sibbes was working along with Featley and Holdsworth to
encourage reconciliation with the continental Protestants, and that they had
adopted Dury as their "legate." I owe these references to Anthony Milton.

[18]Robert Keayne, "Sermon List", in *Proceedings of the Massachusetts
Historical Society*, 2nd series, L (1916-1917) 204-207.

[19]Hugh Peter, *A Dying Father's Last Legacy to an Only Child*, (London, 1660)
99.

[20]*Letters of Davenport*, 31.
[21]Clarke, 144.

Katharine Hall.[22] A careful look at all the evidence suggests an important difference, then, between these two London associates of Sibbes—Gouge was a long-time friend and a contemporary; Davenport was a younger, energetic associate who was anxious to help forward the plans of the godly. In 1633 Davenport resigned his pastoral charge, and left England. Sibbes did not mention him in his will. Yet Sibbes requested that William Gouge, who continued as minister of St. Anne's Blackfriars long after Davenport had left his living, take the trouble to preach his funeral sermon. Records of activities are essential to uncovering Sibbes's associations in London, but taken alone and uncritically, they can mask more than they discover.

Less evidence can be even more misleading. One of the historian's most important sources of knowledge of Sibbes comes through the prefaces he wrote. Yet a careful examination reveals the problems of taking such prefaces as evidential coins of equivalent value. Sibbes's prefaces to Robert Jenison's and Richard Capel's books provide a particularly helpful example. Both Jenison and Capel used Sibbes as an agent in London to commend their works to the press. Both also got in some trouble with the authorities and may, therefore, be taken as "radicals" of some sort. In his 1625 preface to Jenison's book, Sibbes referred to Jenison as a "godly Minister, whom for his soundnesse in Judgement, faithfulnesse in friendship, painfulnesse in his calling, & integrity of his life, I have much esteemed ever since our first acquaintance in the Universitie."[23] In 1633 Sibbes called Richard Capel "this godly minister, my Christian friend."[24] Capel had been at Oxford, and seems to have known Sibbes primarily through his patron Nathaniel Stephens, a member of Middle Temple and friend of Sibbes.

Yet these two prefaces hardly demonstrate similar friendships between Sibbes and the respective authors. Though Capel resigned his living in 1633, and Jenison in 1639, both for nonconformity, and though Sibbes had known Jenison longer, his relationship to Capel was probably closer than his relationship to Jenison. Jenison had written from Newcastle to Samuel Ward on 26 May 1621, complaining contemptuously of Sibbes's "timourousness" in advising him not to

---

[22]Audit Book, 42, Muniments Room, St. Catharine's College, Cambridge.

[23]Robert Jenison, *The Christians Apparelling by Christ*, (London, 1625).

[24]"To the Christian Reader," to Richard Capel's, *Treatise of Temptation*, in *Works*, 1:cx.

publish works that could be taken as so directly critical of royal policy (ie., the Spanish match).[25] Sibbes's kind comments about Jenison several years later in the preface to Jenison's 1625 book are particularly interesting in light of Jenison's frustration. Either Sibbes was unaware of Jenison's earlier complaints about the caution he had advised regarding publication of the earlier book or Sibbes's usefulness to or friendship with Jenison exceeded his irritation. On the other hand, in Sibbes's will, Capel was remembered with a small bequest, as "my worthy friend, Mr Capell, late preacher in Gloucestershire." Shortly after Sibbes wrote this preface in 1633, Capel was suspended for his refusal to read the *Book of Sport.* Yet he was apparently a moderate man like Sibbes. Of Capel, Clarke wrote, "Moderation he professed, and moderation he practised."[26] Thus, Sibbes wrote for those who could well be taken as radical. But the conclusion does not necessarily follow that Sibbes was himself a radical, for the more polemical writer (Jenison) complained of Sibbes's reluctance. The other, though forced out of his preaching post six years earlier, was apparently the more moderate man and was remembered in Sibbes's will.

Of the thirteen volumes of sermons Sibbes prefaced during seventeen years in London, seven of them were sermons of a minister who had died (Paul Baynes, Ezekiel Culverwell [1634], Preston, John Smith) and six were of living ministers (Henry Scudder, Culverwell [1623], Thomas Gataker, Jenison, John Ball, Capel). With the posthumous sermons, he seemed to be discharging debts he felt either to the deceased author (Baynes, Smith[27]) or to a patron of their's (Culverwell) or in the case of the Preston sermons, fulfilling the express request of the deceased. The publications of the sermons of the living ministers seem to have had more various origins. In the case of Scudder's and Capel's sermons, Sibbes was clearly acting not only for the minister but for a mutual patron Sir Thomas Crewe[28] and Nathaniel Stephens,

---

[25]Tanner MS 73.

[26]Clarke, 312.

[27]In Sibbes's preface, he singled out Smith's use of "lively representations" and his Christ–like expressions of heavenly teaching "in an earthly manner" for particular praise. Perhaps Smith was one of Sibbes's models for his own use of illustrations.

[28]Crewe's family home was in Stene, Northants., not far from Drayton, Oxfordshire, where Scudder was minister. The sermons that formed Scudder's

respectively. In three cases, he seemed to publish Gataker's, Ball's, and perhaps Culverwell's sermons for charitable reasons (the first on behalf of Mrs. Winter, the second two for the preachers themselves, both having been deprived). The only other example is his involvement with Jenison's 1625 volume, which could well have been ammends for his refusal to write a foreword to an earlier book. Of these six ministers, four lived away from London (Oxfordshire, Newcastle, Staffordshire, Gloucestershire). Of the two who lived in or around London, Culverwell was advanced in years and had been deprived of his living, and Gataker's sermon was given over specifically to Mrs. Winter to be published for her own support. This would suggest that a part of Sibbes's activity with the press was simply pragmatic—for practical reasons ministers remote from London needed the help of London friends in publishing their sermons.

Sibbes seemed to have known well all of the authors (with the possible exceptions of Scudder and Ball). Of the nine authors whose works Sibbes published, four had been deprived of their livings, (Baynes, Culverwell, Ball, and Capel). Sibbes talked at greater length, and more intimately, about Smith than he did about other authors whose works he prefaced. In tone this preface is most similar to his prefaces for Baynes's Ephesians and Culverwell's second book. This suggests that Sibbes's reticence to write personally about an author may have had as much or more to do with whether the author was alive or dead, than with the depth of Sibbes's friendship with him. In the case of Baynes in particular, Sibbes's aid of Culverwell evidenced his appreciation for the man to whom he felt spiritually indebted, rather than his won religious radicalism. He published the work of another ejected minister—Baynes—despite disagreeing with the book's clearly articulated supralapsarian position.

There is no denying that Sibbes was a close friend of many who espoused more radical reform for the Church of England than did he. He continued friendships with godly ministers who could not in good conscience conform. Baynes, Culverwell, Ball, and Capel were all friends of Sibbes after their open nonconformity. John Cotton, John Norton, John Wilson, Samuel Whiting, Hugh Peter, and Philip Nye—all of whom left England because of their religious views—were also

---

book had been taken down by Crewe. Scudder dedicated that volume to Crewe and his children.

among Sibbes's friends. As the preaching of Baynes had been the means for Sibbes's conversion, so Sibbes's preaching was the means of John Cotton's conversion "which begat in him [Cotton] a singular and constant love to the said doctor, of whom he was also answerably beloved."[29] Indeed, "Mr. Cotton's veneration for Dr. Sibs was after this [his conversion] very particular and perpetual: and it caused him to have the picture of that great man in that part of his house where he might oftenest look upon it."[30] Nor was Sibbes's friendship with men more radical than he limited to mere affection and admiration. Cotton Mather recorded that John Norton was approached by Sibbes, but Norton's "conscience being now satisfied in the unlawfulness of some things then required in order there–unto, would not permit him to do it."[31] As John Wilson lay dying in Boston, Massachusetts, in August 1667, he "thus comforted himself, 'I shall ere long be with my old friends, Dr. Preston, Dr. Sibs, Dr. Taylor, Dr. Gouge, Dr. Ames, Mr. Cotton, Mr. Norton, my Inns of Court friends.'"[32] Mather also mentioned that Samuel Whiting's piety "was further advanced by the ministry of such preachers as Dr. Sibs and Dr. Preston: so that in his age he would give thanks to God for the divine favours which he thus received in his youth...."[33] In his memoir Hugh Peter recalled his [Peter's] early days in London hearing Sibbes.[34] As lecturer at St. Sepulchre's, London, Peter soon became quite involved in the work of the Feoffees, eventually being named a co-defendant in the case against them. And finally, there was Philip Nye, the Oxford graduate who served as perpetual curate of Allhallows, Staining, London from

---

[29]John Norton's life of John Cotton, printed in Clarke, 218.

[30]Cotton Mather, *Magnalia Christi Americana*, (Hartford, 1852) 1:255. Mather's *Magnalia* recounted the lives of the first generations of New England ministers and published information about Sibbes's friendships that has not survived elsewhere. This is in contrast with Daniel Neal's *History of the Puritans* (London, 1732-1738) which drew its information on Sibbes exclusively from Samuel Clarke's brief biographical notice of him. Cf. the preface to Cotton's *An Exposition upon the Thirteenth Chapter of Revelation*, (London, 1655).

[31]Mather, :1:288.

[32]Mather, 1:313.

[33]Mather, 1:502. Cf. comments by Thomas Cawton, *The Life and Death of that Holy and Reverend Man of God, Mr. Thomas Cawton*, (London, 1662) and Thomas Walker, (E. Calamy, *The Nonconformist's Memorial*, [London, 1775], 2:408).

[34]Peter, 99; cf., 31, 57-58; R. P. Stearns, *The Strenuous Puritan: Hugh Peter, 1598-1660* (Urbana, Illinois, 1954) 34.

1627, and as lecturer at St. Michael's Cornhill, London, from 1630. Though he resigned all of his positions in 1633 after embracing congregationalism and eventually left for Holland, he apparently did not leave London immediately after resigning his livings. Hartlib recalled conversations with Nye in London in 1634 and 1635. During this time, Nye apparently attempted to get Sibbes's permission to ready for the press his sermons upon "the Corinth" (It is unclear whether these are his sermons on chapter 1 or 4 of 2 Corinthians).[35] Nye's interest in Sibbes's sermons continued after his death. Nye told Hartlib that "Dr. Sibs hase left much behind him in writing but all broken notes."[36] Nye co-edited many of Sibbes's sermons that were published posthumously. Yet in each of these cases, Sibbes's relationships with these men were always begun while they were cooperating members of the Church of England. In fact, while evidence exists of their continuing affection for Sibbes, it should be noted that there is no evidence of his relationship with Cotton, Norton, Peter or Nye after their decision to separate from the Church of England.

Sibbes certainly countenanced nonconformists. Among his friends were an older generation of them, including Culverwell and John Dod. By the time Sibbes moved to London, he had come to know Dod.[37] Dod gave evidence of his acquaintance with Sibbes in his commendatory epistle prefixed to Sibbes's *Bowels Opened*. Yet, if Sibbes's close fellowship with the suspended ministers Culverwell and Dod suggests religious radicalism on Sibbes's part, then it must be a religious radicalism that encompassed James Ussher as well. Dod, Culverwell and Sibbes all seem to have been part of a circle in London that included Ussher, Preston and Mrs. Mary More, sometimes along with others.[38] In a letter to Ussher dated 21 March, 1622, Sibbes passed on greetings from "Mrs. More...Mr. Dod" and others of Ussher's and Sibbes's common London circle of godly friends.[39] Preston, in one letter to Ussher, gives evidence of his own regular consultations with Sibbes (along with Chaderton and Dod) and assumes that Ussher will see

---

[35]Hartlib, Ephemerides, 1634.

[36]Hartlib, Ephemerides, 1635.

[37]See letter of Sibbes to Ussher, 21 March 1622, Elrington, 16:395–396.

[38]See Elrington, 15:361–366, 369, 375; 16:330–334, 370–373, 395–396, 440–441, 453, 455–456, 522–523.

[39]Sibbes to Ussher, Elrington, 16:395–396.

Sibbes as a matter of course.[40] Ussher clearly esteemed Sibbes and at one point, attempted to persuade him to come to Dublin as provost of Trinity College. Ussher referred to Sibbes as one "with whose learning, soundness of judgment, and uprightness of life I was very well acquainted."[41] Ussher's warm friendship with Sibbes is also evidenced in Clarke. Nicholas Bernard's biography of Ussher (printed in Clarke) reported that when Ussher was in London, "Twelve of the most eminent divines in London, (who at his being here, were wont to apply themselves to him as to a father, as Dr Sibs, Dr Preston, &c., between whom and him there were most entire affections) wrote to him for his directions about a body of practical divinity, which he returned to them accordingly."[42] It seems certain that two of those "eminent divines" were Culverwell and Dod. This godly circle of friends, which included Sibbes with both suspended ministers and an archbishop, demonstrates that the values and concerns that these people had in common, whatever else they may have been, were neither those of conformity, nor radicalism.

Sibbes's London connections often led to associations in other parts of the country. He seemed to have a particular way with "Personages of Quality."[43] Catlin mentioned that Sibbes was often trusted by such persons with "divers sumes of money, for pious and charitable uses." Though such comments were a typical way of commending ministers and their sermons at the time,[44] the evidence of Sibbes's friendships bears out the truth of the assertion, particularly in the cases of Sir Thomas Crewe,[45] Sir Robert and Lady Elizabeth Brooke,[46] Nathaniel

---

[40]Preston to Ussher, 20 July [1621?], in Elrington, 16: 370–372; Preston to Ussher, 16 March, 1619; *ibid.*, 373.

[41]Ussher to Abbot, Elrington, 15:361. Cf. Sibbes's remarks to Ussher in Elrington, 16:440–441.

[42]Clarke, 292; cf. Brook, 2:418.

[43]Zachary Catlin's Memoir of Richard Sibbes, printed as "Appendix to Memoir," in *Works*, 1:cxxvi.

[44]E.g., Clarke's memoir of William Gouge (Clarke, 244).

[45]See Sibbes, letter to Ussher, Elrington, 16:395. Crewe had been at the Pension meeting when Sibbes was chosen preacher of the Inn (5 February 1617), had served with him as one of the Feoffees for Impropriations, and requested Sibbes to preach his funeral sermon.

[46]Sibbes remembered Sir Robert and Elizabeth Lady Brooke in his will as "My very worthy frends." In 1637, in Goodwin and Nye's dedication of their second volume of Sibbes's sermons—*A Fountain Sealed*—they referred to Lady

Stephens, Sir Robert Harley,[47] Sir Henry Yelverton, Christopher
Sherland,[48] Lady Mary Vere,[49] and Mrs. Mary More.[50] "He used
sometimes in the summer-time, to go abroad to the houses of some
worthy Personages, where he was an Instrument of much good, not
only by his private labours, but by his prudent counsell and advice,
that upon every occasion he was ready to Minister unto them."[51] Sibbes
was among the most well-connected of the godly clergy of London,
particularly with those who (like Yelverton and Harley) freely owned
the name "Puritan."[52] His prominent positions in London and Cambridge, which connected him institutionally with both patrons and

---

Elizabeth Brooke as being held in the affection and esteem of Sibbes "more than
any friend alive" and mentioned that "though his tongue was as the 'pen of a
ready writer' in the hand of Christ who guided him, yet your ladyship's hand
and pen was in this his scribe and amanuensis whilst he dictated a first draft of
it in private, with intention for the public" (Thomas Goodwin and Philip Nye's
Dedication of Sibbes, A Fountain Sealed (London, 1637); rpt. in Works, 5:411). Her
chaplain, Nathaniel Parkhurst, published a posthumous memoir of her, recalling
that "Dr. Sibs, an Eminent Divine, Master of K. Hall Cambridg, and Preacher to
the Honourable Society of Grayes-Inn, who frequented her House at Langley in
Hartfordshire, would say, that he went to other places (mostly) to satisfy others,
but thither to please himself," (Parkhurst, The Faithful and Diligent Christian
Described and Exemplified, [London, 1684], 74).

[47]When the living of Brampton Bryan fell vacant in late 1633, Harley wrote
to leading ministers around the country, trying to find a suitable replacement.
Perhaps it was about this matter that Harley wrote to Sibbes, (undated letter of
Sibbes to Harley [BL Add. Ms. 70106]).

[48]Christopher Sherland, Yelverton's nephew, also of Gray's Inn, served with
Sibbes as a Feoffee for Impropriations. Sibbes's close friendship with Sherland is
shown by his request for Sibbes to preach his funeral sermon. In the sermon,
"Christ is Best," Sibbes referred to bequests in his will, which included £400 for
the Feoffees and £100 to Katharine Hall for the training of poor scholars.

[49]See "The Bruised Reed and Smoking Flax," in Works, 1:35-37; Letters of
Davenport, 31.

[50]In his will, Sibbes remembered Mrs. More again, with one of the most
profuse appositions— "my very worthy, religious, and bountifull frend." Cf.
"Epistle Dedicatory," Ezekiel Culverwell, Time Well Spent in Sacred Meditations
(London, 1634); rpt. in Works, 1:xciii-xciv.

[51]Clarke, 145.

[52]G. Ornsby, ed., The Correspondence of John Cosin (Durham, 1869) part I,
155-158; Wilfrid Prest, The Rise of the Barristers (Oxford, 1986) 219-220; J. T.
Cliffe, The Puritan Gentry: The Great Puritan Families of Early Stuart England
(London, 1984) 12.

young clerics, made him a natural agent for both laity and clergy, when either was looking for a minister or a living, (e.g., John King of Abbot's Langley,[53] or William Mew, of Eastington, Gloucestershire[54]). Thus again, Sibbes relationships seem to reveal more about his character as a respected, trusted, and able friend and minister of the gospel, than they do about his conformity.

Dedications of Sibbes's sermons must also be used critically as evidence of Sibbes's friendships. The nobility were natural dedicatees by whom to commend sermons to the reading public. For example, Lincoln, Saye and Sele and Warwick all had volumes of Sibbes's sermons dedicated to them, yet they do not appear all equally to have been friends of Sibbes. Other than Sibbes and Davenport's dedication of the first posthuomous collection of Preston's London sermons to Lincoln and Viscount Saye and Sele, nothing of any friendship between them and Sibbes survives.[55] Dedications of Sibbes's sermons to Robert Rich, Earl of Warwick, on the other hand, are lent more importance by the

---

[53]A posthumous poem about John King, vicar of Abbot's Langley, indicated that Sibbes was instrumental in getting King his living:

Great Doctor Sibbs did with alluring Smile,
Train him into his Toil, and by a wile,
An honest Wile, got him fast fixed there,
where he well spent near three and fifty year.
The first Flight from his Nest ('twas short) he took,
was to the house of old Sir Robert Brook:
whose Lady, Holy and Elect, behind
yet stays and waiteth for a happy Wind.
I did admire to hear, and since, how still
She writes Epistles, as with Angel's Quill.
'Twas She and Sibbs that chiefly laid the Plot,
To mount him in that Pulpit; and when got
Into the Mount, nothing e're moved or drew
Him thence, but black and windy Barthol'mew.

Anon., *A True Picture of Mr. John King* (London, 1680) 3.

[54]Stephens was the patron of the living of Eastington in Gloucestershire, held from 1613-1633 by Richard Capel. When Capel resigned his living, Sibbes may well have aided both Stephens and Mew. In 1635 Stephens appointed Mew to the vacant living. In his will, Sibbes rememebered Stephens as "my very kind friend"; Mew as "my very good frend."

[55]Preston, *New Covenant*, (1629).

other evidence of Sibbes's relationship with Warwick. In 1619 his son
Robert (aged eight) was admitted to an Inn of Court—not to Inner
Temple (where Warwick was a member), but to Gray's Inn. Warwick
had many friends at Gray's Inn, not least of whom was his cousin, Sir
Nathaniel Rich. One reason, however, for Warwick having his son
admitted there, rather than at Inner Temple, may have been Warwick's
esteem for Sibbes's ministry. Warwick—"the greatest patron of the
Puritans"[56]—was especially mindful of ministers in his care for the
godly. Through his considerable influence (he controlled twenty-two
livings) if not his wealth (in 1631 he quietly secured a loan from Sir
Thomas Barrington), he offered support to numerous godly ministers,
including Gouge, William Twisse, Samuel Collins, William Wright,
Stephen Marshall, Jeremiah Burroughs, Dod, Obadiah Sedgwick and
eventually Hugh Peter.[57] Whether through his cousin or through
Gouge,[58] or some other mutual friend, Warwick became a regular
hearer of Sibbes. He took up residence next to Gray's Inn, occupying
the most spacious house on Holborn High Street.[59] In 1631 Warwick got
permission to build another gallery in the south-east corner of the
chapel at Gray's Inn so that he and his friends could be nearer the
pulpit "for the better heareing the sermon."[60] In the first posthumously
published volume of Sibbes's sermons, Thomas Goodwin and Philip
Nye dedicated Sibbes's final two sermons at Gray's Inn to Warwick,
noting Warwick's habit of bringing his family to hear Sibbes preach.[61]
In 1638 John Sedgwick and Arthur Jackson (the other primary
publishers of Sibbes's sermons) also dedicated their first volume of

[56]Neal, 2:3. Cf. Clarendon, Edward Hyde, *The History of the Great Rebellion*
(Oxford, 1819) 2:281.

[57]Derek Hirst, *Authority and Conflict* (London, 1986) 67; Barbara Donagan,
"The Clerical Patronage of Robert Rich," *Proceedings of the American
Philosophical Society*, vol. CXX/5 (1976): 388–419. Arthur Searle, ed., *Barrington
Family Letters 1628–1632* (London, 1983) 204. William Hunt, *The Puritan
Moment: The Coming of Revolution in an English County* (Cambridge,
Massachusetts, 1983) 164.

[58]Hunt, 163.

[59]John Stow, *The Survey of London*, ed. H. B. Wheatley, (London, 1956) p. 389.

[60]See entry for 9 May 1631 (*Pension Book*, 1:300). Cf. Francis Cowper, *A
Prospect of Gray's Inn*, 2nd ed. (London, 1985) 60.

[61]Thomas Goodwin and Philip Nye's Dedication of Sibbes, *Two Sermons
Upon the first words of Christs last Sermon, John 14.1. Being also the last Sermons
of Richard Sibbs* (London, 1636); rpt. in *Works*, 7:335.

Sibbes's sermons to Warwick and his wife Susanna.[62] In Edmund Calamy's funeral sermon for Warwick, Calamy recalled that Warwick had been "a very special friend unto that man of God of famous memory Dr. Sibbs."[63]

Sibbes's friendship with Warwick was reenforced by his close association with Warwick's cousin, Sir Nathaniel Rich. Christopher Thompson has observed that Rich is "a figure whose political importance contemporaries recognized more clearly than later historians have done."[64] Rich, admitted to Gray's Inn in 1610, first sat in parliament in 1614. He was a leader of what may be termed the moderate opposition,[65] having formed by 1628 a close working relationship with Sir Dudley Digges and Viscount Saye and Sele to support the via media of the Petition of Right (rather than the more radical Bill of Rights). Sibbes came to know Rich at Gray's Inn relatively quickly, commending him to Ussher as his "worthy friend" in a letter only a few years after he had arrived at the Inn. In this letter, Sibbes referred to Rich's "sincerity, wisdom, and right judgment."[66] His friendship with Sibbes continued throughout Sibbes's time in London and ended when he was requested to serve as an overseer of his will.

Many of Sibbes's legal friends, however, were outside of Gray's Inn. Two of Sibbes's closest friends (both of whom he remembered in his will) were John Pym and Nathaniel Stephens (both of Middle Temple). Pym was a frequent hearer of Sibbes's sermons. He discussed the publication of some of them with booksellers[67] and told Hartlib that he

---

[62]John Sedewick's [sic] Dedication of Sibbes, *Light from Heaven* (London, 1638); rpt. in *Works*, 4:492.

[63]E. Calamy, *A Patterne for All* (London, 1658) 37.

[64]Christopher Thompson, "The Origins of the politics of the parliamentary middle group 1625-1629," *Transactions of the Royal Historical Society*, 5th series (1972) 22:76.

[65]S. R. Gardiner, *The Constitutional Documents of the Puritan Revolution, 1625-1660*, 3rd ed. (Oxford, 1906) 1; Barry Coward, *The Stuart Age* (London, 1980) 138.

[66]Sibbes to Ussher, 21 March 1622, Elrington, 16:395.

[67]"Mr. Bartlet hase as many Ms. of Dr. Sips as the writing stood him in thrity pounds. as hee told Mr. Pim who hase interest in him," (Hartlib, Ephemerides, 1634). This is John Bartlet, who, cooperating with Thomas Goodwin and Philip Nye, later had these sermons printed and sold them in two collections in 1639: *Christs Exaltation Purchast by Humiliation* (1639) [rpt. in *Works* vol. V, beginning on p. 324]; and *The Excellencie of the Gospel above the*

thought "Dr. Sibs hase preached abundance of most excellent sermons of the highest diversity (hee being one of the most experimental divines now living) upon the subject about the seeling of the spirit and now hee is upon the witnessing."[68] The interest was clearly not all one way. In his will, Sibbes remembered Pym affectionately as "my deare and very worthy frend." Through the Feoffees, Sibbes was also associated with Samuel Browne and Robert Eyre of Lincoln's Inn and John White of Middle Temple, who was host to many of their meetings.[69] Through them, he also worked with a number of city merchants—Francis Bridges (salter), Richard Davies (vintner), John Gearing (grocer), Nicholas Rainton and George Harwood (haberdashers), and Rowland Heylyn (ironmonger). While the records of the Feoffees tell little of Sibbes's personal relationships with the above, it is clear that Sibbes shared with them a concern for the placement of godly preachers and that he met with them often (sometimes twice a week during term time) in pursuing these goals. Some of these sent their sons to be educated at Katharine Hall, Cambridge, after Sibbes became the Master there. John Gearing sent his son there in 1627, John Pym sent two, one in 1628 and another in 1631.

In addition to his London connections, Sibbes also had strong connections with the leading godly families in Suffolk and Essex. Catlin mentioned Sibbes's continuing relationships with his family and childhood friends, which were maintained through frequent returns to the area. The Springs, Barnardistons, D'Eweses and Bacons all were friends of Sibbes. Sir Symonds D'Ewes sent his brother to Katharine Hall in 1631, though Sir Symonds had been at St. John's; while Sir Nicholas Bacon sent his son to Katharine Hall in 1634, though he had been at Christ's. Sir William Spring and Sir Nathaniel Barnardiston—"my worthy and very loveing frends"—Sibbes asked to be the overseers of his will (along with Sir Nathaniel Rich). It was Sir William Spring's son and namesake who requested Catlin to write a memoir of Sibbes. His family home was in Pakenham, Suffolk, where Sibbes went to school as a boy, and near Thurston, where Sibbes's family continued

---

Law (1639) [rpt. in *Works* vol. IV, beginning on p. 202]. The *D.N.B.* records that Bartlet "enjoyed the friendship of Dr. Sibbes whilst studying at St. Katharine's."

[68]Hartlib, Ephemerides, 1634.

[69]Isabel M. Calder, *Activities of the Puritan Faction of the Church of England 1625-1633* (London, 1957) 76-77, 79.

to live. The Barnardistons had a long association with Katharine Hall as benefactors,[70] and Sir Nathaniel sent one of his sons there during Sibbes's mastership in 1632.

Sibbes also had close friendships with the Barringtons. Sir Thomas Barrington and his brothers–in–law, Sir William Masham and Sir Gilbert Gerard, all knew Sibbes. All three were members of Gray's Inn. Sir Thomas was an ardent consumer of Sibbes's printed sermons.[71] Two letters from her sons–in–law Sir William Masham and Sir Gilbert Gerard to his mother survive, Lady Joan Barrington, in which Sibbes is mentioned. Sir William Masham recalled having dined with Sibbes in William Prynne's chambers the previous Sunday.[72] Masham, though educated at Magdalen College, Oxford, sent two sons to Katharine Hall, Cambridge (in 1632 and 1634). Gerard, from a prominent family of governmental officials and noted for his concern for issues of religion, was appointed to the House committee on religion in 1626, along with Sir Francis Barrington (his father–in–law). Gerard's house in Harrow–on–the–Hill often served as a meeting place for the godly (many of whom were related to him). Writing on 19 September 1631, Gerard summarized a sermon of Sibbes ("The Rich Pearl") to Lady Joan. She may well have heard Sibbes preach, perhaps even at her own or Gerard's house. In 1624 the Benchers agreed to Gerard's turning his chambers in the Inn over to Sibbes in return for which "Mr. Gerrard is otherwyse to be gratified by the house."[73] In 1632 Gerard also sent a son to Katharine Hall, Cambridge (not a college previously attended by the Gerard's). Such was the depth of respect and admiration Sibbes had earned from these prominent, though moderate, godly families.

---

[70]R. Almack, "Kedington, alias Ketton, and the Barnardiston Family," *Proceedings of the Suffolk Institute of Archaeology and Natural History* (1864–1874) 4:131. In 1633 his mother, Lady Katharine Barnardiston, left a bequest to the college of land, the proceeds of which were to establish three scholarships at Katharine Hall, (Henry Philpott, *Documents Relating to St. Catharine's College in the University of Cambridge*, [Cambridge, 1861], 117–119).

[71]See Mary E. Bohannon, "A London Bookseller's Bill: 1635–1639," *The Library*, 4th series, vol. XVIII (1938): 417–446.

[72]Searle, 227–228.

[73]*Pension Book*, 266. The benchers may have gratified Gerard by letting him proceed with his plans to build a new range of buildings in the Inn, which were built by him five years later, (see *Pension Book*, 286).

One of the most interesting aspects of Sibbes's friendships is his ability to keep the affections of such disparate people. Two young fellows of Katharine Hall during his tenure there serve as a case in point—Thomas Goodwin and John Ellis. While an undergraduate, Thomas Goodwin heard Sibbes preach.[74] After his election to a fellowship at Katharine Hall, and his conversion, Goodwin became "the instrument of the choice of that holy and reverend man, Dr Sibbs, to be Master of that College, and of most of the Fellows of that College in those times, as Dr Arrowsmith, and Mr Pen of Northamptonshire, to name no more."[75] Goodwin recounted "familiar" conversation with Sibbes, once he took up the mastership of the college.[76] Upon Preston's death, Goodwin succeeded him as the Holy Trinity lecturer and became vicar of the church in 1632. Yet within two years, Hartlib recorded the fact that Goodwin "resigned his living to Dr. Sips et seemes to stagger bec[ause] of the Ceremonies."[77] Goodwin resigned from his position at Holy Trinity and at Katharine Hall and moved to London. Hartlib recorded Goodwin's comment that "Dr. Sips eminency lyes in the knowledge of Christ. And therfore hee should bee set to goe over that place, Christ is made wisdome unto us etc, and though hee bee gone over it already yet it is taken imperfectly and hee at this 2nd time will goe over it 4 times as large."[78] Goodwin was obviously in contact with Sibbes upon his removal from Cambridge and Katharine Hall to London. Hartlib reported Goodwin's comment on Sibbes's series on 1 Peter 4:17-19, which he called "the most fullest that ever hee heard him preach et then upon that that judgment must begin at the House of God."[79]

John Ellis's career, less well known, was entirely otherwise. Ellis had been an undergraduate and fellow at Katharine Hall, being elected

---

[74]Thomas Goodwin, "Memoir ... out of his own papers," *Works of Thomas Goodwin* (Edinburgh, 1861) 2:lii–liii, lx.

[75]Goodwin, 2:lxvi.

[76]Goodwin, 2:lxxi.

[77]Hartlib, Ephemerides, 1634. Cf. Goodwin, 2:lxxi–lxxii; Mather, 1: 264; Robert Baillie, *A Dissuasive from the Errors of our Time* (London, 1645) 55–56, 66–67.

[78]Hartlib, Ephemerides, 1634. Perhaps because of his move to London, Hartlib had more chances to talk with Goodwin, and Goodwin's name appeared more frequently in the Ephemerides after 1634.

[79]Hartlib, Ephemerides, 1634.

fellow during Sibbes's last year as master, and then only after Sibbes had mollified the concerns of the more godly fellows that Ellis was simply a spy for Laud (who had sponsored his education). Sibbes argued that Ellis was still young and could change. Ellis, in fact, did just that. After becoming something of a radical during the Interregnum, Ellis changed again at the Restoration. It is surprising that in attempting to present Sibbes as a radical, no one has taken note of Sibbes's comments recorded by Ellis in his personal apologia. In it, Ellis recounted something of his relationship with Sibbes, remembering that:

> Dr. Sibs (a man whose works do praise him in the gate) the then Master of our Colledge, on occasion of certain opinions started by some at that time amongst us; commended unto me the reading of Austins Seventh Tome. God preserved me from that infection (although I lived for some time in a Holland–like aire (from whence that wind blew) and near that water which was conceived to exhale some such vapours) without that Antidote. But had I read then all that Tome; it had, with his blessing, secured me against Independency; the one half of whose evil consists in Donatism and Separation.[80]

Those to whom Ellis referred as "some among us" certainly would have included Goodwin. A few pages later, Ellis, with fulsome praise for the author, quoted a passage from *The Soul's Conflict*, in which Sibbes enjoined obedience to law except when it clearly contradicted scripture.[81]

Other apparently curious friendships of Sibbes's could be produced.[82] In December of 1640, Sir John Finch, the King's Lord Keeper of the Great Seal, defending himself against impeachment in the House of Commons, decried Arminianism and sought to evidence his forwardness for the health of the church by reminding the house

---

[80]John Ellis, *S. Austin Imitated: or Retractations and Repentings In reference unto the late Civil and Ecclesiastical Changes in this Nation* (London, 1662) 45. Ellis referred to the common renaissance grouping of Augustine's works, with the seventh tome including all of Augustine's anti–Donatist and anti–Pelagian writings.

[81]Ellis, 50–51.

[82]E.g. Sibbes's acquaintance with Neile's chaplain, Augustine Lindsell (see letter of Montagu to Cosin, 23 May 1625, (Ornsby, 1:70).

that "I lived thirty years in the society of Grayes Inne, and if one that were a reverend preacher in my tyme (Dr Sibbes) were now alive, he were able to give testimony to this house."[83] Though this statement was made publicly and for the obvious purpose of gaining support among godly members of the Parliament, that is no reason to discount it. Yet this is the Sibbes who, when Finch had helped manage a huge masque of the Inns of Court for the entertainment of the King, had dined with Prynne in his chambers close to the publication of Prynne's infamous attack on the theatre—Histrio-Mastix. Finch soon after led the proceedings against Prynne in the Star-chamber, advocating brutal punishments. Yet both Prynne and Finch were evidently friends of Sibbes. Again, in a letter of Laud to Wentworth, dated 15 November 1633, Laud refered to "you and your cousin Sibbes."[84] This remark need not be seen as sarcastic; more likely, Wentworth was a friend of Sibbes, or at least, as Laud knew, appreciated Sibbes. Having matriculated to St. John's in 1609, Wentworth would have come to know Sibbes not only as a college lecturer, but he also would have met him in the early stages of his popularity as a preacher in English, first in the college chapel, then after 1610, in Holy Trinity Church. Yet at the same time, Sibbes had the leader of Wentworth's mortal critics in the House—Pym—as one of his closest friends. Though one might question whether Sibbes would have had such combinations of friends, it is often the contemporary historian's concerns and assumptions that can make things appear strange in hindsight that appeared quite normal at the time.

Conclusion

Sibbes clearly had an extensive tree of friendships throughout the London legal, merchant, and clergy communities and beyond. This is hardly surprising given the fact that Sibbes was primarily a preacher and a pastor. Reflecting on Sibbes's successful mastership at Katharine

---

[83]Wilfrid Prest, The Inns of Court under Elizabeth I and the Early Stuarts (London, 1972) 214. Cf. Finch's claim to have protected Sibbes from Laudian persecution (Prest, Barristers, 361). What persecution this was is unclear.

[84]William Laud, The Works of the Most Reverend Father in God, William Laud, D. D. (Oxford, 1857) 6:330.

Hall, W. H. S. Jones wrote that Sibbes was "an able, pious man, with a gift of making friends."[85] His skill as a preacher was to prove pivotal in the initiation and continuation of these relationships. It had been by Sibbes's own lectures that he came to the attention of other fellows, students, ministers, and patrons in Cambridge. It was probably these lectures in Cambridge that had brought him to London. Were it not for his preaching, there is no apparent reason why Sibbes might not have continued on as a fellow of St. John's until his death. Once in London, it was primarily through his lectures there that he came to the attention of the godly throughout the city and the country. From his position, Sibbes undoubtably became one of the most important links between the godly lawyers and the godly ministers in London.

When taken together, Sibbes's connections through the Inns of Court brought him close friendships with an impressive array of parliamentary leaders of the early Stuart era, including particularly the leaders of what would later become known as the "Middle Group" of the Parliamentary opposition.[86] Yelverton, Wentworth, Gerard, Barnardiston, Spring, Sherland, Crewe, Rich, Finch, Stephens, Harley, and of course Pym all appear to have been good friends of Sibbes. Whether simply taking note of him, listening to him preach, working for his promotion, co-operating with him at Gray's Inn, sponsoring godly preaching, or agitating for the concerns of the godly in the House of Commons, these men supported and encouraged Sibbes in his ministry. Sibbes was preaching from experience when he said, "Men willingly look upon examples. The examples of great and excellent persons; the example of loving and bountiful persons; the example of such as are loving and bountiful to us in particular; the example of such as we have interest in, that are near and dear to us, and we to them—these four things commend examples."[87] While many others would have known Sibbes, little else can be said from the sources remaining. Reflection upon the evidence suggests that among his closest friends seem to have been fellow Cantabrigians and London ministers Gouge and Preston; among the lawyers and parliamentarians, Pym and Rich; and among other patrons, Mrs. Mary More, Lady Brooke, and Warwick. All were remembered specially in Sibbes's will (except Preston, who predeceased

---

[85]W. H. S. Jones, *A History of St. Catharine's College* (Cambridge, 1936) 92.
[86]See Thompson, 71–86.
[87]"The Church's Riches by Christ's Poverty," in *Works*, 4:520.

him, and Warwick). All clearly shared Sibbes's zeal for godly preaching. And none during Sibbes's lifetime countenanced separation.

This last point is important. By and large, while Sibbes knew these people, they were cautious. Matters of principle were not to be compromised (note the opposition of many of them to forced loans and ship-money[88]); yet the established form of government called for no compromise of principles in and of itself. It was not seen to be at fault; rather, its working in certain particular instances was misguided. Sovereigns and parliaments could, should and would work for the good of the citizens if they were not hampered by evil men. Sibbes had seen the dangers of even merely perceived radical dissent from Ames and Baynes in Cambridge, to Gouge and Prynne in London, and had learned that to which his nature may have inclined him as well—the system was best changed, if it needed to be changed at all, only slightly, and from within. It is perilous to investigate the decade between the deaths of King James and Sibbes with too much hindsight. To suggest that Sibbes was a nonconformist, not to mention a crypto-separatist, is unwarranted by the alleged Cambridge deprivations; it is also unwarranted by his associations. Gouge, Preston and Sibbes all subscribed to the three articles. With varying degrees of difficulty, all seemed to conform. Sibbes's words to Ellis and his Consolatory Letter show his own ecclesiastical temperament better than that which may be inferred from his associations. The crux of understanding Sibbes must be found in his activities set in their historical context and in his own thoughts, not merely in his associates. Even so, Sibbes's associations do not suggest religious radicalism. Sibbes did preside over an institution in which was breathed "Holland-like aire"; but rather than encouraging it, he provided the "Antidote." He was no Dutch separatist. Christopher Hill has grouped Sibbes with others "who were...conformists with no objection to set forms of worship."[89] As has been shown, this is not entirely the case with Sibbes, (e.g. his hesitations about the sign of the cross in baptism) but Sibbes was apparently a conformist, as were his closest friends.

---

[88]Among whom were Warwick, Saye and Sele, Barnardiston, Pym, Gerard, Sherland, and Nathaniel Stephens.

[89]Christopher Hill, *Society and Puritanism in Pre-Revolutionary England* (London, 1964) 17. Cf. *A Learned Commentary or Exposition Upon The first Chapter of the Second Epistle of S. Paul to the Corinthians*, in *Works*, 3:501.

IV

Sibbes and the Contentious Age, 1617–1635

In a contentious age, it is a witty thing to be a Christian, and to know what to pitch their souls upon; it is an office of love here to take away the stones and to smooth the way to heaven. Therefore we must take heed that, under pretence of avoidance of disputes, we do not suffer an adverse party to get ground upon the truth; for thus may we easily betray both the truth of God and souls of men.[1]

"Change" and Changelessness

TO A PERSON in the seventeenth century, "change" would likely have suggested decline or decay.[2] The "changes" in people's minds would have been not progress, but "falls" — whether of Adam and Eve, or of Rome.[3] There was the desire to imitate classical styles in writing and the popular idealization of the Anglo-Saxon past. Even the introduction from Germany of the widespread use of the coach during this period was seen not as part of the inevitable evolution of transport that would eventually bring the locomotive, the automobile, and the airplane, but rather as a new irritation that gutted the streets and lanes of London

---

[1]Sibbes, "The Bruised Reed and Smoking Flax," in *Works*, 1:54.
[2]Sibbes, "Fountain Opened," in *Works*, 5:512. Cf. J. T. Cliffe, *The Puritan Gentry: The Great Puritan Families of Early Stuart England* (London, 1984) 59; Johann Summerville, "Ideology, Property and the Constitution," in *Conflict in Early Stuart England*, R. Cust and A. Hughes, eds. (London, 1989) 62.
[3]"Fountain Opened," in *Works*, 5: 466.

and made them far more dangerous for most people. Heaven would be a place where man would be "altogether unchangeable."[4] Changes by man were "innovations" – a powerful polemical tool for those in the church decrying change in religion.[5]

The status quo was seen to be fundamentally correct. The fact that Richard Sibbes appeared to share in this common conception may seem to help account for the uncontroversial nature of much of Sibbes's preaching. Yet to see Sibbes as a Puritan mystic detached from history[6] is to ignore the import of his words in their time. A careful reading of his sermons reveals more interaction with opponents than one might at first suppose from so pacific a divine. That such statements do not appear more often may have been due to Sibbes's wariness to offend those in authority, perhaps altering what had been preached to make it more acceptable before publication. Therefore the apparent "timelessness" in Sibbes's sermons reflects, in part, the perils of those very times and Sibbes's awareness of them. In his sermons, Sibbes did present clear images of opposing sides and conflicting interests, yet he was always moderate. His moderation was not a pious apathy, but, rather, more akin to the proper balance of humors in the body. This balance would insure the health of his patient, a selective mixture of conservatism and further reform. Therefore, to better explain and define

---

[4]Sibbes, "Bowels Opened," in *Works*, 2:37-38; and "The Soul's Conflict with Itself," in *Works*, 1:282.

[5]See "Fountain Opened," in *Works*, 5:466, 511; "The Excellency of the Gospel above the Law," in *Works*, 4:241; "Divine Meditations and Holy Contemplations," in *Works*, 7:223; "Judgment's Reason," in *Works*, 4:95, 101; "The Saint's Safety in Evil Times, Manifested by St. Paul, From his Experience of God's Goodness in Greatest Distress," in *Works*, 1:301. Cf. "The Excellency of the Gospel above the Law," in *Works*, 4:303; "Proclamation for the establishing of the peace and quiet of the Church of England," reprinted J. P. Kenyon, *The Stuart Constitution: Documents and Commentary*, 2nd ed. (Cambridge, 1986) 138-139; and "The King's Declaration," reprinted S. R. Gardiner, *Constitutional Documents of the Puritan Revolution*, 3rd ed. (Oxford, 1906) 77-82, 89.

[6]H. P. Shelly, "Richard Sibbes: Early Stuart Preacher of Piety" (Ph.D. diss., Temple University, 1972); G. F. Nuttall, *Holy Spirit in Puritan Faith and Experience* (Oxford, 1946) 14; Alexander B. Grosart, "Memoir of Richard Sibbes, D.D.," in *Works*, 1:lx; Bert D. Affleck, Jr., "The Theology of Richard Sibbes, 1577-1635" (Ph.D. diss., Drew University, 1969) 16; W. K. Jordan, *The Development of Religious Toleration in England from the Accession of James I to the Convention of the Long Parliament (1603-1640)* (London, 1936) 358.

Sibbes's moderation, his work and preaching must be seen in the mixture of those things that he would defend and those which he would not.

Innovations in Immoderate Times

SIBBES CAME TO London as the newly-elected divinity lecturer for Gray's Inn. The "Reader of Divinitie to the house" was to be unmarried, having no other cure of souls, and was to provide two lectures each Sunday in the chapel for members of the Inn. In return, he was given a generous salary, chambers in the Inn, commons with the Ancients, and money for board during vacations.[7] The position had fallen open on 16 January 1616 when Roger Fenton died. Though there had been some discussion of John Burgess obtaining the post, it finally went to Sibbes, perhaps because of the influence of Sir Henry Yelverton,[8] or perhaps simply because he was the more conformable of the two candidates considered. Whatever the reason, at an unusually well-attended meeting of the Pensioners on 5 February 1617 (with Yelverton, his only appearance at their meetings between 8 November 1616 and the following June[9]) Sibbes was elected.[10] Though each of the Inns of Court functioned as "a propaganda base and general nexus for Puritan clergy and laymen," Gray's Inn was the largest and arguably the most influential.[11]

Though Cambridge was becoming more contentious as the Elizabethan theological consensus disintegrated (represented best perhaps by all that Whitgift and Cartwright had *agreed* upon), Sibbes's change from Cambridge to London gave him a wider view of "the miseries of the times."[12] Some have characterized the last half of James's reign as

---

[7]Reginald J. Fletcher, ed., *The Pension Book of Gray's Inn . . . 1569–1669* (London, 1901) 22, 139; cf., 224.

[8]Yelverton served as Counsel to the University from 1614 to 1617. With his reputation as a supporter of godly ministers, it is not surprising that he would have heard of Sibbes or even have heard Sibbes preach in Cambridge.

[9]*Pension Book*, 223–226.

[10]*Pension Book*, 224. Joseph Foster, *The Register of Admissions to Gray's Inn, 1521–1889* (London, 1889) 146.

[11]Wilfrid Prest, *Inns of Court under Elizabeth I and the Early Stuarts* (London, 1972) 38, 207.

[12]"The Soul's Conflict with Itself," in *Works*, 1:244

"uneventful,"[13] yet Nicholas Tyacke has more accurately referred to a darkness descending over Puritanism due more to lack of historical study than events.[14] A number of church issues received public attention: James' perilous allowance of divine-right defenses of episcopacy; the issuance on 24 May 1618 of the *Book of Sport*;[15] the meeting of the Synod of Dort.

Paul Seaver is correct, though perhaps gives the wrong impression, when he writes that Sibbes "preached in the city between 1620 and 1628 quite untroubled by the disciplinary machinary of the church courts."[16] On 26 May 1621, Robert Jenison, lecturer at All Saints', Newcastle, wrote to Samuel Ward, Master of Sidney Sussex, Cambridge, about a book of his, the publication of which Sibbes was supervising in London. In the letter, Jenison, with obvious exasperation, wrote that

> Mr Sibbs his timorousness...now...after his owne perusall, after examined and approbationed, yea after printing, hath bethought himself of some passages in the treatises which, if they be published before the book be corrected, may, as he sayeth, prove dangerous to me and to my friends (himselfe) who had a hand in the printing of it, which are as he generally signified about Spanish crueltie which in a word I touch in that [section] dedicated to you . . . as also concerning marriage with Papists.[17]

In December 1620 James warned the London clergy not to involve themselves in matters of state (as he was to do again in the following July), and Sibbes knew that above all this was specially intended to forbid meddling with the Spanish match. During the preceding month Sibbes had seen his friend William Gouge imprisoned for treason by James (at the urging of Neile, Bishop of Lincoln) for forwarding the

---

[13]Frere, *The English Church in the Reigns of Elizabeth and James I (1558–1625)* (London, 1904) 371, 388. Cf. Godfrey Davies, *The Early Stuarts 1603–1660*, 2nd ed. (Oxford, 1959) 20; S. R. Gardiner, *History of England from the Accession of James I to the Outbreak of the Civil War 1603–1642* (London, 1883) 3:252.

[14]Nicholas Tyacke, *The Fortunes of English Puritanism, 1603–1640* (London, 1990) 3.

[15]Reprinted in J. R. Tanner, *Constitutional Documents of the Reign of James I, 1603–1625* (Cambridge, 1961) 54–56.

[16]Paul Seaver, *The Puritan Lectureships* (Stanford, 1970) 235.

[17]Bodleian, Tanner MS. 73. f.29.

publication of Sir Henry Finch's *The Calling of the Jewes*. After Abbot examined Gouge, he was approved and released, but only after nine weeks in prison. During these weeks Sibbes communicated his reluctance to Jenison. To Jenison, Sibbes's advice seemed to appear at best an annoyance to him and at worst an evidence of Sibbes's unseemly regard for his own reputation. Sibbes, on the other hand, lived in the shadow of the court and knew something of James' tenderness to criticism. So while he was not troubled by the church courts, he was not unconcerned with them either. Meanwhile, Sibbes seemed to prosper well enough during this period. His salary was increased twice, and the chapel at Gray's Inn enlarged to accomodate his many hearers.[18]

By 1622, James had begun the sporadic enforcement of a ban on most pulpit discussions of predestination, which would continue in one form or another throughout the rest of Sibbes's life. On 4 August 1622 James sent his "Directions to the Clergy" (largely composed by Laud at his instruction) to Abbot, limiting Sunday afternoon lecturers and prohibiting preaching (by any other than bishops or deans) on "the deep points of predestination, election, reprobation or of the universality, efficacity, resistibility or irresistibility of God's grace."[19] More ominously for the godly, paragraph five coupled the Puritan with the papist as an "adversary" of the Church of England. (While James was fond of referring to the two together, he was usually careful to refer only to those who specifically disputed his authority.) Godfrey Davies overstated the effectiveness of this royal order when he wrote that this caused "the loss of half the preaching in England."[20] Lectures seemed to continue, though perhaps with more caution as to the topics treated. The following year, James attempted to initiate similar controls through the prohibitions to the press concerning controversy over predestination and grace. On 25 September 1623, James issued a proclamation for the press forbidding the printing or importation of books dealing with religion or matters of state until they had been approved.[21] That same

---

[18]*Pension Book*, 229, 234, 300; Francis Cowper, *A Prospect of Gray's Inn*, 2nd ed. (London, 1985) 60; Prest, 188.

[19]Reprinted in H. Gee and W. J. Hardy, *Documents Illustrative of English Church History* (London, 1896) 516–518; also, Tanner, 80–82.

[20]Davies, 74. Cf. Seaver, 241–242.

[21]Tanner, 143–145.

year, Sibbes told his hearers at Gray's Inn, "Many there are who think it not only a vain but a dangerous thing to serve God; . . . they count . . . that course which God takes in bringing men to heaven by a plain publishing of heavenly truths, to be nothing but foolishness."[22]

In this period of growing concern over public communications, Sibbes uttered what was to be after his death his most controversial statement, in which he enjoined subjection to authority in doubtful matters.[23] Yet as the negotiations for the Spanish match were at their height, Sibbes said in the same sermon in which he enjoined obedience to the government, "Whilst he [Solomon] laboured to find that which he sought for in them, he had like to have lost himself; and seeking too much to strengthen himself by foreign combination, he weakened himself, the more thereby."[24] So, while it may not have been "the calling of those that are subjects, to inquire over curiously into the mysteries of government,"[25] that did not prohibit the timourous Sibbes from making pointed comments. As time wore on the need for such comments increased. Whatever success James may have enjoyed in creating an inclusive church, Charles seemed to spurn. Sibbes and his contemporaries could hardly be expected to anticipate the significance for the church in the change of monarchs, for to perceive Charles as in any way fundamentally antipathetic to the true Protestant religion would be tantamount to doubting God's good providence for the church in England. However, there was no denying as the reign went on that a policy of comprehension had been replaced by one of compression.[26]

During the Montagu controversy, though Sibbes does not appear to have engaged publicly in this controversy by direct attacks on Montagu, he was certainly concerned with the growth of "formalism."[27] In his sermons, "The Church's Complaint and Confidence" Sibbes suggests one reason for the plague that year (1625). "There is an

---

[22]"The Soul's Conflict with Itself," in *Works*, 1:178–179.

[23]Ibid., 209–210. On the controversy surrounding this quotation, see chapter 7.

[24]Ibid., 219–220. Cf. "The Returning Backslider," in *Works*, 2:252 (probably preached in late 1624).

[25] Ibid.

[26]Cliffe, 146; cf. Kenneth Fincham, *Prelate as Pastor: The Episcopate of James I* (Oxford, 1990) 303.

[27]Sibbes, "A Glance of Heaven; or, Precious Taste of a Glorious Feast," in *Works*, 6:194, 203.

hypocrisy among men, among a company of formalists, that are the bane of the times, that God will spue out. They are as ill as a profane person in his nostrils."[28] In early 1626, it was becoming clearer that something more needed to be done to ensure godly preaching for the people, especially as the nature of the English church itself seemed increasingly at stake.[29] Laud, in his sermon to the new parliament as it convened openly attacked Calvinism and the godly were discouraged at Montagu's vindication at York House. Further, to quell the debates about Montagu and his writings which had grown throughout the spring, and to save Buckingham, Charles dissolved parliament and the following day, June 16, issued a "Proclamation for the establishing of the peace and quiet of the Church of England." In this proclamation Charles prohibited controversial or novel preaching that would "in the least degree attempt to violate this bond of peace." Though apparently aimed at the Arminians, Rushworth recorded that "The Effects of which Proclamation (how equally soever intended) were the stopping the Puritans Mouths, and an uncontrouled Liberty to the Arminian Party."[30]

By 1623, in the shadow of the troubles on the continent, Sibbes had called the times, "these times of Jacob's trouble and Zion's sorrow."[31] Very concerned about the fortune of his co-religionists, (at points even seeming to make such concern the test of regeneration), Sibbes eventually circulated a letter, dated 2 March 1627, with Gouge, Taylor,

---

[28]Sibbes, "The Church's Complaint and Confidence," in *Works*, 6:196. Cf. "The Sword of the Wicked," in *Works*, 1:114; "Bowels Opened," in *Works*, 2:41, 50; "The Excellency of the Gospel above the Law," in *Works*, 4:211; "Divine Meditations and Holy Contemplations," in *Works*, 7:228; "The Knot of Prayer Loosed," in *Works*, 7:234, 244, 246.

[29]The first recorded meeting of Sibbes and the other Feoffees was four days after the first meeting of the York House Conference.

[30]Reprinted Kenyon, 138–139. Cf. John Rushworth, *Historical Collections* (London, 1721) 1:265, 413. Daniel Neal (*The History of the Puritans* [London, 1837], 1:507) mistakenly dated this proclamation as being issued on 24 January. This is given further weight by Charles's decision to silence the Oxford Calvinists' attacks on Arminians at the conference at Woodstock on 23 August 1631. The conference was called as the result of attacks in sermons at Magdalen Hall and Exeter College. Charles stopped these attacks decisively by dismissing the three preachers from the university. This left Laud free to reform Oxford. For Laud's accounts of this, see *The Works of the Most Reverend Father in God, William Laud, D. D.* (Oxford, 1853) vol. V pt. i, pp. 47–73.

[31]"The Soul's Conflict with Itself," in *Works*, 1:261.

and Davenport appealing for aid especially for the destitute ministers from the upper Palatinate.[32] Two contradictory errors have grown up around the story of this letter. The first—that the authors were supported by Laud—was reinforced by Hugh Trevor-Roper who wrote that Laud "in the odd company of such prominent Puritans as Sibbes, Gouge, and Davenport...advocated relief for the ejected Calvinist ministers of the Palatinate."[33] Apparently he suggested this (as had Grosart) upon the basis of the *Calendar of State Papers, Domestic* entry about the letter, which has, following the summary of it, "[Indorsed by Bishop Laud]."[34] However, of the two copies listed in the calendar, neither of the originals in the Public Records Office are endorsed by Laud.[35] The second error is that these four were reprimanded for this action by the Star Chamber. While Prynne does say that they were brought "as notorious delinquents," he says that they were brought before the High Commission, not the Star Chamber.[36] This corresponds with a letter of John Davenport's, over a year after the Palatinate letter was circulated,

[32]Public Records Office, SP16/56, items 15 and 16. Summarized in *Calendar of State Papers, Domestic 1627–1628*, ed. John Bruce (London, 1858) 77.

[33]Hugh Trevor-Roper, *Archbishop Laud 1573–1645*, 3rd ed. (London, 1988) 263. So too Grosart, "Memoir of Richard Sibbes, D.D.," in *Works*, 1:lix.

[34]*Calendar of State Papers, Domestic 1627–1628*, 77.

[35]This author, with the help of the librarian in the manuscripts room, checked both copies on 20 April 1989 and could find no evidence of a signature from Laud.

[36]William Prynne, in the midst of a series of polemical rhetorical questions aimed at the High Commission for overstepping its proper authority, asks, "By what Law of the Land did they [the High Commissioners] convent Doctor Souge [sic], Doctor Sibbs, Doctor Taylor, and Master Davenport, as notorious delinquents, onely for setting their hands to a Certificate (upon intreaty testifying the distressed condition of some poore Ministers of the Palatinate) and furthering a private contribution among charitable Christians for their reliefe, when publicke Collections failed," (William Prynne, *A Breviate of the Prelates Intolerable Usurpations...* [London, 1637], 164). Grosart mistakenly cites Prynne's *Canterburies Doome* (London, 1646) for this, (Grosart, "Memoir of Richard Sibbes, D.D.," in *Works*, 1: lix). Gardiner (*History*, 7:261) D. A. Kirby ("The Radicals of St. Stephen's, Coleman Street, London, 1624–1642", *Guildhall Miscellany*, vol. III/2 [1970], 106) and Christopher Hill (*Economic Problems of the Church* [Oxford, 1956], 256) all followed Grosart in this error, Hill later (*Intellectual Origins of the English Revolution* [Oxford, 1965], 100) suggesting that it was the Privy Council. Cf. Ole Peter Grell, *Dutch Calvinists in Early Stuart London: The Dutch Church in Austin Friars 1603–1642* (Leiden, 1989) 179–182.

which reported the situation was still unresolved and was being reviewed by Laud.[37] Also William Gouge, in a letter to Laud in October 1631, made mention of his having been before him to the High Commission Court with Sibbes, Taylor, and Davenport.[38] For their efforts, Sibbes and his copetioners were brought before Laud and the High Commission. While it was not inconsistent with English foreign policy to aid the Protestants on the continent, this action could have been seen as an inappropriately direct involvement of private persons in state affairs and therefore as implicit criticism of government inactivity. Furthermore, the whole question of the Protestant cause on the continent was considered politically dangerous by the court. A presentation of the events on the continent as essentially a Protestant/ Roman Catholic war was dangerous to James because it would severely limit his diplomatic freedom. Therefore, it was in his interest to discourage representations of the war as a war of religion. To the godly, however, that is exactly what it was. Equally important as the plight of their co-religionists on the continent, however, was the plight of the godly in England. As "formalism" in the church at home increased and the clergy's ability to comment critically declined, comment upon the situation abroad grew in importance as such comment became indirect criticism of trends in the English church.[39] Surely, to both court and clergy, the continental war was an on-going illustration of ecclesiastical concerns dominating secular ones—and therefore of apocalyptic interest to both.

By 1628 the godly had seen numerous disappointments. Abroad, the Protestant forces on the continent seemed near complete collapse, having received a number of serious defeats (including Lutter), and Buckingham's expedition to relieve the Protestants of La Rochelle had failed. Fearing popular reaction to this, Charles had forbidden London

[37]John Davenport to Mary, Lady Vere, June 30, 1628, *Letters of John Davenport*, ed. I. M. Calder (New Haven, Connecticut, 1937) 28–29.

[38]*Calendar of State Papers, Domestic, 1631–1633*, ed. John Bruce (London, 1862) 167.

[39]Sibbes, "The Saint's Safety in Evil Times, Manifested by St. Paul, From his Experience of God's Goodness in Greatest Distress," in *Works*, 1:318; cf. "Josiah's Reformation," in *Works*, 6:30–34.

preachers to take note of this in their sermons.[40] At home, Sibbes, Gouge, Taylor, and Davenport had been reprimanded for their circular letter to help Protestant refugees on the continent, while William Laud and Richard Neile had been promoted in the church and had both been made privy councillors. Meanwhile, John Preston and Richard Stock, both leading godly ministers of London (and old friends of Sibbes) had died, and the publication of John Cosin's popish *A Collection of Private Devotions* and the collection of forced loans had provided fresh worries for the godly divines and lawyers. The parliament was incensed. But they were even more incensed by Roger Manwaring's preaching, with Charles' approval, that those who opposed the forced loan would burn in hell. As a result, Charles adjourned parliament, paid Manwaring's fines, formally pardoned him, and gave him the living of Stanford Rivers, Essex. To the godly, these events suggested that the triumph of Roman Catholicism abroad seemed to be imminent at home as well. In November of 1628, Charles issued a Declaration similar to the Proclamation of 1626, commanding it to be prefixed to all copies of the Articles of Religion.[41] The Declarlation forbad anyone "to print, or preach, to draw the Article [any of the 39] aside any way, but shall submit to it in the plain and full meaning thereof: and shall not put his own sense or comment to be the meaning of the Article, but shall take it in the literal and grammatical sense."[42] While on its face intending to promote peace within the church, it served in the minds of the godly only to confirm their fears.

Lectures proliferated throughout early Stuart England, particularly in London. Sibbes may well have been right when he observed about London "I think there is no place in the world where there is so much preaching."[43] With a growing metropolitan population measured in the hundreds of thousands and clergy who believed that "preaching is that

---

[40]Bodleian Tanner MS 72/269 (cited "Arminianism" chapter in Julian Davies, *The Caroline Captivity of the Church: Charles I and the Remoulding of Anglicanism: 1625-1641*, [Oxford, 1992], n. 148).

[41]Neal, 1:519-520. Gardiner, *Constitutional Documents*, 75-76; Gee & Hardy, 518-520. Edward Cardwell, (*Documentary Annals of the Reformed Church of England* [Oxford, 1844], 221-225), for some reason dates the declaration to 1627 (though the notes give 1628).

[42]Gardiner, *Constitutional Documents*, 76.

[43]"Lydia's Conversion," in *Works*, 6:527.

whereby God dispenseth salvation and grace ordinarily,"[44] this is hardly surprising. These lecturers (almost entirely called and supported by the laity) created a situation in which much of the preaching in the city took place outside of normal ecclesiastical lines of authority. Charles and Laud, therefore, seemed to mistrust the class of lecturers in general. As Bishop of London, Laud persuaded Charles to enact certain restrictions on lecturers or, as Laud called them, "the Peoples Creatures."[45] On 30 December 1629 Charles, at Laud's request, issued his "Instructions" which came close to forbidding preaching without cure of souls.[46] In these instructions (reissued in the autumn of 1633 upon Laud's translation to Canterbury), the bishops were enjoined to encourage parishes to turn afternoon sermons to catechizing, "that every lecturer do read divine service according to the liturgy printed by authority, in his surplice and hood, before the lecture," that properly–attired, local lecturers be used in market towns, and that "if a corporation maintain a single lecturer, he be not suffered to preach, till he profess his willingness to take upon him a living with cure of souls within that corporation; and that he actually take such benefice or cure, as soon as it shall be fairly procured for him." As a result, Sibbes's friend and fellow in the work of the Feoffees, Thomas Foxley, was deprived of his lectureship, along with a number of others.[47]

---

[44]"Fountain Opened," in *Works*, 5:507.

[45]Rushworth, (1706), 2:8. Kenyon has wrongly represented these restrictions as forbidding corporations to have lecturers, (Kenyon, *The Stuarts* [Glasgow, 1958], 75). This was probably based on mistaking Laud's "Considerations" (reprinted in Prynne and summarized in Rushworth), which had formed the basis of Charles's "Instructions," for the "Instructions" themselves. Paragraph 5 article 4, of the Instructions merely required a willingness to take up a cure of souls as soon as it may be offered to the lecturer, whereas Laud's "Considerations" had suggested that no lecturer "be suffered to preach till he take upon him Curam Animarum within that Corporation," (Rushworth, 2:8). Seaver noted that this lessening of the requirement was a royal alteration in Laud's more stringent request, (Seaver, 244).

[46]Laud, vol. V, pt. ii, 307–309; Kenyon, *Stuarts*, 75; Rushworth, 2:8–9; cf. Seaver, 243–244; Prynne, *Canterburies Doome*, 368–373; G. E. Gorman, "A London Attempt to 'tune the pulpit': Peter Heylyn and his sermon against the Feofees for the purchase of imporpriations," *Journal of Religious History*, vol. VIII/9 (1975): 336; Trevor-Roper, 104–108.

[47]Prynne, *Canterburies Doome*, 273.

During these eventful early years of Charles' reign, Sibbes was very active, launching the Feoffees scheme, cooperating in sending the letter requesting aid for Protestant refugees on the continent, and reforming Katharine Hall as master. His preaching, though not overtly controversial, contained timely remarks. Of the growing irenicism toward Roman Catholicism, Sibbes lamented, "We see nothing in religion, but are as ready to entertain popery as true religion. Is this the fruit of the long preaching of the gospel, and the veil being taken off so long? . . . We are under the seal of God's judgment."[48] Of those who opposed the furtherance of godly preaching, Sibbes said, "It is an argument that a man is in bondage to Satan when he is an enemy any way of the unfolding of the word of God."[49] Thus Sibbes, through his preaching especially, and through other careful measures, sought to advance the concerns of the godly.

If the newer presentation of Sibbes is one of pacific moderate mystic, the older was one of a battling proto–dissenter, locked in mortal ecclesiastical combat with Laud. Though certainly a distortion of Sibbes's career, one conflict that did involve both Sibbes and Laud was that which surrounded the Feoffees for Impropriations. In 1625 a group of twelve Londoners "formed themselves into an unincorporated, self–perpetuating group of trustees" in order to "raise funds with which to acquire ecclesiastical revenue in the hands of laymen to be used for the maintenance and relief of a godly, faithful, and painstaking ministry."[50] As they gained control of livings, these Feoffees did not simply fill vacancies with any duly–ordained cleric. In a number of instances, they acted to replace holders of benefices with preachers who were clearly of a more radical nature than their predecessors.[51] In his diary, Laud noted, under the heading "Things which I have projected to do if God Bless me in them" as the third of his projects simply "To overthrow the Feoffment, dangerous both to Church and State, going under the specious pretence of buying in Impropriation."[52] Beside this in his

---

[48]"The Excellency of the Gospel above the Law," in *Works*, 4:304; cf. "The Rich Pearl," in *Works*, 7: 260.

[49]"The Excellency of the Gospel above the Law," in *Works*, 4: 228

[50]Isabel M. Calder, *Activities of the Puritan Faction of the Church of England 1625–1633* (London, 1957) vii.

[51]See Calder, *Activities*, 54–59.

[52]William Laud, *History of Troubles* (London, 1695) 68.

diary, Laud recorded the single word "Done" — in February 1633, after lengthy hearings[53] the Feoffees for Impropriations were dissolved in the Court of Exchequer for having formed a self-perpetuating corporation without having obtained a royal charter. These conflicts — over the Palatinate letter and the Feoffees — suggest that Sibbes, while judiciously observing his obligations to the church, was not beyond trying the boundaries of those obligations, or at least working apart from them. Such willingness to work within the church did not, however, mark a number of Sibbes's younger friends. Soon after the dissolution of the Feoffees, with Abbot's death, Laud's translation to Canterbury and the reissuing of the 1629 Instructions that limited lecturers[54] and the *Book of Sport*, John Cotton was confirmed in his separation, and Thomas Goodwin and John Davenport were soon convinced of the necessity of leaving their livings.

It may have been his practise of not "provoking Persons in Power"[55] that led to Sibbes's appointments to the Mastership of Katharine Hall in 1626 and to the vicarage of Holy Trinity, Cambridge, in 1633, when other more vocal opponents of Laud and his reforms were being pushed out.[56] More immediately, it was by the work of Thomas Goodwin that Sibbes had become Master of Katharine Hall in late 1626.[57] It was not a

---

[53]Arthur Searle, ed., *Barrington Family Letters 1628-1632* (London, 1983) 244.

[54]Laud, *Works*, vol. V, pt. ii, 307-309; Kenyon, *Stuarts*, 75; Rushworth, 2:8-9; cf. Seaver, 243-244; Prynne, *Canterburies Doome*, 368-373; Gorman, 336; Trevor-Roper, 104-108.

[55]Edmund Calamy, *An Account of the Ministers, Lecturers, Masters and Fellows of Colleges and Schoolmasters, who were Ejected or Silenced after the Restoration in 1660*, 2nd ed. (London, 1713) 2:605-606.

[56]Ussher had written to Archbishop Abbot in January of 1627, suggesting that he encourage Sibbes to take the position of Provost at Trinity College, Dublin, because, "I dare undertake that he shall be as observant of you, and as careful to put in execution all your directions, as any man whosoever." Ussher to Abbot, 10 January 1626[7]; found in *The Whole Works of the Most Rev. James Ussher, D. D.*, C. R. Elrington, ed. (Dublin, 1864) 16:361.

[57]Thomas Goodwin, "Memoir...out of his own papers," *Works of Thomas Goodwin* (Edinburgh, 1861) 2:lxvi. Irvonwy Morgan suggests that this position was obtained for Sibbes by Preston's influence with Buckingham. This, however, would be unlikely because Preston would have had little influence with Buckingham by the winter of 1626. (See Irvonwy Morgan, *Prince Charles's Puritan Chaplain* [London, 1957], 42).

strange choice. Sibbes had been for many years a senior fellow of St. John's College, one of the largest colleges in the university. As Ussher had recently written of him, Sibbes was "one that hath been well acquainted with an academical life, and singularly well qualified for the undertaking of such a place of government."[58] Ussher's estimation proved correct: Sibbes was a successful master,[59] bringing in students,[60] and benefactions.[61] As a result, his godly influence was felt in the college's religious life at a time when other colleges were experiencing influence of a decidedly different cast. Within a year of his death, the chapel was reported to Laud as being as irregular as Emmanuel's. William Dowsing, several years later, had but little to break down there.

But even as master of Katharine Hall,[62] Sibbes continued to exercise his own peculiar brand of moderate reform. One of the more confusing aspects of the small college at this time is the fact that two persons of the name of John Ellis were admitted in the college in 1630/1631. The older was a Welshman who had taken his B. A. from St. John's and was admitted as a fellow in December of 1631, the same meeting at which William Strong was admitted. The younger John Ellis was a Yorkshireman who matriculated as a student to Katharine Hall in 1630. When a fellowship at Katharine Hall came vacant, Archbishop Laud had recommended John Ellis, whom Edmund Calamy does not name,

---

[58]Ussher, letter to Lincoln's [Gray's] Inn, 10 January 1626/7, reprinted in *Works*, ed. Elrington, 15:363–364.

[59]Under Sibbes's direction the college regularly gave to the poor of the town, and new buildings were built, forming Bull Court in 1629. Muniments Room, St. Catharine's College Audit Book, 53, 64, 72.

[60]In 1626-7 a scholarship was set up with Sibbes's approval to provide for one blind student within the college. Muniments Room, St. Catharine's College Audit Book, 36.

[61]G. F. Browne, *St. Catharine's College* (London, 1901) 99. Mr. Thomas Hobbes of Gray's Inn left a benefaction for the college's catechizing lecture and two or three scholars of either Katharine Hall or Emmanuel, with preference to be given to those from Katharine Hall "especially so long as my worthy friend Doctor Sibbs shall continue Master of the said Hall." Browne, 91.

[62] For having only six fellows, Katherine Hall could boast an amazing number while Sibbes was there who later became noted persons, including Thomas Goodwin, Andrew Perne, John Arrowsmith, William Strong, Samuel Lynford, John Bond, and William Spurstow

but simply identifies as Laud's "bell-ringer."[63] "Meek persons will bow when others break; they are raised when others are plucked down;... these prevail by yielding, and are lords of themselves, and other things else, more than other unquiet-spirited men: the blessings of heaven and earth attend on these."[64] In 1634 Sibbes proved himself to be such a self-governing, quiet spirit, prevailing by yielding and bowing. The election of the younger John Ellis, as recounted by Calamy, the last fellowship election in which Sibbes was to participate, provides a last look at Sibbes's ability to conform. Calamy wrote:

> This was a mighty thing at that time, and intended to be a push upon that Society, with a design either to quarrel with them if they refus'd, or to put a Spy upon them if they accepted. The Doctor [Sibbes], who was not for provoking Persons in Power, told the Fellows, that Lambeth House would be obey'd; that the Person was young, and might prove hopeful, etc. The Fellows yielded....[65]

John Ellis was elected a fellow of the college in December 1634. Ellis turned out to be more pliable than moderate, going through Presbyterian and Independent stages and finally conforming at the Restoration. John Knowles, another fellow of the college at that time whom Sibbes had persuaded to vote for Ellis and later one of the ejected nonconformists of 1662, "Fifty Years after, he said that nothing troubled him more, than his giving his Vote in that Election."[66] Sibbes's moderation did not always endear him to his contemporaries.

The Substance of Moderation: Sibbes's Ecclesiology

---

[63]Ellis recounted his debt to Laud in his *S. Austin Imitated: or Retractations and Repentings In reference unto the late Civil and Ecclesiastical Changes in this Nation* (London, 1662) 112.

[64]"The Soul's Conflict with Itself," in *Works*, 1:280. Cf. "The Saint's Safety in Evil Times," in *Works*, 1:301.

[65]Calamy, 2:605-606. Cf. Benjamin Brook, *The Lives of the Puritans* (London, 1813) 2:419, where the vacancy is mistakenly reported as having occurred in "Magdalen College."

[66]Calamy, 2:606.

MOST OF THE divisions in the last two decades of Sibbes's life came about over the underlying issue of what a true church was. But the divisions of the time shifted according to the perceived needs for and possibilities of continuing reform in accord with one's vision of the true church. Thus, to categorize particular ministers according to whether they favoured further reform of the Church of England in their day, or the status quo, can cause the illusion of equivalence between a Sibbes defending aspects of the existing settlement in the 1620's and a Whitgift's defense in the 1570's, or Simon Patrick's in the 1660's or even other of Sibbes's contemporaries—e.g. Laud's defense in the 1620's. In fact, the substance of Sibbes's defense of the church—much godly preaching, right administration of the sacraments, some discipline—has more theologically in common with many of those attacking the Eliza-bethan settlement of his boyhood, than with many of his contem-poraries' defenses of the establishment of the 1630's. Nevertheless, though Sibbes queried (and probably disagreed with) certain cere-monies, he clearly advocated remaining within the Church of England. By the end of his life, he recognized more clearly than ever that "all Christians in this life have both a different light and a different sight."[67]

There were those, however, who were clearly beyond the pale. As J. Sears McGee has observed, in Sibbes's sermons, any "apparent moderation on the subject of Rome is seen to be ephemeral."[68] Papists came unworthily to the sacraments and were handicapped in the quest for holiness by their ignorance.[69] His sermons are full of attacks on ceremonialism and formalism, all aimed at those within the Church of England, but also at those in the Roman church. His D. D. oration at Cambridge in 1627 was a classic Elizabethan-style confutation of

---

[67]"The Bride's Longing," in Works, 6:549, preached in February, 1634.

[68]J. Sears McGee, The Godly Man in Stuart England: Anglicans, Puritans, and the Two Tables, 1620–1670 (New Haven, Connecticut, 1976) 6. In 1610 Sibbes had been chosen as the B. D. candidate to "respond" at the commencement exercises. He was first to respond to the statement, "Romana Ecclesia est apostatica," (BL Harl. MS. 7038, f. 88).

[69]Sibbes, "The Right Receiving," in Works, 4:65, 68, 73; cf. "The Soul's Conflict with Itself," in Works, 1:138. This piece is an interesting example of Sibbes's understanding of the institution of the University as a bulwark of the defense against Rome, charged with protecting the "good deposit of faith."

Rome.[70] Arminianism, too, was clearly not to be comprehended in Sibbes's understanding of moderation. In citing and disposing of some of Robert Bellarmine's free will objections, Sibbes was also dealing with the Arminians, but in a more politically acceptable way.[71] Although Sibbes's sermons were filled with positive allusions to Luther,[72] his followers proved a more uncertain object of praise. In fact, with the Lutherans, the godly of England had potentially one of their most difficult problems. This was well demonstrated by Christopher Potter (dean of Worcester).[73] In this reprinting of a letter, Potter defended himself in response to a letter from "Mr. V" that charged him with changing his views to Arminianism. Mr. V. makes this charge upon the basis of his [Potter's] sermon at the consecration of Barnabas Potter as Bishop of Carlisle in March 1629. Potter, espousing "moderation," argued that if one accepted the Lutherans, then one must accept the less different Arminians because "how then doth the Arminian erre fundamentally, since the Lutheran maintaines the same Opinion with many more and worse?"[74] While Sibbes was rarely critical of the Lutherans in his sermons, Sibbes in conversation at one point criticized Melanchton, according to Hartlib, for his "errors which hee had about Praedestination, as Luther about the Sacrament."[75]

Sibbes did, of course, favor moderation: "Where most holiness is, there is most moderation, where it may be without prejudice of piety to God and the good of others."[76] Described after his death with the

---

[70]"Antidotum Contra Naufragium Fidei et Bonae Conscientiae," in *Works*, 7:548–560.

[71]"Bowels Opened," in *Works*, 2: 63; "The Church's Riches by Christ's Poverty," in *Works*, 4:500; cf. "The Excellency of the Gospel above the Law," in *Works*, 4:271–272.

[72]"The Returning Backslider," in *Works*, 2:337; *A Learned Commentary or Exposition Upon The first Chapter of the Second Epistle of S. Paul to the Corinthians*, in *Works*, 3:159, 303, 417; "The Excellency of the Gospel above the Law," in *Works*, 4:302; "Violence Victorious," in *Works*, 6:311.

[73]Christopher Potter, *Vindication of Himself... 1629*, printed in John Plaifere, *Apello Evangelium* (London, 1651).

[74]Potter, 426, 428–429.

[75]Hartlib, Ephemerides, 1634. Cf. criticism of the Lutherans as idolaters in *A Learned Commentary or Exposition Upon The first Chapter of the Second Epistle of S. Paul to the Corinthians*, in *Works*, 3:134, because of their doctrine of consubstantiation.

[76]"The Bruised Reed and Smoking Flax," in *Works*, 1:57.

phrase "amiable living,"[77] Sibbes was remembered wistfully in the more contentious 1650s as a type of the Christians of a more pacific age, who "like a skilful physician, applied himself to preserve the vitals and essentials of religion, that the souls of his heareres...might not evaporate and discharge themselves in endless, gainless, soul-unedifying, and conscience-perplexing questions."[78] Sibbes even went so far as to present moderation as the heart of Christianity: "What is the gospel itself but a merciful moderation, in which Christ's obedience is esteemed ours, and our sins laid upon him, and wherein God of a judge becometh the father, pardoning our sins and accepting our obedience, though feeble and blemished!"[79] In keeping with this sentiment, the first book Sibbes introduced to the press was a controversial work by Baynes advocating supralapsarianism, to which Sibbes contributed a moderating preface. He concluded by noting the agreements between supra- and infralapsarians and he reminded his readers that "The worthiness of men on both sides is such, that it should move men to moderation in their censures either way... But for diversity of apprehensions of matters far remote from the foundation; these may stand with public and personal peace."[80]

Throughout his lifetime, Sibbes had seen men he respected resign their livings out of scruples about conformity (Baynes, Ames, Culverwell), but during the last years of Sibbes's life, the church seemed to be hemorrhaging. The occasional conformists were less tolerated, and men began more openly to choose ministry outside the church of England, whether in Holland or New England. But in this especially, moderation was important in Sibbes's response to those who would separate from the Church of England. Such forgot that "The church of Christ is a common hospital, wherein all are in some measure sick of some spiritual disease or other; that we should all have ground of exercising

---

[77]John Sedgwick's Dedication of Sibbes, *Beames of Divine Light* (London, 1639); rpt. in *Works*, 5:221.

[78]Simeon Ash, James Nalton and Joseph Church, "To the Reader," in Sibbes, *A Heavenly Conference Between Christ and Mary after His Resurrection* (London, 1654); rpt. in *Works*, 6:415; cf. Arthur Jackson, James Nalton, and William Taylor, "To the Reader" in Sibbes, *The Glorious Feast of the Gospel* (London, 1650); rpt. in *Works*, 2:439.

[79]"The Bruised Reed and Smoking Flax," in *Works*, 1:58.

[80]"To the Reader," to Paul Baynes, *A Commentary Upon the First Chapter of the Epistle...to the Ephesians*, in *Works*, 1:lxxxv-lxxxvi.

mutually the spirit of wisdom and meekness."[81] Instead, "for private aims" they wounded the church.[82] Yet in his ardor years earlier, Sibbes had reminded his hearers of the necessity of coming out of popery and lamented that "it shews the coldness of the times when there is not heat enough of zeal to separate from a contrary faith."[83] While this was meant as a statement to call men out of a growing ceremonialism in the church, or even out of Rome, it could easily be taken as a pro-separatist statement (which, to an extent, it clearly was). Here Sibbes demonstrates the double-edged nature of the arguments which the godly used against Rome.[84] Moderation was clearly in the eye of the beholder.[85] If Rome could be declared apostate, why not the increasingly corrupted Church of England?

This is precisely the question that Sibbes tried to answer in his brief six-page *Consolatory Letter to an Afflicted Conscience*. In it, he countered the argument he had used against the Roman church: "But you will say England is not a true Church, and therefore you separate; adhere to the true Church."[86] Sibbes's proof of the Church of England as a true church of Christ is that it has all the necessary marks of a true Church — "sound preaching of the Gospell, right dispensation of the Sacraments, Prayer religiously performed, evill persons justly punisht (though not in that

---

[81]"The Bruised Reed and Smoking Flax," in *Works*, 1:57.

[82]"The Bruised Reed and Smoking Flax," in *Works*, 1:76.Cf. *Letters of Davenport*, 39.

[83]"The Soul's Conflict with Itself," in *Works*, 1:270.

[84]Sibbes clearly was aware of this problem; e.g., "An Exposition of the Third Chapter of the Epistle of St. Paul to the Philippians," in *Works*, 5:68.

[85]Cf. "The devil in people is in extremes; he labours to bring people to extremes, to make the sacraments idols or idle, to make the outward sacrament a mere idol, to give all to that or to make them idle signs. The devil hath what he would in both. The apostle knew the disease of the times, especially in his time, they attributed too much to outward things," (The Demand of a Good Conscience," in *Works*, 7:479). While Sibbes could well have had the Laudians in his mind when preaching this, if it were after 1633, he could just as well have had his separating friends — Cotton, Goodwin, and Davenport — in mind. Such a statement would have had the full agreement of Laud (e.g., recounted by E. C. E. Bourne, *The Anglicanism of William Laud* [London, 1947], 79; Laud, *Works*, 7:87–88) and of John Cotton, (e.g., recounted by Cotton Mather, *Ecclesiastical History of New England* [New York, 1967], 2:495–496).

[86] Ibid.

measure as some criminals and malefactors deserve)"[87]—and the production of "many spirituall children to the Lord."[88] "Yea, many of the Separation, if ever they were converted, it was here with us" (a remark which Sibbes could make with Goodwin, and especially Cotton clearly in his memory). Even if it is admitted that England's church was corrupted with ceremonies, Sibbes argued, "must we make a rent in the Church for... circumstantiall evils? That were a remedy worse than the disease."[89] He then pointed out that all churches have corruptions, even those abroad which are more free from ceremonies "yet... are more corrupt in Preachers, (which is the maine) as in prophanation of the Lords day, &c."[90] Sibbes concluded by exhorting the person:

> There will be a miscellany and mixture in the visible Church, as long as the world endures.... So it is no better then soule-murder for a man to cast himselfe out of the Church, either for reall or imaginall corruptions.... So let me admonish you to returne your selfe from these extravagant courses, and submissively to render your selfe to the sacred communion of this truly Evangelicall Church of England.[91]

Sibbes's defense of the "truly Evangelicall Church of England" was a brief, powerful one, no doubt worked out in his own conscience over many years. No wonder Sibbes gained the reputation for ability to "bring them [nonconformists] about, the best of any about the City of London."[92] As he said, "Sympathy hath a strange force. "[93]

---

[87]"Consolatory Letter to an Afflicted Conscience," in *Works*, 1:cxv.

[88]This last was a traditional argument used against the separatists. Sibbes used this argument ("Church's Visitation," in *Works*, 1:375-376) as had Thomas Cartwright decades earlier, (cited in Peter Lake, *Moderate Puritans and the Elizabethan Church* [Cambridge, 1982], 87; cf. Thomas Cartwright's Letter to his Sister-in-Law to Dissuade her from Brownism," reprinted in *The Presbyterian Review*, vol. VI [Jan. 1885], 101-111; William Perkins, *The Workes of that Famous and Worthy Minister of Christ in the University of Cambridge, Mr. William Perkins* (London, 1618) 3:389.

[89] "Consolatory Letter..." *Works* 1:cxv.

[90] "Consolatory Letter..." *Works* 1:cxvi.

[91]"Consolatory Letter to an Afflicted Conscience," in *Works*, 1:cxvi.

[92]John Hacket, *Scrinia Reserata: A Memorial Offer'd to the Great Deservings of John Williams, D. D.*, (London, 1693) part i paragraph 106, pp. 95-96. Cf. John

For all the sympathy Sibbes must have felt for nonconformists, his attitude about those who would in practise separate from the Church of England was slightly different. The former were rightly obeying their conscience. The latter were usurping roles which God had not given them. Sibbes wrote:

> There is therefore in these judging times good ground of St. James's caveat, that there should not 'be too many masters,' James iii.1; that we should not smite one another by hasty censures, especially in things of an indifferent nature; some things are as the mind of him is that doth them, or doth them not; for both may be unto the Lord.[94]

Though separation did not hinder Cotton, Goodwin, Nye, Norton, and Burroughs from remembering Sibbes and his influence very positively, there remains no other evidence of how Sibbes came to terms with his friends leaving the English church for reasons that had not compelled him to do the same.

The Disappearing Middle

IN 1629 BISHOP Neile warned a preacher brought before him in Hampshire, "I have heard you often preach before the king, and you were wonte to be earnest against poperie and your discourse was pleaseinge to your king, but now you must not, for the tymes are altered."[95] It was Sibbes's lot to live through that alteration. As such a person, he becomes more difficult to understand as the categories that would help explain him in Cambridge in the 1590s shift to somewhat different categories appropriate for the 1630s. A presentation of Sibbes as a nonconformist can only be had in the hindsight, which sees every Puritan as a dissenter and everyone who voiced objections to ceremonies or the Book of Common Prayer as a nonconformist. Sibbes worked for reform, perhaps most actively around the beginning of

---

Dury's experience, recounted in John Dury, *The Unchanged, Constant and Single-hearted Peacemaker*, (London, 1650) 7.
[93]"The Soul's Conflict with Itself," in *Works*, 1:193.
[94]"The Bruised Reed and Smoking Flax," in *Works*, 1:56.
[95]Searle, 53.

Charles' reign, when both the need and the opportunity appeared greater than they had before. Soon though, the opportunity for action to promote the godly agendas of preaching and Protestantism declined. Throughout Sibbes's final two years he may well have felt a growing discouragement. He had undoubtedly been frustrated by the shrinking possibility that the Church of England could include those who would be "reformers without being revolutionaries."[96]

In summary, where did Sibbes's moderation leave his ecclesiology amid the shifting sands of Stuart conformity, far from the Elizabethan settlement in which he spent the first half of his life? Certainly time often teases out inherent contradictions and incipient discord. Perhaps this is what has caused the disparate pictures of Sibbes. On the one hand, he has been presented as completely neglecting eccesiology.[97] On the other hand, even among those who may have more carefully read his sermons, it seems that Sibbes adopted the rhetoric of an establishment revolutionary; that is, someone who affirmed the established ecclesiology of the Elizabethan church and yet who increasingly emphasized the more voluntary nature of much continental Reformed ecclesiology—aspects obviously compatible in Sibbes's earlier days in Cambridge. As apparent opposition to what Sibbes understood as the preaching of the gospel increased, he became ever more explicit about the voluntary aspects of the church.[98] Godly preaching, as the means of

---

[96]Brian Burch, "The Parish of St. Anne's Blackfriars, London, to 1665," *Guildhall Miscellany*, vol. III/1 (October, 1969) 30.

[97]R. T. Kendall, *Calvin and English Calvinism to 1649* (Oxford, 1979) 103.

[98]Sibbes, "A Breathing after God," in *Works*, 2:226. William Bartlet in his *Model of the Primitive Congregational Way* (London, 1647) 44–45, later realized the way this voluntaristic section of Sibbes could be taken, and used this to support the thesis that one [Sibbes] who was "little thought by most men to have been of this judgement" was in fact a Congregationalist. Collinson (in his "'Magazine,'" *Godly People* [London, 1983], 516) has mistakenly suggested that Simeon Ashe and John Wall later claimed that Sibbes [along with Preston, Dod, and Hildersham] were "zealously affected towards the Presbyterial Government of the Church." Yet, the passage quoted from Wall and Ashe (from their December 1649 preface to Samuel Clarke's, *The Marrow of Ecclesiastical Historie*, (London, 1650) says only that "the latter of these" were so affected, "these" being a long list of sixteen divines, the last eight of whom were nonconformists. Sibbes appears second in the full list. Sibbes had earlier been described as a "Presbyterian" by George B. Dyer in his *History of the University and Colleges of Cambridge* (London, 1814) 2:170.

the Spirit's activity, rather than historical organizational continuity was the heart of Sibbes's vision of the church.

Victor Morgan has written of the "latent congregationalism inherent in Puritanism;" yet Sibbes clearly did not assert the voluntary nature of the church to the extent of separation, as some of his younger followers did.[99] Why not? Perhaps Sibbes's years—slightly greater than Cotton, much greater than Goodwin or Davenport—provided either a confidence in or a resignation to the establishment, or both, which the younger ones could not as easily have had.[100] For whatever reason, Sibbes held these two aspects together by taking the establishment to be adiaphorous, useful insofar as it served the reformation. In other words, his ecclesiology was clearly subordinated to soteriology in a way Roman Catholics and later dissenters have found largely impossible to imitate. Yet the changes to the church under the Stuarts shifted the issues around a bit—ecclesiology became necessarily more central as it interfered with what strongly Protestant clergy and laity had taken to be the truly central issue of soteriology. As the issues shifted, Sibbes's position as an establishment revolutionary became more precarious, and even compromised. Both sides found him useful as a counter example to ameliorate stringent remarks about the other side.

If any time after 1616 could have driven him to open nonconformity, and even separation, it would have been the last two years of his life, yet even they did not. By 1632 Sibbes had seen four preachers at Lincoln's Inn come and go, and three at the Temple. By 1633 only six of the Cambridge heads were more senior than himself, and by 1635, only four were. In 1634 John Cosin had become Master of Peterhouse, William Strong, one of Sibbes's fellows at Katharine Hall was suspended, and John Ellis was elected in his place. Samuel Ward writing to Ussher in 1634 noted the shifting nature of these heads and lamented "new heads [of houses] are brought in, and they are backed in maintaining novelties, and them which broach new opinion.... It

---

[99]Victor Morgan, "Country, Court and Cambridge University, 1558–1640: A Study in the Evolution of a Political Culture" (Ph.D. diss., University of East Anglia, 1983) 1:59. Note the prevalence of more radical, congregational or independent principles among Sibbes's younger friends.

[100]Peter Lake has written of the essence of moderate Puritanism as the ability to avoid a clash of allegiances between Protestant principle and the national church, (Lake, "Laurence Chaderton and the Cambridge Moderate Puritan Tradition," [Ph.D. diss., University of Cambridge, 1978], 316).

may be you are willing to hear of our University affairs. I may truly say I never knew them in worse condition since I was a member thereof, which is almost forty-six years."[101] The moderation Sibbes had advocated was disappearing. Polarization in the church was increasingly displacing toleration. Yet Sibbes remained a reforming conformist to the end, even if after 1633 there were few opportunities for such moderate reform beyond his own pulpit. Though he clearly grew more alienated from the power structures of the church—at least in spirit—he was perhaps simply too successful and well-established, too old, and too tired to be polarized.

As one who had been a child of eleven not too far from the coast in 1588, Sibbes would have naturally felt the import of the fate of the Protestants on the continent more than some of his younger contemporaries would have. It continued to be a concern of Sibbes's until his death. In his final sermon at Gray's Inn, on 28 June 1635, he said, "When there comes ill tidings of the church abroad and at home, it doth not much dismay him. His heart is fixed; he believeth in God and in Christ, and that keeps him from being like a reed shaken with every wind."[102] That evening Sibbes fell sick. Hartlib noted that in Sibbes's final days, he was unshaken: "Being asked how hee (Dr. Sips) did in his soule replied I should doe God much wrong if I should not say very well."[103] He was obviously in control of his mental faculties. He finished his preface to The Soul's Conflict, and Victory over Itself by Faith, the following Wednesday, 1 July at Gray's Inn. Catlin reported that "his Physitian, that knew his Body best" was "then out of ye Citty..." On Saturday, 4 July, Sibbes clearly knew himself to be dying.[104] That day he revised his will being "weake in body, but of p'fect memory" leaving his goods to family, friends and servants at Gray's Inn. For his last six years, Sibbes's home was a rooftop chamber created some years before for Sir Gilbert Gerard, but that had been yielded to Sibbes when Gerard had decided that he required larger chambers. It was in this

---

[101]Quoted in J. C. Ryle, Light from Old Times (London, 1890) 358. Cf. Prest, 212.

[102]"Two Sermons Upon the first words of Christs last Sermon, John 14.1. Being also the last Sermons of Richard Sibbs," in Works, 7:355-6.

[103]Hartlib, Ephemerides, 1635.

[104]Sibbes's will, Grosart, "Memoir of Richard Sibbes, D.D.," in Works, 1:cxxviii.

chamber at Gray's Inn on 5 July 1635—Commencement Sunday in Cambridge—that Sibbes died. He was buried the next day in St. Andrews Holborn where the members of Gray's Inn had maintained a chapel from medieval times.[105] His funeral sermon, preached by William Gouge, has not survived.

> "Our life is nothing but as it were a web woven with interminglings of wants and favours, crosses and blessings, standings and fallings, combat and victory..."[106]

---

[105]Cowper, 52.
[106]"The Soul's Conflict with Itself," in *Works*, 1:249.

PART II:

"The Vitals and Essentials of Religion":[1]

THE THEOLOGICAL IDENTITY OF

RICHARD SIBBES

IF RICHARD SIBBES has been characterized as being uninvolved with his times, on the one hand, he has just as regularly been presented as being rather unconcerned with theology. Larzer Ziff has written that the difference between Sibbes and William Perkins was that "Sibbes was not a powerful theologian; he was rather, a spiritual counselor, what his colleagues called a 'physician of the soul.'"[2] Norman Pettit has referred to Sibbes's development of the doctrine of the Holy Spirit specifically, "with a minimum of concern for the rigors of dogma." He suggested that Sibbes thought that so long as "divinity could 'warm' the heart, it mattered little what in theory man should not be allowed to do to affect his own salvation."[3] While there is in this conception something of the truth (as there is in the picture of Sibbes as an almost ahistorical figure),

---

[1]Simeon Ash, James Nalton, and Joseph Church, "To the Reader," in Sibbes, *A Heavenly Conference Between Christ and Mary after His Resurrection* (London, 1654); rpt. in *Works*, 6:415.

[2]Larzer Ziff, *The Career of John Cotton: Puritanism and the American Experience* (Princeton, 1962) 31. Cf. G. F. Nuttall, *The Holy Spirit in Puritan Faith and Experience* (Oxford, 1946) 14.

[3]Norman Pettit, *The Heart Prepared* (New Haven, Connecticut, 1966) 67.

it, too, is misleading. Sibbes published no learned theological treatises, except for his sermons. Whatever polemics may lace these sermons, he took no leading part in any theological controversy. Apart from his governing roles in colleges and among the Feofees, he was primarily a preacher and a pastor. Yet in the seventeenth century, ministers were theologians and psychologists, as well as preachers and pastors.

Part Two of this study will examine the theological identity of Sibbes. Three significant areas of Sibbes's theology will be examined: roughly, his theology, anthropology and some aspects of his understanding of the Christian life. More accurately stated, Sibbes's sermons are explored to find that which is fundamental, distinctive, and most often misconstrued. In so doing, the currently popular suggestion that the divinity preached by Sibbes and his friends was a substantial modification of earlier Reformed theology will be called into question, as the theological identity of Sibbes more clearly appears. In turn, Richard Sibbes will be shown to have been a Reformed theologian, an "affectionate" theologian, and a conforming theologian. The first of these tasks involves investigations of matters of predestination and election, covenant, conversion, and preparation — well-worked ground in general, if not in Sibbes. Thus chapter five helps place Sibbes theologically in a group of moderate, though clearly Reformed members of the Church of England. Chapter six undertakes the briefest task, but also that at which Sibbes excelled. An investigation into the roots of Sibbes's "affectionate" theology should further integrate Sibbes's previously disheveled theological appearance. Finally, while Sibbes has been misunderstood in both the previous areas, the last area has been almost completely ignored in the secondary literature (save the vexed issue of assurance). Yet the historical study in Part One of this dissertation demands a reevaluation of Sibbes as a conforming theologian. Although Sibbes has been presented variously in other areas, it is in this final aspect that the issues of self-perception and consequent responsibility — comfort, assurance, providence, and perhaps most importantly, conscience — provide the theological context for Sibbes's continued functioning within the bounds of conformity. The result of chapter seven then, is that Sibbes's theology should, in the process, become more congruent with his life. Moralism, mysticism, and nonconformity aside, Richard Sibbes may then appear — theologically — more authentically than he has for some time.

V

A Reformed Theologian

WHILE AN INVESTIGATION of Sibbes as a Reformed theologian could be informative in any case, it is particularly appropriate because he is often presented as having been vague on theological issues, particularly if they had to do with predestination. It is appropriate also because Sibbes has been presented as a central, though unwitting, figure in the development of moralism, emphasizing sanctification at the expense of justification. This has been argued on the basis of his advocacy of both covenant theology and his understanding of conversion and preparation. Since this second image (of Sibbes as engendering moralism) would seem to fit nicely with the picture of him as lessening the emphasis on divine sovereignty traditional in Reformed theology, these issues are best considered together.

Predestination

THE OBVIOUS PLACE to begin a study of the Reformed nature of Sibbes's theology is with the doctrine of predestination. As Samuel Brooke, Master of Trinity College, Cambridge, told William Laud, the "doctrine of predestination is the root of Puritanism, and Puritanism is the root of all rebellion, and disobedient intractableness in parliament, and all schism and sauciness in the country, nay in the church itself."[1] Yet R. T.

---

[1] State Papers of Charles I, 16/177/13 (Public Records Office, London). Cited by Charles Carlton, *Archbishop William Laud* (London, 1987) 121. Carlton attributes this to Samuel Moore. Yet there was no Master of Trinity College, Cambridge by this name. It well fits, however, Laud's contemporary, Samuel Brooke. Such antipathy is shared by a number of modern historians of the period: e.g., Max Weber, *The Protestant Ethic and the Spirit of Capitalism*, trans. Parsons (London, 1930) 104; William Haller, *The Rise of Puritanism* (New York,

Kendall has noted "Sibbes's small attention to the doctrine of predestination."[2] While Kendall observes that this may have been due to some of the restrictions on preaching mentioned in the previous chapter, he wonders, based on "Sibbes's pastoral concern," if Sibbes "would almost prefer that men forget about the decrees of predestination."[3] Larzer Ziff has clearly implied that Sibbes was "ambiguously inconsistent on the matter of predestination."[4] Small attention, ambiguity, and a desire for his hearers to forget would hardly seem to be the hallmarks of one concerned to present a gospel that was predestined before the foundations of the earth.

Yet while Sibbes's explicit references to predestination may be few, they are not unclear and do not seem to have been made reluctantly. For Sibbes to have been ambiguous or inconsistent on predestination would have been particularly surprising considering the thought he must have given to the matter when he took his Bachelor of Divinity from Cambridge. The manuscript in the British Library records that he was chosen as the B.D. "respondant" for the 1610 commencement exercises in the University and that the second statement to which he had to respond was "*Dei Decretum non tollit libertatum voluntatis.*"[5] The substance of his response is not recorded, though, given that the respondent was to answer all comers for two hours, it could hardly have been slight. Furthermore, in his first introduction of a book to the press eight years later, Sibbes praised Augustine's and Bradwardine's defenses of predestination.[6] Regardless of how frequently he mentioned it expressly in his sermons, he clearly believed:

1938) 83; Pettit, 47; Barry Coward, *The Stuart Age: A History of England, 1603-1714* (London, 1980) 149; Bert Affleck, "The Theology of Richard Sibbes, 1577-1635 (Ph.D. diss., Drew University, 1969) 290.

[2] R. T. Kendall, *Calvin and English Calvinism to 1649* (Oxford, 1979) 103; cf. Charles H. George, "A Social Interpretation of English Puritanism," *Journal of Modern History*, vol. XXXV/4 (December, 1953): 330.

[3] *Ibid.*

[4] Ziff, 219.

[5] BL MS Harl. 7038, f.88.

[6] "To the Reader," to Paul Baynes, *A Commentary Upon the First Chapter of the Epistle...to the Ephesians*, in *Works*, 1:lxxxiv; and again in *A Learned Commentary or Exposition Upon The first Chapter of the Second Epistle of S. Paul to the Corinthians*, in *Works*, 3:331. Cf. his criticism of Melanchton for his "errors which hee had about Praedestination," recorded by Samuel Hartlib,

First, that there was an eternal separation of men in God's purpose. Secondly, that this first decree of severing man to his ends, is an act of sovereignty over his creature, and altogether independent of anything in the creature, as a cause of it, especially in comparative reprobation, as why he rejected Judas, and not Peter; sin foreseen cannot be the cause, because that was common to both, and therefore could be no cause of severing. Thirdly,...that damnation is an act of divine justice, which supposeth demerit; and therefore the execution of God's decree is founded on sin, either of nature, or life, or both.[7]

Sibbes voiced these propositions as ones with which both sides in the then-current debates surrounding the order of decrees would agree.

Order of the Decrees.

MODERN WRITERS' MISUNDERSTANDINGS of the doctrine of predestination in the seventeenth century are perhaps nowhere more plentiful than in discussions of the decrees. Although it has often been represented as such,[8] the question was never one of election being temporally prior to one's birth, or even to the fall itself. Infra- and supralapsarians,

---

Ephemerides, 1634. Cf. *A Learned Commentary or Exposition Upon The first Chapter of the Second Epistle of S. Paul to the Corinthians*, in *Works*, 3:134.

[7]"To the Reader," to Paul Baynes, *A Commentary Upon the First Chapter of the Epistle...to the Ephesians*, in *Works*, 1:lxxxv.

[8]J. Kenyon provides an example of the most common kind of misunderstanding surrounding the debates about the order of the decrees, when he writes that "the heirs of Calvin" held "of their own volition . . . his awful proposition that each man, even before his birth (some said before Adam's Fall) was *elected* to salvation or *reprobated* to damnation ," (J. Kenyon, *Stuart England*, [London, 1978], 99). Even the usually careful John von Rohr confused the issue when he wrote of Jerome Zanchius' theology as consisting of maintaining that the decrees of election and damnation occurred "prior to the fall itself," (John Von Rohr, *The Covenant of Grace in Puritan Thought*, [Atlanta, Georgia, 1986], 4). So, too, Basil Hall, who wrote describing Theodore Beza's supralapsarianism as "the view that God decreed from before creation everything relating to man's future, including his fall and total depravity, which comes near to being thoroughgoing determinism," (Basil Hall, "Calvin against the Calvinists," in *John Calvin*, ed. G. E. Duffield, [Appleford, Abingdon, Berkshire, 1966], 27).

Arminians and Calvinists, all accepted that God elected (and most, that God reprobated or passed over) before the fall of Adam, and indeed, before the creation of the world. The real issue was not *chronological*, but rather *logical* order. The Remonstrants (Arminians) maintained that the decree of salvation was simply an intention of God to save all of those who cooperated with the grace he offered. In the Arminian schema, while God's grace was necessary, it was not sufficient to account for the salvation of any particular individual. The Reformed theologians rejected this position as grounding salvation too much in individual differences, even smacking of Roman merit as the cause of salvation, rather than in God's gracious choice, and thus making a mockery of the whole idea of *divine* election.[9]

Having rejected Arminianism, however, there was still within the Reformed camp a division concerning the order of the decrees. In the quotation from Sibbes above, he makes it clear that both sides in the dispute were eager to affirm that the decree of election logically preceded any envisioning of individual merit or response. The question, rather, was whether the decree of electing some individuals *logically* preceded the decree to permit the fall. Those who said that it did were called "supralapsarians," and those who said that it did not were called "infra-" or "sublapsarians." Stated differently, the question was whether those God elected were envisioned by him as being sinless (the supralapsarian position) or sinful (the infralapsarian position). Essentially the discussion was one of purpose and the conflict between basic tendencies to monism and dualism, neither of which are fully appropriate for Christian theology.

Sibbes was decidedly agnostic in this discussion. Though some have suggested that infralapsarianism should be inferred from the "enormous responsibility that Sibbes imputes to men who hear the Gospel,"[10] both sides would have agreed with Sibbes's words on the necessity of means.[11] Sibbes believed in God's "decrees"[12] and his

---

[9]Canons of the Synod of Dort, particularly I.vi, vii, ix, x. Cf. *A Learned Commentary or Exposition Upon The first Chapter of the Second Epistle of S. Paul to the Corinthians*, in *Works*, 3:331.

[10]Kendall, 105.

[11]*A Learned Commentary or Exposition Upon The first Chapter of the Second Epistle of S. Paul to the Corinthians*, in *Works*, 3:331.

[12]"Bowels Opened," in *Works*, 2:69; "The Privileges of the Faithful," in *Works*, 5:262; "The Rich Poverty; or, The Poor Man's Riches," in *Works*, 6:241.

"counsels."[13] He declared the issues at stake in this dispute "a mystery,"[14] and of little practical consequence.[15] (In this sentiment he was joined by William Twisse, one of the most ardent supraapsarians of the day.[16]) After objecting to the whole discussion on the grounds that there "is the difficulty of understanding, how God conceives things," Sibbes concluded with the observation "that men should in all matters have the same conceit of things of this nature, is rather to be wished for, than to be hoped."[17]

Reprobation

The debates between the infralapsarians and supralapsarians were most heated concerning the doctrine of reprobation—the doctrine that even as God had eternally decreed to save some, so he had also eternally decreed to damn some.[18] If the decrees were to be maintained in strictest parallel (which was the architectonic theological virtue the supralapsarians naturally sought) then both of these decrees—to election and reprobation—must be irrespective of individual merit or demerit, but based on God's sovereignty alone. Ziff has suggested that Sibbes "tended to disregard or skirt about" reprobation and that the "possibility that the listener may have been damned formed no part of Sibbes's public outlook."[19] Yet this is not an accurate picture of Sibbes; he was not so much silent, as quiet, on the doctrine of eternal reprobation. On those occasions when Sibbes did speak of the reprobate, he did so in one of two ways. Sometimes he used the word

---

[13]"The Soul's Conflict with Itself," in *Works*, 1:207.

[14]Ibid.

[15]Cf. "The Church's Riches by Christ's Poverty," in *Works*, 4: 520–521.

[16]See John Gill, *A Complete Body of Doctrinal and Practical Divinity* (London, 1839) 185.

[17] "To the Reader," to Paul Baynes, *A Commentary Upon the First Chapter of the Epistle ...to the Ephesians*, in *Works*, 1:lxxxvi.

[18]Clearly stated by William Perkins in *The Workes of that Famous and Worthy Minister of Christ in the University of Cambridge, Mr. William Perkins* (London, 1616) 1:24–25.

[19]Ziff, 31–32.

simply to refer to those who were presently outside of Christ.[20] Yet
Sibbes also used the word to refer to the fact that Christ "hath
predestinated and elected us, and refused others."[21] Echoing Paul's
words about Pharaoh in Romans 9, Sibbes referred to those who "had
rather lose their souls than their wills" as those who "are but raised up
for Christ to get himself glory in their confusion."[22] He did not assume
that eternal reprobation was the case of any particular individual
listening to him, nor could he, because as he said repeatedly, this was
part of "God's secret purpose" hidden in this world,[23] and their very
presence in the hearing of the word was cause for hope rather than
despair.[24] Discouraging his hearers from delving too deeply into this
discussion,[25] Sibbes exhorted them simply to trust.[26] The problem with
the supralapsarian presentation of the decree of reprobation, pointed out
regularly by critics, was that it seemed effectively to make sin a
necessary means to God's end, and therefore, in some way, God
seemed to become the author of it.[27] Thus the infralapsarians argued
that reprobation can only be a more passive preterition, or passing by,
of those individuals whom God envisioned (not foresaw) as sinful.
Sibbes certainly seemed to agree that damnation must always come

---

[20]E.g., *A Learned Commentary or Exposition Upon The fourth Chapter of the
Second Epistle of Saint Paul to the Corinthians*, in *Works*, 4:323.

[21]"Bowels Opened," in *Works*, 2:181; cf. "Salvation Applied," in *Works*,
5:389.

[22]"The Bruised Reed and Smoking Flax," in *Works*, 1:93; cf. "Salvation
Applied," in *Works*, 5:390; "The Saint's Safety in Evil Times, Manifested by St.
Paul, From his Experience of God's Goodness in Greatest Distress," in *Works*,
1:321.

[23]"Salvation Applied," in *Works*, 5:390; cf. *A Learned Commentary or
Exposition Upon The fourth Chapter of the Second Epistle of Saint Paul to the
Corinthians*, in *Works*, 4:377.

[24]"Description of Christ," in *Works*, 1:23; cf. "The Saint's Hiding-Place in the
Evil Day," in *Works*, 1:410; "The Bruised Reed and Smoking Flax," in *Works*, 1:
48, 72; *A Learned Commentary or Exposition Upon The fourth Chapter of the Second
Epistle of Saint Paul to the Corinthians*, in *Works*, 4:377.

[25]"Salvation Applied," in *Works*, 5:390.

[26]"Fountain Opened," in *Works*, 5:511.

[27]Perkins and other supralapsarians responded to this partially by
maintaining that "there is not anything absolutely evil" that exists (Perkins,
Workes, 1:15).

from God's judgment on sin[28] and thus was concerned that a decree of reprobation presented too starkly would dishonor God. Ultimately, Sibbes insisted that the damned have only themselves to blame for their fate[29] He stated that "there was never any yet came to hell, but they had some seeming pretence for their coming thither."[30]

Particular Redemption.

THE OTHER ISSUE arising from this discussion that could easily create pastoral problems for doubting souls was the issue of the extent of Christ's atonement. In short, if God elected only some, not all, to salvation, then for whom did Christ die? There is some ambiguity in Sibbes's sermons on this point, perhaps simply because of his desire to be a faithful exegete of scripture. One finds statements that "He [Christ] was a public person. Upon the cross he stood in the place of all the world, and all their sins committed, or foreseen to be committed, lay upon him."[31] Yet in context, he clearly only intended by this a reference to show that Christ's resurrection foreshadows the resurrection to life of "every true Christian." Consistent with his Reformed theology presented above, Sibbes taught that "when Christ is said to redeem the world, it must not be understood generally of all mankind."[32] Instead, "Christ died alone and singular in this respect; because in him dying all died that were his, that the Father gave him to die for. For they go in parallel, God's gift and Christ's death."[33] When Sibbes referred to

---

[28]"Fountain Opened," in *Works*, 5:510–511; "Salvation Applied," in *Works*, 5: 389.
[29]"Bowels Opened," in *Works*, 2: 69; cf. "The Matchless Love and Inbeing," in *Works*, 6:406; "Description of Christ," in *Works*, 1:25; "Christ is Best; or, St. Paul's Strait," in *Works*, 1:337–338.
[30]"Bowels Opened," in *Works*, 2:87.
[31]"The Power of Christ's Resurrection," in *Works*, 5:198.
[32]"Fountain Opened," in *Works*, 5:516–17.
[33]"Christ's Exaltation Purchased by Humiliation," in *Works*, 5: 345. Cf. "Salvation Applied," in *Works*, 5:388; "Bowels Opened," in *Works*, 2:179; "Judgment's Reason," in *Works*, 4:103; "Christ's Sufferings for Man's Sin," in *Works*, 5:356. Karl Barth, in his criticism of federal or covenant theology, presented the doctrine of a "limited" atonement as being one of the necessary results. Karl Barth, *Church Dogmatics*, trans. G. W. Bromiley (Edinburgh, 1956)

"God's secret purpose in electing some, and redeeming some," he was not repeating himself in poetic parallelism, but was making two distinct points. God has elected only some, and that Christ, by his death, has redeemed only some.[34] This was not, however, in Sibbes's mind to introduce a smallness into consideration of the atonement. Both the extention and limitation of Christ's atonement were matters of praise.[35] In his only long dicussion of this doctrine extant (in his sermon on Gal 2:20, "Salvation Applied"), Sibbes reasoned from Romans 5:10 that "the greatest part are not saved by his life, therefore they are not reconciled by his death."[36] He assumed that his opponents on this point would not be Protestants, but "papists"[37] who wished to add individual merit into salvation. Yet it must be admitted that Sibbes's affirmation of this doctrine is in most of his sermons more evident in its assumption than in its exposition.[38]

Election

WHEN SIBBES SPOKE of predestination, he usually spoke of election.[39] Election is simply the particular predestination of certain individuals to salvation,[40] and therefore fitted perfectly with Sibbes's desire to speak of Christianity affectionately, as the story of God's love. When Sibbes spoke of the elect, he meant those marvelously, lovingly chosen by God the Father for salvation before time and in time.[41] To be elect meant to be God's. This "world taken out of the world, the world of the elect"[42] is

vol. IV/I, 57. J. B. Torrance follows part way in this assessment, "Covenant or Contract?" *Scottish Journal of Theology*, vol. XXIII/1 (Feb. 1970): 68–69.

[34]"Salvation Applied," in *Works*, 5:390.

[35]"The Rich Pearl," in *Works*, 7:257; "Salvation Applied," in *Works*, 5:389.

[36]"Salvation Applied," in *Works*, 5:388; cf. "The Pattern of Purity," in *Works*, 7:509.

[37]"Salvation Applied," in *Works*, 5:389, 392.

[38]E.g., "Angels' Acclamations," in *Works*, 6:354; "Salvation Applied," in *Works*, 5:389–391; "The Church's Riches by Christ's Poverty," in *Works*, 4:525.

[39]"Lydia's Conversion," in *Works*, 6:523.

[40]"The Privileges of the Faithful," in *Works*, 5:262.

[41]"Description of Christ," in *Works*, 1:9; cf. "Bowels Opened," in *Works*, 2: 73; "The Rich Poverty; or, The Poor Man's Riches," in *Works*, 6:241.

[42]"Fountain Opened," in *Works*, 5:516; "Judgment's Reason," in *Works*, 4:98.

composed of people who are specially favoured, those God calls his "best friends."[43] They are God's before they ever respond to the ministry of the Word.[44] They are not all who professed to be Christians, but rather are those whom the Father had given to the Son before the creation of the world. They are those for whom the Son had died, the "true professors of the truth" drawn by the Spirit through the ministry of the word, moving to perfection "by degrees." They never fall away, but rather who certainly spend eternity together with God.[45] It was only by being in Christ that the believer could have any certainty that he was himself one of the elect.[46]

Election was, for Sibbes, primarily something not to be debated, but demonstrated.[47] If to be one of the elect was to be one to whom God had reconciled Himself, and who had been reconciled to God, then nothing could be more important for the Christian than seeking and securing evidence of election.[48] Yet such assurance was not to be found by speculations of the "dark scruples of his eternal decree! Obey the command, obey the threatening, and put that out of doubt. If thou yield to the command, if thou obey the threatening, if thou be drawn by that, undoubtedly thou art the child of God."[49] By speaking of election in his

---

[43]"A Breathing after God," in *Works*, 2:216; cf. "The Rich Poverty; or, The Poor Man's Riches," in *Works*, 6:232, 235; "The Soul's Conflict with Itself," in *Works*, 1:262.

[44]"Bowels Opened," in *Works*, 2:142; "Of the Providence of God," in *Works*, 5:50-51.

[45]"A Breathing after God," in *Works*, 2:234; "Bowels Opened," in *Works*, 2:36, 83, 179; "The Demand of a Good Conscience," in *Works*, 7:482; "The Excellency of the Gospel above the Law," in *Works*, 4:218; "The Faithful Covenanter," in *Works*, 6:8; "Judgment's Reason," in *Works*, 4:103; "The Difficulty of Salvation," in *Works*, 1:396.

[46]"Description of Christ," in *Works*, 1: 9, 18; "The Soul's Conflict with Itself," in *Works*, 1:132.

[47]"The Church's Riches by Christ's Poverty," in *Works*, 4:520-1; cf. "Bowels Opened," in *Works*, 2:69. Sylvia Roberts, "'Radical Graces': A Study of Puritan Casuistry in the Writings of William Perkins and Richard Sibbes," (M.A. Thesis, University of Melbourne, 1972) 183.

[48]"The Right Receiving," in *Works*, 4:62-63; "The Soul's Conflict with Itself," in *Works*, 1:137.

[49]*A Learned Commentary or Exposition Upon The first Chapter of the Second Epistle of S. Paul to the Corinthians*, in *Works*, 3:156; cf. "A Glance of Heaven; or, Precious Taste of a Glorious Feast," in *Works*, 4:182.

sermons, Sibbes meant not to grow pride, but gratitude,[50] not to ennervate the elect, but rather to energize them to action.[51]

KENDALL'S SUGGESTION THAT "Sibbes's pastoral concern" indicates that he "would almost prefer that men forget about the decrees of predestination," is clearly an overstatement. If the stress is on "decrees" taken to mean the order, this is almost certainly true. However, if the suggestion is that Sibbes might have wished his hearers to forget about predestination, then it is clearly false. However successfully Sibbes avoided controversy over predestination[52] or however sparingly he referred to it, it cannot reasonably be suggested that he had doubts about the doctrine's truth or use. In his sermons, all the doctrines typically associated with predestination were clearly present—election and reprobation, the decrees and definite atonement. Yet this did not give to Sibbes's sermons a grimness that some modern writers present as the necessary concomitant to any espousal of such doctrines. Instead, the discussions of predestination in Sibbes's sermons always had a positive purpose. They were always pastoral and personal. For Sibbes,

---

[50]*A Learned Commentary or Exposition Upon The first Chapter of the Second Epistle of S. Paul to the Corinthians*, in *Works*, 3:331; "The Rich Poverty; or, The Poor Man's Riches," in *Works*, 6:234; "Bowels Opened," in *Works*, 2:142; cf. "A Breathing after God," in *Works*, 2: 234; "Bowels Opened," in *Works*, 2:73; "Divine Meditations and Holy Contemplations," in *Works*, 7:216; "The Excellency of the Gospel above the Law," in *Works*, 4:218; "The Faithful Covenanter," in *Works*, 6:8; "The Privileges of the Faithful," in *Works*, 5:264; "The Soul's Conflict with Itself," in *Works*, 1:184, 264; "Fountain Opened," in *Works*, 5:529; "Description of Christ," in *Works*, 1:9.
[51]"Bowels Opened," in *Works*, 2:36, 83; "The Bruised Reed and Smoking Flax," in *Works*, 1:49; "The Demand of a Good Conscience," in *Works*, 7: 478, 482, 491; "The Excellency of the Gospel above the Law," in *Works*, 4:282; "The Soul's Conflict with Itself," in *Works*, 1:206-207, 250; "The Church's Riches by Christ's Poverty," in *Works*, 4:517; "Fountain Opened," in *Works*, 5:490, 532; "Judgment's Reason," in *Works*, 4:103; "The Rich Poverty; or, The Poor Man's Riches," in *Works*, 6:235, 241; "The Privileges of the Faithful," in *Works*, 5:257; "Of the Providence of God," in *Works*, 5:50-51.
[52]"The Church's Riches by Christ's Poverty," in *Works*, 4:520-1.

the Reformed doctrines of predestination were nothing other than God's love language to his people, a "delightful determinism."[53]

It may fairly be asked, though, if Sibbes believed so clearly in a Reformed understanding of predestination, why was he reluctant to discuss the doctrine explicitly? Four reasons suggest themselves. First, during his time in London, the pulpit and press knew increasing controls. On the other hand, part of the very reason that precipitated him being officially discouraged from preaching on predestination—the doctrine's popularity—may suggest why he could have felt so little need to do so. His clerical circles, and perhaps most of his audiences, were composed perhaps entirely of those who would have agreed with him on predestination. A third reason for apparent reluctance may be the form of address that is almost exclusively left to the modern reader, and that Sibbes most extensively used, the sermon. It is significant that Sibbes's longest discussion of predestination comes in one of the few non-sermonic pieces of his writings—the preface to a book. Sermons were for lay edification, not university disputation. As presented above, some very difficult pastoral issues were involved in contemplation of the doctrines of election and predestination. And finally, there is the matter of his personality. From Jenison's 1621 reference to Sibbes's "timourousness" to his posthumous reputation as being personally humble and non-controversial, the historian is left with the impression of Sibbes as a pacific figure. Regardless of the political situation, the pastoral situation always seems to find predestination an unpacific doctrine (whether for good or ill). It would be consistent with what we know of him to suggest that, given the controversy which so easily arose from it, he felt it a topic better dealt with outside the pulpit.

Covenant, Conversion, and Preparation

Covenant

A NUMBER OF historians and theologians have suggested that the early seventeenth-century English Protestant preachers and theologians were in the forefront of a sea-change in Protestant theology from monergism

---

[53]Harold Shelly, "Richard Sibbes: Early Stuart Preacher of Piety (Ph.D. diss., Temple University, 1972) 137.

to synergism, through the idea of covenant,[54] and that not least among them was Richard Sibbes. Was Sibbes a covenant theologian? If so, was

---

[54]Pettit, 218. It has been suggested that the sheerness of the sixteenth-century reformers' doctrine of the sovereignty of God was effectively, if not formally, undermined by their successors' use of covenant imagery. The number of books and articles on the modification of Reformed theology by the concept of covenant is truly vast; some of the more important ones are cited below. E.g., Christopher Hill's statement that "covenant theology, and the suggestion that a hearty desire for salvation might be the first evidence of grace at work in a man's soul, were desperate attempts to make Calvinism palatable for mass consumption," (*Society and Puritanism in Pre-Revolutionary England*, [London, 1964], 489; elsewhere, Hill has referred to covenant theology as "a means . . . of smuggling 'works' into Calvinism," (Hill, *Puritanism and Revolution*, [London, 1958], 240); Norman Pettit's statement that "the extreme emphasis on covenant ideals . . . contradicted the dogmatic stand that anything done on man's part diminishes God's sovereignty," (218). The most gross misrepresentations concerning the covenant idea as giving one a claim on God are found in Perry Miller, "The Marrow of Puritan Divinity," *Publications of the Colonial Society for Massachusetts* vol. 32 (1933–1937) 268ff, repeated in his *The New England Mind: The Seventeenth Century* (New York, 1939) 395; M. M. Knappen, *Tudor Puritanism* (Chicago, 1939) 395. More theological critiques are provided by G. C. Berkouwer, *Studies in Dogmatics: Sin*, trans. C. Holtrop (Grand Rapids, Michigan, 1971) 206–210; Kendall; and, most seminal, criticizing covenant theology as essentially anthropocentric, Barth, *Church Dogmatics*, vol. IV/I, 54–66 (and popularizing Barth's criticisms have been Torrance, 51–76; and Holmes Rolston III, *John Calvin Versus the Westminster Confession*, [Richmond, Virginia, 1972]). David Zaret, *The Heavenly Contract: Ideology and Organization in Pre-Revolutionary Puritanism* (Chicago, 1985) 153, simply seems to accept that "Puritan covenant theology modified Calvinism in subtle ways" and proceeds to show the use covenant theology was put to, without investigating whether or not it was actually a modification (cf. 161–162). Yet see Jens G. Moller, "The Beginnings of Puritan Covenant Theology," *Journal of Ecclesiastical History*, vol. XIV (1963): 49; Patrick Collinson, *Elizabethan Puritan Movement* (London, 1967) 435; Anthony Hoekema, "The Covenant of Grace in Calvin's Teaching," *Calvin Theological Journal*, vol. II/2 (Nov. 1967): 133–161; George Marsden, "Perry Miller's Rehabilitation of the Puritans: A Critique," *Church History*, vol. XXX (1970): 91–105; William K. B. Stoever, '*A Faire and Easie Way to Heaven': Covenant Theology and Antinomianism in Early Massachusetts* (Middletown, Connecticut, 1978) 81–118; Meredith G. Kline, "Of Works and Grace," *Presbyterion*, vol. XII (Spring–Fall, 1983): 86–87; Von Rohr, *passim*, e.g., 1–2; David B. McWilliams, "The Covenant Theology of the Westminster Confession of Faith and Recent Criticism," *Westminster Theological Journal*, vol. LIII (Spring, 1991): 109–124. What will perhaps come to be regarded as the definitive treatment is Andrew Woolsey, "Unity and Continuity in Covenantal

this covenantal framework in tension with his orthodox Protestant teaching of predestination and election considered above? To trace the history of covenant thought, even in the English reformation, is well beyond the scope of this study.[55] Essentially, the uses of "covenant" among the godly of Sibbes's time seemed to be two: primarily in description of God's saving covenant and secondarily in description of the obligations of the Christian to God and others. The first sense intended no synergism, and the second sense more clearly included the obligations on both parts as fundamental to the existence of the covenant.[56] John Knewstub, Sibbes's early patron at Cambridge, "took the covenant pattern so completely for granted that the word itself appears only now and then, quite casually."[57] For example, throughout his exposition of Exodus 20, Knewstub quite naturally used much legal language. In preaching on the Ten Commandments, he clearly intended that his hearers should understand the obligations under which they stood as God's covenant people. In his epistle dedicatory, he stated that one sermon "will declare with what conditions we have wages promised for our work, and whether the covenant be so favorable as that we need not to doubt but that we shall be able to perform it."[58] Yet Knewstub also used "covenant" interchangeably with the more obviously unilateral "promise"[59] and explicitly denied that the

---

Thought: A Study in the Reformed Tradition to the Westminster Assembly," (Ph.D. diss., University of Glasgow, 1988). His conclusion: "The weight of evidence...leans heavily towards the view that the theology of the covenant does not represent any great divergence on the part of later Reformed covenantal theologians from the theology of the Reformers themselves," (2:291).

[55]Perhaps still the best short summary of the history of this doctrine is Geerhardus Vos, "The Doctrine of the Covenant in Reformed Theology," trans. Voorwinde and Van Gemeren, in *Redemptive History and Biblical Interpretation*, ed. Richard Gaffin, Jr. (Phillipsburg, New Jersey, 1980) 234–267. Two longer excellent histories are Richard A. Muller, *Christ and the Decree: Christology and Predestination in Reformed Theology from Calvin to Perkins* (Durham, North Carolina, 1986) and Andrew Woolsey (cited above). For a good summary of scholarly opinion on the point through the mid-1980s, see Von Rohr, 17–33; or, even more thoroughly, Woolsey, 1:101–200.

[56]E.g., Sibbes, "The Bride's Longing," in *Works*, 6:542; Hebrews 9:16–17.

[57]Leonard Trinterud, *Elizabethan Puritanism* (Oxford, 1971) 313.

[58]Knewstub, *Lectures...upon the Twentieth Chapter of Exodus and Certain Other Places of Scripture* (1577; rpt. in Trinterud, *Elizabethan*) 316.

[59]Knewstub, 321; cf. 322–324.

basis of the covenant could ever be bilateral.[60] William Perkins, like Knewstub before him, spoke of the covenant of grace in a way that showed that it was both essential to be a part of it, yet beyond any one's ability to enter it savingly. In so doing, Perkins was trying both to encourage people to rely on God and to grow gratitude in those who thought themselves already in the covenant of grace.[61] In Perkins's sermons, like Calvin's before him, the "covenant–God offered grace and demanded obedience, but he did not recompense obedience by offering grace."[62] It should, then, come as no surprise to find Sibbes and John Davenport, in their introduction to what is generally considered one of the most important statements of early–seventeenth century English covenant theology, writing, "We send forth these sermons of God's All–Sufficiency, and Man's Uprightness, and the Covenant of Grace first...because the right understanding of these points hath a chief influence into a Christian life."[63] Likewise, in Sibbes's own sermons covenant was central.[64]

Covenant Membership

Entrance and Requirements. Who is in the covenant? Essentially, Sibbes taught, as had the Reformers, that whoever had been baptized was in the covenant.[65] The covenant was "made in baptism"[66] and "renewed in taking of the Lord's supper."[67] That is not to say that all

---

[60]Knewstub, 324.

[61]William Perkins, *A Clowd of Faithfull Witnesses, Leading to the heavenly Canaan: Or, A Commentarie upon the 11. Chapter to the Hebrewes, preached in Cambridge...* (n.l., 1609) 2, 27.

[62]Moller, 67.

[63][Sibbes and John Davenport], "To the Reader", to John Preston, *The New Covenant, or the Saints Portion* (1629); rpt. in *Works*, 1:xcvi.

[64]Miller, "Marrow," 257; Roberts, 108.

[65]"Lydia's Conversion," in *Works*, 6:530–531; cf. "The Knot of Prayer Loosed," in *Works*, 7:249.

[66]"The Demand of a Good Conscience," in *Works*, 7:487; cf. 483; "The Faithful Covenanter," in *Works*, 6:24.

[67]"The Demand of a Good Conscience," in *Works*, 7:490; cf. "The Faithful Covenanter," in *Works*, 6:24; "David's Conclusion; or, the Saint's Resolution," in *Works*, 7:90; "Lydia's Conversion," in *Works*, 6:530–531; "Epistle to the Christian Reader," to Ezekiel Culverwell, *Treatise of Faith* (London, 1623); rpt. in

within the covenant were saved. There was an inward baptism and an outward baptism. "The inward, which is the washing of the soul; the outward doth not save without the inward. Therefore he prevents them, lest they should think that all are saved by Christ that are baptized, that have their bodies washed outwardly with water."[68] Sibbes taught that there were obligations and requirements—"indentures"[69]—in the covenant of grace. The primary requirement, as represented in the baptismal service, is trusting,[70] or faith.[71] He wrote, "We that will answer to the covenant made in baptism must perform it, especially that that we then covenanted. What was that? We answered that we would believe. Dost thou believe? I believe every article of the faith. And do you renounce the devil and all his works? I do. Therefore, unless now we believe in Christ, and renounce the devil, we renounce our baptism. It doth us no good."[72] Any perfection taken to be counseled here was simply sincerity because "Under this gracious covenant sincerity is perfection."[73] "Whosoever hath grace to cast

---

Works, 1: xc–xciii; "The Soul's Conflict with Itself," in *Works*, 1: 212; "Fountain Opened," in *Works*, 5:462, 469; William Perkins, "The Foundation of Christian Religion Gathered into Six Principles," in *The Work of William Perkins*, ed. Ian Breward (Appleford, Abingdon, Berkshire, 1970)163; Perkins, *Workes*, 1:71–77; William Gouge, *A Learned and Very Useful Commentary on the Whole Epistle to the Hebrews* (London, 1655) pt. viii.,45.

[68]"The Demand of a Good Conscience," in *Works*, 7:479; cf. "The Excellency of the Gospel above the Law," in *Works*, 4:219; *A Learned Commentary or Exposition Upon The first Chapter of the Second Epistle of S. Paul to the Corinthians*, in *Works*, 3:462; "Bowels Opened," in *Works*, 2:169. Though *A Learned Commentary or Exposition Upon The first Chapter of the Second Epistle of S. Paul to the Corinthians*, in *Works*, 3:451, could be taken as assuming baptismal regeneration, upon careful reading in context, it clearly does not.

[69]"The Demand of a Good Conscience," in *Works*, 7:482; cf. "Fountain Opened," in *Works*, 5:511.

[70]"The Rich Poverty; or, The Poor Man's Riches," in *Works*, 6:254; cf. "Yea and Amen; or, Precious Promises," in *Works*, 4: 127.

[71]"The Demand of a Good Conscience," in *Works*, 7:482.

[72]"The Demand of a Good Conscience," in *Works*, 7:487; cf. 488–491.

[73]"The Bruised Reed and Smoking Flax," in *Works*, 1:59; cf. 40, 58, 68; "The Demand of a Good Conscience," in *Works*, 7:490; *A Learned Commentary or Exposition Upon The first Chapter of the Second Epistle of S. Paul to the Corinthians*, in *Works*, 3: 221; "Art of Contentment," in Works, 5:187; "The Faithful Covenanter," in *Works*, 6:24; John Preston, *The Breast-Plate of Faith and Love* (London, 1634) pt. i, 111, pt. iii, 145.

himself upon the free love of God, he fulfils the covenant of Grace."[74] Sibbes commonly reminded his hearers that this sincerity was not to lead to inaction, but was to lead one to "perform" the covenant of grace.[75] To this end he could exhort his hearers to "often renew our covenants and purposes every day."[76] Those who so live will in "times of trouble, and at the hour of death, at such times" will become known as "the wisest people" because they "have made conscience of keeping their covenant with God, or renewing their covenant with God."[77]

Benefits. God entered into covenant with his people in order to benefit them[78] and the benefits of the covenant were many. Once someone entered the covenant, "they had right in all the good things by Christ."[79] Fundamentally, in the covenant were to be found both justification and sanctification, both forgiveness of sins and growth in grace.[80] Relationally stated, " the fundamental and principal favour" of the covenant of grace was to have God for your God,[81] to "enter into

---

[74]"Angels' Acclamations," in *Works*, 6:354; cf. "Bowels Opened," in *Works*, 2:18.

[75]"The Bride's Longing," in *Works*, 6:541–542; "The Rich Poverty; or, The Poor Man's Riches," in *Works*, 6:252; "The Pattern of Purity," in *Works*, 7:514–515. Cf. Gouge, pt. viii, 39.

[76]"Angels' Acclamations," in *Works*, 6:345; cf. "Judgment's Reason," in *Works*, 4:94; "The Faithful Covenanter," in *Works*, 6:24; "Bowels Opened," in *Works*, 2:16; "Church's Visitation," in *Works*, 1:381; "The Demand of a Good Conscience," in *Works*, 7:490–1; "Judgment's Reason," in *Works*, 4:111; "Two Sermons Upon the first words of Christs last Sermon, John 14.1. Being also the last Sermons of Richard Sibbs," in *Works*, 7:345; "The Returning Backslider," in *Works*, 2:269.

[77]"The Demand of a Good Conscience," in *Works*, 7:490–1; cf. "Judgment's Reason," in *Works*, 4:95.

[78]"The Soul's Conflict with Itself," in *Works*, 1:263; "The Bruised Reed and Smoking Flax," in *Works*, 1:40; "Angels' Acclamations," in *Works*, 6:350. Cf. Gouge, pt. viii. 40; John Calvin, *The Sermons of M. John Calvin upon the Fifth Booke of Moses Called Deuteronomie*, trans. Arthur Golding (London, 1583) 915.b.40.

[79]"The Demand of a Good Conscience," in *Works*, 7:483; cf. "The Privileges of the Faithful," in *Works*, 5:262. Affleck's anachronistic Barthian reading of Sibbes presents the blessings of the covenant in Sibbes, "The benefits of a free and meaningful life in the covenant" as "the believer's experiential self–authentication of God," (Affleck, 142).

[80]"The Excellency of the Gospel above the Law," in *Works*, 4:258.

[81]"The Faithful Covenanter," in *Works*, 6:8, 20; cf."The Privileges of the Faithful," in *Works*, 5:263; "The Returning Backslider," in *Works*, 2:253–254.

terms of friendship with God,"[82] to know God as Father, and to love and be loved by God.[83] One became a "favourite" who "hath God's ear"[84] and who knows his providential care.[85] The result of such covenant love was also a new found unity within the person. One's heart was united around love to God, instead of diversely allying itself to passing things.[86] Humility and faith, those virtues that carried the person out of themselves to God, were to activate these blessings.[87] Finally, from all these benefits, the believer could derive great comfort.[88]

Mutual. Contrary to the rather cold and scholastic way the federal framework has sometimes been presented, in Sibbes's sermons God's testaments were testimonies of his love, and the conditions of the covenant were the Savior's wooing of the beloved. Consent being an essential part of this covenant, Sibbes used the civil contract of marriage as an illustration of the "spiritual contract between Christ and his church."[89] Any sin, therefore, was "spiritual adultery and a breach of covenant with God."[90] The covenant member, therefore, must keep his

[82]"The Demand of a Good Conscience," in *Works*, 7:482; cf. "The Excellency of the Gospel above the Law," in *Works*, 4:218; "The Returning Backslider," in *Works*, 2:267–268.

[83]"Angels' Acclamations," in *Works*, 6:338, 340. Cf. "Bowels Opened," in *Works*, 2:29 (note the impressive restraint in the exegesis here); "The Bruised Reed and Smoking Flax," in *Works*, 1:68; "The Rich Poverty; or, The Poor Man's Riches," in *Works*, 6:254.

[84]"Bowels Opened," in *Works*, 2:18.

[85]"The Privileges of the Faithful," in *Works*, 5:262–263; cf. "Of the Providence of God," in *Works*, 5:46.

[86]"A Breathing after God," in *Works*, 2:218; cf. "The Bride's Longing," in *Works*, 6:541–542.

[87]"Art of Contentment," in Works, 5:191.

[88]"The Soul's Conflict with Itself," in *Works*, 1:212; cf. "The Saint's Hiding-Place in the Evil Day," in *Works*, 1:410.

[89]"The Spouse, Her Earnest Desire After Christ," in *Works*, 2:201; cf. "The Bride's Longing," in *Works*, 6:541; "Discouragement's Recovery," in *Works*, 7:62; "The Demand of a Good Conscience," in *Works*, 7:482; "The Excellency of the Gospel above the Law," in *Works*, 4:246, 257; "The Faithful Covenanter," in *Works*, 6:4; Preston, *Breast-Plate*, 31–33, 201; Gouge, pt. viii. 39; cf. Calvin, (covenant interchangeably with bargain) 94.a.30, 423, 1028, (covenant as unilateral) 146.b.50, 177.a.30.

[90]"Church's Visitation," in *Works*, 1:379; cf. "The Faithful Covenanter," in *Works*, 6:24; Preston, *Breast-Plate*, pt. iii. 145–146.

marriage to Christ pure and "unviolable."[91] Yet Sibbes also used the
image of marriage to show that "weaknesses do not break covenant
with God. They do not between husband and wife; and shall we make
ourselves more pitiful than Christ, who maketh himself a pattern of
love to all other husbands?"[92] (Sibbes also used the language of parent
and child to make this same point.[93]) The image of marriage also
illustrated the role of the preacher in the life of the covenant. Preaching
ministers were "friends of the Bridegroom, who are to hear what Christ
saith and would have said to the church; and we must pray to him, that
he would teach us what to teach others. We are to procure the contract,
and to perfect it till the marriage be in heaven. That is our work."[94]

Unilateral. Sibbes clearly did teach that there were promises of God
that were conditional. For example, in commenting upon 2 Corinthians
1:20 ("For all the promises of God in him are yea, and in him amen")
Sibbes divided promises which were "absolute, without any condition"
(e.g., the coming of Christ, his return, the final resurrection) and those
that he said were "conditional, in the manner of propounding, but yet
absolute in the real performance of them" (e.g., forgiveness of sins if
one believes and repents). Yet even these latter types, though they are:

> propounded conditionally, in the performance they are
> absolute, because God performs the covenant himself; he
> performs our part and his own too. For since Christ, though he
> propounded the promises of the gospel with conditions, yet he
> performs the condition; he stirs us up to attend upon the means,
> and by his Spirit in the word he works faith and repentance,
> which is the condition. Faith and repentance is his gift.[95]

---

[91]"Bowels Opened," in *Works*, 2:58; "Christ's Sufferings for Man's Sin," in
Works, 1:357.
[92]"The Bruised Reed and Smoking Flax," in *Works*, 1:69.
[93]"Judgment's Reason," in *Works*, 4:104; cf. Preston, *Breast-Plate*, 111.
[94]"Bowels Opened," in *Works*, 2:68; cf. "Fountain Opened," in *Works*,
5:505–506.
[95]*A Learned Commentary or Exposition Upon The first Chapter of the Second
Epistle of S. Paul to the Corinthians*, in *Works*, 3:394; cf. 521; "The Bride's
Longing," in *Works*, 6:541–542; "Yea and Amen; or, Precious Promises," in
Works, 4:122.

Much discussion of the place of covenant theology in the sixteenth and seventeenth centuries has surrounded the use of the words "testament" and "covenant" as representing, respectively, unilateral and bilateral agreements.[96] Although Sibbes allowed the distinction, he suggested that either word could be used appropriately about the gospel.[97] Sibbes frequently echoed the prayer of Augustine, "Lord, give what you command, and command what you will."[98] His sermons were replete with phrases that emphasized the graciousness of the saving covenant: "All is out of us in the covenant of grace."[99] Therefore, when he called believers to respond, he called their response a "reflection" and a "holy echo."[100] "Though it is we that answer, yet the power by which we answer is no less than that whereby God created the world and raised Christ from the dead. The answer is ours, but the power and strength is God's, whereby we answer, who performs both his part and ours too in the covenant."[101] Given this unilateral basis of the covenant, it followed that the foundation of the covenant is not man, but Christ.[102]

---

[96]E.g., Von Rohr, 35–36.

[97]*A Learned Commentary or Exposition Upon The first Chapter of the Second Epistle of S. Paul to the Corinthians*, in *Works*, 3:521; "Christ's Exaltation Purchased by Humiliation," in *Works*, 5:342. Cf. "Angels' Acclamations," in *Works*, 6:342, 350; "Art of Contentment," in Works, 5:188; "The Bride's Longing," in *Works*, 6:541–542; Martin Luther, *Lectures on Galatians 1519*, trans. R. Jungkuntz (St. Louis, 1964) 264; Gouge, pt. vii. 94.

[98]"The Bruised Reed and Smoking Flax," in *Works*, 1:58; "The Demand of a Good Conscience," in *Works*, 7:483; cf. "Christ's Exaltation Purchased by Humiliation," in *Works*, 5:342.

[99]"The Excellency of the Gospel above the Law," in *Works*, 4:296; cf. "Bowels Opened," in *Works*, 2:10; "The Returning Backslider," in *Works*, 2:264–265; "The Rich Poverty; or, The Poor Man's Riches," in *Works*, 6:245; "Yea and Amen; or, Precious Promises," in *Works*, 4:127; "The Soul's Conflict with Itself," in *Works*, 1:125; Preston, *Breast-Plate*, 33.

[100]"The Bruised Reed and Smoking Flax," in *Works*, 1:72; "The Faithful Covenanter," in *Works*, 6:19.; "The Demand of a Good Conscience," in *Works*, 7:487; cf. "The Soul's Conflict with Itself," in *Works*, 1:263.

[101]"Bowels Opened," in *Works*, 2:174, 183; "The Saint's Safety in Evil Times, Manifested by St. Paul, From his Experience of God's Goodness in Greatest Distress," in *Works*, 1:321.

[102]"Angels' Acclamations," in *Works*, 6:340, 350; "Art of Contentment," in Works, 5:189; "The Bruised Reed and Smoking Flax," in *Works*, 1:86; "The Demand of a Good Conscience," in *Works*, 7:481; "Fountain Opened," in *Works*,

Perhaps suggesting the pre-creation intra-trinitarian covenant as the original basis of the covenant of grace, Sibbes said, "He [God] being the foundation of the covenant, there must be agreement in him. Now Christ is the foundation of the covenant, by satisfying God's justice, else God and we could never have come to good terms. . . . God is satisfied with the death of the mediator."[103] It was the satisfaction of Christ that Sibbes presented as most properly the basis of the covenant.[104] This was to give the believer hope when surveying his own proneness to sin and to despair. God set himself in the covenant of grace "to triumph in Christ over the greatest evils and enemies we fear."[105]

Covenant of Works. One of the most vexed issues in discussing covenant theology in the Reformed tradition is the place of the covenant of works.[106] It was at this point that Karl Barth criticized the federal theologians most severely. By positing a covenant of works prior to the covenant of grace, they made law more fundamental than grace, Barth objected, and considered salvation fundamentally anthropocentrically, thus falling from the theocentric insights of Calvin. While Barth's understanding of Calvin does not seem to have been correct,[107] this same criticism might well be leveled at Sibbes. Sibbes spoke of the covenant of works, though rarely by name. The initial covenant of works with Adam, Sibbes taught, resulted only in Adam's fall.[108] The

---

5:482; "The Rich Poverty; or, The Poor Man's Riches," in *Works*, 6:245; Gouge, pt. viii. 24.

[103]"The Demand of a Good Conscience," in *Works*, 7:481-2; cf. "The Faithful Covenanter," in *Works*, 6:7; Muller, 181.

[104]"The Excellency of the Gospel above the Law," in *Works*, 4:246. Cf. "Yea and Amen; or, Precious Promises," in *Works*, 4:119; "The Soul's Conflict with Itself," in *Works*, 1:263; "Bowels Opened," in *Works*, 2:145; Calvin, 915.a.60; Perkins, *Workes*, 1:165; William Ames, *The Marrow of Theology*, trans. J. Eusden (Durham, North Carolina, 1968) I.XX.17.

[105]"The Bruised Reed and Smoking Flax," in *Works*, 1:39; cf. 66.

[106]For a recent survey and treatment, see D. A. Weir, *The Origins of the Federal Theology in Sixteenth-Century Reformation Thought* (Oxford, 1990).

[107]Though he did not use the phrase "covenant of works," Calvin essentially taught the same series of obligations and responsibilities which came to be called the covenant of works. See Woolsey, 2:291ff; Perkins clearly defined the covenant of works in *Workes*, 1:32.

[108]"Christ's Exaltation Purchased by Humiliation," in *Works*, 5:342; cf. "The Privileges of the Faithful," in *Works*, 5:259; "The Returning Backslider," in *Works*, 2:260; "The Ungodly's Misery," in *Works*, 1:389; "Yea and Amen; or,

Mosaic dispensation, too, Sibbes occasionally represented as "the covenant of works" or the "old covenant."[109] Though this identification would seem to sacrifice the unity of the Old and New Testaments, Sibbes's suggestion of a previous agreement within the Trinity would make any such Mosaic "covenant of works" essentially a sub-set of the more fundamental gracious covenant.[110] The distinction between these two covenants, both said to be "of works," was made clear by Sibbes in his more extended and careful treatments of the two covenants: his sermons on 2 Corinthians 3:17-18, "The Excellency of the Gospel above the Law;" and his sermons on Genesis 17:7, "The Faithful Covenanter." In the former, Sibbes compared "the administration of the covenant of grace under the gospel...with the administration of the *same covenant in the time of the law*" (italics added).[111] Sibbes went on to show that the administration of the covenant of grace under the gospel is more excellent than it was under the law in four ways: in its liberty and freedom from ceremonies and the law, in its clarity, in its more intensive grace, and in its more extensive grace.[112]

In the beginning of his sermons on Genesis 17:7, Sibbes was even more careful. He clearly stated that fellowship between man and God "was first founded on a covenant of works made with Adam in paradise."[113] The Mosaic law was a renewal of this covenant of works. Concurrently with this works covenant, however, Sibbes posited a gracious covenant, first made immediately after the fall, and then repeated to Abraham.[114] Along with the Mosaic laws was the testament that had been given to Abraham, represented by the "sacrament" of

Precious Promises," in *Works*, 4:118; Cf. Ames, *Marrow* (1968) I.X.9; Gouge, pt. viii. 42.

[109]"The Bruised Reed and Smoking Flax," in *Works*, 1:58-59; "The Excellency of the Gospel above the Law," in *Works*, 4:204.

[110]"The Demand of a Good Conscience," in *Works*, 7:481-2; cf. "The Bruised Reed and Smoking Flax," in *Works*, 1:43, 45.

[111]"The Excellency of the Gospel above the Law," in *Works*, 4:238. So too, Ames (see Eusden, "Introduction," to Ames, *Marrow*, [1968], 54).

[112]"The Excellency of the Gospel above the Law," in *Works*, 4:239; cf. "The Faithful Covenanter," in *Works*, 6:5-7, 19-21; Gouge, pt. vii. 94.

[113]"The Faithful Covenanter," in *Works*, 6:3.

[114]"The Faithful Covenanter," in *Works*, 6:4. Cf. William Perkins, *A Commentarie, or, Exposition Upon the five first Chapters of the Epistle to the Galatians* (Cambridge, 1617) 303-308, 502; Preston, *Breast-Plate*, 31-32; Gouge, pt. viii. 42.

circumcision and then by the sacrifices. This testament "differeth a little from a covenant; for a testament is established by blood, it is established by death. So was that; but it was only with the blood and death of cattle sacrificed as a type."[115] These merely pointed to its fulfilment in Christ. This period, inaugurated with the life, ministry, death, and resurrection of Christ, marked a new clarity to God's intentions in the covenant of grace and was generally called "the New Testament." This testament "is a covenant, and something more. It is a covenant sealed by death...[and] A testament bequeatheth good things merely of love. It giveth gifts freely. A covenant requireth something to be done." This concurrence of covenants in the Old Testament, Sibbes taught continued to the present.[116] Thus he could refer to all his hearers as having, like Adam, sinned against the first covenant, and so encourage them to seek a better covenant.[117] The difference between the two covenants was crucial to the individual because while these covenants ran concurrently they were quite exclusive of each other. Either one could be relied on, but only one, not both, and only one would save.[118]

Conclusion. In conclusion, it is clear that Sibbes frequently used covenant terminology and that this in no way eclipsed the essentially gratuitous nature of salvation. Quite simply, Sibbes could say that "[i]n the covenant of grace, God intends the glory of his grace above all."[119] As if he knew some of the readings that would be put on his sermons by later scholars, Sibbes rebuked his hearers, saying "it is a childish thing from them to infer that there is power in man, becuase God persuadeth and exhorts."[120] Some earlier studies of Sibbes have fallen short at exactly this point. Though Frank E. Farrell gave a full chapter to consideration of the covenant theme in his dissertation, it was badly marred by an uncritical acceptance of Perry Miller's reading of covenant theology as being a "movement away from pure Calvinism" and thus

---

[115] *Ibid.*

[116]"The Faithful Covenanter," in *Works*, 6:5.

[117]"The Ungodly's Misery," in *Works*, 1:389. Cf. Gouge, pt. viii. 45.

[118]"The Faithful Covenanter," in *Works*, 6:5.

[119]"Divine Meditations and Holy Contemplations," in *Works*, 7:189.

[120]*A Learned Commentary or Exposition Upon The fourth Chapter of the Second Epistle of Saint Paul to the Corinthians*, in *Works*, 4:385.

incorrectly concluded that Sibbes's use of covenant terminology made his theology "rather legalistic."[121]

Others, however, have seen the presence of both the unilateral and in a subordinated way, the bilateral in Sibbes's covenant language.[122] The strain in the unilateral/bilateral relations of God and man present in the Bible were not so much lessened through the covenantal framework, as described. "[t]he covenant of grace is monopleuric or unilateral in its origin, but dipleuric or bilateral in its fulfillment."[123] Sibbes's retention of both these aspects of the covenant was achieved by "combining furious opposites, by keeping them both, and keeping them both furious."[124] In his last sermon to his hearers at Gray's Inn, preached the week before his death, he urged them therefore "above all, labour to know and understand the covenant of grace; the tenor of which requireth no set measures of grace; but 'if we believe, we shall not perish, but have everlasting life,' under so gracious and merciful a covenant are we."[125]

Conversion

PERRY MILLER RIGHTLY observed that the doctrine of conversion "holds in miniature almost every characteristic of Puritan thinking."[126] Conversion was that for which Sibbes exhorted church members to

---

[121]Frank E. Farrell, "Richard Sibbes: A Study in Early Seventeenth Century English Puritanism," (Ph.D. dissertation, University of Edinburgh, 1955) 168, 207.

[122]Affleck, 129-135 rightly criticized Perry Miller on this point. Nevertheless, Affleck then goes on to posit a mistaken difference between covenant theologians and federal theologians, (135-136). Cf. Roberts, 133.

[123]Hoekema, 140; cf. Richard A. Muller, "Covenant and Conscience in English Reformed Theology: Three Variations on a 17th Century Theme," Westminster Theological Journal, vol. XLII (1980): 308-334.

[124]G. K. Chesterton, Orthodoxy in Collected Works (San Francisco, 1986) 1:299. See Stoever, 117; Von Rohr, 1-2, 33.

[125]"Two Sermons Upon the first words of Christs last Sermon, John 14.1. Being also the last Sermons of Richard Sibbs," in Works, 7:352; cf. "The Bride's Longing," in Works, 6:554; . "The Saint's Hiding-Place in the Evil Day," in Works, 1:415.

[126]Miller, Mind, 287. Cf. Alan Simpson, Puritanism in Old and New England (Chicago, 1955) 2-6.

prepare themselves, yet it was also presented as fundamentally God's action. How could the monergism implied in the theology presented above be blended with human action in conversion? Max Weber has declared all the attempts, from Augustine onwards, of relating the doctrines of divine predestination and human responsibility inconsistent failures.[127] This criticism, intuitively obvious in itself, may well seem to be a fair criticism of Sibbes's statements about the Spirit's working in the soul in conversion. Yet even though sometimes it may sound as if Sibbes were suggesting that conversion is essentially persuasion, this position—that he took to be advocated by both Jesuits and Arminians—was clearly not his own.[128] According to Sibbes, the Spirit did not simply persuade; rather He enlightened the elect by opening the eyes of the soul to God because "A carnal eye will never see spiritual things."[129] Miller took Preston's language of reason and persuasion to mean that "conversion is not prostration on the road to Damascus, but reason elevated."[130] Yet the sight of these reasons was not understood as a mere semi-Pelagian option presented to the soul, whether expressed as education, or persuasion.[131] Instead Sibbes presented conversion as a more Augustinian notion—the Spirit's action in enlightenment is a transforming event in the soul.[132] No one will be converted apart from the Spirit's work in his soul, for the ability of the soul to move to God is itself a radical change in the fallen soul. "It is no matter how dull the scholar be, when Christ taketh upon him to be the teacher."[133] Grace was irresistible.[134] "As the minister speaks to the ear,

---

[127]Weber, 221.

[128]Irvonwy Morgan, *Puritan Spirituality* (London, 1973) 32–36; cf. Von Rohr, 142.

[129]"The Bruised Reed and Smoking Flax," in *Works*, 1:59; cf. "The Soul's Conflict with Itself," in *Works*, 1:172, 214, 269.

[130]Miller, *Mind*, 200.

[131]Cf. John Calvin, *The Institutes of the Christian Religion*, trans. F. L. Battles (London, 1960) II.iv.1; III.ii.7–8; Perkins, *Galatians*, 44; *Workes*, 1:79.

[132]See chapters 31 and 32 of Augustine, "On Grace and Free Will," *Anti-Pelagian Writings*, trans. Peter Holmes (Grand Rapids, Michigan, 1971) beginning on 456; *Enchiridion*, trans. Ernest Evans (London, 1953) 28–30; Calvin, *Institutes*, II.iv.8; Perkins, *Galatians*, 44; *Workes*, 1:79.

[133]"The Bruised Reed and Smoking Flax," in *Works*, 1:52; cf. 83, 93–94; "Fountain Opened," in *Works*, 5:468. On conversion in Sibbes, Thomas Hooker and Thomas Shepherd as alteration of judgment, see Stoever, 61–63.

Christ speaks, opens, and unlocks the heart at the same time; and gives it power to open, not from itself, but from Christ.... The manner of working of the reasonable creature, is to work freely by a sweet inclination, not by violence. Therefore when he works the work of conversion, he doth it in a sweet manner, though it be mighty for the efficaciousness of it."[135] In conversion, the Spirit opens the heart,[136] making it to be fruitful,[137] by presenting true knowledge of God to the soul— "the sight of their misery and the sight of God's love in Christ"[138] —thereby enabling the soul to see that to which it was previously blind. Only at conversion is the soul liberated, only then does it become truly free. "Those that take the most liberty to sin are the most perfect slaves," said Sibbes,[139] true freedom only comes in freedom toward the good.[140]

Even more radical images for conversion are common in Sibbes's sermons.[141] Conversion "is an alteration, a change, a new man, a new creature, new birth, &c. We see the necessity of a change."[142] Nevertheless, conversion necessarily incorporated actions of both God and man.[143] Though Kendall perhaps is careless when he states that

---

[134]"The Bruised Reed and Smoking Flax," in *Works*, 1:95; cf. *A Learned Commentary or Exposition Upon The fourth Chapter of the Second Epistle of Saint Paul to the Corinthians*, in *Works*, 4:385.

[135]"Bowels Opened," in *Works*, 2:63; cf. "Fountain Opened," in *Works*, 5:468; "The Bruised Reed and Smoking Flax," in *Works*, 1:81; "The Excellency of the Gospel above the Law," in *Works*, 4:218, 233-4; "The Pattern of Purity," in *Works*, 7:511.

[136]"Bowels Opened," in *Works*, 2:8; cf. "Lydia's Conversion," in *Works*, 6:521-525.

[137]"Bowels Opened," in *Works*, 2:9.

[138]"Bowels Opened," in *Works*, 2:160. Cf. Preston, *Breast-Plate*, pt. i, 47-49, 162.

[139]"The Bruised Reed and Smoking Flax," in *Works*, 1:97; "The Excellency of the Gospel above the Law," in *Works*, 4:226-227.

[140]See Augustine, *De libero arbitrio*, 2:13; Anselm, "Proslogion," in *A Scholastic Miscellany: Anselm to Ockham*, ed. and trans. E. R. Fairweather (London, 1956) 77; Calvin, *Institutes*, II.iii.5; Perkins, *Galatians*, 46, 318.

[141]"The Excellency of the Gospel above the Law," in *Works*, 4:259.

[142]"The Excellency of the Gospel above the Law," in *Works*, 4:259; cf. 221, 272; "Bowels Opened," in *Works*, 2:24-25.

[143]"The Bruised Reed and Smoking Flax," in *Works*, 1:47; cf. "Bowels Opened," in *Works*, 2:24, 179; "The Rich Poverty; or, The Poor Man's Riches," in *Works*, 6:242; Stoever, 8.

Sibbes "encounters men as if the act of faith is in themselves," men are clearly represented as agents in their own, and other's, conversions.[144] Belief was necessary;[145] therefore, Sibbes exhorted his hearers to "get into Christ"[146] and the covenant with him,[147] to "run after him" and to "open unto him,"[148] to "trust God . . . now."[149] Yet even this consent, in that we must "labour to bring our hearts," is nevertheless "wrought:"[150] although "his subjects are voluntaries," they "seek for heaven in hell that seek for spiritual love in an unchanged heart."[151] At conversion, "we had nothing good in us," when the Spirit came to the soul "it met with nothing but enmity, rebellion, and indisposedness,"[152] "we resisted;"[153] our hearts were "unyielding and untractable."[154] Conversion was an even greater work of God's than creation, Sibbes taught, because at creation, "he had to do with simply nothing. But when God comes to make the heart believe, he finds opposition and rebellion. He finds man against himself."[155] Christ must, therefore,

---

[144]"Bowels Opened," in *Works*, 2:36, 69, 167; cf. "Judgment's Reason," in *Works*, 4:85; "The Returning Backslider," in *Works*, 2:255; *A Learned Commentary or Exposition Upon The fourth Chapter of the Second Epistle of Saint Paul to the Corinthians*, in *Works*, 4:449; "Fountain Opened," in *Works*, 5:513; "The Power of Christ's Resurrection," in *Works*, 5:199; "Of the Providence of God," in *Works*, 5:37; Perkins, *Galatians*, 46.

[145]"The Power of Christ's Resurrection," in *Works*, 5:198.

[146]"Bowels Opened," in *Works*, 2:187.

[147]"The Knot of Prayer Loosed," in *Works*, 7:249.

[148]"Bowels Opened," in *Works*, 2:10.

[149]"The Soul's Conflict with Itself," in *Works*, 1:202. Cf. Calvin, *Institutes*, III.ii.1. Perkins, too, exhorted people to "labour for a sound and saving faith," Perkins, *Hebrewes*, 26, 29; cf. 31–32.

[150]"Fountain Opened," in *Works*, 5:486. Cf. Calvin, *Institutes*, III.ii.33; Perkins, *Galatians*, 45; *Work*, ed. Breward, 156–157; Preston, *Breast-Plate*, pt. i. 165; Westminster Confession X.ii; Stoever, 106–109.

[151]"The Bruised Reed and Smoking Flax," in *Works*, vol. I,79–80; cf. "The Christian's End," in *Works*, 5:308; "The Pattern of Purity," in *Works*, 7:510.

[152]"Bowels Opened," in *Works*, 2:48.

[153]"Bowels Opened," in *Works*, 2:73; cf. "The Bruised Reed and Smoking Flax," in *Works*, 1:96.

[154]"The Bruised Reed and Smoking Flax," in *Works*, 1:, 44–45.

[155]"Fountain Opened," in *Works*, 5:519; cf. "The Power of Christ's Resurrection," in *Works*, 5: 198–199; "The Soul's Conflict with Itself," in *Works*, 1:152; "The Excellency of the Gospel above the Law," in *Works*, 4:225, 245; Preston, *Breast-Plate*, pt. i. 165–166.

wound,[156] and must give new life.[157] "It must be all new, as a bell; if there be but a crack in it, it must be new moulded and cast again. It is good for nothing else. So the soul of man, if there be but a flaw, but a crack, all is naught. It must be cast and moulded again anew."[158] Our rebellious spirits must be "overpowered with grace."[159] Again echoing Augustine, Sibbes said, "God knoweth we have nothing of ourselves, therefore in the covenant of grace he requireth no more than he giveth, and giveth what he requireth, and accepteth what he giveth."[160] As he said elsewhere:

> We believe, but it is Christ by his Spirit that opens our hearts to believe.... The understanding is ours, the affections are ours, the will is ours; but the sanctifying of all this, and the carriage of all these supernaturally above themselves, to do them spiritually, that it is not ours, but it is Christ's. So we see what is ours, and what is not ours. We are able to do; but the strength, and the grace, and ability is from Christ. A wind instrument sounds, but the man makes it sound by his breath. We are like wind instruments. Indeed, we sound, but no further than we are blown upon; and we yield music, but no further than we are touched by the Spirit of God.[161]

Preparation

Given that conversion, though a human turning, was enabled and made certain by God, what was the role of man and means in this

---

[156]"The Bruised Reed and Smoking Flax," in Works, 1:46.

[157]"The Bruised Reed and Smoking Flax," in Works, 1:95. Cf. "Fountain Opened," in Works, 5:495; Calvin, Institutes, II.v.14.

[158]"The Excellency of the Gospel above the Law," in Works, 4:256.

[159]"The Ungodly's Misery," in Works, 1:392; cf. "Bowels Opened," in Works, 2: 10, 106, 182, 187; "The Excellency of the Gospel above the Law," in Works, 4:244; "The Soul's Conflict with Itself," in Works, 1:265.

[160]"The Bruised Reed and Smoking Flax," in Works, 1:58.

[161]"Art of Contentment," in Works, 5:190; cf. "To the Christian Reader," John Smith, An Exposition of the Creed (London, 1632); rpt. in Works, 1:civ; [Sibbes and John Davenport], "To the Christian Reader," to John Preston, The Breast-Plate of Faith and Love (1634); rpt. Works, 1:xcvii.

turning? This is precisely the issue that has come to be called "preparationism." Ambiguity is particularly dangerous in this question because one can lose sight of the point of the preparation under discussion. For what is one being prepared? Sibbes spoke of preparation for good works,[162] for self-denial,[163] for trials,[164] for the second coming,[165] for reception of the sacrament,[166] for hearing the word,[167] for prayer,[168] for coming to church,[169] as well as preparation for conversion.[170] Carelessness at this point has led some to take any statement of or call for human action—that will surely be found on every page of Sibbes's works—as proof of "preparationism." Some also have confused the issue by taking descriptive passages in sermons as prescriptive passages. They have understood sections in which the preacher described what were various stages in the Christian's journey as instructions to his hearers about what they should do next.[171] Something like this seems to be going on in Norman Pettit's assertion that, "Of all the preparationists Sibbes was by far the most extreme in terms of the abilities he assigned to natural man."[172] Pettit seems to

---

[162]"The Bruised Reed and Smoking Flax," in *Works*, 1:75.

[163]"An Exposition of the Third Chapter of the Epistle of St. Paul to the Philippians," in *Works*, 5:82; "The Rich Pearl," in *Works*, 7:258.

[164]"Of the Providence of God," in *Works*, 5:53; "The Soul's Conflict with Itself," in *Works*, 1:163, 249.

[165]"The Bride's Longing," in *Works*, 6: 551–552.

[166]*A Learned Commentary or Exposition Upon The first Chapter of the Second Epistle of S. Paul to the Corinthians*, in *Works*, 3: 134, 528; "Angels' Acclamations," in *Works*, 6: 336–7; "Bowels Opened," in *Works*, 2:193; "Judgment's Reason," in *Works*, 4: 88–89; RR.IV.62. This theme is naturally made prominent in Sibbes's sermons due to the fact that so many of his sermons were preached before communion (e.g., "Right Receiving, Judgement's Reason").

[167]"Of the Providence of God," in *Works*, 5:36, 53.

[168]"Bowels Opened," in *Works*, 2:17–18; "The Knot of Prayer Loosed," in *Works*, 7:246.

[169]"Fountain Opened," in *Works*, 5:465.

[170]"Bowels Opened," in *Works*, 2:166; "The Excellency of the Gospel above the Law," in *Works*, 4:296. Perhaps Sibbes's most clear exposition of the "works of preparation" for conversion, is found in Sibbes's sermon "Lydia's Conversion," in *Works*, vol. 6:522–523.

[171]Cf. Lynn Baird Tipson, Jr., "The Development of a Puritan Understanding of Conversion" (Ph.D. Dissertation, Yale University, 1972) 322; "Lydia's Conversion," in *Works*, 6:522.

[172]Pettit, 73; cf. 17, 66–73.

have assumed that an adherence to a theology of predestination would also necessitate a belief in both an immediate conversion, and in a conversion that was, by its violence, inconsistent with natural human faculties.[173] Since he found in Sibbes appeals to the use of means (that necessitated both time and human participation), and to congregations in which Sibbes assumed there were some who were "reprobates," Pettit saw in Sibbes a perfect example of "preparationism."

Yet this reading of Sibbes is faulty for two reasons. First, Sibbes's theology of reprobation discussed above clearly accounted for those in his congregations who would never respond savingly to the gospel. They were termed by Sibbes the "eternal reprobates." Though he thought he would never know who they were, he believed that, whoever they were, his preaching only added to their condemnation. However, he also referred more generally to those living wicked lives at the time, who were not at present in Christ, as reprobates. Again, indiscernable from the others to human eyes, he also assumed their presence in his congregations and it was to them that his exhortations to conversion were addressed. Pettit was also confused by his assumption that obligation always implies ability, when in the Augustinian tradition it by no means need be understood to do so.[174] Any of the "abilities he [Sibbes] assigned to natural man" highlighted by Pettit, Sibbes would explain as only having been possible by the power of the Spirit. While Pettit seems to have some notion of this (he mentions that Sibbes "wants not...to exalt natural man"), he goes on to write as if human preparation were done apart from grace.[175] Sidney Rooy has better expressed what Pettit observed in Sibbes when he said, "Perhaps no theme recurs more frequently in Sibbes's sermons than this: God uses means, he saves through means, he gives grace through means. Men are damned who despise the means."[176]

---

[173]Pettit, 17.

[174]E.g., "The Ungodly's Misery," in *Works*, 1:391. Sibbes encountered this objection in Bellarmine ("Bowels Opened," in *Works*, 2:63).

[175]Affleck has also criticized Pettit in this way, suggesting (consistently with a Barthian Christo-monism) however, that the problem of Pettit's understanding is in his lack of appreciation for Sibbes's Christology (Affleck, 292-293).

[176]Sidney H. Rooy, *The Theology of Missions in the Puritan Tradition: A Study of Representative Puritans: Richard Sibbes, Richard Baxter, John Eliot, Cotton*

David Zaret has suggested that Calvin thought "the conversion experience of regeneration" occurred at one point in time, while "Puritan clerics" taught that it "was a life-long experience of spiritual growing."[177] In the sense that conversion was used as a synonym for regeneration, both Calvin and the clerics to which Zaret referred would have understood it to be the instantaneous gift of God. Yet Sibbes specifically denied that this "first conversion" though instantaneous, was violent (as Pettit seemed to assume instantaneous conversions must have been).[178] Sibbes believed not only that regeneration was punctiliar, but also that conversion could appear instantly.[179] Contrary to the strict preparationist image of Sibbes, he did believe in the possibility of sudden conversions. However, given the pastoral situation of Sibbes—preaching almost entirely to congregations full of members of the covenant, (i.e., those who had been baptized)—it is hardly surprising that he should have said that "God usually prepares those that he means to convert, as we plough before we sow."[180] Sibbes spent the bulk of his time exhorting regular hearers to use the means of grace frequently offered in order to make certain to themselves of their conversion and to "stablish" their faith.[181] Yet he was careful to say that "all preparations are from God. We cannot prepare ourselves, or deserve future things by our preparations; for the preparations themselves are of God."[182] Lest anyone think that any action, however

---

Mather, and Jonathan Edwards (Grand Rapids, Michigan, 1965) 36. See "The Returning Backslider," in *Works*, 2:355; "Bowels Opened," in *Works*, 2:166.

[177] Zaret, 160.

[178] "Bowels Opened," in *Works*, 2:63. Cf. Preston, *Breast-Plate*, pt. i, 160.

[179] "The Rich Poverty; or, The Poor Man's Riches," in *Works*, 6:243; "Witness of Salvation," in *Works*, 7:375; John Ball, *Treatise of the Covenant* (London, 1645) 337-338. On the question of instantaneous conversion, see Stoever, 219, n.16. In one sermon, Sibbes does say that "our nature is not altered on the sudden," but this is clearly a reference to the incomplete nature of sanctification in the believer on earth ("The Returning Backslider," in *Works*, 2:404).

[180] "Lydia's Conversion," in *Works*, 6:522. Calvin, too, it should be noted, was such a "preparationist." See, for example, Calvin, *Deuteronomie*, 423, where he asserts that God "prepareth our hearts to come unto him and to receive his doctrine," clearly referring to conversion.

[181] "The Pattern of Purity," in *Works*, 7: 510-511; "The Fruitful Labour for Eternal Food," in *Works*, 6:380.

[182] "Lydia's Conversion," in *Works*, 6:522; cf. "Josiah's Reformation," in *Works*, 6:33; "The Bruised Reed and Smoking Flax," in *Works*, 1: 51, 72, 74; "The

much required or useful, could be a source of pride, Sibbes preached that "it is a sottish conceit to think that we can fit ourselves for grace, as if a child in the womb could forward its natural birth. If God hath made us men, let us not make ourselves gods."[183]

Sibbes taught that the primary means Christ used to prepare his elect's hearts for salvation was "by the ministry of the gospel."[184] "Hearing begets seeing in religion. Death came in by the ear at the first. Adam hearing the serpent, that he should not have heard, death came in by the ear. So life comes in by the ear."[185] Preaching was the "chariot that carries Christ up and down the world. Christ doth not profit but as he is preached."[186] Thus "it is a gift of all gifts, the ordinance of preaching. God esteems it so, Christ esteems it so, and so should we esteem it."[187] Indeed, all the means of grace for conversion had to do with speech, which could confer the word of God, or drive

Returning Backslider," in *Works*, 2:404; "The Excellency of the Gospel above the Law," in *Works*, 4:219; *A Learned Commentary or Exposition Upon The fourth Chapter of the Second Epistle of Saint Paul to the Corinthians*, in *Works*, 4: 449–450; "An Exposition of the Third Chapter of the Epistle of St. Paul to the Philippians," in *Works*, 5:83; . "The Saint's Hiding-Place in the Evil Day," in *Works*, 1: 409–410; "Lydia's Conversion," in *Works*, 6:523; "A Breathing after God," in *Works*, 2:217. So Perkins, *Galatians*, 10, 43; *Hebrewes*, 31; *Work*, ed. Breward, 156–157. See Stoever, *passim*; Tipson's conclusion (315–341) which provides a careful critique of Pettit, among others.

[183]"Divine Meditations and Holy Contemplations," in *Works*, 7:189.

[184]"Description of Christ," in *Works*, 1: 23–24; "Bowels Opened," in *Works*, 2:63; "A Breathing after God," in *Works*, 2:216; "The Dead Man," in *Works*, 7:404.

[185]"The Excellency of the Gospel above the Law," in *Works*, 4: 251-2; cf. *A Learned Commentary or Exposition Upon The fourth Chapter of the Second Epistle of Saint Paul to the Corinthians*, in *Works*, 4: 367, 377, 386; "Angels' Acclamations," in *Works*, 6:353; "The Matchless Love and Inbeing," in *Works*, 6:409; "The Ruin of Mystical Jericho," in *Works*, 7:476; "The Fruitful Labour for Eternal Food," in *Works*, 6:380; "Lydia's Conversion," in *Works*, 6:523; "The Dead Man," in *Works*, 7: 404–405; "Faith Triumphant," in *Works*, 7:434; "Divine Meditations and Holy Contemplations," in *Works*, 7:198; Calvin, *Institutes*, III.ii.6, 31; Perkins, *Hebrewes*, 28; "Foundation," in *Work*, ed. Breward, 148, 161 (and *Workes*, 1:79); John Coolidge, *The Pauline Renaissance in England* (Oxford, 1970) 142. Cf. Calvin, *Institutes*, III.ii.6, 31. Cf. Perkins, *Hebrewes*, 28; *Work*, ed. Breward, 161, 228.

[186]"Fountain Opened," in *Works*, 5:508; cf. "The Ungodly's Misery," in *Works*, 1:391; Perkins *Workes*, 1:71.

[187]"Fountain Opened," in *Works*, 5:509.

home that which had been learned—"good company,"[188] conversations,[189] reading,[190] meditating,[191] prayer.[192] This is not to suggest that
the word invariably wrought conversions. It too depended on the Spirit.
"For if it were not the Spirit that persuaded the soul, when the minister
speaks, alas! all ministerial persuasions are to no purpose."[193] According
to Sibbes, ignoring such a means would bring no small judgment.[194]
Therefore, "there is somewhat to do to bring our hearts to these
things."[195] One could bring oneself to hear the word preached, even if
not to understand and believe it.[196] The sacraments are notably absent
from the above list of means of grace for conversion. As he had with
preaching, Sibbes also warned against idolizing the sacraments and
further against assuming that "alway God gives grace with the
sacraments."[197] The role of the sacraments was not as preparations for
conversion,[198] to create faith, but rather to strengthen, confirm, or assure
faith already present. Apart from a humble and believing heart, Sibbes

[188]"Bowels Opened," in *Works*, 2:166; "The Matchless Love and Inbeing," in
Works, 6:409.
[189]"The Returning Backslider," in *Works*, 2: 355, 404; cf. "An Exposition of
the Third Chapter of the Epistle of St. Paul to the Philippians," in *Works*, 5:82.
[190]"The Christian Work," in *Works*, 5:7.
[191]"The Christian Work," in *Works*, 5:7; "Lydia's Conversion," in *Works*,
6:530; "David's Conclusion; or, the Saint's Resolution," in *Works*, 7:90.
[192]"David's Conclusion; or, the Saint's Resolution," in *Works*, 7:90.
[193]"The Excellency of the Gospel above the Law," in *Works*, 4:219.
[194]"King David's Epitaph," in *Works*, 6:495. Cf. Preston, *Breast-Plate*, pt. i.
163.
[195]"Fountain Opened," in *Works*, 5:508.
[196]"Judgment's Reason," in *Works*, 4: 99–100.
[197]*A Learned Commentary or Exposition Upon The first Chapter of the Second
Epistle of S. Paul to the Corinthians*, in *Works*, 3:134.
[198]Cf. "The Returning Backslider," in *Works*, 2:379. Sibbes called the
sacraments "means of salvation" in a list of other things in the church, including
preaching, but that was in considering the entire Christian life (e.g., "A Breathing
after God," in *Works*, 2:232). On the other hand, it would have been surprising if
he had called the sacrament a "means of *conversion*." Stoever has noted this
distinction between "salvation" and "conversion," though he has suggested that
salvation was equivalent to glorification (196). Perkins suggested that the use of
the sacrament by the elect before conversion was "utterly unlawful," (Perkins,
Workes, 1:73). Geoffrey Nuttall has been (uncharacteristically) confused on this
matter of the sacraments as means of salvation in Sibbes (90–91).

said that the sacraments were "seals to a blank."[199] Indeed, "The sacrament is bane and poison to us, if we come without repentance."[200]

Conviction, though the beginning of true conversion, was also called a preparation for the changing of the heart.[201] Evoking what must have been a common image for conviction in the minds of his hearers at Gray's Inn, Sibbes said, "A marvellous hard thing it is to bring a dull and a shifting heart to cry with feeling for mercy. Our hearts, like malefactors, until they be beaten from all shifts never cry for the mercy of the Judge."[202] Such despair was "the beginning of comfort; and trouble the beginning of peace. A storm is the way to a calm, and hell the way to heaven."[203] Though an apparently strange work for a saving God,[204] conviction was "a peal of great ordnance, shot off to prepare the way for him, to shew the King his coming. . . . So the Lord rends, tears, and shakes our consciences ofttimes to prepare the way for him, and then he comes unto us in that still and soft voice of consolation."[205] Too

---

[199]A Learned Commentary or Exposition Upon The first Chapter of the Second Epistle of S. Paul to the Corinthians, in Works, 3:134; cf. 528.

[200]"Angels' Acclamations," in Works, 6:329.

[201]"Josiah's Reformation," in Works, 6:33; "An Exposition of the Third Chapter of the Epistle of St. Paul to the Philippians," in Works, 5:82; "Angels' Acclamations," in Works, 6:333; "Fountain Opened," in Works, 5:506; "Lydia's Conversion," in Works, 6:522; "The Rich Poverty; or, The Poor Man's Riches," in Works, 6: 242-243; "Witness of Salvation," in Works, 7:370; "The Excellency of the Gospel above the Law," in Works, 4:219; A Learned Commentary or Exposition Upon The fourth Chapter of the Second Epistle of Saint Paul to the Corinthians, in Works, 4: 340, 368. Note, however, that this preparation was done by God. Cf. Preston, Breast-Plate, pt. i. 160-161.

[202]"The Bruised Reed and Smoking Flax," in Works, 1:44. cf. 47; "The Rich Poverty; or, The Poor Man's Riches," in Works, 6: 243-244; "The Soul's Conflict with Itself," in Works, 1:194. Cf. Perkins, "Foundation," in Work, ed. Breward, 156.

[203]"The Soul's Conflict with Itself," in Works, 1:158; Thomas Hooker, The Soules Preparation (London, 1638) 55. If the distinction between description and prescription is remembered, much (though not all) of the difference between Perkins and Hooker which Pettit and Kendall have suggested may be seen to vanish. Cf. Robert Horn, "Thomas Hooker--The Soul's Preparation for Christ," The Puritan Experiment in the New World (London, 1976) 19-37; Stoever, 192-199.

[204]"The Soul's Conflict with Itself," in Works, 1:262.

[205]"Witness of Salvation," in Works, 7:374.

sudden[206] or too lengthy conviction if not bringing forth repentance, was an ominous sign.[207] Yet Sibbes exhorted, since "there is more mercy in Christ than sin in us, there can be no danger in thorough dealing. It is better to go bruised to heaven than sound to hell. Therefore let us not take off ourselves too soon, nor pull off the plaster before the cure be wrought, but keep ourselves under this work till sin be the sourest, and Christ the sweetest, of all things."[208]

Sibbes assured his hearers that repentance would surely follow the Spirit's conviction.[209] "Let us labour to bring our hearts to wait in the use of the means, for God's good Spirit to enable me to see my state by nature, and to get out of it."[210] The exhortation to believe and repent, when answered by the heart, was the "spiritual echo and answer of the soul" that "comes from the Spirit of God in calling" and was initial conversion.[211] In that men could cooperate with God in this, "bruising," like hearing the word, was both a state into which God brought them and a duty to be performed. "The paschal lamb was to be eaten with sour herbs; so Christ our passover must be eaten with repentance."[212] Once sin was bitter to the sinner, the Spirit would complete his preparatory work by the sinner's forsaking sin.

Conclusion

THE SAME MEANS that Richard Sibbes urged those in the covenant to use in order to be saved, he encouraged any Christian to use in order to become certain of their election, or simply to grow in grace. "There are several ages in Christians....Man, the perfectest creature, comes to

---

[206]"A Glimpse of Glory," in *Works*, 7:497.

[207]Giles Firmin recalled being told that "Doctor Sibbs . . . when he heard of persons under such great legal terrors, he began to fear them, that they would not prove sound," (Firmin, *The Real Christian*, [London, 1670], 80).

[208]"The Bruised Reed and Smoking Flax," in *Works*, 1:47-48; cf. 44, 46. On 47, Sibbes gave eight signs of one "truly bruised." Cf. "The Rich Poverty; or, The Poor Man's Riches," in *Works*, 6:244.

[209]"The Excellency of the Gospel above the Law," in *Works*, 4:219.

[210]"Angels' Acclamations," in *Works*, 6:354.

[211]"The Excellency of the Gospel above the Law," in *Works*, 4:219.

[212]"Bowels Opened," in *Works*, 2:193; cf. "The Saint's Comforts," in *Works*, 6:171-172; "Lydia's Conversion," in *Works*, 6:522.

perfection by little and little," Sibbes preached.[213] Therefore, most of his exhortations could have been and should have been appropriate to different groups of his hearers. It was to believers that he said, "We carry about us a double principle, nature and grace."[214] Aware that some believers constantly needed reassurance of God's graciousness, Sibbes needed to, and did, exhort them to continue to use the means of grace "in a continual dependence upon God." The Christian, no less than the unregenerate, was to say, "I will use these means, God may bless them; if not, I will trust him; he is not tied to the use of means, though I be."[215] And yet the use of means in preparation by the believer in no way meant that the Spirit did not prepare the heart. Even as the Spirit initiated the covenant from before the creation of the world, so the initiative rested with God in both conversion and preparation.

It should also be noted that the kind of exhortatory message for which Sibbes became known was particularly suited for his situation— preaching election and conversion within the framework of a covenant, practically and theologically. Practically, he was preaching to congregations who heard the word so regularly that he could give attention almost exclusively to pastoral issues. With apologetics largely unneeded, or relegated to interests of a fraction of his hearers, Sibbes's sermons quite naturally were addressed to those who had been brought into the covenant as infants and kept in the covenant community, whether by convention or conviction. Either way, they would have been regularly present at the ministry of the word and administration of the sacraments and so were quite naturally inclined to have more gradual, less apparently urgent religious lives. Theologically, Sibbes sermons fit well with the covenant framework. The line between the converted and the unconverted, clearer in churches that taught the coordination of baptism and regeneration (whether Roman or baptistic), was blurred. There was, as a result, great scope in Sibbes's congregations for those who were certain of their obligation, but agnostic of their fate. Sibbes preached that his hearers, by their baptism as infants and inclusion in the covenant community, had become particularly obliged to believe and live as Christians. But such was beyond their

---

[213]"The Bruised Reed and Smoking Flax," in *Works*, 1:49.
[214]*Ibid.*, 50.
[215]"The Saint's Hiding-Place in the Evil Day," in *Works*, 1:421.

powers. Naturally, this brought to the fore the gracious element in Christian theology, as Sibbes implored them with the electing love of God.

Sibbes's understanding of the nature of the covenant community helps to explain his combination of Reformed theology and exhortation to means in conversion. Because of Sibbes's understanding of the covenant community in which the members are pledged to God and are regularly and willingly present at the means of grace, Sibbes could speak with certainty of the Holy Spirit's having "often knocked at their hearts, as willing to have kindled some holy desires in them."[216] Neither a higher estimation of human nature nor a belief in a prevenient grace offered to all enabled Sibbes to make such statements. Instead, the fact that he preached in a time and place, and with an understanding of Christianity in which the concept of the covenant was widely accepted, gave him such license. Parents had taken on responsibilities for their children in baptism and religious training. Ministers did the same as they offered the word to hearers week after week. As a result, to those within the covenanted community who were already obligated and able to avail themselves of the means of grace, preparation could most appropriately be urged, yet not inconsistently with a theology that was thoroughly Reformed. Sibbes was not, then, an unwitting representative of a nascent moralism. He was, rather, one of the last of the great Reformed preachers of England both to believe in theory and to know in practice an officially undivided covenant community.

---

[216]"The Bruised Reed and Smoking Flax," in *Works*, 1:74.

VI

An "Affectionate" Theologian

ONE REASON WHY the Reformed foundations and covenantal framework of Richard Sibbes's theology may have been so easily mistaken is his renowned passionate rhetoric.[1] A number of writers describe this affective element in Sibbes as "mysticism."[2] Martin Thornton has

---

[1]See G. F. Nuttall, *The Holy Spirit in Puritan Faith and Experience* (Oxford, 1946) 14; William Haller, *The Rise of Puritanism* (New York, 1938) 163; Norman Pettit, *The Heart Prepared: Grace and Conversion in Puritan Spiritual Life* (New Haven, Connecticut, 1966) 66. Cf. U. Milo Kaufmann's judgment that "Richard Sibbes is one of the most attractive spirits among Puritan Divines of the seventeenth century," (*The Pilgrim's Progress and Traditions in Puritan Meditation* [New Haven, Connecticut, 1966]) 141; John R. Knott, Jr., *The Sword of the Spirit: Puritan Responses to the Bible* (Chicago, 1980) 61.

[2]So J. F. Maclear, "'The Heart of New England Rent': The Mystical Element in Early Puritan History," Mississippi Valley Historical Review, vol. XLII (1956): 625-626, 637. Maclear was clearly influenced by Nuttall, presenting roughly the same progression from more "conservative" to more radical, and was apparently pointed to the importance of Sibbes in this connection by Nuttall (see Nuttall, 7, 14-15; Maclear, 621, 625-627). Based apparently on Maclear, Sargent Bush has suggested that the "early roots for the mystical elements of American thought" can be readily traced to "the direct influences back through Richard Sibbes in England," (*The Writings of Thomas Hooker: Spiritual Adventure in Two Worlds* [Madison, Wisconsin, 1980], 309). Cf. Gordon Rupp, "A Devotion of Rapture," in *Reformation, Conformity and Dissent*, ed. R. B. Knox (London, 1977) 115-131. Though he never carefully defined mysticism, F. Ernest Stoeffler has presented Sibbes as representing a "pronounced mystical trend," (Stoeffler, The Rise of Evangelical Pietism [Leiden, 1965], 81). Stoeffler suggested that in Sibbes's sermons "the mystical element began to intrude noticeably upon the interstices of his Puritan doctrines. In Sibbes, the older Puritan piety was definitely admixed with mysticism," (Stoeffler, 82-83). Though more restrained in his use of the word "mystic," Kaufmann has seen in Sibbes one of the most important representatives of the Puritan contemplative tradition that was later embodied in Bunyan's *Pilgrim's Progress* (140-146). Cf. Simon K. H. Chan, "The

referred to "mysticism" as "usually undefined and often misunderstood," sometimes to the point "when practically any Christian who said his prayers affectively was a 'mystic.'"[3] This lack of definition is

Puritan Meditative Tradition, 1599–1691: A Study of Ascetical Piety," (Ph. D. diss., University of Cambridge, 1986); Charles Cohen, *God's Caress: The Psychology of Puritan Religious* Experience (Oxford, 1986) 209. Frank E. Farrell used the word "mystical" interchangeably with the word "spiritual" (Sibbes's preferred word for distinguishing experiential knowledge from notional knowledge) and explained the necessity of experience in Christian knowledge for Sibbes (Frank E. Farrell, "Richard Sibbes: A Study in Early Seventeenth Century English Puritanism," [Ph.D. diss., University of Edinburgh, 1955], 120–136). Yet he also at points described Sibbes as a "mystic," as if Sibbes's emphasis on Christian experience resulted in the devaluation of the historical aspects of the Christian faith (Farrell, 216). Bert Affleck's study of Sibbes specifically denied the "mystical" label to him, but did this primarily by affirming Sibbes's orthodox trinitarianism (by which he intended mainly to affirm Sibbes's orthodox Christology) (Bert D. Affleck, Jr., "The Theology of Richard Sibbes, 1577–1635," [Ph. D. diss., Drew University, 1969], 22, 260). He then went on to present Sibbes as almost a seventeenth–century Barthian, complete with a Christocentric theology, couched in terms of entirely existential concerns and an inordinate number of hyphenated adjectives and nouns, and sequential sentences with subject and object reversed. Yet throughout his study, Affleck centered on portraying Sibbes as an "experiential" theologian, contrasting this with the image of a "dogmatic" theologian, in a way that may at times slight, even if not denying, Sibbes's concern with the role of the understanding, and come close to what other writers have intended when calling Sibbes a mystic (e.g., Affleck, 27). One of Stoeffler's students, Harold Shelly, presented Sibbes as a "Puritan, pietist and mystic" and repeatedly used "mystic" and "mystical" as descriptions of Sibbes throughout his study (Harold Patton Shelly, "Richard Sibbes: Early Stuart Preacher of Piety," [Ph. D. diss., Temple University, 1972], 5). Indeed, the purpose of Shelly's study, he wrote, was "to emphasize the spirit of his [Sibbes's] message, the mystical dimension of his orthodox Puritan sermons," (6–7). Shelly suggested that Sibbes's use of reason kept his mysticism in check—even at one point affirming that all of Sibbes's mystical knowledge came through the Word written (71)—but that he clearly desired to "go beyond reason," (62–65, 80–82). By the end of Shelly's study, one may be certain that Sibbes was a mystic, yet uncertain of which Christian theologian was not.

[3]Martin Thornton, *English Spirituality: An Outline of Ascetical Theology According to the English Pastoral Tradition* (London, 1963) 13. Cf. David Knowles, *The English Mystical Tradition* (London, 1960) 2; Gordon S. Wakefield, "Mysticism and its Puritan Types," *London Quarterly and Holborn Review*, vol. XCXI, 6th series, XXXV (1966): 34.

obviously and unhelpfully present in most of the studies that have so presented Sibbes. Nevertheless, something in Sibbes has certainly attracted these repeated comments, something that has often been seen as "mysticism." The task of this chapter is to explore Sibbes as a "mystic" and to suggest that a more helpful adjective for understanding him would be the contemporary word (associated with Sibbes), "affectionate."

Sibbes himself certainly used the word "mystical" sparingly. When he did use it, he intended essentially "mysterious," or something evident that contains a hidden knowledge.[4] Much more commonly, he used the word "mystery."[5] Sibbes referred to the mystery of the incarnation[6] of the church as the body of Christ,[7] of the sacraments,[8] and when referring to allegorical or unclear passages of Scripture.[9] Negatively, he referred to the "mystery of popery,"[10] (recalling the expression "mystery of iniquity" in 2 Thess 2:7). Though "mystic" is little used by Sibbes, and vague enough to make "Puritan" seem a precise term, this general characterization of Sibbes is common enough to draw attention to his theological anthropology, his understanding of man.[11]

---

[4]"Divine Meditations and Holy Contemplations," in *Works*, 7:200.

[5]"Bowels Opened," in *Works*, 2:135, 168; "The Bride's Longing," in *Works*, 6:542–543; "Art of Contentment," in *Works*, 5:178; "Divine Meditations and Holy Contemplations," in *Works*, 7:216, 220; "The Excellency of the Gospel above the Law," in *Works*, 4:289; "Fountain Opened," in *Works*, 5:466–468, 471, 474–475, 482, 511. Geoffrey F. Nuttall has noted the common use of "mystical" as something more akin to "mysterious" in seventeenth-century religious writers (Nuttall, "Puritan and Quaker Mysticism," *Theology*, vol. LXXVIII [Oct. 1975]: 520).

[6]"Fountain Opened," in *Works*, 5:482.

[7]"Bowels Opened," in *Works*, 2:81; "The Bride's Longing," in *Works*, 6:547; "Art of Contentment," in *Works*, 5:192; "Christ's Sufferings for Man's Sin," in *Works*, 1:369; "The Excellency of the Gospel above the Law," in *Works*, 4:242, 255, 264–265; "Fountain Opened," in *Works*, 5:464.

[8]"The Glorious Feast of the Gospel," in *Works*, 2:460–461.

[9]"Bowels Opened," in *Works*, 2:137; "Fountain Opened," in *Works*, 5:513.

[10]"Bowels Opened," in *Works*, 2:42–43; "Fountain Opened," in *Works*, 5:470-2, 475.

[11]On "mysticism" in Puritan religion see Joe Lee Davis, "Mystical Versus Enthusiastic Sensibility," *Journal of the History of Ideas*, vol. IV/3 (June, 1943): 301–319; J. C. Brauer, "Puritan Mysticism and the Development of Liberalism," *Church History*, vol. XIX (1950): 151–170; Trinterud, "The Origins of

"Affectionate" Theology

The Context: The Faculties

THE INSTRUMENT UPON which God's Spirit played was man, "a complicated structure of fluids and spirits, dust and eternal stuff."[12] Perry Miller shrewdly observed that though the early seventeenth-century Puritans "discussed faculties [of the soul] only in passing references, in incidental exegesis...with no deliberate concentration," yet these passing comments taken together could "constitute an extended treatise upon psychology, the outlines of a doctrine upon which all Puritans agreed, of a premise for all their thinking, that can be said to have influenced them all the more extensively because it was unformulated and taken as axiomatic."[13] Noting this tendency in Sibbes for discussions of the faculties to be incidental rather than systematic, Jonathan Harris has referred to Sibbes's "predeliction for description rather than analysis."[14] But as one trained in logic, particularly of the Ramist variety, such "description" would have been the normal way of

---

Puritanism," *Church History*, vol. XX [1951]: 37–57; Maclear; Robert Middlekauff, "Piety and Intellect in Puritanism," *The William and Mary Quarterly*, 3rd series, vol. XXII/3 (July, 1965): 457–470; Wakefield; Nuttall, "Mysticism."

[12]Cohen, 25.

[13]Perry Miller, *The New England Mind: The Seventeenth Century* (New York, 1939) 242–243; cf. Middlekauff. Calvin, too, dismissed intricate disections of the soul (*The Institutes of the Christian Religion*, trans. F. L. Battles [London, 1960], I.xv.6–7; cf. II.ii.12–26). William Gouge's disection of the soul in his comments on Hebrews 12:22–24 (Gouge, *A Learned and Very Useful Commentary on the Whole Epistle to the Hebrews* [London, 1655], pt. xii. 110) is somewhat more elaborate, proof that sermons of the godly could be considerably more systematic than Sibbes's. Cf. William Perkins, *Commentarie on...Galatians* (London, 1617) 562–563; Jeremiah Burroughes, *Excellency of Gracious Spirit* (London, 1638) 8–10; John Preston, *Saints Qualification* (London, 1633) 48–70; Robert Burton, *Anatomy of Melancholy* (London, 1621).

[14]Jonathan Harris, "Richard Sibbes: A Moderate in Early Seventeenth Century Puritanism," (M.A. Thesis, University of Melbourne, 1978) 107. Cf. S. R. Roberts, "'Radical Graces': A Study of Puritan Casuistry in the Writings of William Perkins and Richard Sibbes," (M. A. Thesis, University of Melbourne, 1972) 151.

Sibbes's learning.[15] Since Plato and Aristotle, the soul had been defined and described by being divided into its various faculties—which description Herschel Baker has called "a convenient terminology to explain every man's functioning."[16] Though Sibbes's own lifetime saw some of the biological advances (e.g. Harvey's discovery of the circulation of blood, Kepler's experiments on the eye) which helped to undermine the old Galenic physiology, and thus weaken faculty psychology, Sibbes appeared to know little or nothing of them. Thus, careful examination of Sibbes's understanding of the human faculties brings to light an aspect of his theology that was characteristic of him, and seems immediately to attract his readers—the centrality of the affections.

Sibbes's presentation of faculty psychology seemed to presume the following. The primary faculties of the soul while in the body were the senses, the phantasy, the mind, and the heart. All of these were intermixed with the bodily humors (corresponding to the body's blood, phlegm, yellow bile, and black bile). In order for the outward man to act, the inward man must unite to desire and will the action of its various members. Once that was done, action would follow. This description seemed to present man as both adequately unified to allow culpability on the part of the individual, yet complex enough to explain the various actions individuals might take and their conflicting attitudes toward and motivations for those actions. A slightly more detailed presentation of this is fundamental to understanding Sibbes's conceptions of depravity, conversion, and the further work of God in the soul.

By the word "soul" Sibbes meant the whole inner person. "Our body is but the case or tabernacle wherein our soul dwells; especially a

---

[15]E. g., *A Learned Commentary or Exposition Upon The first Chapter of the Second Epistle of S. Paul to the Corinthians*, in *Works*, 3:448.

[16]Herschel Baker, *The Dignity of Man* (Cambridge, Massachusetts, 1947) 275. Perry Miller sums up the history of faculty psychology (*The New England Mind* [New York, 1939] 244–245). Particularly in his first two chapters, Cohen also looks at the impact of Scriptural concerns upon the Puritan understanding of the faculties of the soul. For a longer, more general treatment see Baker; or J. B. Bamborough, *The Little World of Man* (London, 1952) in which Bamborough sets out to sketch "the psychological theory that was current when Shakespeare wrote" (11).

man's self is his soul."[17] While the soul is in the body, his primary means of gaining information is through the physical senses.[18] The senses, in turn, are immediately connected to the "phantasy,"[19] "imagination" or "opinion."[20] This imagination is no more than a shallow understanding, reflecting the immediate reaction of the senses to either pain or pleasure. As a result, the imagination is the sensual judgment, which naturally bypasses the rational judgment and directly stirs up the affections in the soul.[21] Though the soul was created "in that sweet harmony wherein there is no discord as an instrument in tune, fit to be moved to any duty,"[22] since the fall, the imagination has become the cause of much trouble in the soul. "This imagination of ours is become the seat of vanity, and thereupon of vexation to us because it apprehends a greater happiness in outward good things than there is and sees a greater misery in outward evil things than indeed there is."[23] Thus Sibbes bewailed the "Worldly, sottish men that live here below, they think there is no other state of things than they see; they are only taken up with sense, and pleasures, and goodly shows of things. Alas! poor souls!"[24]

This is not to suggest that the imagination had no positive use. "We should make our fancy serviceable to us in spiritual things," Sibbes taught. "And seeing God hath condescended to represent heavenly things to us under earthly terms, we should follow God's dealing herein....A sanctified fancy will make every creature a ladder to heaven." After God has revealed his truth, it is the imagination's role to

---

[17]"The Saint's Hiding-Place in the Evil Day," in *Works*, 1:408. Cf. Calvin's definition of soul: "an immortal yet created essence, which is his [man's] nobler part. Sometimes it is called 'spirit,'" (I.xv.2).

[18]"Bowels Opened," in *Works*, 2:40; "The Soul's Conflict with Itself," in *Works*, 1:178.

[19]"Bowels Opened," in *Works*, 2:40; cf. "The Soul's Conflict with Itself," in *Works*, 1:137. The "imagination" or "phantasy" seems to be roughly equivalent to what would today be commonly spoken of as "feelings."

[20]"The Soul's Conflict with Itself," in *Works*, 1:178. Kaufmann calls Sibbes's discussion of the imagination in "The Soul's Conflict," "the first detailed engagement with the subject in seventeenth-century Puritanism," (143).

[21]Ibid., 179–182.

[22]Ibid., 173.

[23]Ibid., 178–179. Cf. Baker, 283.

[24]"Angels' Acclamations," in *Works*, 6:319.

"colour divine truths, and make lightsome what faith believes."[25] For just this reason, Sibbes's own sermons are replete with scores of striking illustrations, so much so that one could almost reconstruct life in Stuart England from Sibbes's sermons alone. Everything from the "Gloria Patri" in church to blind men on the streets, from military tactics to the Englishman's view of far-off places, was used by Sibbes to capture the imaginations of his hearers and to "make our fancy serviceable to us in spiritual things."

In contrast, the role of the "mind,"[26] "judgment,"[27] or "understanding,"[28] located in the brain,[29] is to take in the information from the senses through the imagination and by means of rational discourse, to determine what is true. Once that is determined, the understanding naturally chooses what it perceives to be the true, thus showing wisdom or foolishness.[30] This faculty is essentially the image of God in the soul and therefore separates humans from beasts.[31] Thus, while "soul" is usually used to mean the entire person, Sibbes occasionally used it to mean simply that part of man which is unique to him among the creatures — the understanding.[32] Though its proper function is to give decisive reasons and thoughts to the heart, thus ruling the soul,[33] in the unregenerated man, the understanding "since the fall, until it hath a

---

[25]"The Soul's Conflict with Itself," in *Works*, 1:185.

[26]"A Breathing after God," in *Works*, 2:218

[27]"Bowels Opened," in *Works*, 2:92; "The Bruised Reed and Smoking Flax," in *Works*, 1:83; "The Soul's Conflict with Itself," in *Works*, 1:178.

[28]"A Breathing after God," in *Works*, 2:218-219, 221, 227, 237-8; "The Bride's Longing," in *Works*, 6:544; "The Bruised Reed and Smoking Flax," in *Works*, 1:83; "The Soul's Conflict with Itself," in *Works*, 1:178, 246; "The Saint's Safety in Evil Times," in *Works*, 1:297.

[29]"A Breathing after God," in *Works*, 2:218, 227; "The Bride's Longing," in *Works*, 6:544.

[30]"A Breathing after God," in *Works*, 2:221, "The Soul's Conflict with Itself," in *Works*, 1:246; See also "Angels' Acclamations," in *Works*, 6:328. Cf. Thomas Adams, *Mysticall Bedlam* (London, 1629) 493.

[31]"A Breathing after God," in *Works*, 2:216, 227. On the image of God in fallen humanity, see "The Faithful Covenanter," in *Works*, 6:220; "A Learned Commentary or Exposition Upon The first Chapter of the Second Epistle of S. Paul to the Corinthians," in *Works*, 3:40, 135; cf. "The Excellency of the Gospel above the Law," in *Works*, 4:267.

[32]"The Soul's Conflict with Itself," in *Works*, 1:245.

[33]"A Breathing after God," in *Works*, 2:218; "Bowels Opened," in *Works*, 2:9; "The Saint's Safety in Evil Times," in *Works*, 1:297.

higher light and strength, yieldeth to our imagination" and to "bribes" from the unsubdued will working in conjunction with the imagination.[34]

The Centrality of the Heart

SIBBES TAUGHT THAT "it is the bent of our wills that maketh us good or ill."[35] It is on the basis of just such statements that both Harold Shelly and Bert Affleck have built their presentations of Sibbes.[36] Affleck highlighted the heart–centeredness of Sibbes's language, which, he states, enabled Sibbes "to overcome in large measure the divisive thrust of the faculty psychology," and to "transcend the strictures of rationalistic humanism to affirm that men's relation to God is an experiential affair that goes much deeper than Reason can ever know."[37] Similarly, Shelly pointed out the centrality of the will in Sibbes's theology and of the affections in his presentation of Sibbes on the Christian life.[38] To this subordination of the reason to the heart/will, both Affleck and Shelly attribute Sibbes's "experiential" (Affleck), "mystical" (Shelly) religion.

---

[34]"The Bruised Reed and Smoking Flax," in *Works*, 1:83; "A Breathing after God," in *Works*, 2:221.

[35]"The Bruised Reed and Smoking Flax," in *Works*, 1:87; cf. "The Excellency of the Gospel above the Law," in *Works*, 4:258–259; "The Spiritual Jubilee," in *Works*, 5:230; William Ames, *The Marrow of Theology*, 3rd ed., trans. John Dykstra Eusden (Durham, North Carolina, 1968) 224–225; Miller, 249–250.

[36]Affleck, 212–215. Baker makes a similar assessment of Calvin as essentially voluntaristic (as opposed to rational) yet a careful reading of Calvin, II.ii.12–18, 23–27, shows Calvin as presenting both the reason and the will as fallen, yet neither one as extinguished. Again, the confusion results from taking Calvin's statements about what is the case in fallen, unregenerated man to be his statement of man's nature in and of itself.

[37]Affleck, 214–215.

[38]See Shelly, 222–226, 131–158; cf. Sibbes, "Bowels Opened," in *Works*, 2:157; "The Glorious Feast of the Gospel," in *Works*, 2:481. Sibbes suggested that this centrality of the affections in the Christian life (along with their natural weakness and the dangers of childbirth) explains why "for the most part women have sweet affections to religion, and therein they oft go beyond men" ("Lydia's Conversion," in *Works*, 6:520).

Certainly it is not Sibbes's statements of the supreme place of reason in the soul that are remarkable. Rather, what strikes the reader of his sermons is his affectionate language.[39] For Sibbes, Christianity was a love story. God was essentially a husband to his people: "with the same love that God loves Christ, he loves all his."[40] "You see how full of love he was. What drew him from heaven to earth, and so to his cross and to his grave, but love to mankind?"[41] In fact, "religion," said Sibbes, "is mainly in the affections."[42] God is the affectionate, loving sovereign, with every "sincere Christian...a favourite."[43] Given this understanding of Christianity, it is not surprising that Sibbes should publish sermons on three sections of the Song of Solomon. The book's erotic poetry expressed well "the mutual joys and mutual praises of Christ and his church."[44] Sibbes realized that sensual language was a powerful metaphor for the love between God and the soul.

"The putting of lively colours upon common truths hath oft a strong working both upon the fancy and our will and affections,"[45] and it was the will and affections, Sibbes said, that must be reached by the preacher. "By heart I mean, especially, the will and affections."[46] Even as the understanding was in the brain, the will and affections and desires were in the heart. As a result, Sibbes often used the four words interchangably[47] (though he occasionally referred to the heart as

---

[39]E.g., Richard Baxter included Sibbes high on his list of "Affectionate Practical English writiers" which even the poorest students library should include (Richard Baxter, *A Christian Directory, Or, A Summ of Practical Theology and Cases of Conscience* [London, 1673], 922).

[40]"Description of Christ," in *Works*, 1:12; cf. "The Excellency of the Gospel above the Law," in *Works*, 4:242.

[41]"The Excellency of the Gospel above the Law," in *Works*, 4:262.

[42]"The Returning Backslider," in *Works*, 2:368.

[43]"Yea and Amen; or, Precious Promises," in *Works*, 4:131.

[44]"Bowels Opened," in *Works*, 2:5. Cf. "This book is nothing else but a plain demonstration and setting forth of the love of Christ to his church, and of the love of the church to Christ," ("The Spouse, Her Earnest Desire After Christ," in *Works*, 2:200).

[45]"The Soul's Conflict with Itself," in *Works*, 1:184.

[46]"The Matchless Love and Inbeing," in *Works*, 6:403.

[47]"The Bride's Longing," in *Works*, 6:544; "A Breathing after God," in *Works*, 2:218, 227; "The Bruised Reed and Smoking Flax," in *Works*, 1:83; "The Soul's Conflict with Itself," in *Works*, 1:179–180, 184; "Josiah's Reformation," in *Works*, 6:31; "Church's Visitation," in *Works*, 1:374. So too Perkins (e.g.,

synonymous with the entire soul[48] and to the will as "drawing" the affections[49]). The heart is the faculty to which the understanding was to give its thoughts and reasons "as a prince doth his wiser subjects, and as counsellors do a well ordered state."[50] (Though the heart, like the brain, is immediately stirred by the imagination, these sensual judgments were to be ignored.) "Images are approved by the reason because they are true, by the will because they are good."[51] The heart, in turn, affects the understanding. Indeed, Sibbes spoke of the heart as essentially revealing the person.[52] Though the heart, or will, always chooses "with the advisement of reason,"[53] it is the heart, not reason, that is the determining (not judging) faculty of the soul,[54] particularly in the unregenerate man. It is the "fountain of life,"[55] the "inward motion," the "feet," the "wind" of the soul.[56] Therefore, Sibbes could say, "Love is the weight and wing of the soul, which carries it where it goes."[57]

562–563) and John Preston (e.g. *The Breast–plate of Faith and Love* [London, 1634], pt. i. 86–87).

[48]"Bowels Opened," in *Works*, 2:46. Cf. Preston, *Breast–plate*, 47. Gouge noted that "heart" in scripture was used both of the whole soul and of various faculties of the soul, including the will and affections (pt. iii. 79 [cf. 126]).

[49]"Divine Meditations and Holy Contemplations," in *Works*, 7:204. Preston (e.g. *Breast–plate*, pt. I, 204). Sibbes often spoke of the will and the affections, ("The Coming of Christ," in *Works*, 7:312–313; "The Soul's Conflict with Itself," in *Works*, 1:151) but these uses always present the will and affections as inextricably linked facets of the same faculty and are primarily useful as description. They do not represent the kind of distinction in Sibbes's mind that was clearly present between "understanding" and "heart." Sibbes usually used the word "will" to include the "affections" but occasionally spoke distinctly of the disposition to affect something (the affections) and the decision to affect something (the will).

[50]"The Soul's Conflict with Itself," in *Works*, 1:245.
[51]Miller, 248.
[52]"A Breathing after God," in *Works*, 2:219. Cf. Calvin, III.vi.4.
[53]"The Excellency of the Gospel above the Law," in *Works*, 4:225
[54]"A Breathing after God," in *Works*, 2:221.
[55]Ibid., 227.
[56]Ibid., 218, 227; "The Soul's Conflict with Itself," in *Works*, 1:159.
[57]"Bowels Opened," in *Works*, 2:129.

In Depravity

EVEN DEPRAVITY WAS presented by Sibbes in affectionate terms. Though some may be more so, all non–Christians, said Sibbes, were "hard–hearted."[58] Before conversion, all are "full of malice and base affections."[59] The carnal heart, overcast with passion and strong affections to the world, hates God naturally and cherishes corruption and rebellion against Him.[60] Naturally, "the heart of man is a proud piece of flesh."[61] Even "the best worldling sells Christ for a very thing of nought, a toy, a pleasure of sin, or a little profit. Such strongholds hath the king of this world in the hearts of the children thereof."[62]

According to Sibbes, the heart's preeminence was not a result of the fall, but was central according to God's design.[63] And yet, this heart–centered presentation of the soul in Sibbes's sermons should not be taken as revealing a mysticism that is irrational, or a–rational. Sibbes recognized both the desires and the thoughts as the "two primitive issues of the heart [i.e., soul]."[64] Problems occurred, Sibbes said, particularly in the soul where the will was unsubdued. In such souls the will, usurped the rightful role of the understanding, where "the heart being corrupt sets the wit awork, to satisfy corrupt will."[65] Thus, both were dealt with in conversion and sanctification, the heart being the goal, but the judgment always being the entry point.[66] As a result, the

---

[58]"The Soul's Conflict with Itself," in *Works*, 1:177.

[59]"A Breathing after God," in *Works*, 2:234. Cf. Calvin's statement that "our heart especially inclines by its own natural instinct toward unbelief," (III.ii.20).

[60]"Angels' Acclamations," in *Works*, 6:342; "The Bride's Longing," in *Works*, 6:540; "The Demand of a Good Conscience," in *Works*, 7:487; "Fountain Opened," in *Works*, 5:471

[61]"Judgment's Reason," in *Works*, 4:86.

[62]"The Rich Pearl," in *Works*, 7:259.

[63]"The Soul's Conflict with Itself," in *Works*, 1:159; cf. "The Privileges of the Faithful," in *Works*, 5:276; "Church's Visitation," in *Works*, 1:374.

[64]"A Breathing after God," in *Works*, 2:218.

[65]"The Soul's Conflict with Itself," in *Works*, 1:145; cf. "The Bruised Reed and Smoking Flax," in *Works*, 1:83; "A Breathing after God," in *Works*, 2:221; "Divine Meditations and Holy Contemplhations," in *Works*, 7:194.

[66]"A Breathing after God," in *Works*, 2:218-219; "The Bruised Reed and Smoking Flax," in *Works*, 1:83; "Divine Meditations and Holy Contemplations," in *Works*, 7:200-201; "The Saint's Hiding-Place in the Evil Day," in *Works*, 1:419.

role of the understanding was always to "breed" and "lead," to "work upon," to "warm" and "kindle" and even "inflame" the affections.[67] Reason, said Sibbes, "is a beam of God."[68] On the other hand, Sibbes certainly was not content with religion that was contained entirely in the brain. He scorned men that "never see spiritual things experimentally...though they know these things in the brain."[69] "A man knows no more in religion than he loves and embraceth with the affections of his soul."[70] To embrace something in one's affections was to know it experimentally because the "will is the carriage of the soul."[71] "Action follows affection."[72] If the grace of Christ were effectually working in the heart, one would do good, and on the other hand to be warned about evil desires, and yet to persist in pursuing them, was "atheism" in the heart.[73]

In Conversion

CONVERSION MUST, THEN, take place in the heart. Though it must include sanctification of the judgment, it must also include the subduing of the will.[74] "For it is not knowledge that will bring to heaven, for the devil hath that, but it is knowledge sanctified, seizing upon the affections."[75] In the unconverted man, the heart, or will, runs rough-shod over the understanding, bribing it and bringing it along with its carnal desires. In conversion, both the mind and the heart needed changing—the mind must be enlightened, and the very desires

---

[67]"Angels' Acclamations," in *Works*, 6:334, "A Breathing after God," in *Works*, 2:218–219; "The Excellency of the Gospel above the Law," in *Works*, 4:271; "The Privileges of the Faithful," in *Works*, 5:282; "The Soul's Conflict with Itself," in *Works*, 1:201, 245.

[68]"The Excellency of the Gospel above the Law," in *Works*, 4:234; cf. "Fountain Opened," in *Works*, 5:467. Cf. Nutall, *Holy Spirit*, 35–37.

[69]"Divine Meditations and Holy Contemplations," in *Works*, 7:200–201.

[70]"Fountain Opened," in *Works*, 5:478.

[71]"A Breathing after God," in *Works*, 2:218–219.

[72]"Bowels Opened," in *Works*, 2:110.

[73]"The Church's Riches by Christ's Poverty," in *Works*, 4:524; "The Soul's Conflict with Itself," in *Works*, 1:174–175.

[74]"A Breathing after God," in *Works*, 2:218.

[75]Ibid., 240.

and tastes of the heart must be altered.[76] God must come in to the heart to rule it.[77] He must seize on the powers of the soul, subdue the inward rising of the heart and the innate rebellion against the truth of God — he must "bring the heart down"[78] by opening the heart to believe and working in it to cause repentance.[79] God "turns" the heart to Him and "frees the will" to serve Him.[80] Though all is still touched by the fall, from the lowest member to the understanding,[81] the enlightened understanding will increasingly judge correctly and will be obeyed rather than coerced, thus allowing man to show his distinction from the beasts. In Sibbes, then, both depravity and conversion find their core in the heart, but neither in such a way as to deny the essential role of the understanding.

Therefore, while Affleck and Shelly were correct in noting that Sibbes did teach that the will or heart was the most powerful faculty in the soul, that it must be changed at conversion, and that the understanding would never move the soul without the will, they neglected the role of reason in Sibbes. Sibbes never presented religion as essentially a-rational: "all grace come in through the understanding enlightened."[82] It was "the most excelleant part of the soul."[83] The purpose of regeneration was to "reestablish" the "ideal supremacy of

---

[76]"The Returning Backslider," in *Works*, 2:416; "A Breathing after God," in *Works*, 2:220, 222; "Description of Christ," in *Works*, 1:24; "The Privileges of the Faithful," in *Works*, 5:284; "The Bride's Longing," in *Works*, 6:541; "The Excellency of the Gospel above the Law," in *Works*, 4:221; "The Faithful Covenanter," in *Works*, 6:19; "The Soul's Conflict with Itself," in *Works*, 1:268; "Divine Meditations and Holy Contemplations," in *Works*, 7:199; "To the Christian Reader," John Smith, *An Exposition of the Creed* (London, 1632); rpt. in *Works*, 1:clii; "Bowels Opened," in *Works*, 2:173.

[77]"The Bride's Longing," in *Works*, 6:551.

[78]Ibid., 540.

[79]"Yea and Amen; or, Precious Promises," in *Works*, 4:122; "Art of Contentment," in *Works*, 5:190.

[80]"The Knot of Prayer Loosed," in *Works*, 7:251; "The Pattern of Purity," in *Works*, 7:511.

[81]"The Soul's Conflict with Itself," in *Works*, 1:153.

[82]"The Excellency of the Gospel above the Law," in *Works*, 4:258-9; cf. "The Soul's Conflict with Itself," in *Works*, 1:245; "Description of Christ," in *Works*, 1:24.

[83]"Angels' Acclamations," in *Works*, 6:334.

reason over will."[84] In the regenerate man, the Spirit of God subdued the will to His Word coming through the understanding: "all comfort cometh into the soul by knowledge....Indeed, all graces are nothing but knowledge digested."[85] If to be a mystic, or to be "experiential," was fundamentally to exalt the role of the heart and will above that of the mind, then Sibbes was neither.

In Motivation

GIVEN THE CENTRALITY of the heart in Sibbes's presentations of both depravity and conversion, it is no surprise to find him speaking of the Christian life as one driven by holy loves and desires. "The gospel breeds love in us to God."[86] Though this love may first be simply for the salvation Christ has brought, "when she [the soul] is brought to him, and finds that sweetness that is in him, then she loves him for himself."[87] God becomes the one thing the soul most desires. Echoing Augustine's *Confessions*, Sibbes wrote, "The soul is never quiet till it comes to God...and that is the one thing the soul desireth."[88] Only those who so love God, preferring Him to carnal pleasures, riches, and honors, find Him.[89] A desire to do all to honor God and love Him typifies the life of the Christian.[90] "Whatsoever we do else, if it be not stirred by the Spirit, apprehending the love of God in Christ, it is but morality. What are all our performances if they be not out of love to God?"[91] "When the soul hath been with God in the mount, and when it

---

[84]Miller, 260.

[85]"A Learned Commentary or Exposition Upon The fourth Chapter of the Second Epistle of Saint Paul to the Corinthians," in *Works*, 4:459; cf. "The Bruised Reed and Smoking Flax," in *Works*, 1:83.

[86]"Description of Christ," in *Works*, 1:24.

[87]"Divine Meditations and Holy Contemplations," in *Works*, 7:217.

[88]"A Breathing after God," in *Works*, 2:217–218.

[89]"Description of Christ," in *Works*, 1:24; "The Spouse, Her Earnest Desire After Christ," in *Works*, 2:204; "A Breathing after God," in *Works*, 2:222.

[90]"A Breathing after God," in *Works*, 2:220; "The Excellency of the Gospel above the Law," in *Works*, 4:271.

[91]"Description of Christ," in *Works*, 1:24.

is turned from earthly things, then it sees nothing but love and mercy, and this constrains us to do all things out of love to God and men."[92]

For the Christian, to be in this world means to be separated from what he most desires. Christ Himself underwent this lack of *affectione accomoda* during the Incarnation.[93] Therefore, Christians, too, must expect this life to be marked by longing. Like David in the Psalms, the Christian will desire "to see the beauty of God in his house, that his soul might be ravished in the excellency of the object, and that the hightest powers of his soul, his understanding, will, and affections might be fully satisfied, that he might have full contentment."[94] "Therefore, we should press the heart forward to God...."[95] because the Christian will only find rest for his desires in heaven, its proper "element," "where all desires shall be accomplished."[96] Affectionately stated, the point of the Christian life is "to grow in nearer communion with God by his Spirit, to have more knowledge and affection, more love and joy and delight in the best things daily."[97] Therefore, Christians are to "labour to have great affections" for God, and subsequently, for other, lesser goods, particularly his ordinances through which his presence is enjoyed.[98] Whereas the worldling must always finally loose that which he desires, the Christian never does.[99]

Preeminently, the affection God uses in the soul of the believer is love. Once converted, this affection of love becomes the driving force of the soul to God. "Love is a boundless affection."[100] As the "prime and leading affection of the soul,"[101] the "firstborn affection of the soul,"[102] love naturally motivates the rest of the soul to action. "Love is an affection full of inventions," zealously pursuing the pleasure of the

---

[92]"Divine Meditations and Holy Contemplations," in *Works*, 7:221.

[93]"Fountain Opened," in *Works*, 5:533.

[94]"A Breathing after God," in *Works*, 2:237–8.

[95]"The Soul's Conflict with Itself," in *Works*, 1:202.

[96]"A Breathing after God," in *Works*, 2:227–229.

[97]Ibid., 247.

[98]"Fountain Opened," in *Works*, 5:478; "The Returning Backslider," in *Works*, 2:266; "A Breathing after God," in *Works*, 2:229; "Bowels Opened," in *Works*, 2:157; "The Glorious Feast of the Gospel," in *Works*, 2:481.

[99]"The Danger of Backsliding," in *Works*, 7:413.

[100]"Christ is Best; or, St. Paul's Strait," in *Works*, 1:349.

[101]"The Soul's Conflict with Itself," in *Works*, 1:130.

[102]"The Sword of the Wicked," in *Works*, 1:105.

beloved.[103] Thus, love "will constrain us to obedience"[104] because "it studies to please the person loved as much as it can every way."[105] That is why Sibbes exhorted his hearers, "Beloved, get love....It melts us into the likeness of Christ. It constrains, it hath a kind of holy violence in it. No water can quench it. We shall glory in sufferings for that we love. Nothing can quench that holy fire that is kindled from heaven. It is a glorious grace."[106] The phrase "a kind of holy violence" well reflects the powerful image of the heart that Sibbes presented. Similarly, the affection of love performs a "sweet kind of tyranny" that will make a man willing even to die.[107] "Nothing is hard to love; it carries all the powers of the soul with it."[108] Thus, since one who loves will do anything for "the contentation of the person beloved,"[109] one should "labour for a spirit of love....Nothing is grievous to the person that loves."[110]

Furthermore, since love naturally "stirs up the soul to make out for" the beloved, the love for God that Sibbes presented had as its end, not only the pleasure of the beloved, but "union and fellowship with the person we affect."[111] Therefore the Christian has "this further desire of familiarity with Christ" and yearns for "further inward kisses of his love."[112] Love leaves one at rest only in the beloved.[113] "Love is an affection of union. What we love...we are knit unto."[114] One implication of this love is losing oneself. Thus, "the more loving Christian ever the more humble Christian."[115] Yet Sibbes did not infer from this a divinely

---

[103]"The Soul's Conflict with Itself," in *Works*, 1:181; "The Excellency of the Gospel above the Law," in *Works*, 4:274-275; "The Sword of the Wicked," in *Works*, 1:116.
[104]"The Danger of Backsliding," in *Works*, 7:411.
[105]"The Excellency of the Gospel above the Law," in *Works*, 4:271.
[106]Ibid., pp 274-5; "Divine Meditations and Holy Contemplations," in *Works*, 7:221.
[107]"Art of Contentment," in *Works*, 5:182; cf. "Description of Christ," in *Works*, 1:9.
[108]"The Soul's Conflict with Itself," in *Works*, 1:279.
[109]"The Privileges of the Faithful," in *Works*, 5:276-277.
[110]"The Difficulty of Salvation," in *Works*, 1:399.
[111]"The Privileges of the Faithful," in *Works*, 5:276-277.
[112]"The Spouse, Her Earnest Desire After Christ," in *Works*, 2:205.
[113]"The Privileges of the Faithful," in *Works*, 5:276-277.
[114]"Judgment's Reason," in *Works*, 4:98.
[115]"The Privileges of the Faithful," in *Works*, 5:281-2.

sanctioned asceticism. Though he can refer to self-love as "a common corruption that cleaves to the nature of all men,"[116] he also spoke of a self-love that "God hath put in us ... not sinful, but love of preserving our nature."[117] It is this instinct for self-preservation, or "self-love," that naturally causes people to care for themselves in good ways, both physically and spiritually. So, man is compelled to grow spiritually both by love of God, and by a godly love of self.

In Assurance

SIBBES TAUGHT THAT the examination of the heart was essential to indicate the true state of the soul because "there is nothing that charcteriseth and sets a stamp upon a Christian so much as desires. All other things may be counterfeit. Words and actions may be counterfeit, but the desires and affections cannot, because they are the immediate issues and productions of the soul."[118] The heart was the only place the Christian could examine "for the evidence of our good estate in religion. Let us not so much search what Christ hath done, but search our own hearts how we have engaged ourselves to God in Christ, that we believe and witness our believeing, that we lead a life answerable to our faith, renounce all but Christ."[119] Without affections, a "man...is like

---

[116]"The Soul's Conflict with Itself," in *Works*, 1:177.

[117]"The Returning Backslider," in *Works*, 2:266.

[118]"A Breathing after God," in *Works*, 2:219. See also ibid., 220–221. "Bowels Opened," in *Works*, 2:129; "The Danger of Backsliding," in *Works*, 7:413; "The Privileges of the Faithful," in *Works*, 5:282; "The Pattern of Purity," in *Works*, 7:514–515; "The Returning Backslider," in *Works*, 2:264; "The Saint's Hiding-Place in the Evil Day," in *Works*, 1:419. "We may dissemble words and actions, but we cannot dissemble our desires and affections; we may paint fire, but we cannot paint heat. Therefore God judgeth us more by our desires and affections than by our words and actions," ("The Bride's Longing," in *Works*, 6:543). Cf. William Perkins suggestion of gaining assurance through sanctification of the heart because "we knowe it sufficiently to be true, and not painted fire, if there be heate, though there be no flame," (William Perkins, *The Whole Treatise of the Cases of Conscience* [Cambridge, 1606] 77).

[119]"The Demand of a Good Conscience," in *Works*, 7:483; "Bowels Opened," in *Works*, 2:123; "Judgment's Reason," in *Works*, 4:101–102.

mare mortuum, the dead sea that never stirreth;"[120] "for it is affection that makes a Christian."[121]

The brain could not give convincing witness to conversion because religion could be well known to the understanding, and yet a stranger in the heart. Such was the case with hypocrites.[122] As Sibbes observed from the "backsliding" of Demas, "we are not as we know, but as we love."[123] The Christian's assurance will never be greater than his love. "Therefore, when we find our heart inflamed with love to God, we may know that God hath shined upon our souls in the pardon of sin; and proportionably to our measure of love is our assurance of pardon. Therefore we should labour for a greater measure thereof, that our hearts may be the more inflamed in the love of God."[124] Furthermore, affections testified not only of one's conversion, but also, Sibbes taught, of one's sanctification. "If a man ask, how I know that I am sanctified? the answer must be, I believe, I know it to be so. The work of working these things in me comes of God; but the work of discerning them is certain, how our affection stands in this case—comes of us."[125]

In Backsliding

WHILE AFFECTIONS FOR God were to characterize a Christian, Sibbes recognized that they were not the only desires in a Christian's heart. Even the best Christian should know that "if we would examine ourselves...it would bring us on our knees, and make our faces be confounded, to consider what a deal of atheism there is in our heart... that must be mortified and subdued."[126] Worldly-mindedness "will

---

[120]"The Returning Backslider," in *Works*, 2:368.

[121]"The Faithful Covenanter," in *Works*, 6:10, 12.

[122]"Divine Meditations and Holy Contemplations," in *Works*, 7:200–201.

[123]"The Danger of Backsliding," in *Works*, 7:412; cf. "A Glance of Heaven; or, Precious Taste of a Glorious Feast," in *Works*, 4:182.

[124]"The Returning Backslider," in *Works*, 2:264.

[125]"Witness of Salvation," in *Works*, 7:377.

[126]"The Faithful Covenanter," in *Works*, 6:11; cf. "The Danger of Backsliding," in *Works*, 7:409; "Angels' Acclamations," in *Works*, 6:332; "The Knot of Prayer Loosed," in *Works*, 7:248; "Christ's Sufferings for Man's Sin," in *Works*, 1:364; "The Right Receiving," in *Works*, 4:62–63; "The Soul's Conflict with Itself," in *Works*, 1:171; "Judgment's Reason," in *Works*, 4:86–87.

glue thy affections to the earth," Sibbes warned," and will not suffer them to be lifted up to Christ."[127] This is the reason that often those with less worldly goods have "more loving souls" and are more "heated with affection." He has less at stake in this world, and therefore, "a poor Christian cares not for cold disputes. Instead of that he loves; and that is the reason why a poor soul goes to heaven with more joy whilst others are entangled."[128] Therefore, "the life of a Christian should be a meditation how to unloose his affections from inferior things. He will easily die that is dead before in affection....He that is much in heaven in his thoughts is free from being tossed with tempests here below."[129] Sibbes seems to have known the freedom of affections he preached. As he lay dying, Sibbes is reported to have replied to the question, "how hee (Dr. Sips) did in his soule" by saying, "I should doe God much wrong if I should not say very well."[130]

Yet such a peaceful demise was not the certain earthly end of the Christian. The sheer number of references in Sibbes's sermons to the wanderings of Christian hearts shows that real danger lay even in the converted heart. The danger of backsliding was clearly as much an affair of the heart as was growth in grace. The affections were always ready, even in the redeemed man to rebel. And once in rebellion, they were joined by Satan, increasing their revolt. "And therefore we have need to keep our affections of grief and fear within their due bounds."[131] Such a "double heart" was particularly dangerous because "it will regard God no longer than it can enjoy that which it joins together with him."[132] The division of affections was one of the marks of the unconverted heart and was to be changed at conversion. "As soon as a man becomes a Christian, he hath one heart. His heart before was

---

[127]"The Spouse, Her Earnest Desire After Christ," in *Works*, 2:205–206.

[128]"Divine Meditations and Holy Contemplations," in *Works*, 7:194–5.

[129]"The Soul's Conflict with Itself," in *Works*, 1:164, cf. 159, 163, 286; "Bowels Opened," in *Works*, 2:186; "Of the Providence of God," in *Works*, 5:42; "Christ is Best; or, St. Paul's Strait," in *Works*, 1:341; "The Privileges of the Faithful," in *Works*, 5:283; "A Learned Commentary or Exposition Upon The first Chapter of the Second Epistle of S. Paul to the Corinthians," in *Works*, 3:208. Cf. Calvin, II.ix.1.

[130]Samuel Hartlib, Ephemerides, 1635.

[131]"Two Sermons Upon the first words of Christ's last Sermon, John 14.1. Being also the last Sermons of Richard Sibbs," in *Works*, 7:341.

[132]"The Soul's Conflict with Itself," in *Works*, 1:218–219.

divided."[133] The devil may be contented with half the heart, but Christ "will not have it so."[134] Therefore, the Christian should, "Take heed of the pleasures of the world, lest they drown thy soul, as they do the souls of many that profess themselves to be Christians."[135] "Love, it is the light of our life; love we must, something; and he lives not that loves not. Seeing then that we cannot but love, and that the misplacing of our affection is the cause of all sin and misery, what can we do better than attend to directions how to love as we should?"[136] Sibbes taught that if love is the light of life, then love of darkness becomes a blinding affection.[137] Yet even in those who may appear blinded for a time, there may be "a secret love of Christ." If so, the "pulses will beat this way, and good affections will discover themselves"[138] because "his heart is fixed."[139] "Whatsoever we give the supremacy of the inward man to, whatsoever we love most, whatsoever we trust most, whatsoever we fear most, whatsoever we joy and delight most, whatsoever we obey most—that is our god."[140] In the end, one's love indicated one's God,[141] for no human lives without loving.[142]

In Sanctification

FINALLY, EVEN AS depravity and conversion, backsliding and assurance were all affairs of the heart, so too, taught Sibbes, was sanctification. One grows by means of one's affections. One should:

---

[133]"A Breathing after God," in *Works*, 2:218. "Grace confines the soul to one thing," Ibid., 217.
[134]"The Spouse, Her Earnest Desire After Christ," in *Works*, 2:205-206; "The Returning Backslider," in *Works*, 2:261.
[135]"The Spouse, Her Earnest Desire After Christ," in *Works*, 2:205-206.
[136]"The Privileges of the Faithful," in *Works*, 5:284.
[137]Ibid.
[138]"Bowels Opened," in *Works*, 2:48.
[139]"Two Sermons Upon the first words of Christs last Sermon, John 14.1. Being also the last Sermons of Richard Sibbs," in *Works*, 7:355-6. Cf. Preston, *Breast-Plate*, pt. iii. 215.
[140]"The Faithful Covenanter," in *Works*, 6:12.
[141]"The Soul's Conflict with Itself," in *Works*, 1:268; "The Saint's Safety in Evil Times," in *Works*, 1:298.
[142]"The Privileges of the Faithful," in *Works*, 5:281-282.

Labour therefore to know the world, that thou mayest detest it. In religion, the more we know the more we will love; but all the worldly things, the more we know the less we will affect them; as a picture afar off, it will shew well, but come near it and it is not so....The more we know the vanities of the world and the excellencies of grace, the more we will love the one and hate the other.[143]

It is by meditating on the things of religion, and on the things of the world, that one will grow the appropriate affections to each. Fundamental to this task is the believer's decision to "plough up their own hearts."[144] Sibbes said that God will "have us take words unto ourselves, for exciting of the graces of God in us by words, blowing up of the affections, and for manifestation of the hidden man of the heart."[145] Such action will make sure that Christ is made "sweet ... to the soul."[146] Realizing that the affection is particularly stirred by sight,[147] one must labor to "see spiritual things experimentally."[148] This is why examples of men were so useful to the believer, because examples worked most on the affections.[149] Most of all then, the believer should look to Christ: "When we look upon the mercy of God in Christ, it kindleth love, and love kindleth love, as fire kindleth fire;[150] "let us try our love by our labouring for that sight of Christ which we may have."[151]

Preaching was preeminently the means to grow such loving affections, especially affectionate preaching. According to Sibbes, this was that preaching in which "Christ [was] truly laid open to the hearts of people...the knowledge and preaching of Christ in his state and

---

[143]"The Danger of Backsliding," in *Works*, 7:413.

[144]"Church's Visitation," in *Works*, 1:382.

[145]"The Returning Backslider," in *Works*, 2:260.

[146]"Judgment's Reason," in *Works*, 4:92.

[147]"A Breathing after God," in *Works*, 2:243, 237; "Divine Meditations and Holy Contemplations," in *Works*, 7:203–204; "The Excellency of the Gospel above the Law," in *Works*, 4:251; "Fountain Opened," in *Works*, 5:478.

[148]"Divine Meditations and Holy Contemplations," in *Works*, 7:200–201.

[149]"The Christian Work," in *Works*, 5:122–123; cf. 124; "Divine Meditations and Holy Contemplations," in *Works*, 7:193.

[150]"The Excellency of the Gospel above the Law," in *Works*, 4:271.

[151]"The Spouse, Her Earnest Desire After Christ," in *Works*, 2:205.

offices."[152] "Indeed, 'preaching' is the ordinance of God, sanctified for the begetting of faith, for the opening of the understanding, for the drawing of the will and affections to Christ....Therefore, as we esteem faith and all the good we have by it, let us be stirred up highly to prize and esteem of this ordinance of God."[153] Because Sibbes taught that "God has opened His heart to us in His Word,"[154] it followed simply that "those ages wherein the Spirit of God is most, is where Christ is most preached,"[155] and those places "where the ordinances of Christ are held forth with life and power, they have more heavenly and enlarged affections than others have, as the experience of Christians will testify."[156] While preaching was preeminent, the use of other means was also encouraged upon the believer. Though individual study and meditation were never to be substitutes for preaching in stirring the affections, the Christian did have an obligation to "soar much aloft in our meditations, and see the excellencies of Christ."[157] As in conversion, the gospel must proceed from the understanding into the heart if it is to be effective, so too, "comfortable" thoughts must so proceed if they are to be useful to the Christian.[158] In addition, Sibbes exhorted the believer to the "lifting up the heart to God,"[159] since a "Christian, what he desires as a Christian, he prays for, and what he prays for he desires."[160] Prayers that do not reflect the true desires of the heart are mere hypocrisy, and no true prayers.[161] Finally, as it is the heart that leads the Christian to fellowship with God, it is the heart which leads

---

[152]"Description of Christ," in *Works*, 1:24.

[153]"Fountain Opened," in *Works*, 5:514–515.

[154]"The Soul's Conflict with Itself," in *Works*, 1:212.

[155]"Description of Christ," in *Works*, 1:24.

[156]"Bowels Opened," in *Works*, 2:161.

[157]"The Danger of Backsliding," in *Works*, 7:409. Cf. 413; "The Returning Backslider," in *Works*, 2:260; "Divine Meditations and Holy Contemplations," in *Works*, 7:189.

[158]"Two Sermons Upon the first words of Christs last Sermon, John 14.1. Being also the last Sermons of Richard Sibbs," in *Works*, 7:355–6. These were the last words of which we have evidence that Sibbes spoke publicly. He died within the week.

[159]"Fountain Opened," in *Works*, 5:469.

[160]"A Breathing after God," in *Works*, 2:222; "The Bride's Longing," in *Works*, 6:540.

[161]"The Knot of Prayer Loosed," in *Works*, 7:248.

the Christian to fellowship with other believers, which, like the other means, in turn stirs up further his affections for God.[162]

Conclusion

IN HIS AFFECTIONATE language considered above, it becomes clear that Sibbes moved concerns of Christian piety inward.[163] He affirmed that it was actually love that was the root of all good, and of all evil. He wrote:

> We must know it is not the world simply that draws our heart from God and goodness, but the love of the world. Worldly things are good in themselves, and given to sweeten our passage to heaven. They sweeten the profession of religion, therefore bring not a false report upon the world. It is thy falseness that makes it hurtful, in loving so much. Use it as a servant all thy days, and not as a master, and thou mayest have comfort therein. It is not the world properly that hurts us, but our setting our hearts upon it; whenas God should be in our thoughts, our spirits are even drunk with the cares below. Thorns will not prick of themselves, but when they are grasped in a man's hand they prick deep. So this world and the things thereof are all good, and were all made of God for the benefit of his creature, did not our immoderate affection make them hurtful, which indeed embitters every sweet unto us. This is the root of all evil.[164]

Warning against deliberate hypocrisy on the one hand, and foolish pride on the other, Sibbes radically interiorized Christianity.

This inward piety is not seen primarily in an overriding concern for "union experiences" with God, taken by many to be the hallmark of mysticism. Such a concern is certainly not present at all in Sibbes if it is intended to imply any essentially arational spirituality or antinomian ethic. However, if one simply intends that "wherever there is conjoined

---

[162]"Bowels Opened," in *Works*, 2:161; "The Bride's Longing," in *Works*, 6:541–542; "Description of Christ," in *Works*, 1:14.

[163]Haller, 209.

[164]"The Danger of Backsliding," in *Works*, 7:412–413. Cf. Calvin, III.ix.3–4.

with serious Christianity a certain tenderness of heart and a hunger and thirst for God, and the metaphors of Scripture are believed to enshrine definite promise of intimate communion with Him, we are not wrong to speak of Mysticism,"[165] then Sibbes could certainly be classified as a mystic. Perhaps it would be better to speak of the "tender lyricism barely controllable" that is evident in his sermons.[166] In the end, whether the inwardness that marks Sibbes's sermons should be termed "mysticism" is a matter more important to a study of mysticism than to a study of Sibbes.

Yet taking note of Sibbes's "affectionate" theology (a more appropriate name for this interiorization) is important for an accurate understanding of him and his preaching. His understanding of the human psyche necessitated, or at least was congruent with, his heavy emphasis on saving knowledge settling in the heart and then being reflected in experience and practice. In the united heart, the affections affect, the desires desire, the will wills. The heart and the understanding are united, and the heart proceeds to stir up the bodily humors to pursue that which it has perceived as good. The humors regularly obey the will and the outward members work to attain the thing desired. Thus, when the object desired is true and good, the soul is well united in desiring it, and attainment of it brings happiness, contentment, and satisfaction throughout the soul. When the object is neither true nor good, then there is often disruption in the soul, and a lack of contentment even in the attainment of its goal.

By this interiorizing, Sibbes could easily have appeared to be unconcerned about holiness of actions. A case in point is his sermon "Right Receiving" (preached most likely at Gray's Inn, certainly before 1630). In this sermon, Sibbes taught that worthiness to partake of the Lord's Supper was not to be understood as worthiness of the person himself, but "in respect of his affection."[167] Yet for Sibbes, the affections were the person. How, then, could he be saying that one did not need to be worthy "in himself"? The point of the passage Sibbes was expounding (1 Cor. 11: 28-29) is that one must be worthy in one's actions and life so that Christ's sacrifice is not defamed in the hearts of those partaking and to the watching world. Neither Paul nor Sibbes

---

[165]Wakefield, 45.
[166]Nuttall, "Mysticism," 527.
[167]"The Right Receiving," in *Works*, 4:62–63.

suggested that anyone should partake who was neither a Christian, nor lived like one. Nor did either suggest that one must be worthy to partake of communion in the sense of having earned one's right to partake. Both Paul and Sibbes (even given his radical interiorizing of the text) clearly intended a secondary and subsidiary worthiness based upon the work of the Spirit in the soul. Yet Sibbes took this text, which was clearly concerned with actions of professing believers, and pastorally applied it beyond — almost oppositely to — the original intent. The Corinthian unworthiness consisted exactly in their outward and visible unworthiness, not merely an unworthiness of the affections. Sibbes's concern, however, was with hypocritical conformity. In essence, Sibbes suggested that one may never have the certainty of properly receiving communion based on one's actions (though those should certainly be worthy in so far as they can be), since actions can be deceiving, for all the reasons outlined above. Instead, this subsidiary righteousness, or worthiness that gives evidence of the basic worthiness of Christ having been imputed to the soul, can only be known by the affections of the heart.

According to Sibbes, if one found through searching one's affections that one is in Christ, only then should the bread and the wine be taken. Though Sibbes did not suggest that one rightly partakes in the Lord's Supper via Christ's righteousness imparted to us (albeit in our affections) rather than imputed to us (and therefore existing worthily only in Christ), in his attempts to warn against hypocrisy and pride, his language occasionally could be taken to suggest otherwise. While the power and propriety of such an application in the chapel of Gray's Inn in the early seventeenth century can be readily understood, one can glimpse even here some of the difficulties surrounding assurance of salvation which the Protestant community in England experienced. Not least among them would be the natural mental jump from considering this kind of worthiness as evidence of a deeper, provided worthiness to considering it as worthiness in and of itself. The results of such thinking could easily be a moralism of the heart in which need for forgiveness is replaced by need for education and in which sanctification is emphasized at the expense of justification.[168] While such problems did not occur in Sibbes's preaching, the problems he intended to address by

---

[168]See C. FitzSimons Allison, *The Rise of Moralism: The Proclamation of the Gospel from Hooker to Baxter* (Wilton, Connecticut, 1966).

interiorizing the issue—primarily, reliance on self-righteousness—were merely pushed inward by Sibbes's affectionate language; they were not solved.

If a theological anthropology that cemented the relation between the belief of the heart and the action of the members was particularly appropriate in Sibbes's ecclesiastical environment—in the covenant community of the church—it was also a particularly appropriate understanding given Sibbes's sociopolitical environment. Considering this description of the psyche of a person socially, it becomes clear that each person is understood as a microcosm. The senses, imagination, heart, and members are all spoken of as desiring. The imagination, understanding, and heart are all apparently capable of some kind of judgment. It resembles nothing so much as a governing elite, with the council of advisers (the understanding) advising the more powerful ruler (the heart) commanding the lower members. As Sibbes described the inner man, it was "the consistory of the soul."[169] The wise ruler listened to his advisers, particularly when they counsel with God's word (as ministers did) and worked in accord with them. The evil ruler attempted to subvert the judgment of his counselors and work apart from and against them. With such an understanding of man, it followed simply that preaching should be the salvific ordinance and that a well-run kingdom to discover its health should most fundamentally look to its "faithful ministers"—"the pillars of this tottering world."[170]

---

[169]"The Soul's Conflict with Itself," in *Works*, 1:289.

[170]"Of the Providence of God," in *Works*, 5:50. Note his strong statements on this subject in "A Learned Commentary or Exposition Upon The first Chapter of the Second Epistle of S. Paul to the Corinthians," in *Works*, 3:279-280 (not published until twenty years after his death).

VII

A Conforming Theologian

J. T. CLIFFE, AMONG OTHERS, has referred to the tendency in the 1620s and 1630s "for the godly to become more inward–looking in matters of religion."[1] Richard Sibbes can easily be taken to be a central exponent of such an introspective religion, careless of social implications or public interest. As he said, "we should have a double eye: one eye to see that which is amiss in us, our own imperfections, thereby to carry ourselves in a perpetual humility; but another eye of faith, to see what we have in Christ, our perfection in him."[2] This "eye of faith" was crucial for a godly preacher like Sibbes; yet it was crucial not merely for reasons of personal piety.

A kind of spiritual second sight that could see that God was at work, despite what the eye of flesh might see, was essential for assurance of salvation. Yet this eye of faith was not only turned inward. It was also essential to see God's hand at work in the world and, perhaps most importantly, in the church. And it was particularly important to a minister like Sibbes if he would be conforming. The same uneasy balance of piety, patience, and passion was to characterize the believer's internal religious quest—whether it was to find assurance, draw comfort, discern providence, or educate conscience.

The task of this last chapter will be to examine Sibbes's understanding of assurance, which has been recognized as a central

---

[1]J. T. Cliffe, *The Puritan Gentry: The Great Puritan Families of Early Stuart England* (London, 1984) 198; cf. Perry Miller, *The New England Mind: The Seventeenth Century* (New York, 1939) 55.

[2]"Bowels Opened," in *Works*, 2:85; cf. 136; "Divine Meditations and Holy Contemplations," in *Works*, 7:187; "A Learned Commentary or Exposition Upon The first Chapter of the Second Epistle of S. Paul to the Corinthians," in *Works*, 3:448–449. John Calvin, *The Institutes of the Christian Religion*, trans. F. L. Battles (London, 1960) III.ii.25.

feature of his preaching, and the less–noted, but related issue of conscience. While properly the subject of investigation because of their prominence in Sibbes's preaching, this study explores them because they are significant in understanding Sibbes's ability to remain within the Church of England. In so doing, the issue of Sibbes's conformity, raised in the first half of this study, will be clarified as Sibbes's concern for inward piety is shown to have been for him not the avenue to nonconformity, but rather that which allowed continuing conformity.

Assurance

COMFORT, OF COURSE, came most of all from assurance of one's salvation.[3] Sermonic rhetoric about this doctrine could be quite equivocal, intending at one moment to assure the doubting believer that their election was based upon nothing in themselves and that their perseverance was assured by the same God who had begun a good work in them (Phil 1:6) and at the next, exhorting believers to make sure their interest in Christ. Whatever rush of certainty may have attended the initial preaching of the Protestant gospel, by the early seventeenth century, and probably well before, such preaching, intended as a balm after the Roman "doctrine of doubting," had various effects on its hearers. This is well illustrated by two letters Lady Joan Barrington received from younger relations (daughter and nephew) in 1629 and 1630. Lady Elizabeth Masham, in a letter written to her mother, Lady Joan, confessed that "I daly se more and more that there is noe hapynes in any thing but in getting asuranc of God['s] love in Christ, and 'tis the only thing, I thank God, which I take comfort in, and I know that you will say the like your self."[4] A year later Thomas Bourchier, Lady Joan's nephew, wrote to her a pathetic, mainly melancholic letter, lamenting the state of his own soul. Bourchier wrote:

> Madame of late I have had such infinite sadnes springinge from feares of my union with Christe, that truli I have scarce bin able to subsiste. My feares are not about his faithfulnes, with whome I knowe there is no shadowe of chainge, but they arise from

---

[3]"The Spiritual Jubilee," in *Works*, 5:244.
[4]*Barrington Family Letters*, 1628–1632, ed. Arthur Searle (London, 1983) 56.

secret doubtes of the truthe of grace (without which all prophession does but aggravate condemnation).... Tho thus I complaine, (I blesse God) when I am at the poynte of deathe I still hope, and indeed some tymes have such refreshings, that the sweet thereof invites to truste tho God kill.... tho I am confident that that precious blood which some yeares since I have applied does perfectli justifie me and in some measure by its efficaci I am clensed, yet the thoughtes of wastinge my marrow in vaniti does manye tymes produce stronge assaultes.[5]

If sincere confusion could be created in the hearts of earnest listeners who saw their souls at stake in the early seventeenth century, much more easily can confusion creep into the modern reader's discussion of assurance or certainty. The combination of such confusion with controversies (then and now) only serves to make the task of examining Sibbes treatment of assurance more arduous. To understand more clearly Sibbes's own words, something of the tradition in which he preached must be presented.

Any discussion of assurance that is unclear in the object of assurance can hardly be expected to be clear in any other matter. It is vital to know whether one is discussing the objective assurance of faith that Christ is all he professes to be and will freely save whoever believes in him or the subjective assurance of faith in which one is assured of one's own salvation.[6] The former use of assurance was prominent throughout the century following the reformation, particularly in anti–Roman polemics.[7] The latter emphasis, though always present and distinct in the Reformed tradition, becomes more clearly distinguished, and more prominent in the English church due perhaps to the increased attention given to pastoral issues over polemical ones in printed books as the Protestant succession seemed more certain and the Elizabethan settlement more sure. Such a distinction is essential in clearly considering the Reformed background of Sibbes's preaching of the assurance of salvation.

---

[5]Searle, 176.

[6]For a brief, accurate, systematic distinction of these two, see Louis Berkhof, *Systematic Theology* (Grand Rapids, Michigan, 1939) 507–509.

[7]Peter Lake, *Moderate Puritans and the Elizabethan Church* (Cambridge, 1982) 98–106, 166–167.

Robert Middlekauf has written that "the most familiar figure among Puritans is the tormented soul, constantly examining his every thought and action, now convinced that hell awaits him, now lunging after the straw of hope that he is saved, and then once more falling into despair. He wants to believe, he tries, he fails, he succeeds, he fails—always on the cycle of alternating moods."[8] John Calvin had complained that this was exactly the "assurance mingled with doubt" that some "half-papists" were teaching in his own day. They taught that:

> Whenever we look upon Christ, they confess that we find full occasion for good hope in him. But because we are always unworthy of all those benefits which are offered to us in Christ, they would have us waver and hesitate at the sight of our unworthiness. In brief, they so set conscience between hope and fear that it alternates from one to the other intermittently and by turns.... Thus, when Satan once sees that those open devices with which he formerly had been wont to destroy the certainty of faith are now of no avail, he tries to sap it by covert devices.[9]

Was this teaching of "half-papists" that Calvin lamented the teaching of his Reformed heirs, and particularly of Richard Sibbes?

The tradition against which this Reformed understanding of assurance was preached—one of the most truly catholic traditions overturned by the Reformers—was the tradition concerning assurance of salvation codified by the Roman Catholic Church at Trent. In their Sixth Session in 1547, they produced the "Decree on Justification."[10] Following Aquinas, rather than Duns Scotus, the Council defined justification in a non-punctiliar fashion. The Tridentine explanation of the life of a Christian was that the Christian's initial justification in baptism could be lost through mortal sin.[11] Final justification, that justification which most Christians would have in view in their earthly

---

[8]Robert Middlekauff, "Piety and Intellect in Puritanism," *The William and Mary Quarterly*, 3rd series, vol. XXII/3 (July, 1965): 459.

[9]Calvin, *Institutes*, III.ii.24.

[10]"Decree of Justification," reprinted in *The Christian Faith in the Doctrinal Documents of the Catholic Church*, rev. ed., ed. J. Neuner and J. Dupuis (New York, 1982) 554–570.

[11]"Decree on Justification," Chapter XV.

life, necessarily followed sanctification because God could not justify sinners as sinners.[12] Normally, the righteousness of Christ had to be imparted to them and grown throughout their lives by God's grace administered through the seven sacraments of the church. In chapter IX, the Decree stated what logically followed from such an understanding of justification, i.e., that "no one can know with a certitude of faith which cannot be subject to error, that he has obtained God's grace." Chapter XII was directed explicitly against those who thought that they could definitely know they were among the elect, apart from special revelation.[13] To propagate a teaching of assurance of final justification, then, was taken as teaching sinners to think themselves perfect, a damning error.[14]

The Reformed Tradition

John Calvin

John Calvin wrote of salvation one moment as if it included assurance[15] and yet also conceded that "we cannot imagine any certainty that is not tinged with doubt."[16] This was not to suggest, he insisted, the Roman position, "that faith does not rest in a certain and clear knowledge, but only in an obscure and confused knowledge of the divine will toward us,"[17] because "even if we are distracted by various thoughts, we are not on that account completely divorced from faith.... We see him [God] afar off, but so clearly as to know that we are not at all deceived."[18] Instead of experiencing lack of assurance from putting one's faith in an unsure source of salvation, Calvin said believers should "deeply fix all

---

[12]"Decree on Justification," Chapter XIV.
[13]So too "Decree on Justification," Canon 16.
[14]"Decree on Justification," Chapter XIII contained the "doctrine of doubt."
[15]E.g., his comments on Galatians 4:6 in his *Commentaries on the Epistles of Paul to the Galatians and Ephesians*, trans. William Pringle (Edinburgh, 1854) 121 (yet it should be noted that Calvin makes this comment in the context of anti-Roman polemics); Calvin, *Institutes*, III.ii.7.
[16]Calvin, *Institutes*, III.ii.16 and 17. Cf. III.ii.18, 37; xiii.3; xxiv.6.
[17]Ibid., III.ii.18.
[18]Ibid., III.ii.18–19; cf. III.ii.14.

our hope [on God's promise], paying no regard to our works, to seek any help from them" in regards to the basis of salvation. That was not to say, however, that the believer should disregard works when considering the question of whether one has this salvation established on the basis of Christ's righteousness alone.[19] Assurance, in this sense — having a certain basis of salvation — is inherent in true faith.

Calvin taught that while it was theologically necessary to distinguish between justification and sanctification, they were never separable in the true believer's experience.[20] This inseparability of justification from sanctification in Calvin may go some way to explaining a certain amount of confusion regarding Calvin's position on assurance. Calvin has often been taken as affirming that saving faith necessarily included assurance, with the implication being that the two were almost identical.[21] Yet many statements of Calvin (some quoted in this section)

---

[19]Calvin, *Institutes*, III.xiii.4; cf. xiv.18; Lynn Baird Tipson, Jr., "The Development of a Puritan Understanding of Conversion," (Ph.D. diss., Yale University, 1972) 102–104, concluding that "Calvin very cautiously accepted the confirmatory evidence of good *Works* while insisting that true faith was its own assurance."

[20]Calvin, *Institutes*, III.xxiv.1.

[21]This posited identification in Calvin, and their obvious separation in later Reformed thought, has, along with the related issue of covenant, been the moving force behind the idea that Calvin's heirs in England in the century following his death radically altered his theology. E.g., George Fisher, *History of Christian Doctrine* (Edinburgh, 1896) 274, 299. Perry Miller, in what amounts to an extreme form of this understanding of assurance in Calvin, represented him as even denying that people should attempt to look into the matter of their own salvation at all. Yet he did so by quoting a passage from Calvin in which he was reprimanding the desire to search the hidden will of God. (See Perry Miller, "The Marrow of Puritan Divinity," *Publications of the Colonial Society of Massachusetts*, vol. XXXII [1937], 252.) He then went on to suggest that the anxiety arising from this uncertainty was deliberately exploited by the following generations of Reformed theologians. To do so, Miller suggested that they constructed covenant theology with mutual obligations, which both God and the believer were bound to respect. Ingenious as this reading was, it was clearly a misreading not merely of covenant theology (as has been shown in Chapter 5) but also of Calvin on assurance. In his 1956 collection of some of his previously published articles (*Errand into the Wilderness*, [Cambridge, Massachusetts, 1956]) Miller included "Marrow" unchanged and mentioned in his introduction to it his indebtedness to Fisher and A. C. McGiffert for noting the modification in Calvinism brought about by the advent of the covenant idea (48).

Many writers followed Miller, et al., in positing this substantial modification in Reformed theology. Miller has been specifically criticized for exaggerating the difference between Calvin and the later Puritans by his misunderstanding of Calvin by Ian Breward (Breward, *The Work of William Perkins* [Appleford, Abingdon, Berkshire, 1970] 92-93). The most influential work recently to equate saving faith and assurance in Calvin has been R. T. Kendall, *Calvin and English Calvinism to 1649* (Oxford, 1979) 13-28, 196. Kendall presented some idiosyncratic views (e.g., Calvin believed the "atonement" essentially occurred in Christ's intercession after his ascension, rather than on the cross [16], therefore the idea of a limited atonement as classically stated was not held by Calvin.) Such suggestions stirred a large number of critical responses, most of which have been in the theological journals (unfortunately for historians, who, therefore, have tended to rely on Kendall uncritically, e.g. Lake, 322 (n. 217) 329, [for which G. F. Nuttall criticized Lake in his review of Lake's book, in *Heythrop Journal*, vol. XXVI/1 (Jan. 1985): 95] On the other hand, the contemporary master of the history of theology, Jaroslav Pelikan, has recently referred to Perry Miller as "the leading scholar of Puritan thought" [Pelikan, *Reformation of Church and Dogma* (1300-1700) (Chicago, 1984) 372]). One of the best summaries of criticisms of Kendall's thesis, based on a much more careful look at Calvin, was by Roger Nicole, "John Calvin's View of the Extent of the Atonement," *Westminister Theological Journal*, vol. XLVII (1985): 197-225; cf. Paul Helm, *Calvin and the Calvinists* (Edinburgh, 1982). Kendall also suggested that Calvin could allow Christ alone as the ground of assurance because of the universal reference of Christ's death, and that subsequent Reformed theologians had to find other grounds as they limited the effect of Christ's death (32). Yet even if Kendall's treatment of Calvin here were taken as accurate and the inferences about assurance to follow (which is questionable) such a limited intercession then in Calvin would have left him with essentially similar pastoral problems to the ones had by those that followed him. Kendall's main fault in this study, however, is the presentation of Calvin's views exclusively in dialogue with those of his Reformed followers without taking sufficient cognizance of their original context (both textually and historically). Most importantly, there is no significant mention of the Roman Catholic doctrine against which Calvin's presentation of the gospel is made. Therefore, statements about "assurance" are set in the context of a contrast with later statements by Reformed divines in a very flat way, when their respective contexts no doubt helped to shape the ambiguities and assertions of all of their expressions on assurance. It is as if Calvin's dialogue has been kept from a conversation where the partner has been replaced and the topics changed. The most persuasive and thorough treatment of Calvin on faith and assurance is found in Joel R. Beeke, "Personal Assurance of Faith: English Puritanism and the Dutch 'Nadere Reformatie'" From Westminster to Alexander Comrie (1640-1760)" (Ph. D. diss., Westminster Theological Seminary, 1988) 44-78.

show the fallacy of a simple identification of *fides* and *fiducia* in Calvin.[22] Thus while Calvin could be read as including assurance in initial, saving faith only by controverting other clear statements of his, he may more satisfactorily be read as affirming assurance as part of the Christian's normal, life–long experience of saving faith. In such a way, and only in such a way, does assurance become an experience of all Christians—though not at all times—gratuitous and yet clearly related to sanctification.

In 1539 Calvin prayed to God, remembering the situation before the Reformation, a situation in which "that confident hope of salvation, which is both enjoined by thy Word and founded upon it, had almost vanished. Indeed it was received as a kind of oracle; it was foolish arrogance, and, as they said, presumption, for any one to trust in thy goodness and the righteousness of thy Son, and entertain a sure and unfaltering hope of salvation."[23] In Calvin's teaching and preaching, the sudden acquisition of certain salvation—what Max Weber has referred to as the "powerful feeling of light–hearted assurance, in which the tremendous pressure of their sense of sin is released, apparently breaks over them with elemental force"[24]—would have likely been the experience of his previously Roman Catholic hearers as they came into the Protestant evangelical gospel, being taught for the first time that their justification was not dependent in any sense upon their sanctification and that assurance was more available than most of them had previously imagined. The simple perseverance in abstaining from Roman practices and attending Protestant worship became an act of and an evidence of true faith. With such polemic dominating "Calvin's whole development" of faith, according to Wendel, it is only natural that he should stress the primacy of the work of Christ.[25]

---

[22]In Calvin, *Institutes*, III.xiii.5.

[23]John Calvin, "Reply to Sadolet" [1539], trans. J. K. S. Reid, *Calvin: Theological Treatises* (London, 1954) 247. "The *Institutio* was addressed to men suffering under the pastoral cruelty of the mediaeval church" (T. H. L. Parker, *John Calvin: A Biography* [London, 1975], 36).

[24]Max Weber, *The Protestant Ethic and the Spirit of Capitalism*, trans. Talcott Parsons (London, 1930) 101.

[25]Francois Wendel, *Calvin: Origins and Development of His Religious Thought*, trans. Philip Mariet (London, 1963) 262.

Even among those inwardly embracing the promises of God,[26] Calvin clearly spoke of "degrees of assurance" saying that they were "certainly well known in the faith."[27] Calvin encouraged his hearers, in order to get this "assurance of the kingdom of heaven," to look to the "pledge" that God had given believers "in the death and passion of our Lorde Jesus Christ."[28] "Christ...is the mirror wherein we must... contemplate our own election."[29] Yet Calvin also taught that though any assurance of salvation based on one's own righteousness was impossible,[30] "we do not forbid him from undergirding and strengthening this faith by signs of the divine benevolence toward him."[31] Believers should consider their "experience"[32] as a "confirmation of our fayth."[33] Though never saving, a righteous life was essential to "ratify"[34] the covenant God made with believers. Finally, realizing the problems of hypocrisy,[35] Calvin also stressed the need for the witness of the Holy Spirit as the "seale of our adoption."[36] Therefore he wrote:

---

[26]Calvin, Institutes, III.ii.16; cf. xxiv.4.

[27]John Calvin, Sermons on 2 Samuel, trans. Douglas Kelly (Edinburgh, 1992) 199-201; cf. John Calvin, "Catechism of the Church of Geneva," [1545], trans. Reid, 104.

[28]John Calvin, The Sermons of M. John Calvin upon the Fifth Booke of Moses Called Deuteronomie, trans. Arthur Golding (London, 1583) 28.b.40; cf. 913.a.10; Calvin, Institutes, III.xxiv.5.

[29]Calvin, Institutes, III.xxiv.5; cf. III.xvii.10; III.xvi.1; Calvin, Deuteronomie, 532.a.10.

[30]Cf. Calvin, Institutes, III.xvii.5; cf. xiii.3; xiv.20.

[31]Ibid., III.xiv.18; cf. 19-20; Galatians, 121. William K. B. Stoever has maintained that this is the basis for the practical syllogism in Calvin (Stoever, 'A Faire and Easie Way to Heaven': Covenant Theology and Antinomianism in Early Massachusetts, [Middletown, Connecticut, 1978], 223, n. 16).

[32]Calvin, 2 Samuel, 201.

[33]Calvin, Deuteronomie, 240.b.10; Calvin, Institutes, III.viii.1; Cf. Calvin, A Commentary on the Harmony of the Gospels, trans. T. H. L. Parker (Edinburgh, 1972) II.194.

[34]Calvin, Deuteronomie, 316.b.50; cf. 326.b.50; 554.b.50; 915.b.30-60; Institutes, III.vi.1; III.xvi.1; John Calvin, Commentaries on the Catholic Epistles, trans. John Owen, [Edinburgh, 1855], 376-378.

[35]Calvin, Institutes, III.xvii.5.

[36]Calvin, Deuteronomie, 913.b.60; cf. 316.b.50-317.a.10, 915.a.60; Galatians, 121; Institutes, III.ii.24.

Every one of us must have an eie to himself, so as the gospel be not preached in vain nor we beare the bare name of Christians, without shewing the effect of it in our deedes. For until our adoption be sealed by the holy Ghost, let us not thinke that it availeth us any whit to have herd the word of God....But when we have once a warrant in our hearts, that his promises belong unto us, & are behighted unto us, by reason that we receive them with true obedience, & sticke to our Lord Jesus Christ, suffering him to governe us: that is a sure seale of God's chosing of us, so as we not onely have the outwarde apparance of it before men, but also the truth of it before our God.[37]

Calvin taught that subjective assurance was distinct from saving faith and came not through simply reflecting on one's own process of believing, but through looking to Christ as the sole basis of salvation, leading a Christian life, and acknowledging the direct witness of the Holy Spirit in the believer's heart.[38]

The English Reformers[39]

This same tripartite basis of assurance seemed to be typical of the English reformers' presentation of assurance. William Tyndale,[40] John

---

[37]Calvin, *Deuteronomie*, 440.a.30.

[38]Breward has mistakenly portrayed Calvin as only presenting looking to Christ (though through church, word and sacraments) as the avenue of assurance (Breward, 45). Therefore, the later prominence of assurance among the Puritans Breward portrays as coming from Perkins.

[39]For a brief sketch of assurance in the first century of English Protestantism, see Breward (93–99); and Tipson (76–78, 139–142, 180–183, 187–188).

[40]William Tyndale, *Parable of the Wicked Mammon*, reprinted in *Doctrinal Treatises*, ed. Henry Walter (Cambridge, 1848) 89 [Christ], 101; cf. 113; Tyndale, *Exposition of the First Epistle of St. John* (1531) reprinted in *Expositions and Notes*, ed. Henry Walter (Cambridge, 1849) 186, 207 [*Spirit and Works*]. Kendall ignores Tyndale's exhortations to look to Christ for assurance, presenting him as basing assurance merely on obedience to the law (Kendall, 42–43). In the differences Kendall presents between Tyndale, Bradford and Richard Greenham, he might have noticed that his quotations are taken largely from different sources for each (respectively, polemical theology, personal writings, and sermons).

Bradford, Thomas Becon,[41] John Jewel[42], and William Fulke[43] all presented essentially this picture of assurance. In most of the writings of the English reformers, the doctrine of assurance had been important primarily in anti-Roman apologetics. Bradford's writings are typical of the period in that, as in Calvin, faith and assurance seem to be at points identified[44] and at other points distinguished.[45] Yet it was in his public utterances that Bradford seemed to unite both senses of assurance polemically, in order to clear the field of a Roman understanding of the gospel. In his private writings he distinguished pastorally between assurance of Christ's sufficiency alone, and assurance of one's own apprehension of that. The distinction, less clear at points (e.g., in Becon), seemed to be clarified as the church's pastoral experience of doubt in the midst of an assured gospel grew. Thus, while the English Roman Catholic Gregory Martin's assumption that his Protestant opponents were identifying faith and assurance was not entirely unfounded, William Fulke could well respond that assurance is certainly desirable, yet it was not necessary to salvation.[46] In fact, he said, perhaps overstating his case, "that a man shall never be saved, except he have such certainty of this faith, as the truth of God's promises doth deserve, none of us doth teach, none of us doth think. Fore we know our own infirmity...nevertheless we acknowledge...that these things standing upon the immoveable pillars of God's promises...ought to be most certain unto us."[47]

---

[41]Thomas Becon, "The Sick Man's Salve" in *Prayers and Other Pieces of Thomas Becon*, ed. John Ayre (Cambridge, 1844) 174, 176–178. Cf. Becon, "The Actes of Christe and Antichrist," in *Prayers*, 531.

[42]In John Jewel, *A Defense of the Apologie of the Church of England, Conteining an Answer to a certaine Booke lately set forth by M. Harding*, in The *Works* of John Jewel, ed. John Ayre (Cambridge, 1848) 3:241, 245, 247.

[43]William Fulke, *A Discoverie of the Daungerous Rocke of the Popish Church*, in *Stapelton's Fortress Overthrown...*, ed. Richard Gibbings (Cambridge, 1848) 229.

[44]E.g., "Sermon on Repentance" in *The Writings of John Bradford*, ed. Aubrey Townsend (Cambridge, 1848) 76–77; "Fear," in Writings, 344.

[45]E.g., "Meditations" prefixed to Tyndale's New Testament, in *Writings*, 252; Letter to Robert Harrington and His Wife, in *Writings*, 116–117; Letter to Mary Honywood, in *Writings*, 132; cf. 151–156.

[46]William Fulke, *A Defense of the sincere and true Translations of the holie Scriptures into the English tong* (Cambridge, 1843) 415.

[47]Fulke, *Defense*, 415–416.

William Perkins

WILLIAM PERKINS TAUGHT that assurance was the supreme case of conscience.[48] Though believers differed in the degree of assurance they enjoyed, he suggested that one could be sure by examining oneself to see if one's faith did "purifie thy heart, and cleanse thy life, and cause thee to abound in good workes."[49] Not that Perkins suggested that good works could save a person; they merely witnessed to the reality of saving faith.[50] Because, Perkins taught, election, vocation, faith, adoption, justification, sanctification, and glorification, though partially sequential, "are never separated in the salvation of any man, but like inseparable companions, goe hand in hand."[51] Evidence of any one of them could serve as well for all the others. Furthermore, Perkins set forth the internal witness of the Spirit[52] (which comes usually "by the preaching, reading, and meditation of the word of God; as also by praier, and the right use of the Sacraments" and by the "effects and fruits of the Spirit"[53]) and the witness of the believer's sanctified spirit, or conscience (evidenced by grief for sin, resolution to repent, "savouring" the things of the Spirit, and appropriate works) as the two testimonies of adoption. Even if the fruit were small, Perkins encouraged his hearers to believe. He believed it was like

> The man that is in close prison, if he sees but one little beame of the Sunne, by a small crevisse; by that very beame he hath use of the Sunne, though he seeth not the whole body of the Sunne. In like manner, though our faith, the hand of our soule, be mingled with weakness and corruption; though we feele never so little measure of God's grace in us; yea though our

---

[48]William Perkins, *The Whole Treatise of the Cases of Conscience* (Cambridge, 1606) 73–87.

[49]William Perkins, *A Clowd of Faithful Witnesses, Leading to the heavenly Canaan: Or, A Commentarie upon the 11. Chapter to the Hebrewes*, preached in Cambridge (n.l., 1609) 26.

[50]William Perkins, *A Commentarie, or, Exposition Upon the five first Chapters of the Epistle to the Galatians* (Cambridge, 1617) 186, 502.

[51]Perkins, *Cases*, 74. So too, Calvin, *Institutes*, III.xvi.1.

[52]Cf. William Perkins, "The Foundation of Christian Religion Gathered into Six Principles," reprinted in *Breward*, 155–156, 158.

[53]Perkins, *Cases*, 76.

knowledge be never so small; yet it is an argument, that the Spirit of God beginnes to worke in our harts, and that we have by Gods mercie, begunne to lay hold on Christ.[54]

Perry Miller and many following him since have used just this teaching in Perkins to suggest the striking contrast between Perkins and Calvin: "that the minutest, most microscopic element of faith in the soul is sufficient to be accounted the work of God's spirit. Man can start the labor of regeneration as soon as he begins to feel the merest desire to be saved. Instead of [Calvin's position of] conceiving of grace as some cataclysmic, soul-transforming experience, he [Perkins] whittles it down almost, but not quite, to the vanishing point."[55] Yet, compare Perkins' illustration cited here with the illustration Calvin used to make the same point:

When first even the least drop of faith is instilled in our minds, we begin to comtemplate God's face, peaceful and calm and gracious toward us.... It is like a man who, shut up in a prison into which the sun's rays shine obliquely and half obscured through a rather narrow window, is indeed deprived of the full sight of the sun. Yet his eyes dwell on its steadfast brightness, and he receives its benefits. Thus, bound with the fetters of an earthly body, however much we are shadowed on every side with great darkness, we are nevertheless illumined as much as need be for firm assurance when, to show forth his mercy, the light of God sheds even a little of its radiance.[56]

Whatever architectonic differences there may have been between Perkins's presentation of theology and Calvin's, in the substance of their teaching on assurance, there was little difference. So Perkins exhorted his doubting hearers to "beginne with faith, and in the first place, simply beleeve Gods promises; and afterward we come, by the goodnes of God, to feele and have experience of his mercie."[57]

---

[54]Ibid., 347 (cf. 78).
[55]Miller, "Marrow," 255.
[56]Calvin, *Institutes* III.ii.19.
[57]Perkins, *Cases*, 347.

Sibbes's Contemporaries[58]

REFORMED CONFESSIONAL STATEMENTS[59] from the period largely presented assurance in the same way, affirming each of the tripartite bases outlined above. So too did other of Sibbes's contemporaries, such as William Ames,[60] John Preston,[61] and William Gouge.[62] In many ways, the Westminster Assembly's teaching acts as a fine summary to the Reformed doctrine of assurance in the previous century. Instructed by long experience of anti-Roman polemics and pastoral ministry, the Assembly produced a balanced statement protecting against hypocrisy on the one hand and an uncritical identification of saving faith with assurance on the other. Chapter XX, which dealt with assurance, contained four articles. In the first, the possibility of assurance was set forth, though clearly distinguished from the vain deceits of hypocrites. In the second, the foundation of this assurance was said to be the "divine truth of the promises of salvation" and the inward evidence of "the testimony of the Spirit of adoption witnessing with our spirits that we are the children of God." In the third, this assurance was distinguished from the "essence of faith," and yet, since it was attainable, "it is the duty of everyone to give all diligence to make his calling and election sure; that thereby his heart may be enlarged in

---

[58]For the best survey of Sibbes's Reformed contemporaries on assurance of faith, see John von Rohr, *The Covenant of Grace in Puritan Thought* (Atlanta GA, 1986) 155–191. The importance of the issue in contemporary debates is shown throughout Nicholas Tyacke's *Anti-Calvinists: The Rise of English Arminianism, c. 1590–1640* (Oxford, 1987).

[59]"The Lambeth Articles", in Philip Schaff, ed., *The Creeds of Christendom with a History and Critical Notes*, 6th ed. (New York, 1931) 3:524; cf. H. C. Porter, *Reformation and Reaction in Tudor Cambridge* [Cambridge, 1958], 335–336, 365–371); "The Irish Articles of Religion", in Schaff, 3:534; Fifth Head, Article V, "Canons of the Synod of Dort", in Schaff, 3:593.

[60]William Ames, *The Marrow of Theology*, 3rd ed., trans. John Dykstra Eusden (Durham, North Carolina, 1968) 81–83, 148, 163, 167, 223–224, 245, 248–249; cf. Von Rohr, 65.

[61]John Preston, *The Breast-Plate of Faith and Love* (London, 1630) pt. i. 38–39, 110, 112–114, 164–165, 242, pt. iii. 146–147; Thomas Goodwin, "To the Reader," in John Preston, *Life Eternall* (London, 1631).

[62]William Gouge, *A Learned and Very Useful Commentary on the Whole Epistle to the Hebrews* (London, 1655) pt. i.161; cf. pt. iii.61–62; pt. vi.75, 80; pt. x.131.

peace and joy in the Holy Ghost, in love and thankfulness to God, and in strength and cheerfulness in the duties of obedience, the proper fruits of assurance: so far is it from inclining men to looseness." In the final article, the shaking, diminishing, and intermitting of assurance in the experience of believers was clearly allowed.

Sibbes Himself

Definition. U. Milo Kaufman wrote, "It was Christian assurance, of course, about which Sibbes spoke with such widely conceded grace and authority."[63] Max Weber characterized the Reformed call to assurance as "an absolute duty to consider oneself chosen, and to combat all doubts misunderstanding as temptations of the devils, since lack of self-confidence is the result of insufficient faith, hence of imperfect grace."[64] Yet Weber's characterization is an inaccurate representation of Sibbes and of the tradition he represents. That Christians could and should be assured of their faith, Sibbes took as axiomatic, given the gospel he espoused.[65] This persuasion of God's love involved a "double act of faith."[66] First there was "an act whereby the soul relies upon God as reconciled in Christ, and relies upon Christ as given of God, and

---

[63]U. Milo Kaufmann, *The Pilgrim's Progress and Traditions in Puritan Meditation* (New Haven, Connecticut, 1966) 146. Kendall concluded that Sibbes was unable to espouse lucidly a doctrine of full assurance because he did not make it clear at what point one "consciously graduates from the Spirit of bondage to the Spirit of adoption." But this sounds more like the nineteenth-century revivalistic demand to know the moment of one's conversion in order to be sure of it (Kendall, 106; cf. Tipson, 1–12). Kendall did not suggest that Calvin had offered full assurance because conversion had been dramatic, but rather the reverse (note criticisms of this reading of Calvin in the section on Perkins above).

[64]Weber, 111.

[65] "A Learned Commentary or Exposition Upon The first Chapter of the Second Epistle of S. Paul to the Corinthians," in *Works*, 3:466; cf. "Bowels Opened," in *Works*, 2:47.

[66] "A Learned Commentary or Exposition Upon The first Chapter of the Second Epistle of S. Paul to the Corinthians," in *Works*, 3:467; cf. "Yea and Amen; or, Precious Promises," in *Works*, 4:142; "Salvation Applied," in *Works*, 5:393; "Faith Triumphant," in *Works*, 7:430.

relies upon the promise."[67] This was the gift of saving faith every
Christian had. Also, "there is a reflect act, wherby, knowing we do
thus, we have assurance." Yet this second act was not always done by
all Christians. "We first by faith apply ourselves to God, and then
apply God to us, to be ours; the first is the conflicting exercise of faith,
the last is the triumph of faith; therefore faith properly is not
assurance."[68] Saving faith and assurance were not to be confused (as the
Roman Catholics had taken the Protestants to do). "Some think they
have no faith at all, because they have no full assurance" but they were
mistaken.[69] Furthermore, Sibbes readily admitted that there were
"carnal men" who were presumptous, who "would have heaven, if
they might have it with their lusts."[70] In the hour of trial, however,
when these needed true comfort, Sibbes said, their hypocrisy would be
revealed by their lack of assurance.[71]

*The Witness of the Holy Spirit and the Answer of the Believer's
Spirit.* Sibbes taught that one did not get such assurance through
merit,[72] nor through considering election[73] nor for whom particularly
Christ died.[74] Fundamentally, "The Holy Ghost must ascertain this."[75]

---

[67]A Learned Commentary or Exposition Upon The first Chapter of the
Second Epistle of S. Paul to the Corinthians," in *Works*, 3:467.

[68]"The Soul's Conflict with Itself," in *Works*, 1:266; cf. "Yea and Amen; or,
Precious Promises," in *Works*, 4:142.

[69]"The Bruised Reed and Smoking Flax," in *Works*, 1:62; cf. Von Rohr, 65–68.

[70]"Salvation Applied," in *Works*, 5:391; cf. "The Demand of a Good
Conscience," in *Works*, 7:483; "A Learned Commentary or Exposition Upon The
first Chapter of the Second Epistle of S. Paul to the Corinthians," in *Works*, 3:454,
458, 464, 469; "The Bride's Longing," in *Works*, 6:545.

[71]"A Learned Commentary or Exposition Upon The first Chapter of the
Second Epistle of S. Paul to the Corinthians," in *Works*, 3:458.

[72]"The Excellency of the Gospel above the Law," in *Works*, 4:296–297.

[73]"A Learned Commentary or Exposition Upon The first Chapter of the
Second Epistle of S. Paul to the Corinthians," in *Works*, 3:156; "A Glance of
Heaven; or, Precious Taste of a Glorious Feast," in *Works*, 4:182; "A Glimpse of
Glory," in *Works*, 7:496; Calvin, *Institutes*, III.xxi.1.

[74]"Angels' Acclamations," in *Works*, 6:354; "A Glance of Heaven; or,
Precious Taste of a Glorious Feast," in *Works*, 4:182.

[75]"Angels' Acclamations," in *Works*, 6:352; cf. "The Excellency of the Gospel
above the Law," in *Works*, 4:220, 296; "Description of Christ," in *Works*, 1:21–2;
"The Faithful Covenanter," in *Works*, 6:9; "The Soul's Conflict with Itself," in

True, there was the assurance that was the simple reflection of the man's own spiritual understanding.[76] This was not, however, the work of the Spirit. The Spirit's special sealing would come in times of great temptation and trial when "the soul is so carried and hurried that it cannot reflect upon itself, nor know what is in itself without much ado."[77] Nevertheless, even this seal had to be defined, and Sibbes did so by noting four works of the Spirit in the soul: 1) his "secret voice . . . to the soul, that we are 'the sons of God;' " 2) his granting believers boldness to approach God; 3) sanctification; 4) peace of conscience and joy in the Holy Ghost.[78] The testimony of the Holy Spirit was answered, Sibbes taught, in the believer's spirit by "evidences of grace stamped upon his heart."[79] Such heart-evidences included "discontent with our present ill estate,"[80] the simple belief in God as one is drawn to him,[81] finding comfort in the promises of God,[82] familiarity with God and consequent boldness to approach him as Father,[83] desires to be

---

Works, 1:269; "A Learned Commentary or Exposition Upon The first Chapter of the Second Epistle of S. Paul to the Corinthians," in *Works*, 3:455–456.

[76]A Learned Commentary or Exposition Upon The first Chapter of the Second Epistle of S. Paul to the Corinthians," in *Works*, 3:455–456.

[77]Ibid., 456.

[78]A Learned Commentary or Exposition Upon The first Chapter of the Second Epistle of S. Paul to the Corinthians," in *Works*, 3:456; cf. "The Soul's Conflict with Itself," in *Works*, 1:288–289.

[79]A Learned Commentary or Exposition Upon The first Chapter of the Second Epistle of S. Paul to the Corinthians," in *Works*, 3:445; cf. 454, 457; "The Demand of a Good Conscience," in *Works*, 7:483; "The Danger of Backsliding," in *Works*, 7:413; "Divine Meditations and Holy Contemplations," in *Works*, 7:189, 223; "A Glance of Heaven; or, Precious Taste of a Glorious Feast," in *Works*, 4:182; "The Bruised Reed and Smoking Flax," in *Works*, 1:69; Preston, Breast-Plate, pt. ii. 84–85.

[80]"Bowels Opened," in *Works*, 2:117; cf. "The Bruised Reed and Smoking Flax," in *Works*, 1:97.

[81]A Learned Commentary or Exposition Upon The first Chapter of the Second Epistle of S. Paul to the Corinthians," in *Works*, 3:156; "The Soul's Conflict with Itself," in *Works*, 1:198.

[82]A Learned Commentary or Exposition Upon The first Chapter of the Second Epistle of S. Paul to the Corinthians," in *Works*, 3:452; "Bowels Opened," in *Works*, 2:176.

[83]A Learned Commentary or Exposition Upon The first Chapter of the Second Epistle of S. Paul to the Corinthians," in *Works*, 3:456–457; cf. "The Christian Work," in *Works*, 5:25; "The Faithful Covenanter," in *Works*, 6:12–13;

transformed more and more like Christ,[84] both waiting[85] and zeal,[86] comfortable thoughts of death,[87] and willingness to die for God's truth.[88] Even the desire for assurance, said Sibbes, was a ground of it.[89] In times of unusual trial, an extraordinary seal of assurance was given—"the joy of the Holy Ghost and peace of conscience."[90] These were worked by the Spirit in the soul of the believer to give assurance, but neither were the universal experience of believers. Such extraordinary seals God gave, "even as parents, smile upon their children when they need it most."[91] After discoursing of seals and hypocrisy, Sibbes turned to his hearers and with an arresting change of expression to the second person, asked them, "Did you ever feel the joy of the Spirit in holy duties, after inward striving against your lusts, and getting ground of them? This is a certain sign that God hath sealed you."[92]

The Evidence of Good Works. Sanctification, too, Sibbes presented as an evidence of salvation.[93] In one sense, every description of a Christian by Sibbes in a sermon was an invitation to his hearers to evaluate

---

"The Knot of Prayer Loosed," in *Works*, 7:247; "Christ's Sufferings for Man's Sin," in *Works*, 1:364; "The Excellency of the Gospel above the Law," in *Works*, 4:231-233; "Recommendation," Henry Scudder, *A Key of Heaven, The Lord's Prayer Opened* (London, 1620); rpt. in *Works*, 1:lxxxvii-lxxxix.

[84] "A Learned Commentary or Exposition Upon The first Chapter of the Second Epistle of S. Paul to the Corinthians," in *Works*, 3:453.

[85] "The Soul's Conflict with Itself," in *Works*, 1:251.

[86] "The Sword of the Wicked," in *Works*, 1:116.

[87] "A Learned Commentary or Exposition Upon The first Chapter of the Second Epistle of S. Paul to the Corinthians," in *Works*, 3:442; cf. "Yea and Amen; or, Precious Promises," in *Works*, 4:131.

[88] "The Danger of Backsliding," in *Works*, 7:411; "The Soul's Conflict with Itself," in *Works*, 1:252.

[89] "The Spouse, Her Earnest Desire After Christ," in *Works*, vol. II. 204.

[90] "A Learned Commentary or Exposition Upon The first Chapter of the Second Epistle of S. Paul to the Corinthians," in *Works*, 3:457; cf. 458-459; "The Soul's Conflict with Itself," in *Works*, 1:288-289.

[91] "A Learned Commentary or Exposition Upon The first Chapter of the Second Epistle of S. Paul to the Corinthians," in *Works*, 3:458.

[92] "Yea and Amen; or, Precious Promises," in *Works*, 4:136; cf. "A Learned Commentary or Exposition Upon The first Chapter of the Second Epistle of S. Paul to the Corinthians," in *Works*, 3:458; "Description of Christ," in *Works*, 1:22; "The Excellency of the Gospel above the Law," in *Works*, 4:222.

[93] "The Returning Backslider," in *Works*, vol. II. 255-256.

themselves, to find bases of similarity and thus hope, or difference and thus conviction.[94] He wrote:

> When two masters are parted, their servants will be known whom they serve, by following their own master. Blessed be God, in these times we enjoy both religion and the world together; but if times of suffering should approach, then it would be known whose servants we are. Consider therefore beforehand what thou wouldst do. If trouble and persecution should arise, wouldst thou stand up for Christ, and set light by liberty, riches, credit, all in comparison of him?[95]

"If Christ and the world part once, it will be known which we followed."[96] Though he was certain that works in and of themselves were worthless when considering justification, Sibbes pointed out that Paul, in his Corinthian correspondence, "glories not in his conversation and sincerity as a title, but he glories in it as an evidence that his title is good."[97] In that sense, he said, "We must all read our happiness in our holiness."[98] Yet the imperfection of sanctification in this life, and particularly one's perception of one's own sanctification, made it an uncertain evidence. As if echoing Robert Middlekauf's description of the anxiety-ridden Puritan (quoted above), Sibbes said that Christians "have so different judgments of themselves, looking sometimes at the work of grace, sometimes at the remainder of corruption, and when they look upon that, then they think they have no grace."[99] Yet this

---

[94]E.g., "A Learned Commentary or Exposition Upon The first Chapter of the Second Epistle of S. Paul to the Corinthians," in *Works*, 3:447; "The Rich Poverty; or, The Poor Man's Riches," in *Works*, 6:257; "The Difficulty of Salvation," in *Works*, 1:396.

[95]"The Danger of Backsliding," in *Works*, 7:412; cf. "The Faithful Covenanter," in *Works*, 6:14.

[96]"Bowels Opened," in *Works*, 2:26; "A Glimpse of Glory," in *Works*, 7:495.

[97]"A Learned Commentary or Exposition Upon The first Chapter of the Second Epistle of S. Paul to the Corinthians," in *Works*, 3:205.

[98]Ibid., 469; cf. 446, 478 "The Bruised Reed and Smoking Flax," in *Works*, 1:87; "Description of Christ," in *Works*, 1:14, 22; "Yea and Amen; or, Precious Promises," in *Works*, 4:145; "The Excellency of the Gospel above the Law," in *Works*, 4:221, 231; "The Faithful Covenanter," in *Works*, 6:14.

[99]"The Bruised Reed and Smoking Flax," in *Works*, 1:50.

was not, in fact, the "half-papist" teaching that Calvin had earlier lamented. The crucial difference was that Calvin's antagonists were teaching that the Christian should so doubt because of "the sight of our own unworthiness," whereas Sibbes merely taught that the Christian would so doubt because of the "remainder of corruption." The former were teaching that one should look to Christ and oneself in order to be saved; the latter that one should look to Christ and oneself in order to see if one had been saved. Whatever similarities there may have been between the two positions, they were outweighed by their differences. Sibbes taught that, however little in measure, if the sanctification in the believer's life were authentic, it could provide much comfort.[100] As he said, echoing the illustration used before by Perkins and Calvin:

> A spark of fire is but little, yet it is fire as well as the whole element of fire; and a drop of water, it is water as well as the whole ocean. When a man is in a dark place, — put the case it be in a dungeon, — if he have a little light shining in to him from a little crevice, that little light discovers that the day is broke, that the sun is risen.[101]

Therefore, Sibbes encouraged believers to examine "rather the truth, than the measure of any grace."[102] Any opposition to sin was a meaningful sign of grace. "though we shall have much opposition, yet if we strive, he will help us; if we fail, he will cherish us; if we be guided by him, we shall overcome; if we overcome, we are sure to be crowned.... This very belief, that faith shall be victorious, is a means to make it so indeed."[103]

---

[100]"A Learned Commentary or Exposition Upon The first Chapter of the Second Epistle of S. Paul to the Corinthians," in *Works*, 3:465, 470.

[101]Ibid., 470–471; cf. "Bowels Opened," in *Works*, 2:117; "The Bruised Reed and Smoking Flax," in *Works*, 1:99. The use of this example by Calvin, Perkins, and Sibbes shows up the fallacy in the substantial contrast Pettit has suggested between Sibbes and "most before him," (Norman Pettit, *The Heart Prepared: Grace and Conversion in Puritan Spiritual Life* [New Haven, Connecticut, 1966], 70; cf. 73–74).

[102] "A Learned Commentary or Exposition Upon The first Chapter of the Second Epistle of S. Paul to the Corinthians," in *Works*, 3:471.

[103]"The Bruised Reed and Smoking Flax," in *Works*, 1:99, 100.

The Abuse and Use of Assurance. Sibbes realized that the awareness of salvation was not always present in the believer.[104] Whether through sin[105] or Satan,[106] through divine desertions[107] or the believers' carelessness,[108] natural tempers or spiritual maturity,[109] many reasons could account for different experiences of assurance. Contrary to what he felt was the incalculably cruel pastoral doctrine of the uncertainty of salvation—"the popish doctrine that I ought to doubt"—Sibbes taught that it was the duty of each Christian to labor for the assurance of salvation.[110] To ignore the search for assurance was tantamount to ignoring the search for salvation, not because assurance was saving, but precisely because it was assurance of the salvation one needed.[111] Therefore, Sibbes stressed the need for assurance, its benefits, and its comforts in almost every sermon.[112] One labored to gain assurance in

104 "A Learned Commentary or Exposition Upon The first Chapter of the Second Epistle of S. Paul to the Corinthians," in *Works*, 3:466–467.
105Ibid., 478; cf. "Christ is Best; or, St. Paul's Strait," in *Works*, 1:346; "Divine Meditations and Holy Contemplations," in *Works*, 7:211–2.
106"The Sword of the Wicked," in *Works*, 1:110.
107"A Learned Commentary or Exposition Upon The first Chapter of the Second Epistle of S. Paul to the Corinthians," in *Works*, 3:482; "Faith Triumphant," in *Works*, 7:430–431.
108"The Church's Riches by Christ's Poverty," in *Works*, 4:517; cf. "Two Sermons Upon the first words of Christs last Sermon, John 14.1. Being also the last Sermons of Richard Sibbs," in *Works*, 7:353; "The Soul's Conflict with Itself," in *Works*, 1:199; "Faith Triumphant," in *Works*, 7:430.
109"A Learned Commentary or Exposition Upon The first Chapter of the Second Epistle of S. Paul to the Corinthians," in *Works*, 3:467; cf. "The Church's Riches by Christ's Poverty," in *Works*, 4:510; "The Faithful Covenanter," in *Works*, 6:21.
110"A Learned Commentary or Exposition Upon The first Chapter of the Second Epistle of S. Paul to the Corinthians," in *Works*, 3:468; cf.466, 476; "Description of Christ," in *Works*, 1:23; "A Glimpse of Glory," in *Works*, 7:495; "Christ is Best; or, St. Paul's Strait," in *Works*, 1:342; "Two Sermons Upon the first words of Christs last Sermon, John 14.1. Being also the last Sermons of Richard Sibbs," in *Works*, 7:352; "The Soul's Conflict with Itself," in *Works*, 1:124. Some of Sibbes's most regular and most heated anti–Roman rhetoric comes in discussions of this pastoral issue.
111"The Returning Backslider," in *Works*, vol. II. 264.
112E.g., "Church's Visitation," in *Works*, 1:381–382; "The Danger of Backsliding," in *Works*, 7:411; "A Learned Commentary or Exposition Upon The first Chapter of the Second Epistle of S. Paul to the Corinthians," in *Works*, 3:460, 462, 466, 475; "The Sword of the Wicked," in *Works*, 1:107; Frank E. Farrell,

order "that God may have more honour, and that we may have more comfort from him again, and walk more cheerfully through the troubles and temptations that are in the world."[113] For how could believers be thankful, be joyful, willingly endure trials, if not assured of the outcome?[114] To Sibbes, assurance seemed to grant the believer a kind of spiritual invulnerability.[115] He wrote:

> Oh, what should water my heart, and make it melt in obedience unto my God, but the assurance and knowledge of the virtue of this most precious blood of my Redeemer, applied to my sick soul, in the full and free remission of all my sins, and appeasing the justice of God?...What should enable my weak knees, hold up my weary hands, strengthen my fainting and enfeebled spirit in constant obedience against so many crosses and afflictions, temptations and impediments, which would stop up my way, but the hope of this precious calling unto glory and virtue? Down, then, with this false opinion and perverse doctrine, which overthroweth all the comfort of godliness, faith, and obedience to God.[116]

Finally only an assured soul, Sibbes taught, would find comfort at the hour of death, for "death, with the eternity of misery after it, who

---

"Richard Sibbes: A Study in Early Seventeenth Century English Puritanism," [Ph.D diss., Edinburgh, 1955], 221.

[113]"A Learned Commentary or Exposition Upon The first Chapter of the Second Epistle of S. Paul to the Corinthians," in *Works*, 3:468.

[114]"A Learned Commentary or Exposition Upon The first Chapter of the Second Epistle of S. Paul to the Corinthians," in *Works*, 3:483; cf. "A Glimpse of Glory," in *Works*, 7:495; "The Returning Backslider," in *Works*, vol. 2:273; "The Spouse, Her Earnest Desire After Christ," in *Works*, vol. 2:206; "The Saint's Safety in Evil Times, Manifested by St. Paul, From his Experience of God's Goodness in Greatest Distress," in *Works*, 1:330–331; "A Learned Commentary or Exposition Upon The fourth Chapter of the Second Epistle of Saint Paul to the Corinthians," in *Works*, 4:450.

[115]"The Spouse, Her Earnest Desire After Christ," in *Works*, vol. 2:207; "A Learned Commentary or Exposition Upon The first Chapter of the Second Epistle of S. Paul to the Corinthians," in *Works*, 3:91–93; "Art of Contentment," in *Works*, 5:193; "God's Inquisition," in *Works*, 6:213.

[116]"A Glimpse of Glory," in *Works*, 7:495; cf. "Christ is Best; or, St. Paul's Strait," in *Works*, 1:341; "The Returning Backslider," in *Works*, vol. 2:264.

can look it in the face, without hope of life everlasting, without assurance of a happy change after death?"[117]

Gaining Assurance. To grow assurance, Sibbes taught that one should "attend upon the ordinances of God, and use all kinds of spiritual means."[118] This included attending preaching of the word, meditating on it, reading the Bible and other good books, keeping good company, and taking care not to grieve the Holy Spirit.[119] The conscience must be heeded,[120] and the word heard must be obeyed.[121] To those attempting to regain assurance after sin—"wilful breeches in sanctification"—Sibbes taught that "Such must give a sharp sentence against themselves, and yet cast themselves upon God's mercy in Christ, as at their first conversion."[122] In situations where one was not sure of the reason for a lack of assurance, he taught that one first looked for those extraordinary and obvious signs, joy in the Holy Ghost and peace of conscience.[123] Yet, the Christian knew that when he "finds not extraordinary comfort from God's Spirit, that God's love is constant." He could, therefore, reason from God's past love to his present love.[124] The believer should be encouraged by the work of sanctification in life,

---

[117] "A Learned Commentary or Exposition Upon The first Chapter of the Second Epistle of S. Paul to the Corinthians," in *Works*, 3:483; cf. 460, 464; "The Bride's Longing," in *Works*, 6:552; "Christ is Best; or, St. Paul's Strait," in *Works*, 1:342.

[118] "A Learned Commentary or Exposition Upon The first Chapter of the Second Epistle of S. Paul to the Corinthians," in *Works*, 3:480; "Divine Meditations and Holy Contemplations," in *Works*, 7:209.

[119] "A Learned Commentary or Exposition Upon The first Chapter of the Second Epistle of S. Paul to the Corinthians," in *Works*, 3:480–481; cf. Geoffrey F. Nuttall, *The Holy Spirit in Puritan Faith and Experience* (Oxford, 1946) 23–24.

[120] "The Demand of a Good Conscience," in *Works*, 7:486.

[121] "Witness of Salvation," in *Works*, 7:383; cf. "The Excellency of the Gospel above the Law," in *Works*, 4:296–297; "Faith Triumphant," in *Works*, 7:432, 436–437; "Bowels Opened," in *Works*, 2:26; "Angels' Acclamations," in *Works*, 6:354.

[122] "The Bruised Reed and Smoking Flax," in *Works*, 1:70; cf. "The Soul's Conflict with Itself," in *Works*, 1:123–124, 234.

[123] "A Learned Commentary or Exposition Upon The first Chapter of the Second Epistle of S. Paul to the Corinthians," in *Works*, 3:459; cf. "A Glimpse of Glory," in *Works*, 7:496.

[124] "A Learned Commentary or Exposition Upon The first Chapter of the Second Epistle of S. Paul to the Corinthians," in *Works*, 3:459.

however small. "Be not discouraged, when the stamp in wax is almost out, it is current in law. Put the case the stamp of the prince be an old coin (as sometimes we see it on a king Harry groat), yet it is current money, yea, though it be a little cracked."[125] Still other times, friends "can read our evidences better than ourselves."[126]

Nevertheless Sibbes was intent on not minimizing the gratuitous nature of Christian salvation. When comfort was wanting, Sibbes said, "We must judge ourselves . . . by faith, and not by feeling; looking to the promises and word of God, and not to our present sense and apprehension."[127] Like Calvin, Sibbes had taught that even the best actions of the believer "need Christ to perfume them."[128] Relying too much on works was always a danger in the human heart. "Another cause of disquiet is, that men by a natural kind of popery seek for their comfort too much sanctification, neglecting justification, relying too much upon their own performances."[129] When corruption was so strong that one could see nothing of sanctification, the believer should remember that one's salvation did not come from assurance and that:

> God can see somewhat of his own Spirit in that confusion, but the spirit [of the believer] itself cannot. Then go to the blood of Christ! There is always comfort.... Go...to the blood of Christ, that is, if we find sin upon our consciences, if we find not peace in our consciences, nor sanctification in our hearts, go to the blood of Christ, which is shed for all those that confess their sins, and rely on him for pardon, though we find no grace; . . . before we go to Christ it is sufficient that we see nothing in ourselves, no qualification; for the graces of the Spirit they are not the condition of coming to Christ, but the promise of those that receive Christ after. Therefore go to Christ when thou

---

125Ibid., 461; cf. the list of eleven evidences on 472–475; cf. lists in the following: "Bowels Opened," in Works, 2:148, 154–155; "The Bruised Reed and Smoking Flax," in Works, 1:87; "The Returning Backslider," in Works, vol. 2:255–256; "The Rich Poverty; or, The Poor Man's Riches," in Works, 6:254–263; "Witness of Salvation," in Works, 7:380; Nuttall, Holy Spirit, 59.

126"Bowels Opened," in Works, 2:107; cf. 131; "The Soul's Conflict with Itself," in Works, 1:194.

127"Bowels Opened," in Works, 2:103.

128"The Bruised Reed and Smoking Flax," in Works, 1:50.

129"The Soul's Conflict with Itself," in Works, 1:138.

feelest neither joy of the Spirit, nor sanctification of the Spirit; go to the blood of Christ, and that will purge thee, and wash thee from all thy sins.[130]

Though "the evidence indeed to prove our faith to be a true faith, is from works, . . . the title we have is only by Christ, only by grace."[131] This was to be the ultimate basis of assurance for the Christian, because "We are more safe in his comprehending of us, than in our clasping and holding of him. As we say of the mother and the child, both hold, but the safety of the child is that the mother holds him."[132]

Conclusion

IN SUMMARY, SIBBES presented assurance as a secondary act of faith, not given to all Christians, but available depending upon the will of God and the actions of the believer.[133] Since it was possible for true Christians to doubt their salvation and for hypocrites to delude themselves, assurance of salvation was necessarily to be sought. Theologically, the assurance sought by Sibbes was typical of Protestants. It was not, as Roman polemicists necessarily saw it, a prediction so much as a diagnosis. The matter that was uncertain in Sibbes's discussions of assurance was not salvation itself, but rather merely the perception of it. While Sibbes and his friends did teach (as had their Reformed predecessors, including Calvin) that "good works" were confirming of salvation, they did not teach that such works were either present or obvious at all times to the elect or that they were present only in the elect. Sibbes affirmed what might well be called the Reformed tripartite basis of assurance – the consideration of the objective

---

130 "A Learned Commentary or Exposition Upon The first Chapter of the Second Epistle of S. Paul to the Corinthians," in *Works*, 3:464; cf. 476–477; "Bowels Opened," in *Works*, 2:157; "Divine Meditations and Holy Contemplations," in *Works*, 7:211; "The Soul's Conflict with Itself," in *Works*, 1:124, 212–213; "Witness of Salvation," in *Works*, 7:378.

131"The Faithful Covenanter," in *Works*, 6:5.

132"Bowels Opened," in *Works*, 2:184.

133See Stoever, 129–137.

work of Christ, the inner testimony of the Spirit, and the answering works of the regenerated life.[134]

Sibbes's public works were primarily pastoral, and were polemical only in a secondary sense, as were all sermons of the time. Given this, it is not surprising that there should be ambiguity in many of Sibbes's exhortations to assurance. With pastoral issues in the fore, it was not always clear whether his hearers were being exhorted to conversion or to assurance that they had been converted.[135] Yet such ambiguity is to be expected in sermons to a covenanted community composed largely of two sorts of people: those who had been committed by others, but not self-consciously converted by God (who must be exhorted to trust God themselves) and those who had experienced self-conscious conversion, but yet doubted. To both groups within the covenant, Sibbes urged the same action. Since faith is the gracious gift of God based on the work of Christ, and since faith comes by hearing the Word of God with the working of the Spirit, and since faith was strengthened by the sacrament of the table and by excercises — since faith was and came by and was strengthened by all this, Sibbes taught as the Westminster Confession would teach, and as Reformed Protestants before him taught, that assurance had essentially three grounds. Sibbes, citing 1 John 5:7-8, exhorted his hearers to look to these three for assurance: the "sweet motions of the Spirit," sanctification, and the one place where Sibbes said "there was always comfort" — "the blood of Christ."[136]

Consistent with his pastoral setting, Sibbes particularly focused on the continuing reality of doubt in the believer's life. Though this element is present in the works of all of those Reformed preachers mentioned above, it is more prominent in pastoral writings than in polemical writings. The life of the believer is, Sibbes stressed, always

---

[134]Cf. Heinrich Heppe, *Reformed Dogmatics Set Out and Illustrated from the Sources*, trans. G. T. Thomson (London, 1950) 585-589.

[135]"The Saint's Hiding-Place in the Evil Day," in *Works*, 1:415-417; "Angels' Acclamations," in *Works*, 6:353-4; "Divine Meditations and Holy Contemplations," in *Works*, 7:187; "The Faithful Covenanter," in *Works*, 6:8; "The Returning Backslider," in *Works*, 2:264.

[136] "A Learned Commentary or Exposition Upon The first Chapter of the Second Epistle of S. Paul to the Corinthians," in *Works*, 3:464; cf. "Witness of Salvation," in *Works*, 7:376-377; John Downame, *The Chrisitan Warfare* (London, 1608) 231, 277-278; similar passage in Theodore Beza, *A Brief and Pithy Sum of the Christian Faith*, trans. Robert Fyll (London, 1585) 71-72.

evidence of his spiritual state, but not always discernable. At times of particular need, the Spirit witnessed internally to the troubled believer. Yet, throughout his preaching, Sibbes was always clear that the objective work of Christ was the sole basis not merely of salvation in abstraction, but of one's own participation in it. For the certainty of this, Sibbes taught that the conscience played a pivotal role.

Conscience

THE NATURAL FACULTIES mentioned in the previous chapter were not, Sibbes clearly taught, all that composed a person. God had "in great mercy" left the conscience.[137] While the importance of conscience has not gone unnoticed in the secondary literature on the seventeenth century, "conscience" tends to occur in connection with the words "liberty" and "freedom," whereas in Sibbes and his contemporaries, as has been shown above, it occurs more typically in conjunction with the concepts of "obligation" and "judgment." Where the twentieth-century writer has often seen the ground of a civil liberty to come, the seventeenth-century divine saw a remnant of God's law. What is one to make of this difference? Is this a misunderstanding concerning the conscience by later more secular writers, or was Sibbes's teaching on conscience in fact allowing for, even encouraging, social implications that lay unforeseen to him? Furthermore, did Sibbes present conscience as an unerring guide to eternity, or is this the understanding of a more individualistic age cast backwards? What role was conscience seen to play?[138]

Sibbes taught that God had left the conscience in man as his "vicar; a little god in us to do his office, to call upon us, direct us, check and condemn us."[139] This quotation well summarizes the different roles of the conscience, according to Sibbes, in conviction and conversion, in sanctification and guidance. Throughout his sermons, Sibbes spoke of

---

137 "A Learned Commentary or Exposition Upon The first Chapter of the Second Epistle of S. Paul to the Corinthians," in *Works*, 3:209.

138George Yule, "Theological Developments in Elizabethan Puritanism," *Journal of Religious History*, vol. I (1960): 23.

139"Bowels Opened," in *Works*, 2:62; cf. "St. Paul's Challenge," in *Works*, 7:395; "The Demand of a Good Conscience," in *Works*, 7:486; "The Soul's Conflict with Itself," in *Works*, 1:148, 211.

the conscience in such exalted terms, as God's "vicegerent and deputy in us,"[140] God's judge, his throne in the soul, his "hall, as it were, wherein he keeps his first judgment, wherein he keeps his assizes."[141] To his lawyer listeners at Gray's Inn, he expanded Pauline legal imagery of the conscience, speaking of it as the informer, accuser, witness, judge, and executioner[142] together in the under court of God's justice, the lower "court of conscience."[143] The conscience was essentially "to take God's part" in us.[144] It was a "chaplain in ordinary, a domestical divine" within the soul.[145] Drawing from the Greek and Latin etymologies of the words for conscience, Sibbes taught that conscience is a special universal "knowledge together with God," especially a "knowledge of the heart with God" put in the soul by God.[146] Even the illiterate could "read" this "book,"[147] which was "written in their hearts."[148]

[140]"Judgment's Reason," in Works, 4:83; "A Learned Commentary or Exposition Upon The first Chapter of the Second Epistle of S. Paul to the Corinthians," in Works, 3:209.

[141]"Bowels Opened," in Works, 2:107–108; "The Bruised Reed and Smoking Flax," in Works, 1:78, 84; "A Learned Commentary or Exposition Upon The first Chapter of the Second Epistle of S. Paul to the Corinthians," in Works, 3:211.

[142] "A Learned Commentary or Exposition Upon The first Chapter of the Second Epistle of S. Paul to the Corinthians," in Works, 3:210; "The Soul's Conflict with Itself," in Works, 1:144–145; Cf. "Bowels Opened," in Works, 2:94.

[143]"Judgment's Reason," in Works, 4:85, 91–92; "The Soul's Conflict with Itself," in Works, 1:144–145; "A Learned Commentary or Exposition Upon The first Chapter of the Second Epistle of S. Paul to the Corinthians," in Works, 3:210. Cf. Calvin, Institutes, III.xiii.3; III.xix.15; IV.x.3.

[144]"The Soul's Conflict with Itself," in Works, 1:175; cf. "A Fountain Sealed," in Works, 5:419.

[145]"A Learned Commentary or Exposition Upon The first Chapter of the Second Epistle of S. Paul to the Corinthians," in Works, 3:212.

[146]"Yea and Amen; or, Precious Promises," in Works, 4:118; "A Learned Commentary or Exposition Upon The first Chapter of the Second Epistle of S. Paul to the Corinthians," in Works, 3:208–210; Calvin, Institutes, III.xix.15; cf. IV.x.3); Gouge, pt. xiii.155 (Gouge's treatment of the conscience in this section is a model of the Ramist practise of understanding by division.)

[147]"The Demand of a Good Conscience," in Works, 7:489–490.

[148]"A Learned Commentary or Exposition Upon The first Chapter of the Second Epistle of S. Paul to the Corinthians," in Works, 3:210.

Conviction and Conversion

SIBBES TAUGHT THAT the primary way that the conscience took God's part in the soul was "to witness against us for our sins," (reflecting Paul's words in Romans 2:15).[149] Those who live in sins against conscience abuse their Christian liberty,[150] weaken their faith[151] and their affection to goodness, and decay their love to God and their sense of God's favor.[152] They are stopped from going boldly to God because they stop the mouth of their conscience.[153] Such people Sibbes described as "dead to good actions"[154] and "worse than Sodomites."[155] They renounce their baptism, feed their corruptions,[156] deaden their spirits[157] and exceedingly waste their comfort.[158] Furthermore, they give evidence that Christ is not teaching them by his Spirit.[159] They must not think that they love God,[160] that His Spirit is in them, that they have anything to do with Christ, that God is merciful,[161] or that they will go to heaven.[162] Though they are under the livery of Christ, they serve the

---

[149]"Bowels Opened," in *Works*, 2:111; cf. "Angels' Acclamations," in *Works*, 6:333; "Christ's Sufferings for Man's Sin," in *Works*, 1:360; "Art of Contentment," in *Works*, 5:183; John Calvin, *Commentary on Romans*, trans. R. Mackenzie (Edinburgh, 1960) 49; *Institutes*, III.xix.15; IV.x.3; Heinrich Bullinger, too, in his *Decades* (Cambridge, 1849) 1:194–195.

[150]"Divine Meditations and Holy Contemplations," in *Works*, 7:194.

[151]"The Excellency of the Gospel above the Law," in *Works*, 4:254; "The Knot of Prayer Loosed," in *Works*, 7:242.

[152]"The Privileges of the Faithful," in *Works*, 5:283.

[153]"The Demand of a Good Conscience," in *Works*, 7:488; "The Excellency of the Gospel above the Law," in *Works*, 4:254; "The Knot of Prayer Loosed," in *Works*, 7:242.

[154]"The Excellency of the Gospel above the Law," in *Works*, 4:237.

[155]"The Ungodly's Misery," in *Works*, 1:389.

[156]"The Demand of a Good Conscience," in *Works*, 7:487.

[157]"The Knot of Prayer Loosed," in *Works*, 7:242.

[158]"Divine Meditations and Holy Contemplations," in *Works*, 7:194.

[159]"Description of Christ," in *Works*, 1:23.

[160]"The Privileges of the Faithful," in *Works*, 5:281.

[161]"Description of Christ," in *Works*, 1:23.

[162]"Divine Meditations and Holy Contemplations," in *Works*, 7:189; "The Saint's Safety in Evil Times, Manifested by St. Paul, From his Experience of God's Goodness in Greatest Distress," in *Works*, 1:328.

enemy of Christ, the devil,[163] and therefore can look for nothing but vengeance from God.[164] Such "a galled conscience cannot endure God's presence"[165] because it gives us only fear and terror, especially of God.[166] "Conscience saith, If you do this, ye shall die."[167]

Instead of being disregarded, the conviction of conscience was to be heeded. Sibbes taught that there were two kinds of conviction by the conscience: natural and spiritual.[168] The first, common, natural conviction of conscience, is weak; it does not change a man, but merely torments him.[169] All non–Christians experienced this natural conviction of the Spirit.[170] "A wicked man that hath a bad conscience, is imprisoned in his own heart. Though he have never such liberty, though he be a monarch, a bad conscience imprisons him at home, he is in fetters, his thoughts make him afraid of thunder, afraid of everything, afraid of himself; and though there be nobody else to awe him, yet his conscience awes him."[171] With pathetic imagery, Sibbes described this fear of conscience in the unregenerate. The unregenerate man "cannot go home to his own conscience"[172] because he is afraid of his own conscience; they are "strangers at home, afraid of nothing more than

---

[163]"Angels' Acclamations," in *Works*, 6:343; "The Demand of a Good Conscience," in *Works*, 7:487.

[164]"The Demand of a Good Conscience," in *Works*, 7:490–491.

[165]"A Breathing after God," in *Works*, 2:223.

[166]"The Soul's Conflict with Itself," in *Works*, 1:222; "The Rich Poverty; or, The Poor Man's Riches," in *Works*, 6:261.

[167]"Fountain Opened," in *Works*, 5:523.

[168]"Divine Meditations and Holy Contemplations," in *Works*, 7:210.

[169]"The Soul's Conflict with Itself," in *Works*, 1:152; cf. "A Learned Commentary or Exposition Upon The first Chapter of the Second Epistle of S. Paul to the Corinthians," in *Works*, 3:90–91, 209; "The Saint's Safety in Evil Times," in *Works*, 1:298–299; Calvin, *Institutes*, III.xiii.3.

[170] "A Learned Commentary or Exposition Upon The first Chapter of the Second Epistle of S. Paul to the Corinthians," in *Works*, 3:222, 208; cf. "The Excellency of the Gospel above the Law," in *Works*, 4:278; "Angels' Acclamations," in *Works*, 6:348; "The Soul's Conflict with Itself," in *Works*, 1:153; Calvin, *Institutes*, IV.xx.16; *Romans*, 37, 48.

[171] "A Learned Commentary or Exposition Upon The first Chapter of the Second Epistle of S. Paul to the Corinthians," in *Works*, 3:218.

[172]"The Saint's Hiding-Place in the Evil Day," in *Works*, 1:406.

themselves."[173] Sibbes illustrated the tortures of a guilty conscience by the example of Charles IX "who at night, when conscience hath the fittest time to work, a man being retired, then he would have his singing boys, after he had betrayed them in that horrible massacre, after which he never had peace and quiet."[174] One of Sibbes's most often repeated ideas is that the conscience will inevitably fulfill its role as judge, whether in this life or the next.[175] He wrote, "The more their conscience is silenced and violenced in this world, the more vocal it shall be at the hour of death, and the day of judgment."[176] Therefore Sibbes encouraged his hearers to give heed to their consciences now, since God may make their bed their grave.[177] They should befriend their conscience presently, Sibbes urged his hearers, because "Conscience...is either the greatest friend or the greatest enemy in the world."[178]

---

[173]"The Soul's Conflict with Itself," in *Works*, 1:145, 228; cf. "A Learned Commentary or Exposition Upon The first Chapter of the Second Epistle of S. Paul to the Corinthians," in *Works*, 3:224.

[174] "A Learned Commentary or Exposition Upon The first Chapter of the Second Epistle of S. Paul to the Corinthians," in *Works*, 3:226.

[175]"Bowels Opened," in *Works*, 2:111; "The Bruised Reed and Smoking Flax," in *Works*, 1:97; "Christ is Best; or, St. Paul's Strait," in *Works*, 1:342; "The Excellency of the Gospel above the Law," in *Works*, 4:254; "The Soul's Conflict with Itself," in *Works*, 1:150; "A Learned Commentary or Exposition Upon The first Chapter of the Second Epistle of S. Paul to the Corinthians," in *Works*, 3:211. Cf. Bullinger, 1:195–196.

[176]"A Learned Commentary or Exposition Upon The first Chapter of the Second Epistle of S. Paul to the Corinthians," in *Works*, 3:226; cf. 212, 224; "Fountain Opened," in *Works*, 5:494–495; "Angels' Acclamations," in *Works*, 6:345; "Christ is Best; or, St. Paul's Strait," in *Works*, 1:342; "The Saint's Comforts," in *Works*, 6:172; "The Excellency of the Gospel above the Law," in *Works*, 4:276; "Yea and Amen; or, Precious Promises," in *Works*, 4:140; "God's Inquisition," in *Works*, 6:17; "Christ's Sufferings for Man's Sin," in *Works*, 1:363; Calvin, *Institutes*, III.xii.4; IV.x.3.

[177]"Judgment's Reason," in *Works*, 4:85, 91–92; "The Soul's Conflict with Itself," in *Works*, 1:144–145; "A Learned Commentary or Exposition Upon The first Chapter of the Second Epistle of S. Paul to the Corinthians," in *Works*, 3:224, 226.

[178]"The Demand of a Good Conscience," in *Works*, 7:490; "A Learned Commentary or Exposition Upon The first Chapter of the Second Epistle of S. Paul to the Corinthians," in *Works*, 3:224; "Christ's Sufferings for Man's Sin," in *Works*, 1:363; "Judgment's Reason," in *Works*, 4:91; "The Saint's Hiding-Place in the Evil Day," in *Works*, 1:146; cf. Calvin, *Romans*, 49.

The conscience's role in natural conviction, however, was to lead to spiritual conviction, to "make us to make out of ourselves to Christ, it will make us fly to the city of refuge."[179] Such conviction was the "peal of great ordnance, shot off to prepare the way for him, to shew the King is coming."[180] Aided and enlightened by the Spirit, the conscience prevailed upon a man to follow his conscience fully and to take God's part against himself.[181] God's intention in planting the accusing conscience in man was always to triumph over it by Christ.[182] Christ, by his Spirit, takes and purges the conscience, washing it in His own blood and thereby finally pacifying it.[183]

Conviction and Sanctification

Abuse and Examination of Conscience. In what may seem particularly unusual today, Sibbes presented faith not as necessarily presupposing personal security, but as rather fundamentally antithetical to it and as always guarding against it. He taught that "security" was a dangerous state because in it the believer ceased attending to conscience.[184] A security that could dispense with conscience was not for this world. Instead, the conscience had a role not merely in conversion, but also in sanctification. That role required the Christian's attention to his conscience. Sibbes argued this ongoing role for two reasons. First, because conscience is important "every man is to follow most what his own conscience, after information, dictates unto him; because conscience is God's deputy in us, and under God most to be regarded, and whosoever sins against it, in his own construction sins against God."[185] Second, conscience is delicate, Sibbes taught, and can be suppressed or

---

[179]"Fountain Opened," in *Works*, 5:524; Calvin, *Institutes*, IV.x.3.

[180]"Witness of Salvation," in *Works*, 7:374; cf. "The Excellency of the Gospel above the Law," in *Works*, 4:254; Calvin, *Institutes*, I.xv.2.

[181]"Divine Meditations and Holy Contemplations," in *Works*, 7:210.

[182]"Fountain Opened," in *Works*, 5:482.

[183]"Two Sermons Upon the first words of Christs last Sermon, John 14.1. Being also the last Sermons of Richard Sibbs," in *Works*, 7:345; cf. Calvin, *Institutes*, III.xiii.3.

[184]"Judgment's Reason," in *Works*, 4:90–92.

[185]"The Soul's Conflict with Itself," in *Works*, 1:211.

warped.[186] He warned his hearers at Gray's Inn, "you have some that, for frowns of greatness, fear of loss, or for hope of rising, will warp their conscience, and do anything."[187] Therefore, because of both its importance and its delicacy, the conscience was to be carefully examined.[188] Yet, as Richard Muller has observed, "Introspection gains a militant character."[189] A lack of peace in the conscience of a Christian most likely indicated some guilt that needed to be examined.[190] Even for the Christian, the "peace of conscience is above all good that can be desired."[191] Therefore, Sibbes advised a separatist friend who was suffering from an afflicted conscience, "my earnest suit and desire is, that you would diligently peruse the booke of your conscience, enter into a thorow search and examination of your heart and life; and every day before you go to bed, take a time of recollection and meditation."[192] Instead of leading to petty spiritual book-keeping, Sibbes suggested that such "a search into our own conscience and ways will force us to live by faith every day in Christ Jesus"[193] as we see the greatness of our need and of His provision. To "daub with our own conscience" or in any way ignore it was perilous for the believer.[194] It was to be given unique attention by the believer. Indeed, Sibbes said, "All books are written to amend this one book of our heart and conscience."[195] It is by

---

[186]"The Bruised Reed and Smoking Flax," in *Works*, 1:57.

[187]"Bowels Opened," in *Works*, 2:158; cf. "The Bruised Reed and Smoking Flax," in *Works*, 1:57–58; "Bowels Opened," in *Works*, 2:111.

[188]"Bowels Opened," in *Works*, 2:50; cf. "The Church's Riches by Christ's Poverty," in *Works*, 4:517; "A Learned Commentary or Exposition Upon The first Chapter of the Second Epistle of S. Paul to the Corinthians," in *Works*, 3:222–223; Calvin, *Institutes*, III.xii.5.

[189]Richard A. Muller, "Covenant and Conscience in English Reformed Theology: Three Variations on a 17th Century Theme," *Westminster Theological Journal*, vol. XLII (Spring, 1980): 319.

[190]"The Soul's Conflict with Itself," in *Works*, 1:123–124.

[191]"Of the Providence of God," in *Works*, 5:54; "Christ is Best; or, St. Paul's Strait," in *Works*, 1:342.

[192]"Consolatory Letter to an Afflicted Conscience," in *Works*, 1:cxiv; cf. "A Learned Commentary or Exposition Upon The first Chapter of the Second Epistle of S. Paul to the Corinthians," in *Works*, 3:226.

[193]"Fountain Opened," in *Works*, 5:524.

[194]"Angels' Acclamations," in *Works*, 6:343; "The Bruised Reed and Smoking Flax," in *Works*, 1:92.

[195]"The Soul's Conflict with Itself," in *Works*, 1:149.

such daily sifting and examining that believers discharge their conscience, condemning themselves, and allowing conscience to speak.[196] Such "perpetual tenderness of conscience in God's people" was to be a mark of them, even if the conscience were sleepy sometimes, or "deaded in a particular act."[197]

Conscience and Assurance. If security was not for this world, what of assurance? Did attention to conscience necessarily entail a lack of assurance on the part of the believer? Sibbes said, "What good will it do to know in general that Christ came to save sinners, and yet go to hell for all that?"[198] While this whole subject has been examined in detail above, it can be said in regard of the conscience that Sibbes clearly taught that the believer could know his estate and that it was the role of the conscience to try the claims of the believer to be in a state of grace.[199] Two common problems in this regard were on the one hand, false guilt, and on the other, false security. Sibbes noted that sometimes errors of conscience are taken as its witness "when they regard rules which they should not, or when they mistake the matter and do not argue aright."[200] In such a case, one was to reason with oneself, perhaps with the help of Scripture or friends who could see the error, and to see that the basis of a conscience peaceful before God was the blood of Christ, not meritorious works.[201] On the other hand, there was the problem of false security. Any peace that the conscience seemed to give must reflect "grace working" in one's life, not simple carnal security. Christ "first...gives righteousness, and then he speaks peace to the conscience."[202] In this sense, and in this sense only, the role of the conscience was precisely to tell a man whether he was in a state of

---

[196]"Judgment's Reason," in *Works*, 4:91; "Consolatory Letter to an Afflicted Conscience," in *Works*, 1:cxiv.

[197]"Bowels Opened," in *Works*, 2:48; cf. Calvin, *Institutes*, III.ii.22.

[198]"The Church's Riches by Christ's Poverty," in *Works*, 4:517.

[199]"Bowels Opened," in *Works*, 2:50; "A Learned Commentary or Exposition Upon The first Chapter of the Second Epistle of S. Paul to the Corinthians," in *Works*, 3:222; cf. John Ball, *Treatise of Faith* (London, 1632) 95.

[200]"A Learned Commentary or Exposition Upon The first Chapter of the Second Epistle of S. Paul to the Corinthians," in *Works*, 3:219; cf. 219–221.

[201]Ibid., 227; cf. Calvin, *Institutes*, III.xiv.7.

[202]Ibid., 228; cf. Calvin, *Institutes*, III.xiv.18.

grace.[203] The conscience was to bear witness whether the believer was trusting in God more than in anything else.[204] Though the conscience may be dulled or suppressed in this life, it is never finally satisfied until God is satisfied.[205] Thus, only as the Holy Spirit quiets the conscience can the believer have the assurance of God's love.[206] Without such a good conscience no certain hope of salvation and heaven can be had.[207]

How the Conscience is Awakened. Sibbes frequently urged his hearers to labor to have and to know a good conscience.[208] How was the believer to do this? How was he to wake a naturally sluggish conscience? The more obvious means were by prayer and fellowship, preaching and reflection. Sibbes taught that "sore eyes cannot endure the light; and a galled conscience cannot endure God's presence. Therefore it is good to come oft into the presence of God."[209] Listening to others, whether individually ("speech and conference"[210]) or corporately listening to God's Word preached,[211] especially in a searching fashion,[212] awakens the conscience. Yet the believer was also to stir the conscience by means not obviously religious, particularly by considering the judgments of God on themselves, on the church abroad, and on

---

[203]"The Demand of a Good Conscience," in *Works*, 7:486; "A Learned Commentary or Exposition Upon The first Chapter of the Second Epistle of S. Paul to the Corinthians," in *Works*, 3:207.

[204]"The Faithful Covenanter," in *Works*, 6:11.

[205]"The Demand of a Good Conscience," in *Works*, 7:482.

[206]"Angels' Acclamations," in *Works*, 6:352.

[207]"The Demand of a Good Conscience," in *Works*, 7:483; cf. Calvin, *Institutes*, III.xiii.3; Westminster Confession of Faith XX.1; Westminster Larger Catechism, Question 80.

[208]"The Demand of a Good Conscience," in *Works*, 7:489-90; "Divine Meditations and Holy Contemplations," in *Works*, 7:216; "Judgment's Reason," in *Works*, 4:90; "Two Sermons Upon the first words of Christs last Sermon, John 14.1. Being also the last Sermons of Richard Sibbs," in *Works*, 7:345; "The Rich Poverty; or, The Poor Man's Riches," in *Works*, 6:261.

[209]"A Breathing after God," in *Works*, 2:223.

[210]"Bowels Opened," in *Works*, 2:48.

[211]"Angels' Acclamations," in *Works*, 6:333.

[212]"The Soul's Conflict with Itself," in *Works*, 1:135.

the dangers in the church at home.[213] Temporal troubles were to be seen by the believer as spiritual signs. Whenever God opened the conscience by means of particular punishments, it was in order to convict the believer for particular sins and was not to be ignored.[214] Life seemed to confirm to Sibbes and his contemporaries that troubles were significant, both for unbelievers and believers. And the way of understanding them was through attention to the conscience. Therefore, Sibbes warned that "he that sleeps with a conscience defiled, is as he that sleeps among wild beasts, among adders and toads, that if his eyes were open to see them, he would be out of his wits."[215] When the conscience was guilty, it magnified all troubles into God's judgments until the believer heeded conscience's conviction about the cause of the troubles.[216] Thus the believer's perception of God's providence in his conscience was to become the ground of his guidance.

Conscience as a Tool of Growth. Sibbes taught that the conscience had still more uses in the life of a Christian as a tool for spiritual growth. The conscience, being so sensitive to the wrath of God, was to make a man hate sin and thereby aid his sanctification.[217] Likewise, the conscience was to keep the Christian humble by showing him his sinfulness, and to recall particular sins (e.g., Sabbath-breaking or swearing) to the believer for his correction.[218] However, after sin, the restoring of quietness to the conscience may well prove difficult.

---

[213]"Judgment's Reason," in *Works*, 4:90; "Divine Meditations and Holy Contemplations," in *Works*, 7:201; "The Soul's Conflict with Itself," in *Works*, 1:150; cf. Calvin, *Institutes*, III.ii.20.

[214]"Bowels Opened," in *Works*, 2:60–61.

[215]"A Learned Commentary or Exposition Upon The first Chapter of the Second Epistle of S. Paul to the Corinthians," in *Works*, 3:226.

[216]"The Bruised Reed and Smoking Flax," in *Works*, 1:46, 90. See example below of Mr. Pennington's death.

[217]"Christ's Sufferings for Man's Sin," in *Works*, 1:360; "Church's Visitation," in *Works*, 1:375; "The Excellency of the Gospel above the Law," in *Works*, 4:254.

[218]"Divine Meditations and Holy Contemplations," in *Works*, 7:201; "The Returning Backslider," in *Works*, vol. II. 262; "The Ungodly's Misery," in *Works*, 1:387; "The Faithful Covenanter," in *Works*, 6:16; "Two Sermons Upon the first words of Christs last Sermon, John 14.1. Being also the last Sermons of Richard Sibbs," in *Works*, 7:346.

Time,[219] and even private confession to ministers, Sibbes said, would sometimes be part of the quieting of the conscience.[220] Through controlling the peace and comfort of a believer, his conscience also acted as a guide for him to know how to serve God according to His will and command. Thus, Sibbes frequently described the believer's decision to obey God as his decision to "make conscience."[221] To spend the day keeping a good conscience is to spend it well.[222] Indeed, the goal of keeping a good conscience was to be the polestar for the Christian's life, "for why do men live but to live honestly, and to keep a good conscience?"[223] Sibbes preached that such a good conscience came not from perfect obedience, but from a sincere heart laboring to obey the gospel and keep the covenant with God.[224] He wrote:

> We must not look for perfection. For that makes the papists to teach that there may be doubting, because they look to false grounds; but we must look to the ground in the covenant of grace, to grace itself, and not to the measure. Where there is truth and sincerity, there is the condition of the covenant of grace, and there is a ground for a man to build his estate in grace on.[225]

---

[219]"The Knot of Prayer Loosed," in *Works*, 7:242; "The Saint's Hiding-Place in the Evil Day," in *Works*, 1:416.

[220]"The Returning Backslider," in *Works*, vol. II. 261; cf. "The Bruised Reed and Smoking Flax," in *Works*, 1:54.

[221]"The Demand of a Good Conscience," in *Works*, 7:489–491; "The Privileges of the Faithful," in *Works*, 5:283; "The Sword of the Wicked," in *Works*, 1:114–115; cf. Calvin, *Deuteronomie*, 313.a.10.

[222]"Bowels Opened," in *Works*, 2:88; cf. Gouge, pt. xiii.155.

[223]"Of the Providence of God," in *Works*, 5:52–53; cf. "The Demand of a Good Conscience," in *Works*, 7:490.

[224]"The Demand of a Good Conscience," in *Works*, 7:490; "A Learned Commentary or Exposition Upon The first Chapter of the Second Epistle of S. Paul to the Corinthians," in *Works*, 3:204–205, 223. Cf. Calvin: "A good conscience, then, is nothing but inward integrity of heart," (*Institutes*, III.xix.16; cf. IV.x.4).

[225]A Learned Commentary or Exposition Upon The first Chapter of the Second Epistle of S. Paul to the Corinthians," in *Works*, 3:223. The annotations to the Geneva Bible on this verse (and on II Cor. 5:11) included the idea of "sincerity" as the essence of Paul's plea. Cf. annotations on Titus 1:15; Calvin's statement that "if we desire the real approval of our Judge, we must strive for sincerity of heart," (*Romans*, 49).

Regularly, the conscience was to be kept by taking counsel of God in His Word and by the believer's binding his conscience to closer obedience.[226] Though often God also "awakens the consciences of his children, and exerciseth them with spiritual conflicts" and even temporary desertions.[227]

Benefits of a Good Conscience. The maintenance of a good conscience was so important to the Christian that Sibbes referred to it repeatedly as "a heaven on earth," "the paradise of a good conscience,"[228] and encouraged his hearers not to be driven out of it as Adam and Eve were from the original paradise. Since it is the answer of God's children to the Holy Spirit's effectual call, all Christians begin their new life with such a purified and pacified conscience.[229] Sibbes taught that if kept, the benefits of a good conscience were great. A good conscience is easily troubled for sin by the Spirit, easily pacified by the promises of grace, and easily restored to a gracious desire to please God in all things.[230] "When the conscience is clear...there is nothing between God and us to hinder our trust."[231] The believer can then be easily assured that his prayers will be answered[232] and can live courageously and with joy, being certain of his master's approval.[233] "If so be that man's conscience clears him, he cares not a whit for reports; because a

---

[226]"The Privileges of the Faithful," in *Works*, 5:278; "The Demand of a Good Conscience," in *Works*, 7:490–491.

[227]"The Saint's Safety in Evil Times, Manifested by St. Paul, From his Experience of God's Goodness in Greatest Distress," in *Works*, 1:316.

[228]"The Danger of Backsliding," in *Works*, 7:410; "The Soul's Conflict with Itself," in *Works*, 1:134; "A Learned Commentary or Exposition Upon The first Chapter of the Second Epistle of S. Paul to the Corinthians," in *Works*, 3:215–216, 218.

[229]"The Bride's Longing," in *Works*, 6:541; "The Demand of a Good Conscience," in *Works*, 7:485, 489–490.

[230]"The Demand of a Good Conscience," in *Works*, 7:484; "Fountain Opened," in *Works*, 5:493.

[231]"The Soul's Conflict with Itself," in *Works*, 1:241.

[232]"The Demand of a Good Conscience," in *Works*, 7:483; cf. Calvin, *Institutes*, III.xx.10, 12.

[233]"The Excellency of the Gospel above the Law," in *Works*, 4:237; "The Faithful Covenanter," in *Works*, 6:16; "A Learned Commentary or Exposition Upon The first Chapter of the Second Epistle of S. Paul to the Corinthians," in *Works*, 3:206–207, 223.

good man looks more to conscience than to fame."[234] Without such a good conscience, even the stoutest man in the world, Sibbes said, was a slave.[235]

Finally, one conquers only by having an upright conscience.[236] Only a good conscience can bring true comfort.[237] Sibbes wrote:

> In sickness, when a man can eat nothing, a good 'conscience is a continual feast,' Prov. xv.15. In sorrow it is a musician. A good conscience doth not only counsel and advise, but it is a musician to delight. It is a physician to heal. It is the best cordial, the best physic. All other physicians of no value, comforts of no value. If a man's conscience be wounded, if it be not quieted by faith in the blood of Christ; if he have not the Spirit to witness the forgiveness of his sins, and to sanctify and enable him to lead a good life, all is to no purpose, if there be an evil conscience. The unsound body while it is sick, it is in a kind of hell already.[238]

"Surely sin," said Sibbes, "is the only make-bait of our souls, and weakener of our comforts."[239] A good conscience arms the believer against all discouragements[240] and allows him to "look God in the face,"[241] even being mollified by God when it would threaten for sins

---

[234]A Learned Commentary or Exposition Upon The first Chapter of the Second Epistle of S. Paul to the Corinthians," in *Works*, 3:217.

[235]"The Excellency of the Gospel above the Law," in *Works*, 4:237; "The Soul's Conflict with Itself," in *Works*, 1:228.

[236]"Divine Meditations and Holy Contemplations," in *Works*, 7:207; "The Saint's Safety in Evil Times, Manifested by St. Paul, From his Experience of God's Goodness in Greatest Distress," in *Works*, 1:322.

[237]"The Demand of a Good Conscience," in *Works*, 7:490-491; "Divine Meditations and Holy Contemplations," in *Works*, 7:216; "The Rich Poverty; or, The Poor Man's Riches," in *Works*, 6:261; "Yea and Amen; or, Precious Promises," in *Works*, 4:130; "A Learned Commentary or Exposition Upon The first Chapter of the Second Epistle of S. Paul to the Corinthians," in *Works*, 3:215-216. Cf. Calvin, *Institutes*, III.xiv.18.

[238]A Learned Commentary or Exposition Upon The first Chapter of the Second Epistle of S. Paul to the Corinthians," in *Works*, 3:217.

[239]"The Privileges of the Faithful," in *Works*, 5:283.

[240]"The Faithful Covenanter," in *Works*, 6:16.

[241]"The Demand of a Good Conscience," in *Works*, 7:490. Cf. other related visual imagery "Angels' Acclamations," in *Works*, 6:333; "Christ's Sufferings

already forgiven.[242] "At the hour of death, when nothing else will be regarded, when nothing will comfort, then conscience doth....A good conscience is above the king of fears, death....Therefore a good conscience is joyful in death."[243] In the end then (again evoking Everyman) those who have kept a good conscience are the truly wise,[244] the truly rich[245] people. "So you see how the witness of conscience causeth glory and joy in all estates whatsoever, in life, in death, after death." It follows then quite naturally for Sibbes to exclaim:

> If it be so, that we cannot do anything nor suffer anything as we should, that we cannot praise God, that we cannot live nor die without joy, and the ground of it, the testimony of a good conscience; let us labour, then, that conscience may witness well unto us.[246]
>
> "Therefore how much should we prize and value the testimony and witness of a good conscience! . . . Of all persons and all things in the world, we should reverence our own conscience most of all."[247]

Conclusion: When Conscience Conflicts. Just as the reformers had been critical of the Roman church's binding of men's consciences where the gospel had left them free, so, too, this same issue was a recurring source of dispute in the English church from the controversies between Cranmer and Hooper up through the reign of Charles I. Though this concern is rarely met explicitly in Sibbes's sermons (probably because of the problems of conscientious nonconformity the Church struggled with throughout the time of his ministry), it is present implicitly in his frequent exhortations to heed conscience's dictates above all the counsels

---

for Man's Sin," in *Works*, 1:357–358; "The Demand of a Good Conscience," in *Works*, 7:486; "Divine Meditations and Holy Contemplations," in *Works*, 7:194.

[242]"The Rich Pearl," in *Works*, 7:256.

[243]"A Learned Commentary or Exposition Upon The first Chapter of the Second Epistle of S. Paul to the Corinthians," in *Works*, 3:218–219.

[244]"The Demand of a Good Conscience," in *Works*, 7:490–491; "The Soul's Conflict with Itself," in *Works*, 1:145.

[245]"The Rich Pearl," in *Works*, 7:259.

[246]"A Learned Commentary or Exposition Upon The first Chapter of the Second Epistle of S. Paul to the Corinthians," in *Works*, 3:223; cf. 228.

[247]Ibid., 219.

of men. One can see in Sibbes's pastoral writings—though often explicitly pleading for religious conformity—the ground of nonconformity, religious and civil. In September 1631, Sibbes preached to those gathered in Gray's Inn Chapel, encouraging them to part with "riches, pleasures, and honours, life, world . . . for conscience' sake."[248] Words reminiscent of Jesus' words in Matthew 19:29 might be preached at any time by a popular preacher. In the year 1631, however, such words may have had special import to Sibbes's auditors. To the godly, signs of God's judgment seemed imminent, not least of all in the church. From the godly leaving England because of Laud's innovations to the making of illegal soap because of objections to the Crown's giving the lucrative soap money to a group of the Queen's Roman Catholic friends, godly consciences were being heeded.[249] Earlier that year, Sibbes had introduced a book by John Ball, who had been deprived for conscientiously rejecting conformity. Though Sibbes did not share Ball's conclusion, he could not fail to respect it. He himself had clearly taught that a man should never "enthral his conscience to please another man."[250] Instead, "a good man looks first to God, who is above conscience; and then he looks to conscience, which is under God; and then, in the third place, he looks to report amongst men. And if God and his conscience excuse him, though men accuse him, and lay imputations upon him, this or that, he passeth little for man's judgment."[251] Conscience is to be treated as above all things other than God[252] because "conscience is above me and above all men in the world"[253] and should be revered even "more than any monarch in the world."[254] Therefore, "every man is to follow most what his own conscience, after information, dictates unto him; because conscience is

---

248"The Rich Pearl," in *Works*, 7:259.

249Robert Ashton, *The City and the Court, 1603–1643* (Cambridge, 1979) 141–143.

250"The Excellency of the Gospel above the Law," in *Works*, 4:234.

251"A Learned Commentary or Exposition Upon The first Chapter of the Second Epistle of S. Paul to the Corinthians," in *Works*, 3:217.

252"The Excellency of the Gospel above the Law," in *Works*, 4:220; cf. "Angels' Acclamations," in *Works*, 6:352.

253"A Learned Commentary or Exposition Upon The first Chapter of the Second Epistle of S. Paul to the Corinthians," in *Works*, 3:210.

254Ibid., 225; cf. 500; Calvin, *Institutes*, III.xix.14–15; IV.x.4, 8; Perkins, *Galatians*, 325–326, 361–362.

God's deputy in us, and under God most to be regarded, and whosoever sins against it, in his own construction sins against God."[255]

It is important to note, however, the words "after information" and "in his own construction" in the preceding quotation, for they reveal an important caveat in Sibbes's teaching on conscience. Though Sibbes taught that the conscience was the moral guardian in the soul, and that it was therefore perilous to ignore it, he did not suggest that the conscience was always right;[256] indeed, he specifically denied that it was.[257] He taught that since conscience could be misled, one could and should work to educate the conscience primarily through the Word, but also through the implications of the two tables of the law worked out (fallibly) by the church and the state.[258] Thus for Sibbes, conscience was not the ground of nonconformity, but the avenue to conformity. Indeed, "it will be the heaviest sin that can be laid to our charge at the day of judgment, not that we were ignorant, but that we refused to know, we refused to have our conscience rectified and instructed."[259] Such words

---

[255]"The Soul's Conflict with Itself," in Works, 1:211; cf. "A Learned Commentary or Exposition Upon The first Chapter of the Second Epistle of S. Paul to the Corinthians," in Works, 3:211.

[256]"In the Reformers' use of the term 'conscience,' the static condition of an inclination to good is completely dispelled by the reality of man's inclination to evil, which is experienced with fear, as the divine law is used by the Holy Spirit to tear away man's pretensions," (G. C. Berkouwer, Man: the Image of God, trans. D. Jellema, [Grand Rapids, Michigan, 1962], 172).

[257]"A Learned Commentary or Exposition Upon The first Chapter of the Second Epistle of S. Paul to the Corinthians," in Works, 3:219. "The judgments of the individual conscience are as much subject to argument and correction as any other intellectual proposition; they are not immune to criticism as if based on an inward and private apprehension of God's will," (Conrad Wright, "John Cotton Washed and Made White," Continuity and Discontinuity in Church History, ed. Church and George, [Leiden, 1979], 342).

[258]"The Soul's Conflict with Itself," in Works, 1:211; "Angels' Acclamations," in Works, 6:329; "Divine Meditations and Holy Contemplations," in Works, 7:201; "A Learned Commentary or Exposition Upon The first Chapter of the Second Epistle of S. Paul to the Corinthians," in Works, 3:209, 213–214, 374. Cf. Bernard Verkamp, The Indifferent Mean: Adiaphorism in the English Reformation to 1554 (Athens, Ohio, 1977) 9; Yule, 16–25.

[259]"A Learned Commentary or Exposition Upon The first Chapter of the Second Epistle of S. Paul to the Corinthians," in Works, 3:213; cf. "The Unprosperous Builder," in Works, 7:31; "The Excellency of the Gospel above the Law," in Works, 4:257–8; "Judgment's Reason," in Works, 4:110.

were not those of one of the original generation of the English Reformation. Among them, the category of indifference was one that was used to focus attention away from divisive secondary issues, and onto the central concerns of the gospel of grace through faith, and those practices of the church that completely eclipsed this gospel. The category of adiaphora was largely a knowing, if charitable, wink between reformers, while they waited for preaching to educate the consciences of the weak laity so that reform could precede apace. Yet by Sibbes's time, the consciences of the masses still seemed not to have been completely educated. Thus, without attacking the adiaphorous matters themselves, Sibbes called people to the responsibility of rightly educating their consciences through the Word, and secondarily, through the laws of church and state.

Unlike the Word itself, both the church and the civil law were themselves open to abuse as avenues of education. While they both were to instruct the conscience, neither the church nor the civil government should follow the example of the Roman Church and attempt to usurp the place of the conscience in man.[260] In his popular sermons, *The Soul's Conflict with Itself*, first published the year of his death, Sibbes told his hearers at Gray's Inn:

> We must look to our place wherein God hath set us. If we be in subjection to others, their authority *in doubtful things ought to sway with us. It is certain we ought to obey; and if the thing wherein we are to obey be uncertain unto us, we ought to leave that which is uncertain and stick to that which is certain; in this case we must obey those that are gods under God.* Neither is it the calling for those that are subjects, to inquire over curiously into the mysteries of government; for that, both in peace and war, breeds much disturbance, and would trouble all designs. The laws under which we live are particular determinations of the law of God *in*

---

[260]"Bowels Opened," in *Works*, 2:120; "A Learned Commentary or Exposition Upon The first Chapter of the Second Epistle of S. Paul to the Corinthians," in *Works*, 3:214, 500–504; "The Unprosperous Builder," in *Works*, 7:24. Cf. Calvin, *Reply*, 243); Calvin, *Romans* (283); Verkamp, 9–54. Sibbes's insistence on the authority of the conscience should be seen in the light of a growing number of adiaphorous matters being advocated as part of the faith in the English church.

some duties of the second table. For example, the law of God says, 'Exact no more than what is thy due,' Luke iii.13. But what in particular is thy due, and what another man's, the laws of men determine, and therefore ought to be a rule unto us so far as they reach; though it be too narrow a rule to be good only so far as man's law guides unto. Yet law being the joint reason and consent of many men for public good, hath a use for guidance of all actions that fall under the same. Where it dashes not against God's law, what is agreeable to law is agreeable to conscience. [Italics added].[261]

In the first edition of *Soul's Conflict*, the underscored words in the quotation above were present, but not the italicized words. In the second edition of *Soul's Conflict*, the italicized words were added, and the underscored words deleted. John Ellis in 1662 claimed that this insertion had been done without Sibbes's authorization.[262] Simon Patrick seven years later evidently picked up this same suggestion from Ellis, paraphrasing him in his own account of these mysterious emendations.[263] Though Grosart has adequately refuted Patrick's suggestion (he apparently did not know of Patrick's dependence on Ellis) that the words were added without Sibbes's consent, the simple fact that Ellis and Patrick were so concerned shows both the import of the issue and the widespread respect accorded to Sibbes at the time.[264] It also suggests that Sibbes's legacy on conscience was less than clear.[265] Like the English reformers before him, Sibbes seemed to have assumed that the godly would, under the tuition of the Word, come to agreement concerning which adiaphorous matters were helpful and which were not, and instruct their consciences accordingly.[266]

To discover what Sibbes thought to be the essence of the church theologically — godly preaching, right administration of the sacraments, some discipline — is to discover what Sibbes thought to be essential to

---

[261]"The Soul's Conflict with Itself," in *Works*, 1:209–210.

[262]John Ellis, *S. Austin Imitated: or Retractations and Repentings In reference unto the late Civil and Ecclesiastical Changes in this Nation* (London, 1662) 50–51.

[263]Simon Patrick, *A Friendly Debate betwixt two Neighbours*, Second Part (London, 1669) 219–222.

[264]See Grosart, *Works of Richard Sibbes*, 1:291–294.

[265]See Verkamp, 52.

[266]See Verkamp, 148–149; "The Returning Backslider," in *Works*, vol. 2:355; Calvin, *Institutes*, III.xix.7; Perkins, *Galatians*, 325.

the church practically (and by implication, those things, too, that were non-essential).[267] Divisions caused in the church for reasons other than these essential matters Sibbes relegated to divisions for merely "private aims." Even if the divider was right on the particular, he was wrong to cause division about anything that was not "necessary."[268] Though he did not consider the Elizabethan settlement perfect, Sibbes felt it should be left to those to whom it had been entrusted to govern the church.[269] Furthermore, the cause of much unnecessary division, Sibbes said, was a lack of faith in God's future provision based on his promises, a childish kind of peevishness that, "when they have not what they would have, like children, they throw all away."[270] Such childishness, combined with ignorance of true Christian liberty led to unnecessary scruples. Sibbes said, "they will not have their consciences awaked."[271] Instead of despairing separation, Sibbes said that one should have faith because "faith makes things to come present."[272] No doubt Sibbes's own experience in the church had encouraged his willingness and strengthened his ability to see with the eye of faith and to trust that good things, though unseen at the time, were yet coming. "Look with other spectacles, with the eye of faith, and then you shall see a spring in the winter of the church."[273] Just as the true believer could be assured of his destination by the authenticity of his present experience, so the corrupt church, Sibbes believed, if authentic, could be sure of God's ultimate and complete sanctification and vindication, perhaps uncertain of the means, but not of the end.[274] Therefore, "in some cases peace...is

[267]"Consolatory Letter to an Afflicted Conscience," in *Works*, 1:cxiii–cxvi; cf. "Church's Visitation," in *Works*, 1:375–376.

[268]"The Bruised Reed and Smoking Flax," in *Works*, 1:76.

[269]"If there had been a thorough reformation in the church after her former trouble, and a thorough closing with Christ, she would not thus have fallen into a more dangerous condition," ("Bowels Opened," in *Works*, 2:38).

[270]"The Soul's Conflict with Itself," in *Works*, 1:136.

[271]"A Breathing after God," in *Works*, 2:243; cf. "The Soul's Conflict with Itself," in *Works*, 1:139.

[272]"A Learned Commentary or Exposition Upon The first Chapter of the Second Epistle of S. Paul to the Corinthians," in *Works*, 3:93.

[273]"Fountain Opened," in *Works*, 5:491; cf. "Bowels Opened," in *Works*, 2:136, 180; "Church's Visitation," in *Works*, 1:375; Preston, *Breast-Plate*, pt. i. 113; Stoever, 159.

[274]"Bowels Opened," in *Works*, 2:85, 23; "The Soul's Conflict with Itself," in *Works*, 1:209, 225, 244, 262; "The Saint's Safety in Evil Times," in *Works*, 1:312;

of more consequence than the open discovery of some things we take to be true;...open show of difference is never good but when it is necessary."[275] While some "for a little smoke will quench the light; Christ ever we see cherisheth even the least beginnings."[276] Sibbes concluded for himself, "I had rather hazard the censure of some, than hinder the good of others."[277]

If the choice of conformity had been difficult enough for Sibbes's conscience in December 1616 (even requiring a second meeting with the Vice-Chancellor's court, before subscribing), it could hardly have been less so in 1633, for a number of those close to Sibbes then decided that they could no longer conscientiously conform. Yet by 1633, however disturbed he may have been at the ill signs for the future of the Reformed church in England, Sibbes's conscience was already educated. This self-education had been aided not only by Sibbes's "eye of faith," but also by his belief in providence. On the first Sunday in February 1632, Sibbes and Sir William Masham dined with William Prynne in his rooms at Lincoln's Inn. The conversation had been of the providential control of God over all affairs. In a letter, dated 7 February 1632 to his mother-in-law Lady Joan Barrington, Sir William Masham wrote, recounting their conversation:

> Now I ame in this greate subject of God's workes of justice upon his enimyes, I cannot omitt a strange example of his judgment upon a gentleman of Grays Inne, Mr. Pennington, who in his health usinge much that excration of the divill take him, now in his sicknesse was much trobled with the presentation of a black dogge, sutable to his master, and at last found deade much torne and distorted, his eyes clawed out (as some thinke) by the divill. This Mr Dr Sibbs told me at my brother Prine's chamber on sabboth daye last, where we dyned together and where you were kindly remembered.[278]

"The Saint's Safety in Evil Times, Manifested by St. Paul, From his Experience of God's Goodness in Greatest Distress," in *Works*, 1:318.
   [275]"The Bruised Reed and Smoking Flax," in *Works*, 1:76.
   [276]Ibid., 51.
   [277]Ibid., 41; cf. 55.
   [278]Searle, 227–228.

This recounting of talk of grisly judgements and pleasant greetings in an evening's interesting conversation among the godly—Sibbes, Masham, and Prynne—is one of the rare glimpses of Sibbes outside the pulpit. It is confirming of Sibbes's belief in his ability to read providence. Again, after the plague was particularly severe in Cambridge in 1630, Sibbes preached in Great St. Mary's that God "hath given us our lives more than once, every one of us in particularly especially in regard of the last heavy visitation."[279] God was active in history; his people were to be "warned by public dangers."[280] It was only "worldly, sottish men that live here below, they think there is no other state of things than they see; they are only taken up with sense, and pleasures, and goodly shows of things. Alas! poor souls!"[281] But Christians should use such providential happenings to awake their consciences.[282] Even as in Acts 5 God had judged his enemies and delivered his church from their deceit, so he would ultimately provide revenge for his enemies and salvation for his church.[283] Observing God's providence could prepare his people, "we know not what times God may call us to ere long."[284] Through such observations, God's faithfulness could be discerned, and the believer's faith strengthened. In a Gunpowder sermon, probably preached in 1630 after a particularly bad harvest, Sibbes compared the enemies of the church to "the grass on the house-top, which perks above the corn in the field, but yet no man prays for a blessing upon it. When men come by a goodly corn-

---

[279]"The Saint's Safety in Evil Times," in *Works*, 1:311.

[280]"The Demand of a Good Conscience," in *Works*, 7:491; cf. "Bowels Opened," in *Works*, 2:43, 65–67; "Divine Meditations and Holy Contemplations," in *Works*, 7:208; "Fountain Opened," in *Works*, 5:512; "The Soul's Conflict with Itself," in *Works*, 1:197, 204–206, 210, 231, 244; "The Privileges of the Faithful," in *Works*, 5:269; and, of course, "Of the Providence of God," in *Works*, 5:35–54; Miller, *Mind*, 38–40; Keith Thomas, *Religion and the Decline of Magic* (London, 1971) 90–132.

[281]"Angels' Acclamations," in *Works*, 6:319.

[282]"Judgment's Reason," in *Works*, 4:90.

[283]Sibbes allowed that God's government of the church was more "outward in the primitive times of the church ("Judgment's Reason," in *Works*, 4:83).

[284]"Art of Contentment," in *Works*, 5:193; cf. "Bowels Opened," in *Works*, 2:181; "The Danger of Backsliding," in *Works*, 7:412; "Fountain Opened," in *Works*, 5:466; "Judgment's Reason," in *Works*, 4:95; "The Saint's Hiding-Place in the Evil Day," in *Works*, 1:425.

field, every one is ready to say, God bless this field, &c."[285] The church's enemies, like the grass on the roof, may be raised up for a time, but they were ultimately dead.

Yet it was not the reading of God's providence, but the relying on God's promises that Sibbes taught should ultimately strengthen the believer's faith, and thus instruct his conscience. Informed by his own experience of fruitful ministry within the church and aided by the gradualism that typified his understanding of the action of God's grace in conviction and conversion, in comfort and assurance within the covenant community, Sibbes conscientiously conformed. Seen in this light, the consolation and tender comfort of *The Bruised Reed* were far more than pastoral encouragements in individual piety; they were observations about the nature of grace in covenant. As Sibbes said, "Weaknesses do not break covenant with God."[286] What was true of the individual was also true of the church.[287] "The church of Christ is a common hospital, wherein all are in some measure sick of some spiritual disease or other; that we should all have ground of exercising mutually the spirit of wisdom and meekness."[288] Peter Lake has noted how experimental Calvinism's emphasis on inward sincerity and the supreme place given the invisible distinction between the godly and the ungodly could easily have seemed subversive, at least to "Arminians," of notions of hierarchy and order in the institutional church.[289] However it may have seemed, though, in Sibbes, the inward piety of comfort, assurance, and the conscience was tied up closely with the fallible, visible church, regardless of whether it needed to be. As noted earlier, for Sibbes, this inward piety was not the avenue to nonconformity, but that which allowed continuing conformity.

Perry Miller identified a "hidden difficulty" in "Puritan philosophy" as the conflict between two philosophical inheritances from Aristotle and Plato. Though Sibbes denied that such philosophers were adequate to

---

285"The Saint's Safety in Evil Times," in *Works*, 1:305.

286"The Bruised Reed and Smoking Flax," in *Works*, 1:69.

287"A Breathing after God," in *Works*, 2:242; "The Bruised Reed and Smoking Flax," in *Works*, 1:43, 46; "Church's Visitation," in *Works*, 1:374; "Divine Meditations and Holy Contemplations," in *Works*, 7:203; "Judgment's Reason," in *Works*, 4:99–100; "The Saint's Safety in Evil Times," in *Works*, 1:299.

288"The Bruised Reed and Smoking Flax," in *Works*, 1:57.

289Peter Lake, "Calvinism and the English Church," *Past and Present*, vol. 114 (February, 1987): 75.

"struggle with the difficulties of religion,"[290] just such tensions were present in Sibbes's own thinking. Sibbes seemed to agree with Aristotle that "whatsoever enters into the heart of man, it must be by those passages and windows, the gates of the soul, the sense."[291] This emphasis on the need for education of conscience and the role of reason in that education were clearly useful in Sibbes's discussions with nonconforming friends. To Sibbes, any conscientiousness that led to separation was over-scrupulousness and the consciences of such were to be educated. At this Sibbes was truly talented. As John Hacket recalled his reputation, Sibbes was known for his ability to "bring them [nonconformists] about, the best of any about the City of London."[292] The conscientious John Dury—who felt "bound in Conscience" for pursuing peace among the Protestant churches[293]—had experienced the truth of Sibbes's reputation. Dury had been for "five our [sic] six years before I went into Germany under a scruple of conscience" about the nature of pastoral ministry and his own call.[294] Such scruples appeared again when considering ordination in the Church of England, but they were resolved, at least partially, through conversation with Sibbes.[295] John Ellis, too, at Katharine Hall, had experienced Sibbes's pastoral concern and its effectiveness in "securing" him "against Independency."[296] No doubt these principles had been worked out in Sibbes's own mind and experience in December 1616, when he had submitted his more radical objections to the use of the sign of the cross to the church's tacit declaration of their adiaphorous nature. Once admittedly adiaphorous in and of themselves, it became a matter of his own judgment of their use in the particular circumstance, and the church's judgment. Thus Sibbes had effectively educated his own conscience.

---

[290]"Fountain Opened," in *Works*, 5:467.
[291]"A Glance of Heaven; or, Precious Taste of a Glorious Feast," in *Works*, 4:156–157.
[292]John Hacket, *Scrinia Reserata: A Memorial Offer'd to the Great Deservings of John Williams, D. D.* (London, 1693) part i paragraph 106, 95–96.
[293]John Dury, *The Unchanged, Constant and Single-hearted Peacemaker* (London, 1650) 3.
[294]Dury, 4.
[295]Dury, 7.
[296]Ellis, 45.

Yet, true to Miller's identification of "conscience" as the "one sub-ject... in which Platonism had most frequently blended with Christian thought,"[297] Sibbes could also refer to an "inbred light in the soul" and an "infused establishing by the Spirit," both of which were intelligences gained apart from the senses.[298] This understanding of the nature of conscience led to Sibbes's other and conflicting emphasis on accounta-bility to conscience alone, under God, and gave to conscience such authority that it was never to be dismissed. Though it could not save, it must be heeded; though it needed instruction, it could not be ignored.[299] It was this equivocation, seen in hindsight, that aided Sibbes's representation in the eighteenth century as a non–conformtist, despite his actual conformity. While there is no dispute that Sibbes taught that "where it [law] dashes not against God's law, what is agreeable to law is agreeable to conscience," this was merely a statement of what should be. The years after Sibbes's death revealed the profound conflicts that could emerge between the obligations of humbly educating one's conscience on the one hand and on the other, of heeding it at all costs.

---

[297]Miller, *The New England Mind*, 192.

[298]"A Learned Commentary or Exposition Upon The first Chapter of the Second Epistle of S. Paul to the Corinthians," in *Works*, 3:427; cf. 260.

[299]"A Glance of Heaven; or, Precious Taste of a Glorious Feast," in *Works*, 4:159; cf. Breward, 33.

Conclusion

THREE AND A HALF centuries after his death, Richard Sibbes continues to be a celebrated Puritan. For almost thirty years at this writing, the nineteenth-century edition of his collected works has continued to be in print and to line the shelves of some Anglican, Reformed, and evangelical ministers. In academic circles, he has enjoyed an almost unbroken line of celebrity from the writings of Miller, Haller, and Nuttall down to the most recent works on English religious life in the early seventeenth century. Recently, Janice Knight has once again given Sibbes prominence in her treatment of New England.[1] Sibbes seems to have been accorded central, if protean, importance. Yet, between the vast tract of those necessarily lost to history and those few who have been the subject of painstaking study, Sibbes has inhabited an awkward academic no-man's land marked by the combination of ignorance and prominence. He has been known by inclusion in short lists and citations of apt sayings, complete with biographical phrases. A man so wrested from obscurity should at least be granted the privilege of a thorough study.

Though most of a public person's life remains private and hidden to the view of others, the mists of history might seem to enclose such a person as Sibbes as to render him historically invisible, or at least so obscure as to be necessarily an indistinct or equivocal figure. Sibbes has suffered from being accurately, yet partially, described on scores of issues, with the result that he has been a widely, though not universally, mistaken character. Other representations recounted in this study have been even less accurate on the particulars. Given both the nature and the large number of his writings extant, it would seem that almost any casual interpretation of him and his theology can be sustained. The task of this study has been to recover Sibbes as an historical and theological whole.

---

[1] Janice Knight, *Orthodoxies in Massachusetts: Rereading American Puritanism* (Cambridge, Massachusetts, 1994).

Of course, the fear of a study such as this one is that it will be what
Anthony Milton has praised Nicholas Tyacke's work for not
being—another "amble through well-thumbed texts which has
previously typified work on the religious thought of this period."[2] Most,
though not all, of the study's sources have been printed, and its subject
well-known. Though Sibbes was popular, even celebrated during his
life, his thought could hardly be said to have been seminal, nor his
career determinative for the fortunes of the godly in early Stuart
England. Yet the disadvantage of the limited extent this study, which
has focused on Sibbes alone, may be somewhat offset by the resulting
care that can be given to specifics. While there remains much work to
do on Sibbes—any of the topics explored in the second half of this study
could be the subject of their own dissertation—this study has attempted
to present Sibbes more clearly in both his historical and theological
contexts than has previously been done.

Contrary to previous presentations of him, it appears that Sibbes did
subscribe to the three articles and, presumably, conform. There is no
reason to believe that he was deprived of his lectureship at Holy
Trinity, Cambridge, and it is certain that he was not put out of his
fellowship at St. John's. Sibbes then should no longer be seen to have
been as obstreperous as John Dod or Paul Baynes, but strangely more
fortunate in retaining official positions in the church. Rather, he
becomes more like a Laurence Chaderton than a Thomas Cartwright, a
William Perkins more than a William Ames.

The origin of the great reversal in Sibbes's reputation from a
conforming moderate, to a deprived nonconformist has been briefly
noted in chapter two. The development of the myth of Sibbes as a
Puritan martyr is full of assumptions innocently presented as fact and
dependence on sources secondary rather than primary. Though the full
story is too long to recount here,[3] it is enough to note that from Daniel
Neal's *History of the Puritans* (1732), the most recent historical studies,
the image of Sibbes has been one of a Puritan martyr. Though this is
understandable given the universally reported deprivations he
suffered, it is surprising that it had not previously raised more

---

[2]Anthony Milton, Review of Nicholas Tyacke's *Anti-Calvinists: The Rise of
English Arminianism, Journal of Ecclesiastical History*, vol. XXXIX (October,
1988): 613-614.

[3]See chapter 2, *supra*, especially note 55.

questions, given his subsequent preferment and reputation. The tradition of reporting the history of the Puritan movement as simply the earliest chapter of dissenting history—widely challenged in recent years—has remained intact in Sibbes's case, to the detriment of an accurate portrayal of him. Ensconced in two standard reference works often cited by later historians—James Venn's *Alumni Cantabrigienses* and Alexander Gordon's article on Sibbes in the *Dictionary of National Biography*—the errors surrounding Sibbes and his leaving Cambridge for London were joined together, and canonized. They became biographical "facts" about Richard Sibbes. The normal course for historical writers since then has been to repeat the story of Sibbes's deprivation, almost whenever his name is mentioned.[4]

---

[4]E.g., Rooy, "Because of his Puritan views he was deprived of both his lectureship and his professorship in 1615" (Sidney H. Rooy, *The Theology of Missions in the Puritan Tradition* [Grand Rapids, Michigan, 1965], 15); Pettit, "Sibbes...by 1615...had been sufficiently non-conforming to lose the lectureship of Holy Trinity, Cambridge" (Norman Pettit, *The Heart Prepared: Grace and Conversion in the Puritan Spiritual Life* [New Haven, Connecticut, 1966], 66); Shelly, "After receiving his B.D. he served as lecturer at Holy Trinity, Cambridge, until deprived by the Ecclesiastical Court of High Commission" (Harold P. Shelly, "Richard Sibbes: Early Stuart Preacher of Piety" [Ph.D. diss., Temple University, 1972], 3); Hopkins, "So many students began to desert Great St. Mary's, the university church, for Holy Trinity, that in 1620 it was made out of bounds to them" (Hugh Evan Hopkins, *Holy Trinity Church Cambridge* [n.d. (1975?)], 5); Harris, "We do not know the precise grounds and circumstances of Sibbes'ss 'outing', but it has been possible to sketch a reasonably coherent outline.... The implication is that Richard Sibbes, after six years at the Trinity lectureship, was unable to obtain the necessary licence from the Bishop, and authority from the Vice-Chancellor to continue when the Whitehall-inspired tightening in ecclesiastical jurisdiction occurred...It is...improbable that he was forcibly 'outed' from his fellowship at St. John's; more likely he resigned the position upon taking his new lectureship in London" (Jonathan Harris, "Richard Sibbes: A Moderate in Early Seventeenth Century Puritanism" [M.A. Thesis, University of Melbourne, 1978], 19; Harris' thesis is by far the most careful and considered of all of these studies in looking at some of the questions surrounding Sibbes'ss deprivation); Kendall, "In 1611 he was made lecturer at Holy Trinity Church, Cambridge, remaining in this position until 1615" (R. T. Kendall, *Calvin and English Calvinism to 1649* [Oxford, 1979], 103); Knott, "In 1615 Sibbes was removed from this position [the Trinity lectureship] by a royal prohibition

Sibbes's move from Cambridge to London in 1617 is much more likely explained by his talent for fostering friendships, combined with his obvious gifts as a preacher, than by his previously supposed deprivations. Sibbes's skill at making and retaining friendships certainly helps to account for at least his successful involvement with the feoffees (before their dissolution) and his successful mastership of Katharine Hall, and perhaps for much more. They do not, however, suggest any religious radicalism that would encourage separation. This is clearly ruled out not only negatively by the weakness of the argument itself, but also by noting Sibbes's explicit defenses of the Church of England, together with the general tone of his writing and his career.

Yet as that which Sibbes had taken to be quite literally the salvation of the Church of England—godly preaching—became increasingly hindered by those in authority, his own position in the church certainly appeared more incongruous. This study suggests, however, that his faithful adherence to the Church of England was consistent with his own experience and theology. His experience of authority was not almost wholly negative, as one might assume from earlier presentations of Sibbes's career. Rather, from his education at the expense of some godly Suffolk Johnians to his expiration in the chambers given him by Sir Gilbert Gerard, Sibbes knew the benefits of wealthy patrons. Certainly not all of even those few of Sibbes's experiences with authority, which the modern historian can reconstruct, were positive. Nevertheless, Sibbes had often experienced human help from those in authority. Perhaps this was why he was able to continue to trust a hierarchy which

---

against new lectures" (John R. Knott, Jr., *The Sword of the Spirit: Puritan Responses to the Bible* [Chicago, 1980], 42); Poe, " ... he lost his fellowship and lectureship in 1615 .... Christopher Hill probably correctly concluded that the deprivation resulted from the King's prohibition of new lectureships 'that might draw scholars away from catechizing'" (Harry Lee Poe, "Evangelistic Fervency Among the Puritans in Stuart England, 1603–1688" [Ph.D. diss., The Southern Baptist Theological Seminary, 1982], 56); Prest, "... the High Commission had deprived him [Sibbes] of the Trinity Church lectureship in Cambridge" (Wilfrid R. Prest, in *The Rise of the Barristers* [Oxford], 219). Even in the most recent reprinting of Sibbes's *Bruised Reed*, the anonymous 'Publisher's Foreword' states "He was removed from the post five years later, however, because of his Puritan tendencies," (Edinburgh, 1998) viii.

could be seen to be turning against what he took to be the very means of grace.

Sibbes's loyalty to the Church of England was also consistent with his theology. Sibbes understood the church to be a covenant community far more extensive than the elect, intended to be filled with people in various spiritual states. Therefore, imperfection was expected and tolerated, though not excused, and the use of means vigorously encouraged. Indeed, even more than creation, the covenant obliged one to live a life of holiness. Sibbes's interiorization of piety—not unique to Sibbes, but powerfully communicated in his sermons—accounts at the same time for his popularity with disparate groups, his ability to conform to the demands of the church, and yet also for the potential for a Christianity lived in disobedience to ungodly earthly authorities. Sibbes was not a mere moralist—a pre-incarnation of restoration Anglicanism. He understood the church to be a supernatural, sovereign creation of God. The theology of God's sovereignty was not effectively eclipsed by Sibbes's use of covenant terminology, nor by any of his exhortations to the use of means. Nor was the ultimate accountability of the individual before God eclipsed by his affirmation of the need to educate one's conscience. Sibbes clearly taught that only the ultimate authority was fully trustworthy; and full trustworthiness always characterized the ultimate authority—God.

That Sibbes was able to remain within the Church of England until his death in 1635 should not, however, be used woodenly to suggest that his conformity appeared uniform throughout his life, nor that Sibbes was as representative of the Church in 1635 as he may have been a quarter of a century earlier. Whereas in his early days as a fellow of St. John's, Sibbes may well have been typical of a great many, perhaps even the majority, of the religious types in his college and university, one suspects that by his last two years he was a noted representative of an important, though shrinking and aging group of moderate Puritans within the Church. This is not, however, too puzzling. Just as the deprivations he did not suffer were for so long taken to be the natural expression of a separatist ecclesiology he did not hold, so this study suggests that the conformity he embraced initially, perhaps at his graduation or ordination, crucially in the Vice-Chancellor's court, and finally in his casuistry for the Church, was the natural expression of his own experience and beliefs. It is hoped that this study, in allowing the various aspects of his life and theology to rest more easily together, will go some way to refurbishing the pacific reputation Sibbes enjoyed among his contemporaries.

If this study has been historically helpful in representing Sibbes more accurately as one of what appear today to be a growing number of moderate Puritans in the early seventeenth-century Church of England, it can perhaps be most helpful theologically in suggesting some shortcomings in the well-established tradition of assuming that the covenant framework somehow undermined the bases of Reformed theology. In this century, an interesting confluence of historical and theological studies has suggested this. Both drawing on earlier observations, but apparently independently of each other, in the middle of this century Perry Miller and Karl Barth suggested that this undermining had, in fact, occurred. Though the two men and their concerns could hardly have been more different—Miller, a confidently atheistic American historian, Barth, a devout Swiss Reformed theologian—both came to strikingly similar conclusions about the effects of covenant theology on Reformed thought, albeit for different reasons. Miller's optimistic rationalism clearly left him puzzled by the Reformed roots of his own New England. Looking back at Calvin, and disliking what he took to be the irrationalism he saw, Miller observed a growing reliance on and confidence in reason in Calvin's later heirs, particularly among the covenant theologians. Barth, on the other hand, as an unabashed champion of Calvin, saw in the more explicit covenant formulations that followed a creeping anthropocentrism which obscured grace. Though Miller in particular has influenced later theological interpretations of seventeenth-century Puritanism, and many following him, it was the even more powerful combination of these concerns by church historians such as Basil Hall and J. B. Torrance that gave them particular weight with other historians who were ready to cede all knowledge of things theological to experts trained in that field.

The most influential recent study to reinvigorate debate on this issue was R. T. Kendall's *Calvin and English Calvinism to 1649*. Though Kendall's work has been mentioned repeatedly in the footnotes of this study, it should be noted here that his work, though widely quoted as theologically authoritative by recent historians of the period, is flawed by factual, interpretive, and methodological errors in his treatment at least of Sibbes and almost certainly of others. If one of the advantages of large studies like Miller's and Kendall's is that they can be enormously helpful in digesting, summarizing, and organizing information, one of the disadvantages conversely is the potential for consequent ignorance of particulars and slighting of specifics. Factually, Kendall was incorrect in dating Sibbes's birth and admission to St. John's, in accepting his deprivations, and in suggesting that Sibbes's sermons "do not delve into ecclesiology at all."[5] His interpretation of Calvin and the subsequent Reformed tradition on assurance has been questioned earlier in chapter seven. Finally, by simple constraints of space and time, such a sweeping synthetic study as Kendall undertook is easily flawed in its methodology. To extract figures from different eras and situations in order to compare their views is a task as difficult to do well as it is needful. That it can be done and done well, this author has no doubt. Yet, Kendall's scant attention to the historical setting—at least in the case of Sibbes—would seem to have rendered his study less helpful than it appears. It becomes, in fact, misleading, as Calvin's statements, which were uttered in the context of polemic against the form of Christianity all around him and ever-beckoning to the inhabitants of Geneva, are put "in conversation" as it were, with statements made by English preachers fifty and one hundred years later in a national Protestant church. The hermeneutics involved in getting the two situations to "speak" to one another do not present insuperable barriers; yet they have not been overcome in Kendall's work. Though this present study is in no way as sweeping a work as Kendall's, it does at least raise a serious question against the ready acceptance of his work, and of the ever-popular "Calvin against the Calvinists" theme, at least in so far as it has been built upon the assumption of the fundamental incompatibility of covenant and Reformed theology in godly preachers such as Richard Sibbes.

In 1697, John Higginson, 81-year-old minister of the church in Salem, Massachusetts, looked back on the first generation of ministers (which included his father) who came from England to New England, and remarked, "Our fathers did in their time acknowledge, there were many defects and imperfections in our way, and yet we believe they did as much as could be expected from learned and godly men in their

---

[5]Kendall, 103.

circumstances."[6] Such was the respect accorded Sibbes by those after his death who differed from him, yet esteemed him. To Richard Baxter, Sibbes was one of those "old moderate sort" of "Episcopal men . . . who were commonly in Doctrine Calvinists."[7] Not that Sibbes was a moderate man when preaching of the necessity of justification by faith, the certainty of God's salvation of the elect, or the duty of all members of the covenant to fulfill their obligations. No record remains of his being put in a position by those in authority over him to equivocate on such doctrinal essentials. His moderation was reserved for those externals of religion, which he deemed adiaphorous and which his church deemed edifying—the sign of the cross, the use of the surplice, and perhaps even an unworthy recipient of a fellowship. Given the changes that were about to come in England, hindsight suggests that, as Lord Clarendon later wrote about one of Sibbes's contemporaries (the Lord Keeper Thomas Coventry), "he dyed in a season most opportune, and in which a wise man would have prayed to have finished his course, and which in truth crowned his other signal prosperity in this worlde."[8] Even in his last years when he must have felt most circumscribed and could have most easily despaired, he remained until his dying day a member of "the sacred communion of the truly Evangelicall Church of England."[9] Reflecting a lifetime of fruitful experience, it is understandable that in his will Sibbes should commend his soul to God "with humble thankes that he hath vouchsafed I should be borne and live in the best tymes of the gospell...."[10]

---

[6]John Higginson, "An Attestation to the Church-History", prefixed to Cotton Mather, *Magnalia Christi Americana*(Hartford, Conn., 1853) 1: 17.

[7]Richard Baxter, *Reliquae Baxterianae*, ed. Matthew Sylvester (London, 1696) ii.149. Christopher Hill has noted "the middle way of Archbishops Grindal and Abbott in the church, to which late seventeenth century noncon-formists looked back as the true Church of England" (*A Turbulent, Seditious, and Factious People: John Bunyan and His Church* [Oxford, 1988], 32).

[8]Henry Hyde, Lord Clarendon, *History of the Rebellion* (London, 1702) 1: 38.

[9]"Consolatory Letter to an Afflicted Conscience," in *Works*, 1: cxvi.

[10]"King David's Epitaph," in *Works*, 6: 495.

APPENDIX I:

Richard Sibbes's Family Tree

A. Thomas Sibis, Labourer of Pakenham, m. Elizabeth
        had two children.
        Thomas d. May 1559.
        Elizabeth d. uncertain.
        —B. Paul
        —C. Robert

*****

B. Paul Sibbs, Yeoman (wheelwright) of Thurston, m. Joane
        had six children.
        Paul (b. between 1538–1558, d. Feb. 1610)
        Joane (d. between 1618–1635)
        —D. RICHARD
        —E. John
        —F. Thomas
        —G. Margaret
        —H. Susan
        —I. Elizabeth

C. Robert Sibbs, Thatcher of Tostock, m. Alice (in 1637 called her his "now wife")
        no surviving children (?)
        Robert (b. between 1538–1559, d. Jan 1637)
        Alice (d. 1650)

*****

D. RICHARD SIBBES (1577–1635)
        never married

E. John Sibbs, of Thurston, m. (?)
        one surviving child (?)
        John (b. after 1577 before 1610, d. after 1610 before 1635)
        wife (?)
        —J. John

F. Thomas Sibbs, yeoman of Rattlesden, m. Barbara

no surviving children
Thomas (b. after 1577, d. 1669)
Barbara (d. after 1669)

G. Margaret, m. Mr. Mason
       Children (?)
       Margaret (b. after 1577, d. after 1635)
       Mr Mason (?) H. Susann, m. Mr. Lopham
       children
       Susann (b. after 1577, d. before 1635)
       Mr. Lopham (?)

I. Elizabeth, m. Mr. King (after 1610)
       children
       Elizabeth (b. after 1577, d. between 1610–1635)

*****

J. John Sibbs, gentleman of Thurston, m. Frances Hunt (daughter of
George Hunt of Saxham)
       had six children
       John (b. ~1610–1615, matric. Kath. Hall 1632, BA 1635/6, d. July
1673)
       Frances (d. after 1673)
       – K. John
       – L. Thomas
       – M. Richard
       – N. Robert
       – O. Martha
       – P. Anne

*****

K. John Sibbs, m. (?)
       Children (?)
       John, (b. 1640, matric. Kath. Hall 1660, d. after 1673)

L. Thomas Sibbs, yeoman of Tostock, m. Elizabeth
       had six children

Thomas (buried 18 Jan 1690)
Elizabeth (buried 9 August 1706)
—Q. Ann
—R. Elizabeth
—S. Sarah
—T. Hannah
—U. Francis
—V. Richard

M. Richard Sibbs, Rector of Gedding, (m.?)
    Children (?)
    Richard (b.1645, attended Bury Free School, matric. Kath. Hall
        1661, BA 1664/5,
    MA 1668, Curate of Great Ashfield, Suffolk 1671, Rector of
        Gedding 1672–1738, d. 1738)

N. Robert Sibbs, Rector of Barningham Northwood, Norfolk, m. (?)
    one child (?)
    Robert (b. after 1645, matric. Kath. Hall 1672, BA 1675/6, ord
        deacon (Norwich)
    1678, ord priest 1678/9, Rector of Barningham Northwood,
        Norfolk 1680–1697, d. 1697(?)
    —W. Richard

O. Martha, m. John Skepper
    two children (?)
    Martha (?)
    John (?)
    —Flower
    —John

P. Anne Sibbs, m. (?)
    Children (?)
    Anne (?)

*****

CHILDREN of L. Thomas and Elizabeth Sibbs

Q. Ann Sibbes, m. (?)
     Unmarried in 1690
     Ann (?)

R. Elizabeth, m. John Limner of Chevington on 23 Aug, 1700
     one child(?)
     Elizabeth (?)
     John (?)
     — Esther (baptized 15 Oct 1701)

S. Sarah, m. John Nunn, of Thurston, on 12 Apr 1697
     three children
     Sarah (buried 28 Apr 1719)
     John (?)
     — Mary (baptized 30 Dec 1702)
     — John (baptized 9 Jan 1706)
     — Esther (baptized 26 May 1708)

T. Hannah Sibbs, m. (?)
     Children (?)
     Hannah (baptized 6 Jan 1679)

U. Francis, m. Robert Steggles of Thurston, on 23 Apr 1707
     children(?)
     Francis (baptized 5 June 1683, d. ?)
     Robert (?)

V. Richard, m. (?)
     children (?)
     Richard (baptized 1 May 1688)

CHILD of Robert Sibbs

W. Richard Sibbs, Rector of Mannington, m. (?)
     children (?)
     Richard (b. 1693, matric. Kath. Hall 1711, BA 1716/17, ord
             deacon (Ely) 1717, ord priest (Norwich) 1718, Rector of
             Barningham Northwood, Norfolk 1721–1730, Rector of
             Mannington 1730–1761, P.C. of Sustead 1738–1761, d.
             1761)

APPENDIX II:

PAUL SIBBES'S WILL

Regu or oxu
In the name of god Amen the last day of Januarie, in the year
of our Lord God one thousand six hundred and ten 1610
I Paul Sibbs of Thurston in the county of Suffolk yeoman
being at this present time of a good perfect and of a disposing
mind and memory though weak in body God be praised
for the same do ordain and make this my last will and testament
in form following. First and principally I bequeath my soul
into the hands of almighty God my creator trusting assuredly that
through the death and passion of his son Jesus Christ my
redeemer, all my sins be forgiven me and my body I commend
to the earth from whence it came, to be buried in decent manner
in the churchyard of Thurston aforesaid at the discretion of my
executors hereafter named. And as touching my lands and goods
wherewith it hath pleased God to bless endow or enrich me
I geve bequeath devise and dispose of them in form following
And first my desire and mind is, that the messuage or tenament
wherein I now dwell and all the lands to me and Joane my wife
and the heyres of our two bodies begotten or to be begotten devised
or menconed or intended to be to us of such estate devised by and
in the last will and testament of Richard Fylde deceased, upon
condition for the payment of Fifty — —- and five pounds
to divers and sundry persons in the same last will named, shall
be enjoied by my said wife and that after her death the
same may remaine and be unto Richard th'eldest son of
me and my said wife of such estate and according to the —-
purport and true meaning of the last will of the said
Richard Filde. And because I have been at great charge
in the education of my said son in learning as also for that
I have truly satisfied and paid the said sum of fifty and five
pounds, partly in the nature of a purchase and for the better
preservation of mine and my wife's estate and for the good benefit and advantage of my said son, I therefore entreat my said
son Richard to rest satisfied, well-pleased and contented
with the guift devise and legatie aforesaid. Item I geve devise
and bequeath all that my messuage or tenament with all the lands

homestall ground and land and tenement and hereditaments thereunto belonging
[PAGE 2]
or therewith now used or occupied situate lying and being in Pakenham in the said countie of Suffolk conteyning together by estimacion ten acres be they more or less now in the occupacion of William Brooke being copihold or customarye tenure holden of the Mannor of Pakenham Hall in Paken- ham aforesaid together with all other my copihold or costomarye lands holden of the same Mannor unto John Sibbs my sonne his heyres and assignes for ever. And also I geve devise and bequeath all that my messuage or tenement with all the homestall ground lande tenement and hereditand thereunto belonging nighe or adjoining situate lying and being in Thurston aforesaid in a strete there called Overstrete which I late had and purchased of John Page and Thomas Page his brother or one of theme thereof the said Messuage or tenement is called Cuttinge and all or most of the same grounde doe lye as well on the north and south parte of a waye there called the Shepherde's waye and also all that any I enclose of pasture called Denbyes of late also bought of the said John Page unto my said sonne John his heyres and assigns forever. And my meaning is that my said sonne John his heyres and assigns shall yearly and evrie yeare at the feastes of Th'annunciasion of our Blessed Lady St. Marye the virgin and St. Michaell th'archangell well and truly paye or cause to be payd unto the saide Joane my wife for and during her naturall life one annuitie or yearly rent of fortye shillings of lawfull english money by even portions. The first of the said payments to beginne at the first of the said feastes which first and next shall happen and come after my death provided alwayes that if it shall happen the said yearly rent of fortye shillings to be behind in parte or in all at anie of the saide feastes in which it ought to be payd, that then and so often it shall and maie be lawfull to and for the said Joane my wife and her assignes into the said messuage or tenement called Cuttinges and all the lands thereto belonging, and the said close called Denbyes to enter and distreyne and the distresse
[PAGE 3]
there had and found to take leade drive cary awaye and reteyne and keepe untill she be fully satisfied and paid the Annuitie or yearly rent aforesaid together with th'arreragaes thereof if annie

shall happen then to be behinde and unpaiyd. Item I give devise
and bequeathe all those my twoe messuage or tenement with the
homestall grounde thereunto belonging now in the severall occu-
pacouns of John Wright and William Sowter situate lying and
being at the comon pasture of Thurston aforesaid called the
great grene sometyme Clerkes, unto Thomas Sibbes
my sonne his heyres and assignes forever. Item. I give devise
and bequeathe all that my inclose lying at Stoklye conteyning by estimacion four acres be it more or lesse called
the newclose now sowen with wheat which I purchased of William
Cooke, unto Elizabeth my daughter her heyres and assignes with
this proviso that if the said Richard Sibbs my sonne his heyres
or assignes shall at anie tyme within one yeare [at] most after
my death, well and truly and bona fide paye or cause to be
payd unto my said daughter Elizabeth her executors
or assignes the some of fortye poundes of lawfull english monie at one whole and entire payment at or in the
now dwelling house of me the said Paul Sibbs in
Thurston aforesaid that then and from thenceforth alwayes after
true payment so made of the said fortye pounds, it shall and
maie be lawfull to and for my said sonne Richard his heyres
and assignes to enter into the said Inclose called new close
and the same hold to him and his heyres and that then the
guift and devise thereof to my said daughter Elizabeth made
shall be utterly voyde frustrate and of none effect aniethinge
in this my last will to the contrary notwithstanding. Item. I
geve and bequeath unto my said sone John all my tooles and instru-
ments belonging to my trade of wheelewright and all my timber
and weeles now in my yarde. The residue of all my goods
cattels chattels readye money, debtes owing me hows-hold stuffe
and ymplemente of hows-hold stuffe. I geve them to Joane my said
wife –
and I make the said Joane my wife and my said sonne John my
[PAGE 4]
executors of this my last will and testament and thereof I entreat
Robert Sibbs my brother to be supervisor to whom I geve
for his paynes therein to be taken ten shillings. In witness
whereof and for the better approbacon confirmacion and allowance
of this my last will and testament I have caused the same to
be playnly openly and distinctly redd in my hearing and
understanding and in the presence of the witnesses hereunder

named and after the ready and full understanding thereof
I the said Paul Sibbs have hereunto sette my hand
and seale the daie and yeare first above written.

Redd sealed openly published
and delivered into th'andes of my
executors herein named as my
last will and testament in the presence
of
        signed X Andrewe Wright
        Signed Pauli Sibbes
           signed Johis Vorbe Jnr.
               Andrew Wrighte
           signed Robti Sibbes
           signed Robt Bulner

        (Latin statement of probate)
        (Proved at Bury St. Edmunds, 15 Feb., 1610)

Bibliography

I. Alphabetical Bibliography of Sibbes's Works
II. Chronological (by publication) Bibliography of Sibbes's Works
III. Printed Primary Sources
IV. Manuscript Primary Sources
V. Secondary Sources

I. Alphabetical Bibliography of Sibbes' Works

The following is an alphabetical list of Sibbes' works both by individual sermons and by title of volumes of collected volumes. Titles of sermons not published separately or collections later published in larger collections, are in parentheses. All editions were published in London unless otherwise noted. The bracketed roman and arabic numerals give the location of the sermon in the collected works of Sibbes edited by A. B. Grosart. Where possible, dates entered in the Stationers' Register are included.

+ (works not in Grosart)
= (early editions not noted in Grosart)
italicized numbers, e.g., 1111 (STC numbers)

VB (Listed in William London's *Catalogue: Most Vendible Books,* 1657)
("Angels Acclamations" in *Light*) [VI.316] VB again, as "The Nativity of Christ" in J. Wesley, *A Christian Library* vol. 6, 1819.
Antidotum Contra Naufragium Fidei (preached in 1627) 1657, [VII.547] *3729* VB.
("The Art of Contentment" in *The Saint's Cordials*) [V.176]
   Ms. of this in British Library, Lansdowne 684.3, says preached by Sibbs "Aug 8, 1627 at Black Friars."
   GERMAN TRANSLATION, *Wahrer Seelenfriede, in Beruhigung der verunruhigte seele,* Eisenach, 1740.
("Balaam's Wish" in *Evangelical*) [VII.2] VB.
Beames of Divine Light (XXI Sermons) ed. & epistle dedicatory by J. Sedgwick,
   "To the Christian Reader" by Arthur Jackson, 2 pts., (Ent SR 12 Jan 1638) 1639 [V.220] *22475* VB
   "A Description of Christ" in three sermons 1639, 1–75 [I.2].
   "God's Inquisition" 2 sermons, 77–133 [VI.206].

"The Dead–Man, or The State of Every Man by Nature" 1 sermon, 135–160 [VII.398].

"The Fruitfull Labour for Eternall Food" 2 sermons, 161–220 [VI.358].

"Violence Victorious" 2 sermons, 221–273 [VI.294].

"The Churches Complaint and Confidence" in three sermons 1638, 275–330 [VI.182].

"The Spirituall Jubilee" in 2 sermons, 1–61 [V.220].

"Saint Paul's Challenge" 1 sermon 1638, 63–95 [VII.386].

"The Churches Eccho" 1 sermon 1638, 97–126 [VII.535].

"David's Conclusion, or The Saints Resolution" 1 sermon 1638, 127–156 [VII.80].

"King David's Epitaph" in 3 sermons, 161–232 [VI.488].

("The Beast's Dominion" in *Evangelical*) [VII.517] VB.

Bowels Opened ed. Tho. Goodwin & Philip Nye, "To the Christian Reader" by John Dod, (Ent SR 10 Oct 1632) 1639 [II.2] *22476* VB

again, 2nd ed., 1641 (N. B. This is what STC is referring to when it lists *Union Between Christ and the Church*, 1641– LDW) *3730*.

again, 3rd ed., 1648 *3731*.

again, 4th ed., 1658 *(3731A)*.

(again, as "A Discovery of the Near Union and Communion" sermons on Canticles V & VI, in J. Wesley, *A Christian Library* vol. 6, 1819).

A Breathing After God, I. Dawson, (Ent SR 27 Nov 1638) 1639 [II.210] *22477*.

The Bride's Longing (Sermon preached at the funeral of Sir T. Crew, Knight) E. P. 1638 [VI.536] *22478* (STC lists two slight 1638 variants *22478a, 22478b*) VB.

The Bruised Reed (Ent SR 13 July) 1630 [I.32] *22479* VB

again, [1973 FACSIMILE, Intro. P. A. Slack 1630.

again, 2nd enlarged, 1631 *22480*.

again, 3rd ed., 1631 *22481*.

again, 4th ed., 1632 *22482*.

again, 5th ed. corrected for R. Dawlman and L. Faune, 1635 *22483*.

again, 6th ed. corrected, 1638 *22484*.

again, Dutch Translation, Amsterdam, 1646.

again, Dutch Translation, Amsterdam, 1649.

again, Dutch Translation, Amsterdam, 1650.

again, Dutch Translation, Amsterdam, 1657.

again, 6th ed., 1658 *3732*.

again, Dutch Translation, n. l., 1659.

again, 5th ed., (along with The Soul's Conflict), Glasgow, 1768.

again, 8th ed., revised, Bath, 1794 *2330S1*.

again, new ed., n. d..

again, Philadelphia, 180?.

again, 9th ed., with a life of the author by E. Middleton, 1808 *S1885*.

again, again, 1818.

again, again, 1821.

again, again, 1822.

again, n. l., (L. B. Seeley & Son), 1824.

again, n. l., (Pickering), 1828.

(again, in *The Bruised Reed, A Fountain Sealed, A Description of Christ*, n.l., [Pickering], 1838).

again, Intro. Alexander Beith, Edinburgh, 1878.

again, Edinburgh, 1998.

("The Christian Work" in *Exposition*) [V.2].

+"The Christian's Armor against the Feare off Death. Also the Christian's Preparation for Death. With Divers Profitable Meditations." Discourses on Luke 5:4–6, Ps. 90:12, Unpublished, 1637, British Library, Additional Ms. 25,037.

The Christian's End (Ent SR 18 Oct 1638) 1639 [V.288] *22485*.

The Christian's Portion, ed. Goodwin & Nye, (Ent SR 10 Nov) 1637 [IV.2] *22486* VB.

again, corrected and enlarged Tho Goodwin & Philip Nye, J. O. 1638 *22487*.

again, Philadelphia, 1842.

+"The Christian's Preparation for Death" with "The Christian's Armor against the

Feare off Death". Ps. 90:12, Luke 5:4–6, UNPUBLISHED, 1637, British Library, Additional Ms. 25,037.

("The Christian's Watch" in *Exposition*) [VII.298].

("Christ is Best" in *The Saint's Safetie*, 1633) [I.335].

(again, in *The Saint's Safetie*, 1634).

(again, 2nd ed., in *The Saint's Cordials*, 1637).

(again, 3rd ed., in *The Saint's Cordials*, 1658).

Christ's Exaltation Purchased by Humiliation publ by Goodwin & Nye, T. Cotes, sold by I. Bartlet, 1639, [V.324] *22488* VB.

("Christ's Sufferings for Man's Sin" in *The Saint's Safetie*, 1633) [I.336, 352].

(again, in *The Saint's Safetie*, 1634).

(again, 2nd ed., in *The Saint's Cordials*, 1637).

(again, 3rd ed., in *The Saint's Cordials*, 1658).

("The Churches Complaint and Confidence" in *Beames*) [VI.182] VB.

("The Churches Eccho" in *Beames*) [VII.535] VB.

("The Churches Riches" in *Light*) [IV.490] *22489 (Listed as part of 22498)* VB.

("The Church's Blackness" in *The Saint's Cordials*, 1629) [VII.94].

("The Church's Visitation" in *The Saint's Safetie*, 1633) [I.372].

(again, in *The Saint's Safetie*, 1634).

(again, 2nd ed., in *The Saint's Cordials*, 1637).

(again, 3rd ed., in *The Saint's Cordials*, 1658).

("The Coming of Christ" in *Exposition*) [VII.306].

A Consolatory Letter to an Afflicted Conscience...for Francis Coules, 1641, [I.cxv] 3733.

("The Danger of Backsliding" in *The Saint's Cordials*, 1637, 1658) [VII.408].

("David's Conclusion" in *Beames*) [VII.80] VB.

("The Dead Man" in *Beames*) [VII.398] VB.
("The Demand of a Good Conscience" in *Evangelical*) [VII.478] VB.
("A Description of Christ" in *Beames*) [I.2] VB.
  (again, in *The Bruised Reed, A Fountain Sealed, A Description of Christ*, n.l.,
  [Pickering], 1838).
("The Difficulty of Salvation" in *The Saint's Cordials*) [I.395].
("Discouragement's Recovery" in *The Saint's Cordials*, 1629) [VII.50].
(*A Discovery of the Near Union and Communion* see *Bowels Opened*).
("The Discreet Ploughman" in *The Saint's Cordials*, 1629) [VII.140].
Divine Meditations epistle to reader by E. Culverwell (Ent 27 July) 1638 [VII.180]
  22490.
  again, 2nd ed., 1651 (N.B., Not in STC, see Grosart VII.180).
  again, 3rd ed., 1658 *3734*
  again, new ed., ed. W. Miller, 1775 *2327S1*.
  again, new ed., to which is prefaced a life of the author, Newport, 1779.
  again, Lang & Ustick: Philadelphia, 1796.
  again, Bonsal & Niles: Wilmington, Del., 1797.
  again, new ed., life of author by G. Burder, H. P. Silvester, Newport 1799?
  2327S1 [perhaps this is the same as the 1779 edition listed above].
  again, new ed., 1808 *S1886*.
  again, 1840.
  again, 2nd ed., n.l., [Religious Tract Society], 1850.
  again, in *Apples of Gold, First Series*, Zoar Publications, Ossett, UK, 1975.
Evangelical Sacrifices (In XIX sermons) 2 pts. (Ent SR 20 Aug 1638) 1640 *22491*.
  "The Beast's Dominion over Earthly Kings" (A sermon preached November
  5) 1639,
  1–55, [VII.517].
  "The Ruine of Mysticall Jericho" a sermon preached on November 5., title
  page, 1639, 57–99 [VII.462].
  "The Unprosperous Builder" 1 sermon, 101–134 [VII.18].
  "The Successefull Seeker" in 2 sermons, 135–192 [VI.110].
  "Faith Triumphant" in 5 sermons 1639, 193–318 [VII.414].
  "The Hidden Life" in 2 funeral sermons 1639, 1–34 [V.203].
  "The Redemption of Bodyes" in 1 funeral sermon 1639, 35–67 [V.156].
  "Balaam's Wish" in 1 funeral sermon 1639, 69–104 [VII.2].
  "The Faithful Covenanter" in 2 sermons, 105–165 [VI.2].
  "The Demand of a Good Conscience" 1 sermon, 167–202 [VII.478].
  "The Sword of the Wicked" in 2 sermons 1639, 203–238 [I.104].
The Excellencie of the Gospel above the Law publ. Tho Goodwin & Philip Nye, pri.
  Tho Cotes, (Ent SR 10 Aug 1633) 1639 [IV.202] *22492*.
Exposition of Third Chapter of Philippians + other sermons, T. Cotes, (Ent SR 2 Aug
  1637) 1639 [V.56] *22493* VB.
  "The Christian Work" [V.2].
  "Of the Providence of God" [V.35].
  VB "The Sun of Righteousness" [VII.166].

VB "The Christian's Watch" [VII.298].

VB "The Coming of Christ" [VII.306].

=again, 1647 *3735*.

("Faith Triumphant" in *Evangelical*) [VII.414] VB.

("The Faithful Covenanter" in *Evangelical*) [VI.6] VB.

("The Fountain Opened" in *Light*) [V.458] VB.

(again, in John Wesley, *The Christian Library*, vol. 6, 1819).

A Fountain Sealed (substance of Divers sermons preached at Grayes Inne), ed. Goodwin & Nye, T. Harper, (Ent 27 Aug 1633) 1637 [V.410] *22494* VB.

again, 2nd ed., T. Harper for L. Chapman, 1637 *22495*.

again, 3rd ed., 1638 *22496*.

again, Amstelredam, 1638 *22496.5*.

again, Dutch Translation, Schoonhoven, 1651.

again, Dutch Translation, Leiden, 1652.

(again, in *The Bruised Reed, A Fountain Sealed, A Description of Christ*, n.l., [Pickering], 1838).

("The Fruitful Labor for Eternal Food" in *Beames*) [VI.358] VB.

("The General Resurrection" in *The Saint's Cordials*, 1629) [VII.316].

A Glance of Heaven E. Griffin for J. Rothwell, sold by H. Overton, (Ent SR 7 Apr) 1638 (two different imprints, both done in 1638) [IV.152] *22497 (22497.5)* VB.

("A Glimpse of Glory" in *The Saint's Cordials*) [VII.492].

The Glorious Feast of the Gospel 1650 [II.438] *3736* VB.

("God's Inquisition" in *Beames*) [VI.206] VB.

A Heavenly Conference 1654 [VI.414] *3736B*.

(again, in *A Learned*, 1656) *3737*.

again, Dutch Translation, 1664.

("The Hidden Life" in *Evangelical*) [V.203] VB.

("Josiah's Reformation" in *The Saint's Cordials*) [VI.28; cf.VII.563–564].

("Judgement's Reason" in *The Saint's Cordials*) [IV.76].

("King David's Epitaph" in *Beames*) [VI.488] VB.

("The Knot of Prayer Loosed" in *The Saint's Cordials*, 1629) [VII.230].

A Learned Commentary on Second Corinthians One, Ed. and "To the Reader" by Tho. Manton 1655 [III] *3738* VB.

A Learned Commentary upon Second Corinthians 4 preface by Simeon Ash, Ja. Nalton, Joseph Church 1656 [IV.308] *3739*.

"A Heavenly Conference" [VI.414].

"A Miracle of Miracles" Preached to Grayes Inne 1656 [VII.106].

"The Spirituall–Mans Aime" 1656 [IV.40].

("The Life of Faith" in *The Saint's Cordials*) [V.358].

Light From Heaven in 4 treatises ed. J. Sedgwick, E. Purslow & R. Badger for N. Bourne & R. Harford, (Ent SR 12 Jan) 1638 *22498*.

"Angels Acclamations" 1638 [VI.316].

"The Churches Riches" 1638 [IV.490].

"The Fountain Opened" 1638 [V.458].

"Rich Poverty" 1638 [VI.230].

=again, another edition, 1638 *22498a*.

again, Dutch Translation, Amsterdam, 1661.

again, Dutch Translation, Utrecht, 1664.

("Lydia's Conversion" in *The Riches of Mercie*) [VI.518].

("Mary's Choice" in *The Saint's Comforts*) [VII.288] VB.

("Matchless Love and Inbeing" in *The Saint's Cordials*, 1629; reprinted in 1637 ed. under title "The Saints Assurance") [VI.384].

("The Matchless Mercy" in *The Saint's Cordials*, 1629) [VII.152].

A Miracle of Miracles (Ent SB 26 Oct) 1638 [VII.106] *22499*.

(again?, 1656, STC lists as being held by C, O, yet more likely this was simply part of *A Learned Commentary on IICor 1*) *3740*.

("The Nativity of Christ" see "Angels Acclamations").

("Of the Providence of God" in *Exposition*) [V.35].

("The Pattern of Purity" in *The Saint's Cordials*) [VII.505].

("The Power of Christ's Resurrection" in *Two Sermons*) [V.195].

("The Privileges of the Faithful" in *Yea*) [V.250].

("The Redemption of Bodyes" in *Evangelical*) [V.156].

("A Rescue from Death" in *The Riches of Mercie*) [VI.134].

The Returning Backslider (Ent SR 10 Oct 1632) 1639 [II.250] *22500* (STC lists another imprint *22500.5*) VB.

again, 2nd ed., 1641 *3741*.

again, 3rd ed., 1650 *3742*.

("The Rich Pearl" in *The Saint's Comforts*) [VII.254] VB.

("Rich Poverty" in *Light*) [VI.230] VB.

The Riches of Mercie in 2 treatises I. D., 1638 *22501* VB.

"Lydia's Conversion" [VI.518] (Ent SR 11 May 1638).

"A Rescue from Death" [VI.134] (Ent SR 12 Apr 1638).

("The Right Receiving" in *The Saint's Cordials* 1629) [IV.60].

("The Ruine of Mysticall Jericho" in *Evangelical*) [VII.462] VB.

("St. Paul's Challenge" in *Beames*) [VII.386] VB.

(*The Saint's Ark* 2 sermons abridged from *Saint's Cordials* by W. Batson, n.d. [1810?]).

(*The Saint's Assurance*, abridged ed. of *The Saint's Cordials* by W. Batson, 1809).

The Saint's Comforts (Ent SR 18 Sept 1637) 1638 [VI.160] *22502* VB.

"The Saint's Happiness" [VII.66].

"The Rich Pearl" [VII.254].

"Success of the Gospel" [VII.280].

"Mary's Choice" [VII.288].

The Saint's Cordials as delivered in sundry sermons upon special occasions, pr. by M. Flesher for R. Dawlman, (Ent SR 2 Apr) 1629 [IV.60] *22503* VB.

[N.B., The Congregational Library at Dr. Williams's Library, London, in their cat. vol II 446 mistakenly lists a 1621 ed.]

again, delivered in sundry sermons at Grayes Inne & in the City of London, now added *The Saints Safety in Evil Times*, preached in Cambridge, 1637 *22504*.

again, "another edition", 1658 *3743*.

(*The Saint's Ark* 2 sermons abridged from *Saint's Cordials* by W. Batson, n.d. [1810?]).

(*The Saint's Assurance*, abridged ed. of *The Saint's Cordials* by W. Batson, 1809 *S1888*).

("The Saint's Happiness" in *The Saint's Comforts*) [VII.66] VB.

("The Saints Hiding–Place in the Evil Day" in *The Saints Cordials*) [I.401, 411].

The Saints Priviledge, 1638 (cf. Grosart's note [VII.357]) *22505* (STC lists another 1638

imprint *22505.5*) VB.

again, another edition, 1639 *22506*.

again, another edition, 1641 *3744 (Entry cancelled in Wing Revised because says it is in the Returning Backslider, 1641)*.

(again, in *The Returning Backslider*).

The Saints Safetie in Evil Times (Ent SR 16 Oct) 1633 [I.296] *22507*.

again, M. Flesher for R. Dawlman, 1634 *22507.5*.

Included in part 2

"The Church's Visitation"

"The Ungodly's Misery"

"The Difficulty of Salvation"

"The Saints Hiding Place in the Evil Day."

(again, 2nd ed., in *The Saint's Cordials*, 1637).

(again, 3rd ed., in *The Saint's Cordials*, 1658).

("Saint's Safety in Evil Times Manifested by St. Paul" in *The Saints Safetie in Evil Times* 1633, and in *The Saint's Cordials* 1637, 1658; appeared under title "Experience Triumphing" in 1629 ed. of *Cordials*).

("Salvation Applied" in *The Saint's Cordials*) [V.386].

("Sin's Antidote" in *The Saint's Cordials*, 1629) [VII.262].

The Soules Conflict with Itself, (Ent SR 16 May 1632) 1635 [I.120] *22508* VB.

again, "Victory" re–issue, 1635 *(Noted in STC, but no separate number)*.

again, 2nd ed., 1635 *22508.5*.

again, 2nd ed., 1636 *22509*.

again, 3rd ed., 1636 *22510*.

again, 4th ed., 1638 *22511*.

again, 4th ed., 1651 *3745*.

again, 5th ed., 1658 *3746*.

again, Dutch Translation, Haarlem, 1659.

again, *Der Seelen Selbstreit und derselben Uberwindung ubersich selbst* (*Soules Conflict*) GERMAN TRANSLATION, Kassell & Dresden, 1675.

again, 5th ed., life of the author by S. Clarke, Glasgow, 1768 *2327S2*.

again, 10th ed., 1808 *S1889*.

again, 1830.

again, n.l., [William Pickering], 1837.

again, Philadelphia, 1842.

again, n.l., [Religious Tract Society], 1854.

The Spiritual Favorite at the Throne of Grace, T. Paine, (Ent SR 20 Oct 1639) 1640 [VI.92] *22512*.
("The Spirituall Jubile" in *Beames*) [V.220] (N.B., mistakenly listed as separate work in
   the DNB) VB.
The Spiritual–Mans Aime, ed. Goodwin & Nye, (Ent SR 12 June) 1637 [IV.40] *22513* VB.
   again, 2nd ed corrected, 1637 *22513.5 (was 22512a)*.
   again, 3rd ed., publ. Tho Goodwin & Philip Nye, I. N., 1638 *22514*.
   (again, in *A Learned Commentary*, 1656).
   again, ed. E. Palmer, in *Palmer's Select Pocket Divinity* vol 2, 1827.
("Spiritual Mourning" in *The Saint's Cordials*, 1629) [VI.266].
("The Spouse, Her Earnest Desire After Christ" in *Two Sermons*) [II.198].
("The Success of the Gospel" in *The Saint's Comforts*) [VII.280].
("The Successefull Seeker" in *Evangelical*) [VI.110] VB.
("The Sun of Righteousness" in *Exposition*) [VII.166].
("The Sword of the Wicked" in *Evangelical*) [I.104] VB.
+*Threnoikos* The House of Mourning Furnished delivered in 47 sermons preached at the funeralls of divers faithfull servants of Christ by D. F., M.
   Day, Richard Sibbs, Thomas Taylor, 1640 (N.B., not clear which of the 47 sermons is/are by Sibbes) *24048*.
("The Touchstone of Regeneration" in *The Saint's Cordials*, 1629) [VII.128].
Two Sermons (Ent SR 12 Apr) 1638 *22519*.
   "The Spouse, Her Earnest Desire after Christ" [II.198].
   "The Power of Christ's Resurrection" [V.195].
   =again, "another ed.", T. Cotes for A. Kembe, 1639 *22520*.
Two Sermons upon the First Words (The Last sermon of R. Sibbs preached at
   Grayes Inne, June 21 & 28, 1635) T. Harper for L. Chapman, (Ent SR 14
   Apr) 1636 [VII.338] *22515* VB.
   again, 2nd ed., 1636 *22516*.
   again, 3rd ed., T. Harper for L. Chapman, 1637 *22517*.
   again, 4th ed., 1638 *22518*.
("The Ungodly's Misery" in *The Saint's Cordials*) [I.385].
(*Union Between Christ and the Church* 1641 – listed by STC is referring to the
   1641 edition of *Bowels Opened*) *3747*.
("The Unprosperous Builder" in *Evangelical*) [VII.18] VB.
("The Vanity of the Creature" in *The Saint's Cordials*, 1629) [VII.34].
("Violence Victorious" in *Beames*) [VI.294] VB.
("The Witness of Salvation" in *The Saint's Cordials*, 1629) [VII.367].
Works, ed. W. Baynes, life of author, 3 vols. Aberdeen, 1809 *S1887*.
   again, Aberdeen, 1812.
Works, ed. & life of author Alexander Balloch Grosart, 7 vols. Edinburgh, 1862–1864.
   reprinted, Edinburgh, 1973–1983.
Yea and Amen perused by Tho Goodwin & Philip Nye, R. Bishop, (Ent SR 11 Jan)

1638 [IV.113] *22521* VB.
Works edited and epistles dedicatory with John Davenport
Preston, John, *The Breastplate of Faith and Love* W. J. for N. Bourne, (Ent SR 13 Oct 1629) 1630 [I.xcvi] *20208*.
  again, 2nd ed. corrected, 1630–1631 *20209*.
  again, 1631 *20210*.
  again, 3rd ed., W. Jones for N. Bourne, 1631–1632 *20211*.
  again, 4th ed., R. Young for N. Bourne, 1634 *20212*.
  again, 5th ed., 1634 (–'37') *20213*.
  again, 1643 *3300*.
  again, 5th ed., 1651 *3301*.
  again, 6th ed., G. Purslow, sold in the companie of Stationers, 1651 *3301a*.
Preston, John, *The New Covenant* J. D. for N. Bourne, 1629 [I.xcv] *20241*.
  again, 2nd ed., 1629 *20241.3*.
  again, 3rd ed., 1629 *20241.7*.
  again, 4th ed., 1630 *20242*.
  again, 5th ed., 1630 *20243*.
  again, 6th ed., 1631 *20244*.
  again, 7th ed. corrected, 1633 *20245*.
  again, 8th ed. corrected, 1634 *20246*.
  again, 9th ed., 1639 *20247*.
  again, Dutch Translation, Amsterdam, 1649.
  again, 10th ed., 1655 *3304*.
  again, Dutch Translation, Amsterdam, 1660.
Preston, John, *The Saints Daily Exercise* 1629 [I.xcviii] *20251*.
  again, 2nd ed., 1629 *20252*.
  again, 3rd ed., 1629 *20253*.
  again, 4th ed., 1630 *20254*.
  again, 5th ed., 1631 *20255*.
  again, 6th ed., 1631 *20256*.
  again, 7th ed., 1632 *20257*.
  again, 8th ed., 1633 *20258*.
  again, 1634 *20258.5 (was 20260)*.
  again, 9th ed., 1634 *20259*.
  again, 1635 *20260a (was 20261)*.
  again, Dutch Translation, Dordrecht, 1639.
  again, Dutch Translation, Dordrecht, 1660.
Preston, John, *The Saints Qualification* 1633 [I.xcix] *20262*.
  again, 2nd ed., 1634 *20263*.
  again, 3rd ed., 1634 *20264*.
  again, 3rd ed., 1637 *20265*.
  again, another, 1637 *20265.5*.
Works with epistles dedicatory by Sibbes
Ball, John, *A Treatise of Faith*, 1631 [I.cv] *1319*.
  again, 2nd ed., 1632 *1320*.

again, 3rd ed., 1637 *1321.*
Baynes, Paul, *A Commentary Upon the First Chapter of the Epistle . . . to the Ephesians*, 1618 [I.lxxxiii] *1535.*
    again, to Baynes, P., *An Entire Commentary . . . Ephesians*, 1643 *1549.*
    again, another ed., 1647 *1550.*
    again, 5th ed., 1658 *1551.*
Capel, R., *Tentations, Their Nature* 1633 [I.cvii] *4595.*
    again, 2nd ed., 1635 *4596.*
    again, 3rd ed., 1636 *4597.*
    again, 4th ed., 1650 *472.*
    again, 5th ed., 1655 *473.*
    again, 6th ed., 1658 *474.*
    again, "Sixth" ed., 1659 *475.*
    again, Dutch Translation, Utrecht, 1659.
Culverwell, E., *Time Well Spent in Sacred Meditation* 1634 [I.xciii] *6112.*
    again, 1634 *6113.*
Culverwell, E., *A Treatise of Faith*, 1623 [I.xc] *6113.5.*
    again, 2nd ed., 1623 *6114.*
    again, 3rd ed., 1623 *6115.*
    again, 4th ed., 1624 *6115.5.*
    again, 5th ed., 1625 *6116.*
    again, 6th ed., 1629 *6117.*
    again, Dutch Translation, Delft, 1632.
    again, 7th ed., 1633 *6118.*
    again, Dutch Translation, n.l., 1670.
Gataker, Thomas, *Christian Constancy* A funeral sermon for William Winter, I Haviland for W. Bluden, 1624 [VII.561] *11653.*
    again, 1637 – [Grosart VII.561] *(Not in STC)*
Jenison, Robert, *The Christians Apparelling by Christ*, 1625 [Not in Grosart] *14488.*
Scudder, Henry, *A Key of Heaven* R. Field for T. Man, 1620 [I.lxxxvii] *22121.*
    again, 2nd ed., 1633 *22122.*
Smith, John, *An Exposition of the Creed*, 1632 [I.ci] *22801.*
    again, DUTCH TRANSLATION, Amsterdam, 1661.

II. Chronological (by publication) Bibliography of Sibbes' Works
First editions appear in bold print.
SIBBES, Richard, (all London unless otherwise noted)
1618 **"To the Reader" to Baynes, Paul, *A Commentary Upon the First Chapter of the Epistle . . . to the Ephesians*, 1618** *1535.*
1620 **"Recommendation" to Scudder, Henry, *A Key of Heaven* R. Field for T. Man, 1620** [I.lxxxvii] *22121.*
1623 **"Epistle to the Christian Reader" to Culverwell, E., *A Treatise of Faith* 1623** [I.xc] *6113.5.*
    "Epistle to the Christian Reader" to Culverwell, E., *A Treatise of Faith*, 2nd ed., 1623 *6114.*

"Epistle to the Christian Reader" to Culverwell, E., *A Treatise of Faith*, 3rd ed., 1623 *6115*.

1624 "Epistle to the Christian Reader" to Culverwell, E., *A Treatise of Faith*, 4th ed., 1624 *6115.5*.

Epistle Dedicatory to Gataker, Thomas, *Christian Constancy* A funeral sermon for William Winter, I Haviland for W. Bluden, 1624 [VII.561] *11653*.

1625 "Epistle to the Christian Reader" to Culverwell, E., *A Treatise of Faith*, 5th ed., 1625 *6116*.

To the Christian Reader to Jenison, Robert, *The Christians Apparelling by Christ*, 1625 [Not in Grosart] *14488*.

(1627 delivered *Antidotum Contra Naufragium Fidei* pub in 1657 [VII.547]).

(1627 Aug 8. Delivered "The Art of Contentment" at Black Friars, London, Ms in British Library, Lansdowne 684.3).

1629 "Epistle to the Christian Reader" to Culverwell, E., *A Treatise of Faith*, 6th ed., 1629 *6117*.

The Saint's Cordials **as delivered in sundry sermons upon special occasions, pr. by M. Flesher for R. Dawlman, 1629 [Ent SR 2 Apr 1629] *22503* VB.**

Epistle Dedicatory and ed. with J. Davenport for Preston, John, *The New Covenant* J. D. for N. Bourne, 1629 [I.xcv] *20241*.

Epistle Dedicatory and ed. with J. Davenport for Preston, John, *The New Covenant*, 2nd ed., 1629 *20241.3*.

Epistle Dedicatory and ed. with J. Davenport for Preston, John, *The New Covenant*, 3rd ed., 1629 *20241.7*.

"To the Reader" and ed. with J. Davenport for Preston, John, *The Saints Daily Exercise*, 1629 [I.xcviii] *20251*.

"To the Reader" and ed. with J. Davenport for Preston, John, *The Saints Daily Exercise*, 2nd ed., 1629 *20252*.

"To the Reader" and ed. with J. Davenport for Preston, John, *The Saints Daily Exercise*, 3rd ed., 1629 *20253*.

1630 *The Bruised Reed* (Ent 13 July) 1630 [I.32] *22479* VB.

Epistle Dedicatory and ed. with J. Davenport for Preston, John, *The Breastplate of Faith and Love* W. J. for N. Bourne, 1630 [I.xcvi] *20208*.

Epistle Dedicatory and ed. with J. Davenport for Preston, John, *The New Covenant*, 4th ed., 1630 *20242*.

Epistle Dedicatory and ed. with J. Davenport for Preston, John, *The New Covenant*, 5th ed., 1630 *20243*.

"To the Reader" and ed. with J. Davenport for Preston, John, *The Saints Daily Exercise*, 4th ed., 1630 *20254*.

1631 *The Bruised Reed*, 2nd enlarged, 1631 *22480*.

The Bruised Reed, 3rd ed., 1631 *22481*.

"The Preface to the Reader" to Ball, John, *A Treatise of Faith*, 1st ed, [I.cv] *1319*.

Epistle Dedicatory and ed. with J. Davenport for Preston, John, *The Breastplate of Faith and Love*, 2nd ed. corrected, 1630–1631 *20209*.

Epistle Dedicatory and ed. with J. Davenport for Preston, John, *The Breastplate of Faith and Love*, another imprint 20210.
Epistle Dedicatory and ed. with J. Davenport for Preston, John, *The New Covenant*, 6th ed., 1631 20244.
"To the Reader" and ed. with J. Davenport for Preston, John, *The Saints Daily Exercise*, 5th ed., 1631 20255.
"To the Reader" and ed. with J. Davenport for Preston, John, *The Saints Daily Exercise*, 6th ed., 1631 20256.
1632 *The Bruised Reed*, 4th ed., 1632 22482.
"The Preface to the Reader" to Ball, John, *A Treatise of Faith*, 2nd ed., 1632 1320.
"Epistle to the Christian Reader" to Culverwell, E., *A Treatise of Faith*, Dutch Translation, Delft, 1632.
"To the Christian Reader" to Smith, John, *An Exposition of the Creed*, 1632 [I.ci] 22801.
Epistle Dedicatory and ed. with J. Davenport to Preston, John, *The Breastplate of Faith and Love*, 3rd ed., W. Jones for N. Bourne, 1631–1632 20211.
"To the Reader" and ed. with J. Davenport for Preston, John, *The Saints Daily Exercise*, 1632 20257.
1633 **"To the Christian Reader" to Capel, R., *Tentations, Their Nature* 1633 [I.cvii] 4595.**
"Epistle to the Christian Reader" to Culverwell, E., *A Treatise of Faith*, 7th ed., 1633 6118.
Epistle Dedicatory to Scudder, Henry, *A Key of Heaven*, 2nd ed., 1633 22122.
The Saints Safetie in Evil Times (Ent SR 16 Oct) 1633 [I.296] 22507.
"To the Reader" and ed. with J. Davenport for Preston, John, *The New Covenant*, 7th ed. corrected, 1633 20245.
"To the Reader" and ed. with J. Davenport for Preston, John, *The Saints Daily Exercise*, 8th ed., 1633 20258.
Epistle Dedicatory and ed. with J. Davenport for Preston, John, *The Saints Qualification* 1633 [I.xcix] 20262.
1634 **Epistle Dedicatory to Culverwell, E., *Time Well Spent in Sacred Meditation* 1634 [I.xciii] 6112.**
Epistle Dedicatory to Culverwell, E., *Time Well Spent in Sacred Meditation* 1634 6113.
Epistle Dedicatory and ed. with J. Davenport for Preston, John, *The Breastplate of Faith and Love*, 4th ed. R. Young for N. Bourne, 1634 20212.
Epistle Dedicatory and ed. with J. Davenport for Preston, John, *The Breastplate of Faith and Love*, 5th ed. R. Young for N. Bourne, 1634 ('–37')? 20213.
=*The Saints Safetie in Evil Times*, M. Flesher for R. Dawlman, 1634 22507.5.

Epistle Dedicatory and ed. with J. Davenport for Preston, John, *The New Covenant*, 8th ed. corrected, 1634 *20246*.

"To the Reader" and ed. with J. Davenport for Preston, John, *The Saints Daily Exercise*, 1634 *20258.5* (was *20260*).

"To the Reader" and ed. with J. Davenport for Preston, John, *The Saints Daily Exercise*, 9th ed., 1634 *20259*.

Epistle Dedicatory and ed. with J. Davenport for Preston, John, *The Saints Qualification*, 2nd ed., 1634 *20263*.

Epistle Dedicatory and ed. with J. Davenport for Preston, John, *The Saints Qualification*, 3rd ed., 1634 *20264*.

1635 *The Bruised Reed*, 5th ed. corrected for R. Dawlman and L. Faune, 1635 *22483*.

"To the Christian Reader" to Capel, R., *Tentations, Their Nature*, 2nd ed., 1635 *4596*.

The Soules Conflict with Itself (Ent SR 16 May 1632) 1635 [I.120] *22508* VB.

The Soules Conflict with Itself, "Victory" reissue, 1635 *(Noted in STC, but no separate number)*.

The Soules Conflict with Itself, 2nd ed., 1635 *22508.5*.

(delivered *Two Sermons upon the First Words* (The Last sermon of R. Sibbs preached at Grayes Inne, June 21 & 28, 1635) T. Harper for L. Chapman, 1636 [VII.338]).

"To the Reader" and ed. with J. Davenport for Preston, John, *The Saints Daily Exercise*, 1635 *20260a* (was *20261*).

1636 "To the Christian Reader" to Capel, R., *Tentations, Their Nature*, 3rd ed., 1635 *4597*.

The Soules Conflict with Itself, 2nd ed., 1636 *22509*.

The Soules Conflict with Itself, 3rd ed., 1636 *22510*.

Two Sermons upon the First Words (The Last sermon of R. Sibbs preached at Grayes Inne, June 21 & 28, 1635) T. Harper for L. Chapman, (Ent SR 14 Apr) 1636 [VII.338] 22515 VB.

Two Sermons upon the First Words, 2nd ed., 1636 *22516*.

1637 **+"The Christian's Armor against the Feare off Death. Also the Christian's Preparation for Death. With Divers Profitable Meditations."**
Discourses on Luke 5:4–6, Ps. 90:2, unpublished, 1637, British Library, Additional Ms. 25,037.

The Christian's Portion, ed. Goodwin and Nye, (Ent SR 10 Nov) 1637 [IV.2] *22486*
VB.

"The Preface to the Reader" to Ball, John, *A Treatise of Faith*, 3rd ed., 1637 *1321*.

Epistle Dedicatory to Gataker, Thomas, *Christian Constancy* A funeral sermon for William Winter, I. Haviland for W. Bluden, 1637 [Grosart VII.561] *(Not in STC)*

A Fountain Sealed (substance of Divers sermons preached at Grayes Inne), ed. Goodwin and Nye, T. Harper, (Ent 27 Aug 1633) 1637 [V.410]

22494 VB.

A Fountain Sealed, 2nd ed., T. Harper for L. Chapman, 1637 *22495.*

The Saint's Cordials, delivered in sundry sermons at Grayes Inne & in the City of London, now added *The Saints Safety in Evil Times*, preached in Cambridge, 1637 *22504.*

The Spiritual–Mans Aime, ed. Goodwin and Nye, (Ent SR 12 June) 1637 [IV.40]

22513 VB.

The Spiritual–Mans Aime, 2nd ed., corrected, 1637 *22513.5 (was 22512a).*

Two Sermons upon the First Words, 3rd ed., T. Harper, 1637 *22517.*

Epistle Dedicatory and ed. with J. Davenport for Preston, John, *The Saints Qualification*, 3rd ed., 1637 *20265.*

Epistle Dedicatory and ed. with J. Davenport for Preston, John, *The Saints Qualification*, another, 1637 *20265.5.*

1638 **The Bride's Longing (Sermon preached at the funeral of Sir T. Crew, Knight) E.**

P.1638 [VI.536] 22478 (STC lists two slight 1638 variants *22478a, 22478b*) VB.

The Bruised Reed, 6th ed. corrected, 1638 *22484.*

The Christian's Portion, corrected and enlarged Tho Goodwin & Philip Nye, J. O. 1638 *22487.*

Divine Meditations epistle to reader by E. Culverwell (Ent 27 July) 1638 [VII.180] 22490.

A Fountain Sealed, 3rd ed., 1638 *22496.*

A Fountain Sealed, Amstelredam, 1638 *22496.5.*

A Glance of Heaven E. Griffin for J. Rothwell, sold by H. Overton, (Ent SR 7 Apr) 1638 [IV.152] 22497 (22497.5) VB.

Light From Heaven in 4 treatises ed. J. Sedgwick, E. Puslow & R. Badger for N. Bourne & R. Harford, (Ent SR 12 Jan) 1638 [IV.491] 22498.

=*Light From Heaven*, another edition, 1638 – C, O *22498a.*

A Miracle of Miracles (Ent SR 26 Oct) 1638 [VII.106] 22499.

The Riches of Mercie in 2 treatises I. D., 1638 [VI.518] 22501 VB.

The Saint's Comforts (Ent SR 18 Sept 1637) 1638 [VI.160] 22502 VB.

The Saints Priviledge, 1638 (N.B., Grosart's note [VII.357]) 22505 (STC lists another 1638 imprint 22505.5) VB.

The Soules Conflict with Itself, 4th ed., 1638 *22511.*

The Spiritual–Mans Aime, 3rd ed., publ. Tho Goodwin & Philip Nye, I. N., 1638 22514.

Two Sermons (Ent SR 12 Apr) 1638 [II.198] 22519.

Two Sermons upon the First Words, 4th ed., 1638 *22518.*

Yea and Amen perused by Tho Goodwin & Philip Nye, R. Bishop, (Ent SR 11

Jan) 1638 [IV.113] 22521 VB.

1639 **Beames of Divine Light (XXI Sermons) ed. & epistle dedicatory by J. Sedgwick, to** the reader by Arthur Jackson 2 pts., (Ent SR 12 Jan 1638) 1639 [V.220] 22475 VB.

Bowels Opened ed. Tho. Goodwin & Philip Nye, "To the Christian Reader" by John Dod (Ent SR 10 Oct 1632) 1639 [II.2] 22476 VB.

A Breathing After God I. Dawson, (Ent SR 27 Nov 1638) 1639 [II.210] 22477.

The Christian's End (Ent SR 18 Oct 1638) 1639 [V.288] 22485.

Christ's Exaltation Purchased by Humiliation, publ. by Goodwin & Nye, T. Cotes, sold by I. Bartlet, 1639 [V.324] 22488 VB.

The Excellencie of the Gospel above the Law publ. Tho Goodwin & Philip Nye,

pri. Tho Cotes, (Ent SR 10 Aug 1633) 1639 [IV.202] 22492.

Exposition of Third Chapter of Philippians + two other sermons, T. Cotes, (Ent SR 2 Aug 1637) 1639 [V.56] 22493 VB.

The Returning Backslider (Ent SR 10 Oct 1632) 1639 [II.250] (STC lists another

1639 imprint 22500.5) 22500 VB.

The Saints Priviledge, another edition, 1639 22506.

=*Two Sermons*, "another ed.", T. Cotes for A. Kembe, 1639 22520.

Epistle Dedicatory and ed. with J. Davenport for Preston, John, *The New Covenant*, 9th ed., 1639 20247.

"To the Reader" and ed. with J. Davenport for Preston, John, *The Saints Daily Exercise*, Dutch Translation, Dordrect, 1639.

1640 *Evangelical Sacrifices (In XIX sermons)* 2 pts. (Ent SR 20 Aug 1638) 1640 [V.157]

22491.

The Spiritual Favorite at the Throne of Grace, T. Paine (Ent SR 20 Oct 1639) 1640 [VI.92] 22512.

+*Threnoikos* The House of Mourning Furnished delivered in 47 sermons preached at the funeralls of divers faithfull servants of Christ byz D. F., M. Day, Richard Sibbs, Thomas Taylor, 1640 (Not clear which of the 47 sermons is/are by Sibbes) 24048.

1641 *Bowels Opened*, 2nd ed., 1641 (This is what STC is referring to when it lists *Union Between Christ and the Church*, 1641) 3730; 3747.

A Consolatory Letter to an Afflicted Conscience for Francis Coules 1641 3733 [I.cxv].

The Returning Backslider, 2nd ed., 1641 3741.

The Saints Privilege, another edition, 1641 3744.

1643 "To the Reader" to Baynes, P., *An Entire Commentary . . . Ephesians*, 1643 (formerly attached to Baynes' *Commentary on the First Chapter* 1635) 1549.

Epistle Dedicatory and ed. with J. Davenport for Preston, John, *The Breastplate of Faith and Love*, 1643 3300.

1646 *The Bruised Reed*, Dutch Translation, Amsterdam, 1646.

1647 "To the Reader" to Baynes, P., *An Entire Commentary . . . Ephesians*, another edition, 1647 1550.

=*Exposition of the Third Chapter of Philippians* + two other sermons, 1647 3735.

1648 *Bowels Opened,* 3rd ed., 1648 *3731.*
1649 *The Bruised Reed,* Dutch Translation, Amsterdam, 1649.
   Epistle Dedicatory and ed. with J. Davenport for Preston, John, *The New Covenant,* Dutch Translation, Amsterdam, 1649.
1650 "To the Christian Reader" to Capel, R., *Tentations, Their Nature,* 4th ed., 1650 *472.*
   The Bruised Reed, Dutch Translation, Amsterdam, 1650.
   The Glorious Feast of the Gospel 1650 [II.438] 3736 VB.
   The Returning Backslider, 3rd ed., 1650 *3742.*
1651 *Divine Meditations* 2nd ed., *1651* [Grosart VII.180] *(Not in STC).*
   Epistle Dedicatory and ed. with J. Davenport for Preston, John, *The Breastplate of Faith and Love,* 5th ed., 1651 *3301.*
   Epistle Dedicatory and with J. Davenport for Preston, John, *The Breastplate of Faith and Love,* 6th ed. G. Purslow, sold in the companie of Stationers, 1651 *3301a.*
   A Fountain Sealed, Dutch Translation, Schoonhoven, 1651.
   The Soules Conflict with Itself, 4th ed., 1651 *3745.*
1652 *A Fountain Sealed,* Dutch Translation, Leiden, 1652.
1654 *A Heavenly Conference* **1654 [VI.414] (3736B; 1656 edition in A Learned Commentary**
   on II Cor 4 is listed separately as 3737).
1655 *A Learned Commentary on Second Corinthians One* **Ed. and "To the Christian**
   Reader by Tho. Manton 1655 [III] 3738 VB.
   "To the Christian Reader" to Capel, R., *Tentations, Their Nature,* 5th ed., 1655 *473.*
   Epistle Dedicatory and ed. with J. Davenport for Preston, John, *The New Covenant,* 10th ed., 1655 *3304.*
1656 ? *Miracle of Miracles* (STC lists as being held by C, O; was perhaps simply listed separately, but was published as part of *A Learned Commentary on II Cor 1)* 3740.
   A Learned Commentary upon Second Corinthians 4 preface by Simeon Ash, Ja.
   Nalton, Joseph Church 1656 [IV.308] 3739.
   "To the Reader" and ed. with J. Davenport for Preston, John, *The Saints Daily Exercise,* Dutch Translation, Dordrect, 1656.
1657 *Antidotum Contra Naufragium Fidei* **(given in 1627) 1657 [VII.547] 3729 VB.**
   The Bruised Reed, Dutch Translation, Amsterdam, 1657.
1658 =*Bowels Opened,* 4th ed., 1658 *3731A.*
   The Bruised Reed, 6th ed., 1658 *3732.*
   Divine Meditations, 3rd ed., 1658 *3734.*
   "To the Reader" to Baynes, P., *An Entire Commentary . . . Ephesians,* 5th ed., 1658 *1551.*
   "To the Christian Reader" to R. Capel, *Tentations, Their Nature,* 6th ed.,

1658 474.

The Saint's Cordials, "another edition", 1658 3743.

The Soules Conflict with Itself, 5th ed., 1658 3746.

1659 *The Bruised Reed,* Dutch Translation, n.l., 1659.

"To the Christian Reader" to R. Capel, *Tentations, Their Nature,* "Sixth" ed., 1659 475.

"To the Christian Reader" to R. Capel, *Tentations, Their Nature,* DUTCH TRANSLATION, Utrecht, 1659.

The Soules Conflict with Itself, "*Der Sielen Selfstrijdt*", DUTCH TRANSLATION (by Johannes Grindal), Haarlem, 1659.

1660 Epistle Dedicatory and ed. with J. Davenport for Preston, John, *The New Covenant,* Dutch Translation, Amsterdam, 1660.

1661 "To the Christian Reader" to John Smith, *An Exposition of the Creed,* DUTCH TRANSLATION, Amsterdam, 1661.

Light from Heaven, Dutch Translation, Amsterdam, 1661.

1662 +*Threnoikos The House of Mourning Furnished delivered in 47 sermons preached at the funeralls of divers faithfull servants of Christ* by D. F., M. Day, Richard Sibbs, Thomas Taylor, "*Ruyter op het fael paerd, ofte doen en bedrijf van den koning der verschrickingen, in dertig uytgeleesene lijckpredikatien*" (Dutch Translation) yet this says only of 30 separately published funeral sermons, 1662.

1664 *A Heavenly Conference,* "*Een hemelsche t'samenspraecke*" Dutch Translation, 1664.

Light from Heaven, Dutch Translation, Utrecht, 1664.

Miracle of Miracles, "*De wonderbare ontfanckenisse*" (Dutch Translation), Utrecht, 1664.

"Epistle to the Christian Reader" to Culverwell, E., *A Treatise of Faith,* Dutch Translation, n., 1670.

1675 *Der Seelen Selbstreit und derselben Uberwindung ubersich selbst (Soules Conflict)* GERMAN TRANSLATION Kassell & Dresden, 1675.

1735 *The Soules Conflict with Itself "Der Zielen Zelfstryjdt",* DUTCH TRANSLATION, by Obbo Copinga, 1735.

1750 *Wahrer Seelenfriede, in Beruhigung der verunruhigte seele* GERMAN TRANSLATION Eisenach, 1750.

1768 *The Soules Conflict with Itself, and The Bruised Reed,* 5th ed., life of the author by S. Clarke, Glasgow, 1768 2327S2.

1775 *Divine Meditations,* new ed., ed. W. Miller, 1775 2327S1.

1779 *Divine Meditations,* new ed., to which is prefaced a life of the author, Newport, 1779.

1794 *The Bruised Reed,* 8th ed., revised, Bath, 1794 2330S1.

1796 *Divine Meditations,* Lang & Ustick: Philadelphia, 1796.

1797 *Divine Meditations,* Bonsal & Niles: Wilmington, Del., 1797.

1799? *Divine Meditations,* new ed., life of author by G. Burder, H. P. Silvester, Newport 1799? 2327S1.

180? *The Bruised Reed,* Presbyterian Board of Publication: Philadelphia, 180?.

1808 *The Bruised Reed*, 9th ed., with a life of the author by E. Middleton, 1808 *S1885*.
Divine Meditations, new ed., Berwick, 1808 *S1886*.
The Soules Conflict with Itself, 10th ed. (with *The Bruised Reed*), 1808 *S1889*.
1809 *The Saint's Assurance*, abridged ed. of *The Saint's Cordials* by W. Batson, 1809 *S1888*.
Works, ed. W. Baynes, life of author, 3 vols. Aberdeen 1809 *S1887*.
1810? *The Saint's Ark* 2 sermons abridged from *Saint's Cordials* by W. Batson, 1810?.
1812 *Works*, ed. W. Baynes, Aberdeen, 1812.
1818 *The Bruised Reed*, 9th ed., with a life of the author by E. Middleton, 1818.
1819 *A Discovery of the Near Union and Communion* sermons on Canticles V & VI, *A Fountain Opened, The Nativity of Christ* in J. Wesley, *A Christian Library* vol. 6, 1819.
1821 *The Bruised Reed*, 9th ed., with a life of the author by E. Middleton, 1821.
1822 *The Bruised Reed*, 9th ed., with a life of the author by E. Middleton, 1822.
1824 *The Bruised Reed*, L. B. Seeley & Son, 1824.
1827 *The Spiritual–Mans Aime*, ed. E. Palmer, in *Palmer's Select Pocket Divinity* vol 2, 1827.
1828 *The Bruised Reed*, Pickering, 1828.
1830 *The Soules Conflict with Itself*, 1830.
1837 *The Soules Conflict with Itself*, William Pickering, 1837.
1838 *The Bruised Reed, A Fountain Sealed, A Description of Christ*, Pickering, 1838.
1840 *Divine Meditations*, 1840.
1842 *The Christian's Portion*, Presbyterian Board of Publication, Philadelphia, 1842.
The Soules Conflict with Itself, Philadelphia, 1842.
1850 *Divine Meditations*, 2nd ed., Religious Tract Society, 1850.
1854 *The Soules Conflict with Itself*, Religious Tract Society, 1854.
1862–1864 *Works*, ed. & life of author Alexander Balloch Grosart, 7 vols. Edinburgh 1862–1864.
1878 *The Bruised Reed*, Intro. Alexander Beith, Edinburgh, 1878.
1973 *The Bruised Reed*, [1973 FACSIMILE, Intro. P. A. Slack] 1630
1973–1983 Reprint of *Works* ed. by Grosart, Banner of Truth, Edinburgh 1973 1983.
1975 *Divine Meditations* in *Apples of Gold, First Series*, Zoar Publications, Osset, UK, 1975.
1998 *The Bruised Reed*, Banner of Truth, Edinburgh, 1998.

III. Printed Primary Sources

Adams, Thomas. *Mysticall Bedlam*. London, 1629.

Ames, William. *An Analytical Exposition of both the Epistles of the Apostle Peter.* London, 1641.

_____. *The Marrow of Theology.* John D. Eusden, trans. Durham NC, 1968.

Anselm. "Proslogion," in *A Scholastic Miscellany: Anselm to Ockham,* ed. and trans. E. R. Fairweather. London, 1956.

Arminius, Jacobus. *The Works of James Arminius,* 3 volumes. trans. by James and William Nichols. London, 1825, 1828, 1875.

Augustine. *Anti-Pelagian Writings.* trans. Peter Holmes. Grand Rapids MI, 1971.

_____. *Enchiridion.* trans. Ernest Evans. London, 1953.

Baillie, Robert. *A Dissuasive from the Errors of our Time.* London, 1645.

Ball, John. *Treatise of Faith.* London, 1632.

_____. *Treatise of the Covenant.* London, 1645.

Ball, Thomas. *The Life of the Renowned Doctor Preston.* ed. E. W. Harcourt. Oxford, 1885.

Bartlet, William. *Model of the Primitive Congregational Way.* London, 1647.

Barton, Thomas F. transcribed, *The Registrum Vagum of Anthony Harison,* 2 volumes. Norwich, 1963–1964.

Baxter, Richard. *A Christian Directory, Or, A Summ of Practical Theology and Cases of Conscience.* London, 1673.

_____. *Reliquae Baxterianae.* ed. Matthew Sylvester. London, 1696.

Baynes, Paul. *The Diocesans Triall.* London, 1621.

Becon, Thomas. *Prayers and Other Pieces of Thomas Becon.* ed. John Ayre. Cambridge, 1844.

Beza, Theodore. *A Brief and Pithy Sum of the Christian Faith.* trans. Robert Fyll. London, 1585.

Bradford, John. *The Writings of John Bradford.* ed. Aubrey Townsend. Cambridge, 1848.

Bullard, J. V. *Constitutions and Canons Ecclesiasitcal.* London, 1934.

Bullinger, Heinrich. *Decades.* 4 volumes Cambridge, 1849.

Burroughes, Jeremiah. *Excellency of Gracious Spirit.* London, 1638.

Burton, Robert. *Anatomy of Melancholy.* London, 1621.

Calamy, Edmund. *An Account of the Ministers, Lecturers, Masters and Fellows of Colleges and Schoolmasters, who were Ejected or Silenced after the Restoration in 1660.* 2nd ed.. 2 volumes. London, 1713.

_____. *The Nonconformist's Memorial.* 2 volumes. London, 1775.

_____. *A Patterne for All.* London, 1658.

Calder, Isabel M. ed. *Letters of John Davenport.* New Haven: CT, 1937.

Calendar of State Papers, Domestic, 1627–1628. ed. John Bruce. London, 1858.

Calendar of State Papers, Domestic, 1631–1633. ed. John Bruce. London, 1862.

Calvin, John. *Calvin: Theological Treatises.* trans. J. K. S. Reid. London, 1954.

_____. *Commentary on Romans.* trans. R. Mackenzie. Edinburgh, 1960.

_____. *Commentaries on the Catholic Epistles.* trans. John Owen. Edinburgh, 1855.

_____. *Commentaries on the Epistles of Paul to the Galatians and Ephesians*. trans. William Pringle. Edinburgh, 1854.

_____. *The Institutes of the Christian Religion*. trans. F. L. Battles. 2 volumes. London, 1960.

_____. *The Sermons of M. John Calvin upon the Fifth Booke of Moses Called Deuteronomie*. trans. Arthur Golding. London, 1583.

_____. *Sermons on 2 Samuel*. trans. Douglas Kelly. Edinburgh, 1992.

Cardwell, Edward. *Documentary Annals of the Reformed Church of England*. Oxford, 1844.

Cartwright, Thomas. "Letter to his Sister-in-Law to Dissuade her from Brownism." in *The Presbyterian Review*. VI (January 1885): 101–111.

Clarendon, Edward Hyde, Earl of. *The History of the Great Rebellion*. Oxford, 1819.

Clarke, Samuel. *A general martyrologie...Whereunto are added the lives of sundry modern divines*. London, 1651.

_____. *A general martyrologie, containing a collection of all the greatest persecutions which have befallen the church of Christ . . . . Whereunto is added the lives of thirty-two English Divines*. 3rd ed.. London, 1677.

_____. *The Marrow of Ecclesiastical Historie, conteined in the Lives of the Fathers, and Other Learned Men, and Famous Divines, which have Flourished in the Church since Christs Time, to this Present Age*. London, 1650.

_____. *A Martyrologie, containing a collection of all the persecutions which have befallen the church of England...Together with the lives of ten of our English divines...*, London, 1652.

Cooper, C. H. *Annals of Cambridge*. 5 volumes. Cambridge, 1845.

Cosin, John. *A Collection of Private Devotions*. London, 1627.

Cotton, John. *The Bloudy Tenent, Washed*. London, 1647.

_____. *An Exposition upon the Thirteenth Chapter of Revelation*. London, 1655.

_____. *Way of Congregational Churches Cleared*. London, 1648.

Downame, John. *The Chrisitan Warfare*. London, 1608.

Dury, John. *The Unchanged, Constant and Single-hearted Peacemaker*. London, 1650.

Ellis, John, *S. Austin Imitated: or Retractations and Repentings In reference unto the late Civil and Ecclesiastical Changes in this Nation*. London, 1662.

Elrington, C. R. ed. *Whole Works of the Most Rev. James Ussher*. 16 volumes. London, 1847–1864.

Finch, Henry. *The Calling of the Jewes*. London, 1621.

Firmin, Giles. *The Real Christian*. London, 1670.

Fletcher, Reginald J. ed. *The Pension Book of Gray's Inn...1569–1669*. London, 1901.

Foster, Joseph. *The Register of Admissions to Gray's Inn, 1521–1889*. London, 1889.

Fulke, William. *A Defense of the sincere and true Translations of the holie Scriptures into the English tong*. Cambridge, 1843.

_____. *Stapelton's Fortress Overthrown...*ed. Richard Gibbings. Cambridge, 1848.

Gardiner, S. R. *The Constitutional Documents of the Puritan Revolution, 1625–1660*. 3rd ed.. Oxford, 1906.

Gee, H. and Hardy, W. J. *Documents Illustrative of English Church History*. London, 1896.

Goodwin, Thomas. *Works of Thomas Goodwin*. 12 volumes. Edinburgh, 1861.

Gouge, William. *A Learned and Very Useful Commentary on the Whole Epistle to the Hebrews*. London, 1655.

Hacket, John. *Scrinia Reserata: A Memorial Offer'd to the Great Deservings of John Williams, D. D.*. London, 1693.

Harrison, William. *The Description of England*. ed. G. Edelen. Ithaca NY, 1968.

Heppe, Heinrich. *Reformed Dogmatics Set Out and Illustrated from the Sources*. trans. G. T. Thomson. London, 1950.

Hooker, Richard. *Of The Laws of Ecclesiastical Polity*. ed. Ronald Bayne. London, 1907.

Hooker, Thomas. *The Application of Redemption*. London, 1659.

_____. *The Soules Preparation*. London, 1638.

Jenison, Robert. *The Christians Apparelling by Christ*. London, 1625.

_____. *The Height of Israel's Heathenish Idolatrie*. London 1621.

Jewel, John. *A Defense of the Apologie of the Church of England, Conteining an Answer to a certaine Booke lately set forth by M. Harding*, in *The Works of John Jewel*. 3 volumes. ed. John Ayre Cambridge, 1848.

Kenyon, J. P. *The Stuart Constitution: Documents and Commentary*. 2nd ed.. Cambridge, 1986.

Knewstub, John. *An aunsweare unto certaine assertions, tending to maintaine the Churche of Rome*. London, 1579.

_____. *A confutation of monstrous and horrible heresies, taught by H. N.*. London, 1579.

_____. *Lectures...upon the twentith chapter of Exodus*. London, 1577.

_____. *A sermon preached at Paules Crosse the Fryday before Easter*. London, 1579.

Laud, William. *History of Troubles*. London, 1695.

_____. *The Works of the Most Reverend Father in God, William Laud, D. D.* 7 volumes. Oxford, 1847–1860.

[Anonymous]. *Life and Death of that Holy and Reverend Man of God, Mr. Thomas Cawton*. London, 1662.

Luther, Martin. *Lectures on Galatians 1519*. trans. R. Jungkuntz. St. Louis, 1964.

Mather, Cotton. *Magnalia Christi Americana*. 2 volumes. Hartford, 1853.

_____. _____ as *Ecclesiastical History of New England*. 2 volumes. New York, 1967.

Mayor, J. E. B. "Materials for a Life of Dr. Richard Sibbes." *Antiquarian Communications: Being Papers Presented At the Meetings of the Cambridge Antiquarian Society*, I (1859), 253–264.

Mew, William. *The Robbing and Spoiling of Jacob and Israel*. London, 1643.

Montagu, Richard. *Appello ad Caesarem, A Just Appeale from Two Unjust Informers* London, 1625.

Neuner, J. and J. Dupuis, eds. *The Christian Faith in the Doctrinal Documents of the Catholic Church*. New York, 1982.

Ornsby, George. ed. *The Correspondence of John Cosin, D. D.*. Durham, 1869.

Owen, John. *The Nature, Power, Deceit, and Prevalency of the Remainders of Indwelling Sin in Believers*. London, 1668.

Parkhurst, Nathaniel. *The Faithful and Diligent Christian Described and Exemplified*. London, 1684.

Patrick, Simon. *A Friendly Debate betwixt two Neighbours*. Second Part London, 1669.

Perkins, William. *A Clowd of Faithfull Witnesses, Leading to the heavenly Canaan: Or, A Commentarie upon the ll. Chapter to the Hebrewes, preached in Cambridge...*(n.l. 1609).

_____. *A Commentarie, or, Exposition Upon the five first Chapters of the Epistle to the Galatians*. Cambridge, 1617.

_____. *The Whole Treatise of the Cases of Conscience*. Cambridge. 1606.

_____. *The Work of William Perkins*, ed. Ian Breward. Appleford, Abingdon, Berkshire, 1970.

The Workes of that Famous and Worthy Minister of Christ in the University of Cambridge, Mr. William Perkins. 3 volumes. London, 1616, 1617, 1618.

Peter, Hugh. *A Dying Father's Last Legacy to an Only Child*. London, 1660.

Philpott, Henry. *Documents Relating to St. Catharine's College in the University of Cambridge*. Cambridge, 1861.

Plaifere, John. *Apello Evangelium*. London, 1651.

Potter, Christopher. *Vindication of Himself . . . 1629*. London, 1651.

Preston, John. *The Breastplate of Faith and Love*. London, 1630.

_____. *Life Eternall*. London, 1631.

_____. *The New Covenant, or the Saints Portion*. London, 1629.

_____. *The Saints Daily Exercise: a Treatise Unfolding the Whole Duty of Prayer*. London, 1629.

_____.*The Saints Qualification*. London, 1633.

Prynne, William. *A Breviate of the Prelates Intolerable Usurpations...*London, 1637.

_____. *Canterburies Doome*. London, 1646.

Pym, John. "Report on Mr. Montague's Books" in *Debates in the House of Commons in 1625*. ed. S. R. Gardiner. London, 1873, 179–186.

Robinson, Hastings, ed. *Original Letters Relative to the English Reformation...chiefly from the the Archives of Zurich*. 2 volumes Cambridge, 1846, 1847.

_____. *The Zurich Letters*. Cambridge, 1842.

Rushworth, John. *Historical Collections*. 6 volumes. London, 1703.

Schaff, Philip, ed. *The Creeds of Christendom*, 6th ed. 3 volumes. Grand Rapids, Michigan, 1931.

Searle, Arthur, ed. *Barrington Family Letters 1628–1632*. London, 1983.

"The Statutes of St. John's College Cambridge," printed in *Reports from Committees: Education of the Lower Orders*, IV London, 1818), 405.

Stow, John, *The Survey of London*, ed. H. B. Wheatley. London, 1956.

Tanner, J. R. *Constitutional Documents of the Reign of James I, 1603–1625*. Cambridge, 1961.

Taylor, Thomas. *Three Treatises: The Pearle of the Gospel, The Pilgrims Profession: And a Glasse for Gentlewomen to Dresse Themselves By*. London, 1633.

Texeda, Fernando. *Texeda Retextus: Or the Spanish Monke.* London, 1623.

[Anonymous]. *True Picture of Mr. John King.* London, 1680.

Tyndale, William. *Doctrinal Treatises,* ed. Henry Walter. Cambridge, 1848.

_____. *Expositions and Notes.* ed. Henry Walter. Cambridge, 1849.

Whitaker, William. "An. 1588. Maii 17. A Decree, by Will. Whitaker, Master, and the seniors." printed in *Reports from Committees: Education of the Lower Orders,* IV London, 1818), 405.

Whittingham, William. *A Brief Discourse of the Troubles at Frankfort.* ed. E. Arber. London, 1908.

Williams, J. F. ed. *Diocese of Norwich: Bishop Redman's Visitation, 1597: Presentments in the Archdeaconries of Norwich, Norfolk and Suffolk.* Norwich, 1946.

IV. Manuscript Primary Sources

British Library
    Additional Ms. 4274, no. 18.
    Additional Ms. 70106.
    Harleian Manuscript 7038.
    Lansdowne MSS. vol. LXXIX, no. 69.
    Sloane MS 654, fols. 351–352.
    Sloane MS 1465, fol. 2.

Cambridgeshire County Records Office
    Parish Records of Holy Trinity, P22/6.2.
Norwich and Norfolk Record Office
    ORR/1/2.
Public Records Office, London
    State Papers Domestic, James I, SP10/68.
    State Papers Domestic, James I, SP14/89.
    State Papers Domestic, Charles I, SP16/56.
St. Catharine's College, Cambridge
    Audit Book.
St. John's College Archives, Cambridge
    C12.1 (Prizing Book).
    SB4.3 (Rental Books, 1600–1618).
    SB4.4 (Rental Books, 1619–1633).
St. John's College Library, Cambridge
    Alumnus Sheet for Richard Sibbes.
    Letter of William Whitaker to Lord Burghley, October 26, 1590.
Sheffield University
    Samuel Hartlib Manuscripts, Ephemerides, 1634, 1635.
    Samuel Hartlib Manuscript 5d/10.
Suffolk County Records Office

Sibbes, Paul, Will (W1/67/176).
Statutes of King Edward VI Free Grammar School at Bury St.Edmunds (E5/9/201.7).

University of Cambridge
Catlin, Zachary. "Memoir of Richard Sibbes." (Add. Ms. 48).
Catlin, Zachary. "Memoir of Richard Sibbes." (Add. Ms. 103).
Catlin, Zachary. "Memoir of Richard Sibbes." (Mm.1.49).
Vice-Chancellor's Court, University Archives, I.42.
Viscount Dorchester letter to Vice-Chancellor Butts. May 11, 1630 (Mm.1.38).
Vice-Chancellor John Hills' letter to James Montagu. December 7, 1616 (University Archives Lett. 11.A.A.8.d.).
University of Oxford
Bodleian Library, Tanner Ms. 72/269.
Bodleian Library, Tanner Ms. 73.

V. Secondary Sources

Affleck, Bert D. Jr. "The Theology of Richard Sibbes, 1577–1635." Ph.D. diss., Drew University, 1969.

Allison, C. FitzSimons. *The Rise of Moralism: The Proclamation of the Gospel from Hooker to Baxter.* Wilton CT, 1966.

Almack, R. "Kedington alias Ketton, and the Barnardiston Family," *Proceedings of the Suffolk Institute of Archaeology and Natural History,* IV (1864–1874), 123–182.

Ashley, Maurice. *England in the Seventeenth Century.* 2nd ed.. New York, 1978.

Ashton, Robert. *The City and the Court, 1603–1643.* Cambridge, 1979.

Atkins, Jonathan M. "Calvinist bishops, church unity, and the rise of Arminianism." *Albion,* XVIII/3 (Fall, 1986), 411–427.

Babbage, S. B. *Puritanism and Richard Bancroft.* London, 1962.

Baker, Herschel. *The Dignity of Man.* Cambridge MA, 1947.

Baker, J. Wayne. *Heinrich Bullinger and the Covenant: The Other Reformed Tradition.* Athens OH, 1980.

Baker, Thomas. *History of the College of St. John the Evangelist, Cambridge.* 2 volumes. ed. J. E. B. Mayor. Cambridge, 1869.

Bamborough, J. B. *The Little World of Man.* London, 1952.

Bangs, Carl. "All the best bishops and deaneries: the enigma of Arminian politics." *Church History* XLII/1 (March, 1973), 5–16.

———. "Arminius and the Reformation." *Church History,* XXX (1961), 155–170.

Barth, Karl. *Church Dogmatics IV.1 The Doctrine of Reconciliation.* trans. G. W. Bromiley. Edinburgh, 1956.

Barton, J. "Notes on the Past History of the Church of Holy Trinity, Cambridge." *Cambridge Antiquarian Society Communications,* IV Cambridge, 1869–1870), 313–335.

Bauckham, Richard. 'Marian Exiles and Cambridge Puritanism: James Pilkington's 'Halfe a Score'." *Journal of Ecclesiastical History*, XXVI (1975), 137–148.

Beeke, Joel R. "Personal Assurance of Faith: English Puritanism and the Dutch 'Nadere Reformatie'" From Westminster to Alexander Comrie (1640–1760)." (Ph. D. diss.,. Westminster Theological Seminary, 1988.

Bell, M. Charles. *Calvin and Scottish Theology: The Doctrine of Assurance.* Edinburgh, 1985.

Berkhof, Louis. *Systematic Theology.* Grand Rapids MI, 1939.

Berkouwer, G. C. *Studies in Dogmatics: Man: the Image of God.* trans. D. Jellema. Grand Rapids MI, 1962.

_____. *Studies in Dogmatics: Sin.* trans. P. C. Holtrop. Grand Rapids, Michigan, 1971.

Berkovitch, Sacvan. "Typology in Puritan New England: The Williams–Cotton Controversy Reassessed." *American Quarterly*, XIX/2 part 1 (Summer, 1967), 166–191.

Betteridge, Maurice S. "The Bitter Notes: The Geneva Bible and its Annotations." *The Sixteenth Century Journal*, XIV (1983), 41–62.

Bierma, Lyle D. "Federal Theology in the Sixteenth Century: Two Traditions?" *Westminster Theological Journal*, XLV (1983), 304–321.

Blagden, Cyprian. *The Stationers' Company A History, 1403–1959.* London 1960.

Bohannon, Mary E. "A London Bookseller's Bill: 1635–1639." *The Library.* 4th series. XVIII (1938), 417–446.

Bondos–Greene, Stephen A. "The End of an Era: Cambridge Puritanism and the Christ's College Election of 1609." *The Historical Journal*, XXV (1982): 197–208.

Boulton, J. "The Limits of Formal Religion: the administration of Holy Communion in late Elizabethan and early Stuart London." *London Journal*, X/2 (1984), 135–154.

Bourne, E. C. E. *The Anglicanism of William Laud.* London, 1947.

Bowden, P. J. "Agricultural Prices, Farm Profits, and Rents." in *The Agrarian History of England and Wales, Vol. IV. 1500–1640.* ed. J. Thrisk. Cambridge, 1967, 593–695.

Brachlow, Stephen. *The Communion of Saints: Radical Puritan and Separatist Ecclesiology, 1570–1625.* Oxford, 1988.

Bratt, John H. ed. *The Heritage of John Calvin.* Grand Rapids MI, 1973.

Brauer, J. C. "Puritan Mysticism and the Development of Liberalism." *Church History*, XIX (1950), 151–170.

_____. "Reflections on the Nature of English Puritanism." *Church History*, XXIII (1954), 99–108.

_____. "Types of Puritan Piety." *Church History*, LVI (March, 1987), 39–58.

Breward, Ian. "The Abolition of Puritanism." *Journal of Religious History*, VII (1972), 20–34.

_____. "The Significance of William Perkins." *Journal of Religious History*, IV (1966), 113–128.

Broeyer, F. G. M. *William Whitaker (1548–1595) Leven En Werk Van Een Anglocalvinistisch Theoloog.* Utrecht, 1982.

Browne, G. F. *St. Catharine's College.* London, 1901.

Brook, Benjamin. *The Lives of the Puritans.* London, 1813.

Burch, Brian. "The Parish of St. Anne's Blackfriars, London, to 1665." *Guildhall Miscellany*, III/1 (October, 1969), 1–55.

Bush, Sargent. *The Writings of Thomas Hooker: Spiritual Adventure in Two Worlds.* Madison WI, 1980.

Calder, Isabel M. *Activities of the Puritan Faction of the Church of Enland 1625–1633.* London, 1957.

_____. "A Seventeenth Century Attempt to Purify the Anglican Church." *American Historical Review*, LIII (1948), 760–775.

_____. "The St. Antholin Lectures." *Church Quarterly Review*, CLX (1959), 49–70.

Cam, Helen C. "The City of Cambridge." in *A History of the County of Cambridge* in the *Victoria History of the Counties of England*. London, 1959.

Carlton, Charles. *Archbishop William Laud.* London, 1987.

Carter, Edmund. *The History of the University of Cambridge.* London, 1753.

Chan, Simon K. H. "The Puritan Meditative Tradition, 1599–1691: A Study of Ascetical Piety." Ph. D. dissertation, University of Cambridge, 1986.

Chesterton, G. K. *Collected Works*, I. San Francisco, 1986.

Chilton, C. W. "The Inventory of a Provincial Bookseller's Stock of 1644." *The Library.* 6th series, I/2 (June 1979), 126–143.

Christianson, Paul. "Reformers and the Church of England under Elizabeth I and the Early Stuarts" in *Journal of Ecclesiastical History*, XXXI (1980), 463–482.

Clancy, Thomas H. "Papist-Protestant-Puritan: English Religious Taxonomy, 1565–1665." *Recusant History*, XIII (1976), 227–253.

Clark, Peter. "Josiah Nichols and religious radicalism 1553–1639' *Journal of Ecclesiastical History*, XXVIII/2 (April, 1977), 133–150.

_____. "Thomas Scott and the Growth of Urban Opposition to the Early Stuart Regime." *Historical Journal*, XXI (1978), 1–26.

Cliffe, J. T. *The Puritan Gentry: The Great Puritan Families of Early Stuart England.* London, 1984.

Cohen, Charles. *God's Caress: The Psychology of Puritan Religious Experience.* Oxford, 1986.

_____. "Two Biblical Models of Conversion: An Example of Puritan Hermeneutics." *Church History*, LVIII/2 (June, 1989), 182–196.

Collinson, Patrick. "A Comment: Concerning the Name Puritan." *Journal of Ecclesiastical History*, XXXI/4 (October, 1980), 483–488.

_____. *The Elizabethan Puritan Movement.* London, 1967.

_____. *Godly People.* London, 1983.

_____. "The Jacobean Religious Settlement: The Hampton Court Conference" in *Before the English Civil War*. ed. Howard Tomlinson. London, 1983), 27–52, 189–192.

_____. *The Religion of Protestants: The Church in English Society 1559–1625*. Oxford, 1982.

Coolidge, John. *The Pauline Renaissance in England*. Oxford, 1970.

Cooper, J. P. *The Decline of Spain and the Thirty Years War 1609–48/59*. Cambridge, 1970.

Costello, William T. *The Scholastic Curriculum at Early Seventeenth-Century Cambridge* Cambridge MA, 1958.

Coward, Barry. *The Stuart Age: A History of England, 1603–1714*. London, 1980.

Cowper, Francis. *A Prospect of Gray's Inn*. 2nd ed.. London, 1985.

Cressy, David. "Describing the social order of Elizabethan and Stuart England.' *Literature and History*, 3 (1976), 29–44.

Cross, Claire. *Church and People, 1450–1660*. London, 1976.

Cunningham, William. *The Reformers and the Theology of the Reformation*. Edinburgh, 1862.

Cust, R. and A. Hughes, eds. *Conflict in Early Stuart England*. London, 1989.

Daly, J. W. "John Bramhall and the Theoretical Problems of Royalist Moderation." *Journal of British Studies*, XI (1971), 26–44.

Davies, Godfrey. *The Early Stuarts 1603–1660*. 2nd ed.. Oxford, 1959.

Davies, Horton. *Worship and Theology in England from Andrewes to Baxter and Fox, 1603–1690*. Princeton, 1975.

Davies, Julian. *The Caroline Captivity of the Church: Charles I and the Remoulding of Anglicanism: 1625–1641*. Oxford, 1992.

Davis, Joe Lee."Mystical Versus Enthusiastic Sensibility." *Journal of the History of Ideas*, IV/3 (June, 1943), 301–319.

Dever, Mark. "Moderation and Deprivation: A Re-appraisal of Richard Sibbes." *Journal of Ecclesiastical History*, XLIII (1992) 396-413.

Donagan, Barbara. "The Clerical Patronage of Robert Rich." *Proceedings of the American Philosophical Society*, CXX/5 (1976), 388–419.

_____. "A Coutier's Progress: Greed and Consistency in the Life of the Earl of Holland." *Historical Journal*, XIX/2 (1976), 317–353.

Doriani, Daniel. "The Puritans, Sex, and Pleasure." *Westminster Theological Journal*, LIII (Spring, 1991), 125–143.

Duffield, G. E. ed. *John Calvin*. Appleford, Abingdon, Berkshire, 1966.

Dyer, George B. *History of the University and Colleges of Cambridge*. 2 volumes. London, 1814.

Emerson, Everett H. "Calvin and Covenant Theology." *Church History*, XXV (1965): 136–144.

Farrell, Frank E. "Richard Sibbes: A Study in Early Seventeenth Century English Puritanism." Ph.D. diss., Edinburgh, 1955.

Fincham, Kenneth. "Prelacy and politics: Archbishop Abbot's defence of Protestant Orthodoxy." *Historical Research*, LXI, 144 (February 1988), 36–64.

_____. *Prelate as Pastor: The Episcopate of James I*. Oxford, 1990.

Fincham, Kenneth and Peter Lake. "The Ecclesiastical Policy of King James I." *Journal of British Studies*, XXIV (April, 1985), 36–64.

Fisher, George. *History of Christian Doctrine.* Edinburgh, 1896.

Fisher, R. M. "The Origins of Divinity Lectureships at the Inns of Court, 1569–1585" *Journal of Ecclesiastical History,* XXIX/2 (April, 1978), 145–162.

Fletcher, Anthony. *Outbreak of the English Civil War.* London, 1981.

Fletcher, H. F. *The Intellectual Development of John Milton.* Urbana, Illinois, 1961.

Frere, W. H. *The English Church in the Reigns of Elizabeth and James I (1558–1625).* London, 1904.

Fulcher, J. Rodney. "Puritans and the Passions: The Faculty Psychology in American Puritanism." *Journal of the History of the Behavioral Sciences,* IX/2 (April, 1973), 123–139.

Gane, Erwin R. "The Exegetical Methods of Some Sixteenth-Century Puritan Preachers: Hooper, Cartwright, and Perkins." *Andrews University Seminary Studies,* XIX/1–2 (Spring, Summer, 1981), 21–36, 22–114.

Gardiner, S. R. *History of England from the Accession of James I to the Outbreak of the Civil War 1603–1642.* London, 1883.

George, Charles H. "A Social Interpretation of English Puritanism." *Journal of Modern History,* XXXV/4 (December, 1953), 327–342.

Gill, John. *A Complete Body of Doctrinal and Practical Divinity.* London, 1839.

Godfrey, W. Robert, "Reformed Thought on the Extent of the Atonement to 1618." *Westminster Theological Journal,* XXXVII (Spring, 1975), 133–171.

Gorman, G. E. "A London Attempt to 'tune the pulpit': Peter Heylyn and his sermon against the Feoffees for the purchase of imporpriations." *Journal of Religious History,* VIII/9 (1975), 333–349.

Grayson, Christopher. "James I and the Religious Crisis in the United Provinces 1613–1619." in *Reform and Reformation: England and the Continent c1500–c1750.* ed. Derek Baker Oxford, 1979.

Greaves, Richard. "The Origins and Development of English Covenant Thought." *The Historian,* XXXI (1968), 21–35.

_____. "The Puritan Nonconformist Tradition in England, 1560–1700: Historiographical Reflections." *Albion,* XVII/4 (Winter, 1985), 449–486.

Greaves, Richard and Robert Zaller, eds. *Biographical Dictionary of British Radicals in the Seventeenth Century.* 3 volumes. Brighton, 1984.

Green, Ian. "Career Prospects and Clerical Conformity in the Early Stuart Church." *Past and Present,* 90 (1981), 71–115.

Green, James B. ed. *A Harmony of the Westminster Presbyterian Standards.* Richmond VA, 1951.

Grell, Ole Peter. *Dutch Calvinists in Early Stuart London: The Dutch Church in Austin Friars 1603–1642.* Leiden, 1989.

Haller, William. *The Rise of Puritanism.* New York, 1938.

Hambrick-Stowe, Charles E. *The Practice of Piety: Puritan Devotional Disciplines in Seventeenth-Century New England.* Chapel Hill NC, 1982.

Harris, Jonathan. "Richard Sibbes: A Moderate in Early Seventeenth Century Puritanism." M. A. Thesis, University of Melbourne, 1978.

Hawkes, R. M. "The Logic of Assurance in English Puritan Theology." *Westminster Theological Journal,* LII (1990), 247–261.

Helm, Paul. *Calvin and the Calvinists*. Edinburgh, 1982.

_____. "Calvin, English Calvinism and the Logic of Doctrinal Development." *Scottish Journal of Theology*, XXXIV (April, 1981), 179–185.

Hill, Christopher. *The Century of Revolution 1603–1714*. London, 1961.

_____. *Collected Essays*. Amherst MA, 1985.

_____. *Economic Problems of the Church*. Oxford, 1956.

_____. *Intellectual Origins of the English Revolution*. Oxford, 1965.

_____. *Puritanism and Revolution*. London, 1958.

_____. "Puritans and 'The Dark Corners of the Land'" *Transactions of the Royal Historical Society*. 5th series, XIII (1963), 77–102.

_____. *Society and Puritanism in Pre-Revolutionary England*. London, 1964.

_____. *A Turbulent, Seditious, and Factious People: John Bunyan and His Church*. Oxford, 1988.

Hirst, Derek. *Authority and Conflict*. London, 1986.

Hoekema, Anthony. "The Covenant of Grace in Calvin's Teaching." *Calvin Theological Journal*, II/2 (November. 1967), 133–161.

Hoffman, John G. "The Puritan Revolution and the 'Beauty of Holiness' at Cambridge: The Case of John Cosin, Master of Peterhouse and Vice-Chancellor of the University" *Proceedings of the Cambridge Antiquarian Society*, LXXII (1982–1983), 94–105.

Holden, William P. *Anti-Puritan Satire 1572–1642*. New Haven CT, 1954.

Holifield, E. Brooks. *The Covenant Sealed: The Development of Puritan Sacramental Theology in Old and New England, 1570–1720*. New Haven CT, 1974.

Horn, Robert. "Thomas Hooker—The Soul's Preparation for Christ." *The Puritan Experiment in the New World*. London, 1976, 19–37.

Hopkins, Hugh Evan. *Holy Trinity Church Cambridge*. n.d. [c.1975].

Hoyle, David. "A Commons Investigation of Arminianism and Popery in Cambridge on the Eve of the Civil War." *The Historical Journal*, XXIX/2 (1986), 419–425.

_____. "'Near popery yet no popery': theological debate in Cambridge 1590–1644." Ph. D. diss., University of Cambridge, 1991.

Hudson, Roy F. "Richard Sibbes's Theory and Practice of Persuasion." *Quarterly Journal of Speech*, XLIV/2. April, 1958), 137–148.

Hunt, William. *The Puritan Moment: The Coming of Revolution in an English County*. Cambridge MA, 1983.

Irwin, Joyce. "Music and the Doctrine of Adiaphora in Orthodox Lutheran Theology." *The Sixteenth Century Journal*, XIV (1983), 157–172.

Jones, W. H. S. *A History of St. Catharine's College*. Cambridge, 1936.

Jordan, W. K. *The Development of Religious Toleration in England From the Beginning of the English Reformation to the Death of Queen Elizabeth*. London, 1932.

Jordan, W. K. *The Development of Religious Toleration in England from the Accession of James I to the Convention of the Long Parliament (1603–1640)*. London, 1936.

Kalu, Ogbu. "Bishops and Puritans in Early Jacobean England: A Perspective on Methodology." *Church History*, XLV (1976), 469–489.

_____. "Continuity and Change: Bishops of London and Religious Dissent in Early Stuart England." *Journal of British Studies*, XVIII (Fall 1978), 28–45.

Karlberg, Mark W. "The Original State of Adam: Tensions Within Reformed Theology." *Evangelical Quarterly*, LIX (1987), 291–309.

Kaufmann, U. Milo. *The Pilgrim's Progress and Traditions in Puritan Meditation.* New Haven CT, 1966.

Keayne, Robert. "Sermon List." in *Proceedings of the Massachusetts Historical Society.* 2nd series. L (1916–1917), 204–207.

Keddie, Gordon J. "'Unfallible Certenty of the Pardon of Sinne and Life Everlasting': The Doctrine of Assurance in the Theology of William Perkins (1558–1602)" *Evangelical Quarterly*, XLVIII (1976), 230–244.

Keeler, Mary F. *The Long Parliament, 1640–1641: A Biographical Study of its Members.* Philadelphia, 1954.

Kendall, R. T. *Calvin and English Calvinism to 1649.* Oxford, 1979.

_____. "John Cotton—The First English Calvinist?" *The Puritan Experiment in the New World.* Ripon, 1976, 38–50.

Kenyon, J. P. *Stuart England.* London, 1978.

_____. *The Stuarts.* Glasgow, 1958.

Kevan, Ernest F. *The Grace of Law.* London, 1964.

Kirby, D. A. "The Radicals of St. Stephen's, Coleman Street, London, 1624–1642." *Guildhall Miscellany*, III/2 (1970), 98–119.

Kirby, E. W. "The Lay Feofees: A Study in Militant Puritanism." *Journal of Modern History*, XIV (1942), 1–25.

Kline, Meredith G. "Of Works and Grace." *Presbyterion*, XII (Spring–Fall, 1983), 85–92.

Knappen, M. M. *Tudor Puritanism.* Chicago, 1939.

Knott, John R. Jr. *The Sword of the Spirit: Puritan Responses to the Bible*, Chicago, 1980.

Knowles, David. *The English Mystical Tradition.* London, 1960.

Knox, R. B. ed. *Reformation, Conformity and Dissent.* London, 1977.

Lake, Peter. *Anglicans and Puritans? Presbyterianism and English Conformist Thought from Whitgift to Hooker.* London, 1988.

_____. "Calvinism and the English Church." *Past and Present*, 114 (February, 1987), 32–76.

_____. "Constitutional Consensus and Puritan Opposition in the 1620's: Thomas Scott and the Spanish Match." *Historical Journal*, XXV (1982), 805–825.

_____. "The Dilemma of the Establishment Puritan: The Cambridge Head and the case of Francis Johnson and Cuthbert Bainbrigg" *Journal of Ecclesiastical History*, XXIX/1 (Jan, 1978), 23–35.

_____. "Laurence Chaderton and the Cambridge Moderate Puritan Tradition." Ph.D. diss., University of Cambridge, 1978.

_____. *Moderate Puritans and the Elizabethan Church.* Cambridge, 1982.

_____. "Puritan Identities." *Journal of Ecclesiastical History*, XXXV (1984), 112–123.

Lamont, William M. *Godly Rule: Politics and Religion, 1603–1660.* London, 1969.

_____. "The Rise of Arminianism Reconsidered: A Comment." *Past and Present*, 107 (May 1985), 227–231.

Leader, Damian. *History of the University of Cambridge*. Cambridge, 1989.

Leith, John H. *John Calvin's Doctrine of the Christian Life*. Louisville KY, 1989.

Letham, Robert. "The *Foedus Operum*: Some Factors Accounting for its Development." *The Sixteenth Century Journal*, XIV (1983), 457–467.

Lewis, C. S. *Fern–seed and Elephants and other Essays on Christianity*. ed. Walter Hooper. London, 1975.

Lillback, Peter A. "The Binding of God: Calvin's Role in the Development of Covenant Theology." Ph.D. diss., Westminster Theological Seminary, 1985.

Lockyer, Roger. *Buckingham: The Life and Political Career of George Villiers, First Duke of Buckingham 1592–1628*. London, 1981.

Looney, J. "Undergraduate Education at Early Stuart Cambridge" *History of Education*, X/1 (March 1981), 9–19.

Maclear, J. F. "'The Heart of New England Rent': The Mystical Element in Early Puritan History." *Mississippi Valley Historical Review*, XLII (1956), 621–652.

_____. "The Influence of the Puritan Clergy on the House of Commons: 1625–1629." *Church History*, XIV (1945), 272–289.

_____. "Puritan Relations with Buckingham" *Huntington Library Quarterly*, XXI (1957–8): 111–132.

Marsden, George. "Perry Miller's Rehabilitation of the Puritans: A Critique." *Church History*, XXX (1970), 91–105.

Mathew, David. *The Age of Charles I*. London, 1951.

Matthews, A. G. *Calamy Revised: Being a Revision of Edmund Calamy's Account of the Ministers and Others Ejected and Silenced*. Oxford, 1934.

_____. *Walker Revised: Being a Revision of John Walker's Sufferings of the Clergy during the Grand Rebellion 1642–1660*. Oxford, 1948.

McElwee, William. *England's Precedence*. London, 1956.

McGee, J. Sears. *The Godly Man in Stuart England: Anglicans, Puritans, and the Two Tables, 1620–1670*. New Haven CT, 1976.

_____. "William Laud and the Outward Face of Religion." in *Leaders of the Reformation*. ed. Richard L. DeMolen. London, 1984, 318–345.

McGiffert, Michael. "Grace and Works: The Rise and Division of Covenant Divinity in Elizabethan Puritanism." *Harvard Theological Review*, LXXV (1982), 463–505.

McGrath, Alister E. *Iustitia Dei: A history of the Christian doctrine of Justification: II From 1500 to the present day*. Cambridge, 1986.

McNeill, John T. *The History and Character of Calvinism*. Oxford, 1954.

McWilliams, David B. "The Covenant Theology of the Westminster Confession of Faith and Recent Criticism." *Westminster Theological Journal*, LIII (Spring, 1991), 109–124.

Michaelsen, Robert S. "Change in the Puritan Concept of Calling or Vocation." *New England Quarterly*, XXVI (1953), 315–336.

Middlekauff, Robert. "Piety and Intellect in Puritanism." *The William and Mary Quarterly*. 3rd series, XXII/3 (July, 1965), 457–470.

Miller, Edward. *Portrait of a College*. Cambridge, 1961.

Miller, Perry. *Errand into the Wilderness*. Cambridge MA, 1956.

_____. "The Marrow of Puritan Divinity." *Publications of the Colonial Society for Massachusetts*, XXXII (1933-1937), 247–300.

_____. *The New England Mind: The Seventeenth Century*. New York, 1939.

Milton, Anthony. "The Laudians and the Church of Rome. c. 1625-1640." Ph. D. diss., University of Cambridge, 1989.

_____. Review of Nicholas Tyacke's *Anti-Calvinists: The Rise of English Arminianism, Journal of Ecclesiastical History*, XXXIX (October, 1988), 613–616.

Milward, Peter. *Religious Controversies of the Elizabethan Age: A Survey of Printed Sources*. London, 1978.

_____. *Religious Controversies of the Jacobean Age: A Survey of Printed Sources*. London, 1978.

Moller, Jens G. "The Beginnings of Puritan Covenant Theology." *Journal of Ecclesiastical History*, XIV (1963), 46–67.

Morgan, Edmund S. *Visible Saints: The History of a Puritan Idea*. Ithaca NY , 1963.

Morgan, Irvonwy. *Prince Charles's Puritan Chaplain*. London, 1957.

_____. *Puritan Spirituality*. London, 1973.

Morgan, John. *Godly Learning: Puritan Attitudes towards Reason, Learning and Education, 1560-1640*. Cambridge, 1986.

Morgan, Victor. "Cambridge University and 'The Country' 1560-1640." in *The University in Society, volume I*. ed. Lawrence Stone. London, 1975, 183–245.

_____. "Country, Court and Cambridge University: 1558-1640: A Study in the Evolution of a Political Culture." 6 volumes. Ph.D. diss., University of East Anglia, 1983.

Morrill, John S. ed. *Reactions to the English Civil War 1642-1649*. London, 1982.

Muller, Richard A. *Christ and the Decree: Christology and Predestination in Reformed Theology from Calvin to Perkins*. Durham NC, 1986.

_____. "Covenant and Conscience in English Reformed Theology: Three Variations on a 17th Century Theme." *Westminster Theological Journal*, XLII (1980), 308–334.

Mullinger, James B. *St. John's College*. London, 1901.

Neal, Daniel. *The History of the Puritans*. 3 volumes. London, 1837.

Nicole, Roger. "John Calvin's View of the Extent of the Atonement." *Westminister Theological Journal*, LXVII (1985), 197–225.

Niesel, Wilhelm. *The Theology of Calvin*. trans. Harold Knight. London, 1956.

Nuttall, Geoffrey F. *Holy Spirit in Puritan Faith and Experience*. Oxford, 1946.

_____. "Puritan and Quaker Mysticism." *Theology*, LXXVIII (October. 1975), 518–531.

_____. Review of Peter Lake. *Moderate Puritans, Heythrop Journal*, XXVI/1 (January 1985), 95.

O'Day, Rosemary. *The English Clergy: The Emergence and Consolidation of a Profession 1558-1642*. Leicester, 1979.

Packer, J. I. *Among God's Giants: The Puritan Vision of the Christian Life*. London, 1990.

Parker, T. H. L. *John Calvin: A Biography*. London, 1975.

Patterson, W. B. "The Peregrinations of Marco Antonio de Dominis, 1616–1624." in *Studies in Church History*, XV, ed. D. Baker. Oxford, 1978, 241–252.

Paul, Robert S. *The Assembly of the Lord: Politics and Religion in the Westminster Assembly and the 'Grand Debate'*. Edinburgh, 1985.

Pearl, Valerie. "Oliver St. John and the 'middle group' in the Long Parliament: August 1643–May 1644." *English Historical Review*, LXXXI (1966), 490–519.

Pelikan, Jaroslav. *Reformation of Church and Dogma (1300–1700)*. Chicago, 1984.

Pendrill, Charles. *Old Parish Life in London*. Oxford, 1937.

Pettit, Norman. *The Heart Prepared: Grace and Conversion in the Puritan Spiritual Life*. New Haven CT, 1966.

_____. "Hooker's Doctrine of Assurance: A Critical Phase in New England Spiritual Thought." *The New England Quarterly*, XLVII/4 (December. 1974), 518–534.

Platt, John. "Eirenical Anglicans at the Synod of Dort." in *Reform and Reformation: England and the Continent c1500–c1750*. ed. Derek Baker. Oxford 1979), 221–243.

Poe, Harry Lee. "Evangelistic Fervency Among the Puritans in Stuart England, 1603–1688". Ph.D. diss., The Southern Baptist Theological Seminary, 1982.

Porter, H. C. *Reformation and Reaction in Tudor Cambridge*. Cambridge, 1958.

Prest, Wilfrid. *The Inns of Court under Elizabeth I and the Early Stuarts*. London, 1972.

_____. *The Rise of the Barristers*. Oxford, 1986.

Prestwich, Menna, ed. *International Calvinism 1541–1715*. Oxford, 1985.

Roberts, Sylvia. "'Radical Graces': A Study of Puritan Casuistry in the Writings of William Perkins and Richard Sibbes." M. A. Thesis, University of Melbourne, 1972.

Rolston, Holmes, III. *John Calvin Versus the Westminster Confession*. Richmond VA, 1972.

Rooy, Sidney H. *The Theology of Missions in the Puritan Tradition: A Study of Representative Puritans: Richard Sibbes, Richard Baxter, John Eliot, Cotton Mather, and Jonathan Edwards*. Grand Rapids MI, 1965.

Rose, Elliot. *Cases of Conscience: Alternatives Open to Recusants and Puritans under Elizabeth I and James I*. Cambridge, 1975.

Russell, Conrad. *The Causes of the English Civil War*. Oxford, 1990.

_____. "The Parliamentary Career of John Pym, 1621–1629." in Peter Clark, Alan G. R. Smith and Nicholas Tyacke, eds. *The English Commonwealth 1547–1640: essays in politics and society presented to Joel Hurstfield.*(1979), 147–165.

Ryle, J. C. *Light from Old Times*. London, 1890.

Schoneveld, C. W. *Intertraffic of the Mind*. Leiden, 1983.

Schwarz, Marc L. "Lay Anglicanism and the crisis of the English Church in the Early Seventeenth Century." *Albion*, XIV/1 (1982), 1–19.

Scott, R. F. "Some Aspects of College Life in Past Times" in *The Eagle*; rpt. in R. F. Scott. *Notes from the Records of St. John's College, Cambridge.* 4th series. privately printed, 1913–1934.

Seaver, Paul. *The Puritan Lectureships.* Stanford, 1970.

Seeberg, Reinhold. *The History of Doctrines.* trans. Charles Hay. Grand Rapids MI, 1977.

Selement, George. "Perry Miller: A Note on His Sources in *The New England Mind: The Seventeenth Century.*" *William and Mary Quarterly.* 3rd series. XXXI/3 (July, 1974): 453–464.

Sharpe, Kevin, ed. *Faction and Parliament: Essays on early Stuart history.* Oxford, 1978.

Shaw, Mark R. "Drama in the Meeting House: The Concept of Conversion in the Theology of William Perkins." *Westminster Theological Journal,* XLV (1983): 41–72.

Shelly, Harold Patton. "Richard Sibbes: Early Stuart Preacher of Piety." Ph.D. diss., Temple University, 1972.

Shriver, Frederick. "Hampton Court Re-visited: James I and the Puritans." *Journal of Ecclesiastical History,* XXXIII (1982), 48–71.

_____. "Orthodoxy and Diplomacy: James I and the Vorstius Affair." *English Historical Review,* 336 (1970), 449–474.

Shuffelton, Frank. *Thomas Hooker 1586–1647.* Princeton, 1977.

Simpson, Alan. *Puritanism in Old and New England.* Chicago, 1955.

Smith, Alan G. R. ed. *The Reign of James VI and I.* London, 1973.

Sommerville, C. J. "Conversion Versus the Early Puritan Covenant of Grace." *Journal of Presbyterian History,* XLIV (1966), 178–197.

Sommerville, J. P. "The royal supremacy and episcopacy 'jure divino', 1603–1640." *Journal of Ecclesiastical History,* XXXIV/4 (October 1983), 548–558.

Sprunger, Keith. "Ames, Ramus, and the Method of Puritan Theology." *Harvard Theological Review,* LIX (1966), 133–151.

_____. *The Learned Doctor William Ames: Dutch Backgrounds of English and American Puritanism.* Urbana IL, 1972.

Spufford, Margaret. "The Quest of the Heretical Laity in the Visitation Records of Ely in the Late Sixteenth and Early Seventeenth Centuries." *Studies in Church History,* IX (1972), 223–230.

Stachniewski, John. *The Persecutory Imagination: English Puritanism and the Literature of Religious Despair.* Oxford, 1991.

Stearns, R. P. "Assessing the New England Mind." *Church History,* X (1941), 246–262.

_____. *The Strenuous Puritan: Hugh Peter, 1598–1660.* Urbana IL, 1954.

Stoeffler, E. F. *The Rise of Evangelical Pietism.* Leiden, 1965.

Stoever, William K. B. *'A Faire and Easie Way to Heaven': Covenant Theology and Antinomianism in Early Massachusetts.* Middletown CT, 1978.

_____. "Nature, Grace and John Cotton." *Church History,* XLIV/1 (March, 1975), 22–33.

Stout, Harry S. *The New England Soul: Preaching and Religious Culture in Colonial New England.* Oxford, 1986.

_____. "Theological Commitment and American Religious History." *Theological Education,* XXVI (Spring 1989), 44–59.

Strehle, Stephen. "The Extent of the Atonement and the Synod of Dort." *Westminster Theological Journal,* LI/1 (Spring, 1989), 1–23.

Tawney, R. H. *Religion and the Rise of Capitalism.* London, 1930.

Thomas, Keith. *Religion and the Decline of Magic.* London, 1971.

Thompson, Christopher. "The Origins of the politics of the parliamentary middle group 1625–1629." *Transactions of the Royal Historical Society,* 5th series, XXII (1972), 71–86.

Thornton, Martin. *English Spirituality: An Outline of Ascetical Theology According to the English Pastoral Tradition.* London, 1963.

Tipson, Lynn Baird, Jr. "The Development of a Puritan Understanding of Conversion." Ph.D. diss., Yale University, 1972.

_____. "Invisible Saints: The 'Judgment of Charity' in the Early New England Churches." *Church History,* XLIV (1975), 460–471.

Todd, Margo. "'An act of discretion': Evangelical Conformity and the Puritan Dons." *Albion,* XVIII/4 (Winter, 1986), 581–599.

_____. *Christian Humanism and the Puritan Social Order.* Cambridge, 1987.

Tolmie, Murray. *The Triumph of the Saints: The separate churches of London 1616–1649.* Cambridge, 1977.

Torrance, J. B. "Covenant or Contract?" *Scottish Journal of Theology,* XXIII/1 (February, 1970), 51–76.

Trevelyan, G. M. *England Under the Stuarts.* 21st ed.. London, 1949.

Trevor-Roper, Hugh. *Archbishop Laud 1573–1645.* 3rd ed.. London, 1988.

_____. *Men and Events.* New York, 1957.

Trinterud, Leonard. *Elizabethan Puritanism.* Oxford, 1971.

_____. "The Origins of Puritanism." *Church History,* XX (1951), 37–57.

Turnbull, G. H. *Hartlib, Dury and Comenius.* Liverpool, 1947.

Twigg, John. *A History of Queens' College, Cambridge 1448–1986.* Cambridge, 1987.

Tyacke, Nicholas. *Anti-Calvinists: The Rise of English Arminianism, c. 1590–1640.* Oxford, 1987.

_____. "Arminianism and English Culture." in A. C. Duke and C. A. Tamse, eds. *Britain and the Netherlands,* VII (The Hague, 1981), 94–117.

_____. *The Fortunes of English Puritanism, 1603–1640.* London, 1990.

Van der Molen, Ronald J. "Providence as Mystery, Providence as Revelation: Puritan and Anglican Modifications of John Calvin's Doctrine of Providence." *Church History,* XLVII (1978), 27–47.

Venn, John and J. A. *Alumni Cantabrigienses.* Part I. 4 volumes. Cambridge, 1922–1927.

Verkamp, Bernard. *The Indifferent Mean: Adiaphorism in the English Reformation to 1554.* Athens OH, 1977.

_____. "The Zwinglians and Adiaphorism." *Church History,* XLII/4 (December, 1973), 486–504.

Von Rohr, John. "Covenant and Assurance in Early English Puritanism." *Church History*, XXXIV (1965), 195–203.

_____. *The Covenant of Grace in Puritan Thought*. Atlanta GA, 1986.

Vos, Geerhardus. *Redemptive History and Biblical Interpretation*. ed. Richard Gaffin, Jr. Phillipsburg NJ, 1980.

Wakefield, Gordon S. "Mysticism and its Puritan Types." *London Quarterly and Holborn Review*, XCXI. 6th series. XXXV (1966), 34–45.

Wallace, Dewey D. Jr. *Puritans and Predestination: Grace in English Protestant Theology 1525–1695*. Chapel Hill NC , 1982.

Warfield, B. B. *Calvin and Augustine*. Philadelphia, 1956.

Watts, Michael. *The Dissenters: From the Reformation to the French Revolution*. Oxford, 1978.

Weber, Max. *The Protestant Ethic and the Spirit of Capitalism*. trans. T. Parsons. London, 1930.

Weir, D. A. *The Origins of the Federal Theology in Sixteenth–Century Reformation Thought*. Oxford, 1990.

Weisiger, Cary Nelson II. "The Doctrine of the Holy Spirit in the Preaching of Richard Sibbes." Ph.D. diss., Fuller Theological Seminary, 1984.

Welsby, Paul A. *George Abbot: the Unwanted Archbishop 1562–1633*. London, 1962.

_____. *Lancelot Andrewes 1555–1626*. London, 1958.

Wendel, Francois. *Calvin: Origins and Development of His Religious Thought*. trans. Philip Mariet. London, 1963.

White, B. R. *The English Separatist Tradition from the Marian Martyrs to the Pilgrim Fathers*. Oxford, 1971.

White, Eugene E. "Master Holdsworth and 'A Knowledge Very Useful and Necessary.'" *Quarterly Journal of Speech*, LIII (1967), 1–16.

White, Peter. "The Rise of Arminianism Reconsidered." *Past and Present*, 101 (November. 1983), 34–54.

Wiener, Carol Z. "The Beleaguered Isle. A Study of Elizabethan and Early Jacobean Anti–Catholicism." *Past and Present*. 51 (May, 1971), 27–62.

Willey, Basil. *The Seventeenth Century Background: The Thought of the Age in Relation to Religion and Poetry*. New York, 1935.

Williams Whitney, Dorothy. "London Puritanism: the Haberdashers' Company." *Church History*, XXXII/3 (1963), 298–321.

Williams, Dorothy Ann. "London Puritanism: The Parish of St Botolph without Aldgate." *Guildhall Miscellany*, II/1 (1960), 24–38.

_____. "London Puritanism: The Parish of St. Stephen Coleman Street." *Church Quarterly Review*, CLX (1959), 464–482.

_____. "Puritanism in the City Government, 1610–1640." *Guildhall Miscellany* I/4 (1955), 3–14.

Williams, Franklin B. Jr. "The Laudian Imprimatur" *The Library*, 5th series, XV/2 (June, 1960), 96–104.

Williams, George H. "Called by Thy Name, Leave us Not: The Case of Mrs. Joan Drake." *Harvard Library Bulletin*. 1968), 111–128, 278–300.

_____. *The Radical Reformation*. Philadelphia, 1962.

Woolsey, Andrew. "Unity and Continuity in Covenantal Thought: A Study in the Reformed Tradition to the Westminster Assembly." Ph.D. Diss., University of Glasgow, 1988.

Wormald, Jenny."James VI and I: Two Kings or One?" *History*, LXVIII (1963), 187–209.

Wright, Conrad. "John Cotton Washed and Made White." *Continuity and Discontinuity in Church History.* eds. F. Church and T. George. Leiden, 1979, 338–350.

Wright, Louis B. "William Perkins: Elizabethan Apostle of 'Practical Divinity." *Huntington Library Quarterly*, III (1940), 171–1962.

Wrightson, Keith. *English Society 1580–1680.* London, 1982.

Yule, George. "Theological Developments in Elizabethan Puritanism." *Journal of Religious History*, I (1960), 16–25.

Zakai, Avihu. "The Gospel of Reformation: The Origins of the Great Puritan Migration.' *Journal of Ecclesiastical History*, XXXVII/4. October 1986), 584–602.

Zaret, David. *The Heavenly Contract: Ideology and Organization in Pre–Revolutionary Puritanism.* Chicago, 1985.

Ziff, Larzer. *The Career of John Cotton: Puritanism and the American Experience.* Princeton, 1962.

Person Index

Subject Index

Scripture Index